FROM POWER TO SERVICE

THE STORY OF LAWYERS IN ALABAMA

Pat Boyd Rumore

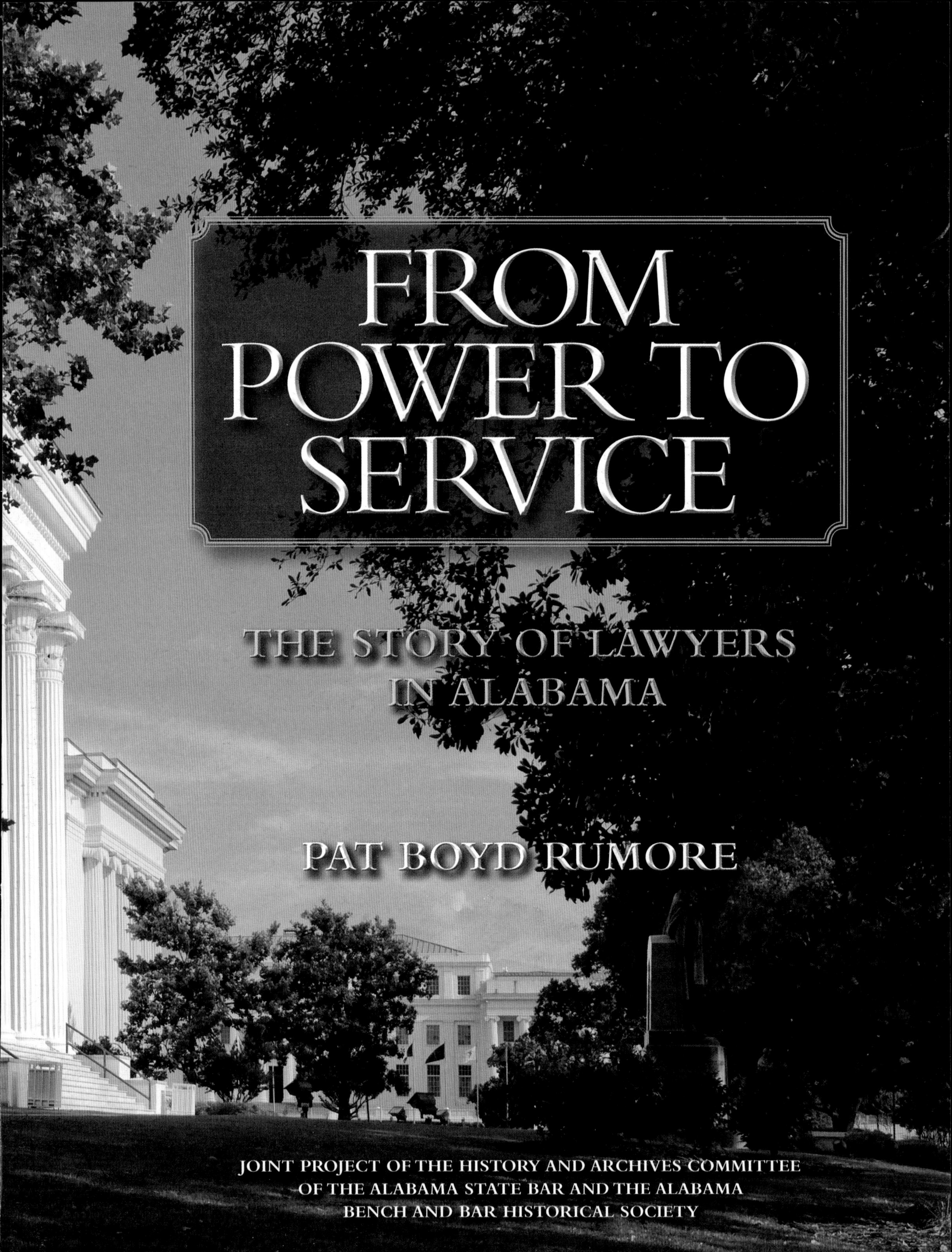

FROM POWER TO SERVICE

THE STORY OF LAWYERS IN ALABAMA

PAT BOYD RUMORE

JOINT PROJECT OF THE HISTORY AND ARCHIVES COMMITTEE
OF THE ALABAMA STATE BAR AND THE ALABAMA
BENCH AND BAR HISTORICAL SOCIETY

FROM POWER TO SERVICE

Published By
The HISTORY AND ARCHIVES COMMITTEE *of the* ALABAMA STATE BAR
in conjunction with the ALABAMA BENCH AND BAR HISTORICAL SOCIETY

Written By
PAT BOYD RUMORE

Project Manager
JOHN COMPTON, *Legacy Publishing*

Design & Picture Research
ROBIN McDONALD

Editor
ALISON M. GLASCOCK

Index
JIM SUMMERVILLE

Printed in the United States of America by
TAYLOR PUBLISHING COMPANY, DALLAS, TEXAS

FIRST EDITION

Library of Congress Control Number: 2010900271
ISBN 978-0-6153465-9-5

ALABAMA STATE BAR
415 Dexter Avenue, Montgomery, Alabama 36104

Frank M. Johnson U.S. Courthouse Complex, Montgomery

TABLE OF CONTENTS

FROM POWER TO SERVICE

FOREWORD

When 2004-2005 Alabama State Bar President Douglas McElvy asked me to chair the History and Archives Committee and make publication of a history of Alabama lawyers the committee's number one project, I immediately responded that I would want Pat Rumore for the book's author. He said that was good since he had already asked her! We are so very lucky that Pat agreed to write this book.

We are also so very lucky that Pat Rumore wrote *Lawyers in a New South City: A History of the Legal Profession in Birmingham* in 2000 (followed by a second edition in 2006) for the Birmingham Bar Association, when Harold Williams was chair of that bar association's history

and archives committee. The resulting friendship led to Harold Williams's tremendous support and encouragement of Pat in her research and writing of this book and his invaluable service on the Alabama State Bar's History and Archives Committee.

Good fortune continued to smile on this book when Tim Lewis and the Alabama Bench and Bar Historical Society agreed to support the book and make its publication a joint project of the historical society and the history and archives committee.

As the title indicates, *From Power to Service: The Story of Lawyers in Alabama* tells the story of lawyers in Alabama's history, including the many pivotal leadership roles played by lawyers in the state's development. This book is also a history of the legal profession in Alabama as well as a history of the organized bar in the state.

This story of lawyers is a story of heroes and villains, a story of bright, curious, energetic, multitalented, disciplined people, who sometimes attempted to do "as adversaries do in law—strive mightily, but eat and drink as friends," (Shakespeare, *The Taming of the Shrew*, Act I, scene ii).

This is also a story of work performed by the Alabama State Bar to serve the good of individual lawyers, the profession itself, and the people of the state of Alabama.

From Power to Service has been a long time coming. It may be even longer before we see anything like it again. So we should savor this book. The journey one takes through it leads to the conclusion that the story of lawyers and the history of this state cannot be separated. I urge you to take that journey.

—Benjamin B. Spratling, III
Chair, History and Archives Committee
Alabama State Bar
January 2010

The eight massive columns around the rotunda of the the Heflin-Torbert Judicial Building are made of Carrara marble from Italy.

ACKNOWLEDGMENTS

FROM ITS EARLIEST HISTORY, ALABAMA'S STORY has been one of division, between sections, between classes, between political philosophies, and, most importantly, between races. Part of the motivation for these divisions was the maintenance of political, social, and economic power by the "haves" against the "have nots." Another part of the divisiveness sprang from a stubbornness of character which took a defensive posture against any group who questioned the conduct and motives of those who "had" against those who "had not." Lawyers have been advocates for both groups. Historically, though, the organized bar was dominated by the "haves" and not particularly sympathetic to the "have nots."

This story began to change when an Alabama attorney was appointed to the United States Supreme Court and joined the majority to declare that the doctrine of "separate but equal" practiced for many decades did not fulfill constitutional requirements for equality of opportunity under law. Other Alabama attorneys took this decision and challenged Alabama's segregation laws at every opportunity, with the support of an Alabama federal district judge and an Alabama federal circuit court judge who were willing to expand the concept declared by the Supreme Court to address similar circumstances. Those civil rights lawyers and judges moved the profession toward service and away from power. An Alabama Supreme Court chief justice took this same service orientation and applied it to reforming the state judicial and legal system for the betterment of the state. Many other Alabama lawyers joined him in this historic effort.

As large numbers of young people, including many who had no previous connections to the power base within the profession, graduated from law schools, the organized bar has become a platform for rendering service to not only the "have nots" but to the public as a whole. The organized bar has adopted a motto that "lawyers render service" and a stance that it will promote that which is good for all the people of the state. That is the goal and that is the hope.

The promise of that early service orientation of civil rights lawyers and judges in Alabama has been borne out in the 2008 presidential election. There is a direct link between the struggles of blacks in Alabama and the election of an African American president—a link that can be looked to with pride, even though the struggle was sometimes violent and pitted citizen against citizen. The struggle and its victims have been justified. And telling the story of lawyers in Alabama illustrates that struggle and that movement from power to service. I am proud to be able to record that history.

With that said, I would like to thank the Alabama State Bar for giving me the opportunity to research and tell the story of lawyers in Alabama. Doug McElvy, president from 2004 to 2005, asked me to join the History and Archives Committee and undertake the writing of this book. Ben Spratling, the committee chairman, has been a guiding energy, and committee member Harold Williams has been a guardian angel throughout. Others on the committee who have taken an active role in shepherding the book include Frank Donaldson, former Chief Justice Perry Hooper, Joe Bolton, Harlan Prater, Supreme Court Judge Greg Shaw, and former state bar president Sam Rumore (who also happens to be my husband.) And, of course, I appreciate all the other committee members who have given input towards this project, including Everette Price, Adrian Johnson, Karlos Finley, Hampton Boles, and David Bright.

While the committee was considering how to fund the publication of the book, Sam was invited to join the board of the Bench and Bar Historical Society. At the time, the Society was looking for a project to sponsor

The Supreme Court of Alabama meets in this elegant courtroom beneath the dome of the Heflin-Torbert Judicial Building on Dexter Avenue in Montgomery, just two blocks down the hill from the Alabama State Capitol, the early home of the court.

and it accepted the invitation of the History and Archives Committee to join forces and became a cosponsor of this book, guaranteeing the production costs. For this action, my great appreciation goes to its president Tim Lewis, and board members Billy Melton, Leah Atkins, former Chief Justice Sonny Hornsby, Lynne Kitchens, Edward Pattillo, William E. Smith, Jr., Fred Gray, Fred Simpson, Sandra Lewis, and Sam Rumore. A special thanks goes to historian Leah Atkins for her review of the manuscript prior to its publication.

Acknowledgement also goes to Executive Director Keith Norman, Assistant Executive Director Ed Patterson, and the Board of Bar Commissioners of the Alabama State Bar for their support and the freedom given me to explore and present fully the story I found, including access to archival materials. Thank you to Reginald Hamner, Rod Nachman, Bill Hairston, Oakley Melton, George Azar, Judge Harold Albritton, Atley Kitchings and, posthumously, to Howell T. Heflin, George Peach Taylor, and Ira Burleson, whose informal conversations gave me direction and insights I might not otherwise have had.

I thank Paul M. Pruitt, Howard P. Walthall, Tony A. Freyer, and Timothy W. Dixon for sharing their unpublished manuscript entitled *Alabama's Supreme Court and Legal Institutions: A History,* which provided me with a wealth of information to incorporate into the book. I also thank Mike Hall for allowing me to keep his sets of Alabama history books containing biographical sketches of many of Alabama's lawyers throughout the several years it took to write the book. Finally, I must give credit to my husband's habit of collecting Alabama history books, journals, and biographies, thereby guaranteeing that I had ample research resources in our home library.

—Pat Boyd Rumore
November 2009

FROM POWER TO SERVICE

INTRODUCTION

Alabama's professional historians have often noted the many paradoxes and idiosyncrasies in the state's history in attempting to explain its failures to act in its own seeming best interests when the trends of history have called it to make political, social, and cultural changes.[1] Reaching consensus about needed change has often been difficult and, in some important respects, has so far not come about. Alabama's legal profession has had its role in these failures and its story contains demagogues and villains as well as heroes, all depending on one's personal historical outlook.

As a writer and a lawyer, I have been interested in the power of words to both describe and to inspire attitudes and actions. I have always thought that Alabama's state motto "Audemus jura nostra defendere" perfectly describes the attitude of the people who have created most of Alabama's history. I assumed that Alabama's early settlers must have ordained the motto, which most people interpret to mean "We dare defend our rights," since most of the early arrivals to the state were yeoman farmers and slave owners who did not want anyone to tell them what to do. As state government was formed and interacted with the developing power of the federal government, Alabama's would-be leaders, who were usually lawyers, tended to promote their own ambitions by using words and phrases to create issues that played to the prejudices of their targeted constituents. These were men who hungered for power and who wielded that power for themselves and the segment of the population with the same interests and prejudices as theirs. The "rights" they defended were their own, making Alabama a state with

The Alabama State Bar headquarters building in Montgomery was completed in 1963 and was, at the time, the most expensive public building per square foot ever built in Alabama.

many "special" interest groups who "dared to defend their rights," usually without seeking commonality or compromise. Those groups without power, particularly the almost fifty percent who were black slaves or former slaves and poor whites, ultimately found themselves without rights. The result has been a modern-day reluctance to trust even elected legislators to make important changes, since they are susceptible to special interests in the form of their personal constituents, financial supporters, and lobbyists.

In research for this introduction, I was surprised to find that Alabama's motto actually dates back to 1923, when Marie Bankhead Owen, then director of the Alabama Department of Archives and History, was working on a state crest and wanted a motto to put on the crest. She later was quoted as saying that she sought "a phrase that would interpret the spirit of our peoples in a terse and energetic sentence." She found inspiration in a poem written in 1781, which contained the words "Men, who their duties know, but know their rights, and knowing, dare maintain." The motto she crafted, which was adopted by the legislature in 1939, was literally the phrase "We dare maintain our rights." When the phrase was translated

into Latin to put on the crest, the translator chose the Latin verb "defendere" rather than one of several others which could represent the word "maintain." Because of that choice, the motto is usually translated as "defend" rather than "maintain."

Since Alabama and its political leaders have often taken a defensive posture when challenged by non-Alabamians, whether they be "carpetbaggers" or "outside agitators" or the federal government, it seems appropriate that the official motto has been transmuted so that it suggests Alabamians' historical willingness to "stand up for Alabama"—regardless of whether Alabama was right or wrong.

And it is a fair assessment that, during much of its history, the state bar as an association was at the forefront of representing the powerful "special" interests in Alabama and has at times stood for Alabama even when it was not right. The profession, when small, parochial, and uniform, often represented power more than service.

Since its inception, the Alabama State Bar as an organization has also represented a movement toward increasing professionalism. Over time, ethical norms and professional expectations have become institutionalized, and in a great thrust of energy generated by the expansion and diversification of the profession after World War II, a call to service has swept the profession. This call was probably first manifested in the use of the legal system by a small group of black civil rights attorneys to secure the civil rights of African Americans. Thereafter, white attorneys joined them to equalize the balance of power in the Alabama legislature by bringing redistricting actions to guarantee "one voter, one vote" throughout the state, giving more power to its urban areas. Then judicial reform swept the state, with impetus provided by the Alabama State Bar, bringing with it procedural and legal reforms as well.

In this new millennium, a new motto is powering the activities of the legal profession through its association. The motto of the Alabama State Bar is "Lawyers render service." With over 16,000 members, representing every possible interest group within the state, the Alabama State Bar has become an institution well positioned to weigh in on behalf of the interests of all Alabamians. The legal profession has moved from a small group wielding power to a large and diverse force of men and women rendering service.

As I worked through the writing of this history of the profession, I was not sure what exactly I would find. Obviously most lawyers make their livings representing individual or institutional clients, but it is impossible to talk about this most important aspect of the profession in other than the most general terms. More important for purposes of this book was the role of lawyers in shaping Alabama's political and social, as well as legal, history. I noted the important role of Alabama lawyers in the development of constitutional law in the United States, especially in the realm of civil rights and civil liberties. I quickly became intrigued by the many lawyers who were also politicians, journalists, writers, orators, educators, church leaders, and historians, many of statewide and even national importance. Lawyers manifest their presence in myriad ways. The courthouse is only one of their stages.

I found that each generation of the profession has had a different story to tell with an interesting cast of characters. I am glad to see that the story being told by members of the profession during my tenure within its ranks is a more promising story than ever before in the state's history. And the profession has created a forum for its youngest potential leaders to prepare for a future of service in the interest of all citizens of the state. So there is reason to hope that the best is yet to come.

Of course, there are still those lawyers whose ambitions for power may not serve the best interests of the state, but they find it difficult to usurp the profession for their purposes. The organized bar has reached a level of development where its contributions are made without hidden agendas and its intentions are aimed at service. History will tell us of the contributions made by individual lawyers, and, for Alabama's currently practicing lawyers, history is still in the making.

—Pat Boyd Rumore
November 2009

FROM POWER TO SERVICE

DEDICATION

DEDICATED TO ATTORNEY HAROLD WILLIAMS,
WHOSE BELIEF IN AND SUPPORT FOR
THIS PROJECT GUARANTEED
ITS COMPLETION.

CHAPTER ONE

PRELUDE TO STATEHOOD: LAWYERS IN THE TERRITORIES

LAND BROUGHT SETTLERS TO THE territory of Alabama—virgin wilderness land that was part of the public domain of the United States, ceded by treaty from Spain, from Georgia, and from various Indian tribes. A major issue for pioneers was how to acquire legal title to the lands they settled. The federal government tried several approaches to land distribution, first hoping to sell large tracts of land for cash to developers who would then subdivide their plots for sale to individuals, with the idea of using this wholesaling approach to raise revenue for the Treasury. There were a few early takers who established land companies to sell the lands they acquired, but not enough to satisfy the demands of those entering the territory. The government ultimately devised a new approach, finalized in 1803, where an individual could buy a tract as small as 160 acres, taking four years to pay required installments. This credit plan helped attract large numbers of farmers and planters from other settled areas as part of the expansion to the west, but it also precipitated disputes when purchasers failed to meet credit obligations and invited frauds and swindles before a legal structure was in place to resolve claims.

Questions had to be answered: What would happen when there were conflicting claims to a piece of property that had passed through the hands of several governments before becoming part of the United States, or when a purchaser failed to pay a credit installment? Who would administer land offices to sell the land, draft mortgages to finance the sale, and draft deeds to evidence the sale? Who would set up and run local governments to record deeds and courts to settle land disputes? Who would advocate on behalf of various interest groups as decisions were made about county lines and county seats, as well as state boundaries? Who would draw up the constitution and laws to establish the legal order in both the territory and the state? Who would represent citizens as political and judicial leaders?

Among the flood of pioneers, most of whom intended to farm, came a group trained in the law, ready to address these questions. Many of the lawyers who arrived on the frontier were seasoned attorneys and statesmen who brought with them the legal culture they had learned in other places. Several became famous in Alabama history. These lawyers had enormous influence while Alabama lands were part of the Mississippi Territory and in Ala-

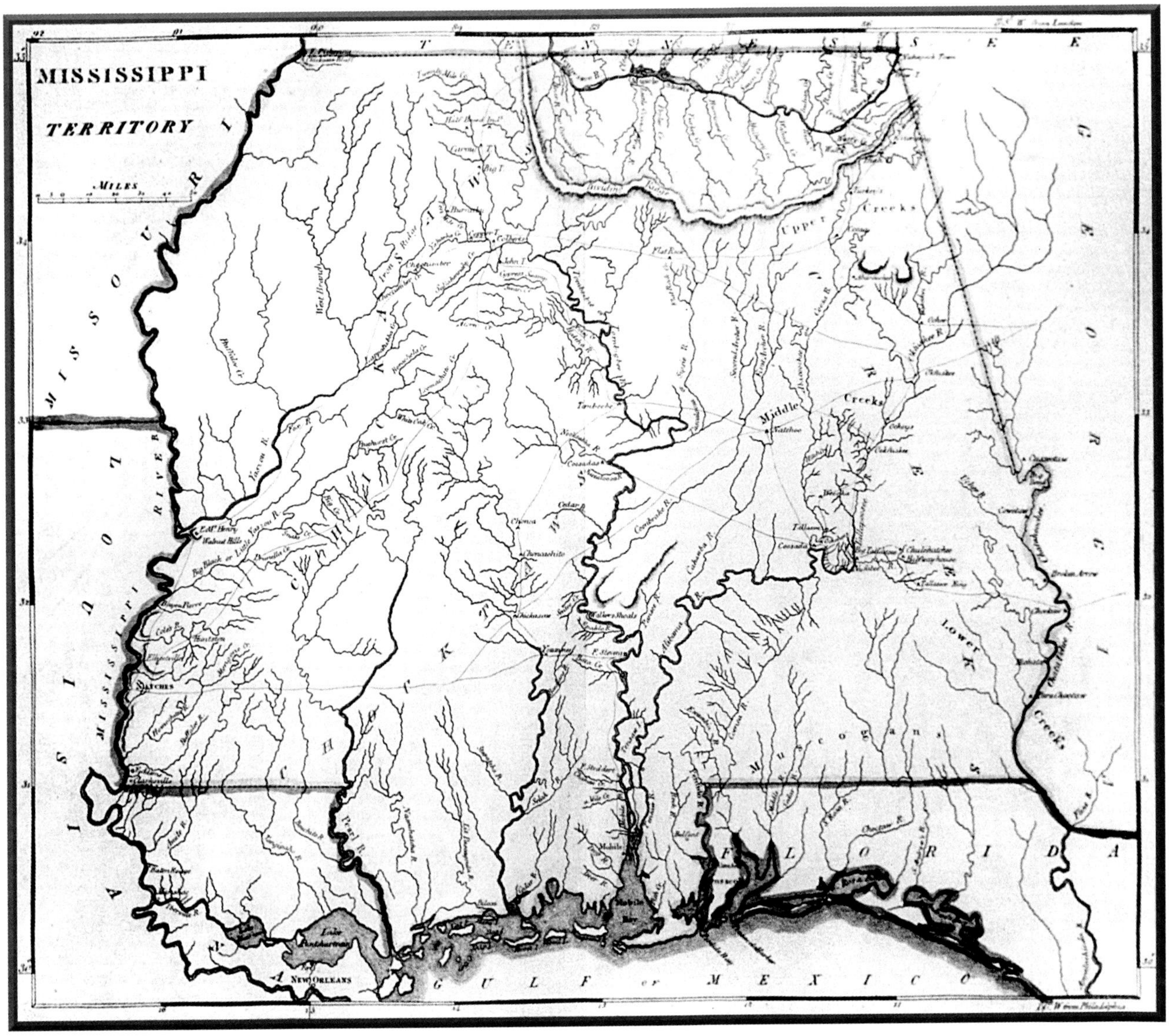

OPPOSITE PAGE: *A native Englishman, Harry Toulmin, was appointed to the superior judgeship of the Mississippi Territory by President Thomas Jefferson in 1804.* ABOVE: *Toulmin settled at Fort Stoddert, which can be found located just to the north of Mobile on this map of the Mississippi Territory.*

bama's separate territorial days, they played significant roles in bringing Alabama to statehood. One of the first was Harry Toulmin.

HARRY TOULMIN OF TOMBIGBEE

In the huge expanse that was the Mississippi Territory in 1798, there were only two white settlements in an area dominated by Native American tribes, including Creek, Choctaw, Chickasaw, and Cherokee. The largest settlement was on the Mississippi River at Natchez. A much smaller settlement was located on the lower Tombigbee River, with the primitive village of St. Stephens being the focal point of trade. In 1798, territorial governor Winthrop Sargent created Washington County, which included the Tombigbee settlement, to provide a governmental presence in that area. In 1799, the U.S. government built Fort Stoddert, about 50 miles above Spanish Mobile, as its southernmost fortification. A land office was established at St. Stephens in 1804, under the provisions of an act that outlined the rules to validate claims of settlers who had come to the area under grants from the English and Spanish in earlier years. This act also handled the disposal of land under prior Georgia territorial claims and established the priorities of claims by those entering the area after the Spanish left.

In 1804, a federal territorial court was established at St. Stephens and President Thomas Jefferson appointed

Harry Toulmin as its judge. Toulmin subsequently became the first federal judge of what was then called the Tombigbee District. His jurisdictional district was approximately 340 miles long and 330 miles wide and eventually included seven territorial counties comprising most of today's Alabama.

Harry Toulmin was born in 1766 in Taunton, England, son of Reverend Joshua Toulmin who was an independent clergyman before serving both the Baptist and Unitarian churches in Taunton and Birmingham, England. Harry Toulmin was educated in England and licensed to preach. He came to America in 1793 and established a seminary at Norfolk, Virginia, later moving to Lexington, Kentucky where he became president of Transylvania University for four years. He gained a reputation as a free thinker and had problems with members of his board of trustees at Transylvania. He subsequently retired and, in 1796, became secretary of state of Kentucky for two terms, during which time he studied law and became a member of the Kentucky Bar. In 1804, his friend Thomas Jefferson appointed him to the superior judgeship in the Mississippi Territory upon the untimely death of Ephraim Kirby, his first appointee.

Toulmin settled at Fort Stoddert in Washington County, but his first court was held in the fall of 1804 at a place he named Wakefield. He not only served as judge, but also as minister, postmaster, and physician to his territorial neighbors. He authored several important legal books during his career, including *Mississippi Magistrate's Guide* (1807), *The Statutes of the Mississippi Territory* (1807), and *Digest of the Laws of the State of Alabama* (1823), books that helped establish the rule of law through their widespread use during the territorial and early statehood periods.

Toulmin is remembered in Alabama history as the most famous citizen of the Tombigbee settlement, representing the settlement in most of its relations with the outside world for many years, probably because he was the most educated in an area where the average settler was a farmer, cattle herder, or Indian trader. He served as territorial judge from his appointment in 1804 until Alabama became a state in 1819.

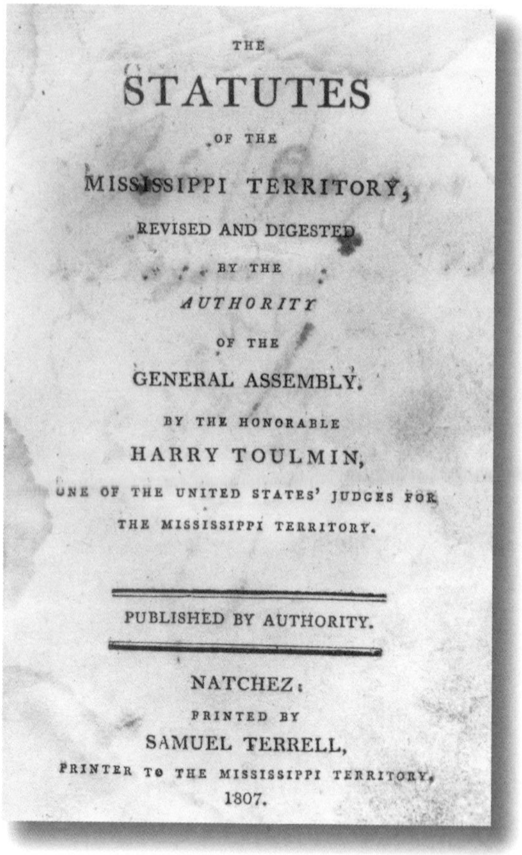
THE
STATUTES
OF THE
MISSISSIPPI TERRITORY,
REVISED AND DIGESTED
BY THE
AUTHORITY
OF THE
GENERAL ASSEMBLY.
BY THE HONORABLE
HARRY TOULMIN,
ONE OF THE UNITED STATES' JUDGES FOR
THE MISSISSIPPI TERRITORY.

PUBLISHED BY AUTHORITY.

NATCHEZ:
PRINTED BY
SAMUEL TERRELL,
PRINTER TO THE MISSISSIPPI TERRITORY,
1807.

Harry Toulmin was the author of several important early legal books widely used in the Mississippi Territory and in the early state of Alabama.

LeRoy Pope and the Georgia Faction, Gabriel Moore and the Tennesseans

Between 1801 and 1804, land cessions by the Chickasaws and Cherokees opened up the area that is today's Madison County to settlement. As early as 1804, large numbers of yeoman farmers from Tennessee, as well as some from North Carolina and Virginia, entered the area as squatters. In 1808, shortly after Robert Williams, governor of the Mississippi Territory, issued a proclamation creating Madison County, the lands officially became available for purchase. Many of the farmers were too poor to afford the cost of the land on which they had squatted. Their lands were bought up by a group of wealthy Georgians, who succeeded in purchasing much of the best land in the area. As described by Alabama historian J. Mills Thornton in his book *Politics and Power in a Slave Society*, "The net result of the land sales…was to create a population with an overwhelming majority of small Tennessee farmers, but to place most of the best land in the hands of a wealthy and clannish band of Georgia planters. The situation was ready-made for class conflict." It was a preview of one thread in the fabric of life in Alabama—the conflict between the haves and the have-nots.

The "Broad River" group of Georgians who supplied these wealthy immigrants to Madison County had originally come from the Piedmont area of Virginia and had moved as a group to Georgia in 1784, settling near the Broad River. They had a strong sense of group identity, strong social relationships, and much kinship through intermarriage. They had grown accustomed to wielding

political and economic power from their days in Virginia and members of their group became governors, senators, and prominent leaders in both Georgia and Alabama as they dispersed from their Broad River beginnings in the Deep South. Many of their number were lawyers, including LeRoy Pope and his son-in-law John Williams Walker, who dominated life in early Huntsville.

Even from the beginning, the aristocratic ways of LeRoy Pope and his kin aroused the animosity of the Tennessee settlers who had come into the area before them. In its earliest days, what is today's Huntsville had been a small settlement of squatters known as Hunt's Spring, named after the first man who built a cabin in the area. In 1809, Pope bought up the lands comprising the community and laid out his own town there, deciding to call it Twickenham, in honor of his family connection

LEFT: *LeRoy Pope was a lawyer and a leader of the "Broad River" group from Georgia who settled in Madison County in the early 1800s.* BELOW: *The aristocratic manners and lifestyle of the Georgians, exemplified by LeRoy Pope's mansion, Poplar Grove, angered the less-wealthy settlers from Tennessee.*

In the 1810 election, the Tennessee faction demonstrated its political clout by electing three Tennesseans, Hugh McVay, above, Peter Perkins, and Gabriel Moore, to represent the newly created Madison County in the Mississippi territorial legislature.

to English author Alexander Pope, who lived in a town of the same name. The squatters who had been expelled from Pope's land, but who had bought other lands in the vicinity, were outraged that he eliminated any reference to the town's first settler. In 1810, when the new Madison County became entitled to send three representatives to the Mississippi territorial legislature, the Georgians nominated John Williams Walker, as well as Louis Winston, the county attorney, and Tennessean Peter Perkins, to balance the ticket. The Tennesseans, who were in the majority, responded by nominating and electing their own, attorneys Hugh McVay and Gabriel Moore, in addition to Perkins. Thus the Georgians were shut out of this early elective opportunity, even though they controlled the economic and social life of the community. They were able to do nothing when the legislators immediately acted to change the name of Twickenham to Huntsville. The seeds of class conflict were sown and attorney Gabriel Moore, one of the territorial representatives, soon became known throughout the territorial period as a leader of the opposition to the Georgia faction.

The Georgia group was able to have one of their supporters appointed territorial judge when the position was created in 1810. Obadiah Jones, an intimate friend of Georgia's senator William H. Crawford, one of the leaders of the Broad River Georgians, was appointed judge of Madison County. He is remembered for the pomp with which he opened court and maintained its dignity.

The Massacre at Fort Mims and the End of the Mississippi Territory

As roads were built through the Mississippi Territory, more and more white settlers entered the area. Although there were periods when the native Indian populations cooperated and even emulated their white counterparts, the constant pressure of white immigration caused tensions over time that resulted in violence. One such incident, which inspired armed resistance, was the attack at Fort Mims, involving isolated settlers in the Tombigbee area. Earlier skirmishes had resulted in the settlers coming together and building a stockade around the home of wealthy settler Samuel Mims. Troops from Fort Stoddert were sent to Fort Mims to help the settlers, under the leadership of Major Daniel Beasley, an attorney from Mississippi who had been given a military title through his political clout but who proved himself an inept soldier. Having no military training or experience, he was unable to organize those defending the fort and even ignored warnings that Red Stick Creeks were planning to attack the fort. By leaving the gates to the stockade propped open with loose sand and even drinking and playing cards with his men on the day of the attack, he guaranteed a victory for the Red Sticks when they attacked on August 30, 1813, and massacred almost everyone there.

This Creek War ended at the Battle of Horseshoe Bend where militia were under the leadership of General Andrew Jackson. The American victory forced the Creeks to cede most of their tribal lands to the United States, precipitating a flood of settlers into the territory after the signing of the Treaty of Fort Jackson in 1814. As the population increased, pressure began to build for the territory to petition Congress for statehood. The big question of the time was whether the whole Mississippi Territory would enter as one state or whether it should be divided.

These issues had been discussed as early as 1803, when Tombigbee settlers in Alabama had sent a petition to Congress asking to be separated from Natchez, a petition renewed in 1809, primarily because they felt entirely neglected by the territorial government based near the Mississippi River. There were proposals to divide the territory either longitudinally or latitudinally, but nothing came of these proposals before the War of 1812 distracted both Congress and territorial settlers from resolving them.

After the War of 1812 and the Creek War ended, the interests of the Tombigbee settlers changed. They saw a large increase in population in their area and the real prospect that they could dominate territorial and state politics. In October 1816, a group from the areas of Tombigbee and east of the Pearl River met at the home of John Ford on the lower Pearl River and adopted a petition asking Congress to admit the whole territory as one state. Called the Pearl River Convention, Judge Harry Toulmin was chosen as their spokesman and he went to Washington to plead their cause. Toulmin was not successful. Instead, the House committee considering the question came out in favor of a north-south division of the territory with the west to come in immediately as a state and the east to continue under territorial government. Toulmin then represented his neighbors in arguing that the territorial counties of Wayne, Greene, and Jackson should be included in the east

LEFT: *William H. Crawford, a leader of the Broad River Georgians, served as U.S. senator from Georgia, and later as secretary of war and secretary of the treasury. Along with Georgia senator Charles Tait, he was deeply involved in the creation of the Alabama territory, and in securing statehood for Alabama.* BELOW: *The attack on Fort Mims by the Red Stick Creeks resulted in the deaths of approximately 250 men, women, and children. It still stands as one of the worst massacres on American soil.*

It is hard to picture this quiet path through the woods as the bustling main street of the territorial capital of St. Stephens. A town of several thousand inhabitants at the time of statehood, it had virtually disappeared only 50 years later.

territory with the Pascagoula River as a boundary. Again, Toulmin's arguments failed.

Others argued in favor of an east-west boundary, which would have created two more states comparable to Tennessee. John Williams Walker was one of the men who supported this approach, recognizing the possibility of future conflicts of interest between counties in the north and counties in the south of the original territory. Ultimately, though, the act creating the Alabama Territory, approved March 3, 1817, established boundaries very close to those of today's Alabama.

Georgia senator Charles Tait, another Broad River Georgian and an attorney, shepherded the act which created the Alabama Territory through the Congress, with the help and influence of William H. Crawford of Georgia, who was the secretary of the treasury at the time. Tait and Crawford would again be intimately involved in the process which would bring Alabama to statehood two years later, as the Broad River group continued to play a critical role in Alabama's formative years. In the meantime, Tait's son, along with other Broad River Georgians, bought land in South Alabama in about 1817, when Creek lands became available, bringing a Georgia influence to south Alabama's Black Belt politics as well as to north Alabama.

John Williams Walker Influences both Territorial Government and the Drive for Statehood

When Alabama became a territory, it was governed by a legislature consisting of two houses, one an appointed council and the other a lower house elected by popular vote. The first representatives were carryovers from the previous Mississippi territorial legislature and all Mississippi territorial laws were to apply in the new territory unless specifically repealed. The dominating figures among the first 12 members of the lower house were Huntsville attorneys Clement Comer Clay, John Williams Walker, and Gabriel Moore. Moore was chosen speaker at the first session, but Walker dominated the action preparing for statehood due to his Washington connections as a member of the Georgia faction.

During the session, the territorial legislature repealed the law setting a maximum rate of interest on loans, created three judicial circuits and 13 new counties, incorporated a steamboat company, an academy, and a bank at St. Stephens, and appointed a commission to propose to the next session a permanent seat of territorial government. The legislature also passed a law authorizing the taking of a census preparatory to statehood.

PRIVATE VERSUS STATE BANKS—THE BEGINNING OF AN IMPORTANT POLITICAL ISSUE

Attorney Abner Lipscomb, one of the 12 house members, who would in the future serve as chief justice of the Alabama Supreme Court, proposed that the Alabama Territorial Legislature repeal the application of the Mississippi Territorial Act against Usury in the new territory. His goal was to attract credit to the new territory, which was without ready sources of currency. His proposal was adopted and thereafter there was no legal limit on the interest that could be charged those borrowing money in the Alabama Territory. Since most of those immigrating to the area were yeoman farmers, who had to borrow to finance their moves, this bill soon came to represent oppression to the majority of the inhabitants of the new territory, especially when land speculation and bank failures resulted in a panic in 1819.

As a member of the Alabama Territorial Legislature, Abner Lipscomb proposed the repeal of the law against usury.

At the time, there was one dominant bank in the territory, the Bank of Huntsville, a private bank owned by LeRoy Pope, which had been chartered in 1816. John Williams Walker proposed to have its charter confirmed during the first session of the Alabama Territorial Legislature, renaming it the Huntsville Planters and Merchants Bank and committing the territorial government to accept its notes and allow it to expand by establishing new branches. Although Governor Bibb expressed reservations that Walker's bill would give the bank's directors in Huntsville disproportionate power over the commerce of the territory, the bill ultimately was adopted. Historian Leah Rawls Atkins described Walker's action in supporting both of these pieces of legislation: "It is abundantly clear that the Georgia faction represented the interests of the creditors and that they were acting out the time-honored use of political power to protect their own interests at the expense of their constituents. This procreditor legislation became extremely unpopular with more democratic groups who proceeded to make private banks and public credit important political issues."[1] Another thread was woven into the fabric called Alabama—the use of government by interest groups to preserve economic power.

The ordinary territorial citizen viewed banks and bankers "as the agents of the upper classes, the holders of a money monopoly, and the instruments by which the rich grew richer."[2] It soon became known that Pope treated the Huntsville bank's funds as his own and that he underwrote much of his elegant lifestyle by his free use of bank funds. This conduct resulted in a scandal that ended the political clout of the Broad River Georgia faction in the politics of early Alabama when, as a result of the 1819 panic, Pope's bank suspended the payment of specie for its notes in 1820.

CHAPTER TWO

ALABAMA'S EARLY STATEHOOD AND THE ROLE OF ATTORNEYS

THE DEFEAT OF THE CREEK INDIANS IN 1814 inspired a rush to Alabama during the rest of the decade, which resulted in a one thousand percent increase in population from the decade's beginning. By 1819, the population was more than sufficient to support statehood. During the second term of the territorial legislature, John Williams Walker, who had been selected speaker of the House, used his clout to present a petition for statehood to Congress through Senator Charles Tait of Georgia. He also led the political wrangling involved in apportioning legislative representation, based on the recent territorial census, so that this apportionment could be used to allocate delegates to a constitutional convention.

At this point, political strains between the interests of Madison County in the north and those of south Alabama counties began to appear, strains which would presage another thread in the fabric of Alabama—the rivalry between north and south Alabama. The census showed a state population of 127,901, but these raw numbers did not answer the question of which section of the state would dominate. First, the method of apportionment had to be decided upon, either representation based on white population only or representation that placed a limit on the number of seats given to any individual county. By the first method, Madison County would be entitled to twice as many representatives as any other county. Counties in south Alabama advocated the second method, but finally accepted the white-population-only method after Madison County agreed to the passage of an amendment locating the permanent capital in the southern part of the state at Cahaba. Huntsville was made the temporary capital until a capital city could be organized and constructed at Cahaba. This compromise rendered redundant the legislative commission's proposal that Tuscaloosa be made the capital.

The enabling act to create the state of Alabama was pushed through Congress by Georgia Senator Tait and signed into law on March 2, 1819. Thereafter, Tait moved to Alabama and, in 1820, was appointed by President James Monroe as the first federal district judge in the state. Once the enabling legislation was enacted, an election was held to choose delegates to a constitutional convention, which assembled in Huntsville on July 5, 1819.

ALABAMA'S FIRST CONSTITUTION— THE CONSTITUTION OF 1819

Alabama's first constitutional convention had 44 delegates representing 22 counties. Madison County had eight of those delegates, twice as many as the next largest delegation. The president of the convention was John Williams Walker. Many of the delegates became famous in Alabama history, including attorneys William Rufus King (who

This mural by Roderick MacKenzie in the Alabama State Capitol rotunda depicts the drafting of Alabama's first constitution.

became vice president of the United States after serving as Alabama's first U.S. senator); Clement Comer Clay (eighth governor of Alabama as well as its eighth U.S. senator); Gabriel Moore (Alabama's fifth governor and seventh U.S. senator); Marmaduke Williams (a member of Congress); Israel Pickens (third governor and fifth U.S. senator); James Dellett (member of Congress); Henry Hitchcock (who wrote the first book published in Alabama and became chief justice of the Alabama Supreme

Court); Harry Toulmin (a territorial judge and leader of the Tombigbee settlement); John Murphy (fourth governor); Arthur F. Hopkins (chief justice of the Alabama Supreme Court); John M. Taylor (a judge on the Alabama Supreme Court); Beverly Hughes (a territorial judge); Reuben Saffold (chief justice of the Alabama Supreme Court); Richard Ellis (who subsequently migrated to Texas and was a principal figure in the Texas rebellion); John D. Bibb (a legislator, judge, and planter and brother of William Wyatt and Thomas Bibb, Alabama's first two governors who were also physicians); and John Williams Walker. The 44 delegates provided the state with a total of six governors, six senators, and six Alabama Supreme Court justices.

Attorney Arthur F. Hopkins was a delegate to the 1819 constitutional convention and a member of the Committee of 15. He later served on the Alabama Supreme Court, including one year as chief justice.

A Committee of Fifteen, chaired by Clement Comer Clay, provided a draft of a constitution for the convention to consider. Eleven of these 15 were attorneys, including Judge John M. Taylor, William Rufus King, Judge Henry Hitchcock, John Murphy, Beverly Hughes, Arthur F. Hopkins, Clement Comer Clay, Reuben Saffold, Richard Ellis, John D. Bibb, and Israel Pickens. These men were socially prominent, well educated, and politically experienced, and drafted a constitution that, in many respects, was considered liberal for its day. It contained no discrimination on the grounds of religion, no political discrimination between rich and poor, and provided for a liberal suffrage for the times, in that all white men aged 21 or older could vote and hold office, if they were U.S. citizens and had lived in the state for one year. The constitution drafted by the Committee of Fifteen was adopted by the convention with few significant changes. It was not ratified by the people, but became official after adoption by the convention.

JOHN WILLIAMS WALKER
1783-1823

EVEN THOUGH JOHN WILLIAMS WALKER DIED IN his fortieth year, his political successes and his progeny have had a lasting impact on the state.

Walker was born to the Reverend Jeremiah and Mary Jane Walker, devout Baptists who were persecuted for their beliefs in the predominantly Anglican area of Virginia where they first lived. They moved to Petersburg, Georgia, and both soon died, leaving John an orphan at age nine. John was raised by his four brothers. He attended Moses Waddell Academy and Princeton University, where he was an excellent student and prolific writer on the subjects of religion, philosophy, and politics. During this time, he was afflicted with tuberculosis and acquired a somewhat fatalistic approach to life and achievement. Still, he persisted and graduated from Princeton with honors in 1806, returned to Petersburg to practice law, and married Matilda Pope.

After the Popes and the Walkers moved to the Tennessee Valley, Walker's restless nature and inclination to dissent made him a natural leader in the politics of frontier Alabama, and his contacts among the Georgia politically connected elite led the way for the formation of a state and his selection as one of Alabama's first two United States senators.

Walker left a legacy of sons, including Percy Walker, LeRoy Pope Walker, and Richard Wilde Walker, who each gained prominence as attorneys in Alabama in the years following their father's death.

Two provisions in the constitution were unusual: the power it gave to state government to establish a state bank and its decree that "schools and the means of education shall forever be encouraged in this state." It established three branches of government, with the legislative branch the most powerful, including the power to elect the United States senators, secretary of state, state treasurer, comptroller of public accounts, supreme court judges, circuit judges, inferior judges, and other lesser positions.

In an effort to enhance popular sovereignty, the constitution authorized annual elections and annual legislative sessions. The framers deliberately created a weak executive, in reaction to earlier experiences with an overly strong territorial executive. Although the governor had the power to veto legislation, a mere majority could override a veto.

Because the drafters wanted to secure an independent judiciary, they provided that judges would be selected by the legislature. A proposal to limit appointments to six years was rejected, and the constitution established lifetime appointments in the name of judicial independence.

The constitution proposed by the Committee of Fifteen contained apportionment by the federal constitutional ratio, that is, counting only three-fifths of the black population for determining representation in the state legislature. Ultimately, this proposal was defeated and the convention set up the white population as the basis for apportionment, for both the House and the Senate. The question of apportionment of senators presented one of the bitterest fights of the convention because south Alabama wanted each county to have a senator regardless of population, while north Alabama wanted senatorial districts of equal population. In each instance, white-only apportionment meant more influence for north Alabama and, in each instance, north Alabama won and continued to win until the end of the Civil War.

Territorial governor William Wyatt Bibb, top, a member of the Georgia faction, defeated Marmaduke Williams, representing the North Carolina faction, in a close election to become the first governor of Alabama. Taking office in December 1819, Bibb died on July 10, 1820, following a fall from a horse. He was automatically succeeded by his brother Thomas, above, who was serving as the president of the Alabama Senate.

Alabama Becomes a State and the North Carolina Faction Presents a Challenge

On August 2, 1819, all 44 members of the convention signed the Constitution of 1819. It was submitted to the U.S. Congress, and, after certain actions were accomplished to establish a government, Congress passed a resolution of admission, which in turn was signed by President James Monroe on December 14, 1819. Alabama became a state on that day.

William Wyatt Bibb became the first governor of the state after defeating attorney Marmaduke Williams, a former congressman from North Carolina, in the state's first gubernatorial election in September 1819. Williams, who was a member of the constitutional convention, representing Tuscaloosa County, would serve as secretary of the Board of Trustees of the University of Alabama from its incorporation in 1821 until 1840. His wife was a first cousin of Dolly Madison. He ran against Bibb on the basis that Bibb had forced through the choice of Cahaba as the state capital in the face of the choice of Tuscaloosa by the appointed legislative committee. Williams could not overcome the advantage that Bibb had as a member of the Georgia faction or as the incumbent territorial governor. The election was close and demonstrated the potential clout of another faction in Alabama politics, the North Carolina faction. It dominated the politics of central Alabama, where Tuscaloosa was the largest center of population, and openly opposed the interests of the Georgia faction.

Factionalism, Sectionalism, and Demagoguery: William Rufus King and William B. Long Come to Prominence

Just like the country as a whole at the time, Alabama did not have political parties in its first elections, but it did have factions: The Georgia faction, called the Royal Party by many, strong in both north Alabama and in the Black Belt; its opposition, the Tennessee faction led by Gabriel Moore and his followers; and the North Carolina faction, led by Marmaduke Williams of Tuscaloosa. In addition to political factions, there was the natural animosity between the people of north and south Alabama demonstrated by the fight for control over how the legislature would be apportioned and where the state capital would be located.

In his first address as governor of the state, Governor William Wyatt Bibb urged the legislators to avoid factionalism and sectionalism. He also urged them to elect Alabama's two senators as soon as possible, so that when statehood was finalized, Alabama could provide two more votes for the South on the important issues that were coming before the Congress. Missouri's bid for statehood, which had raised the difficult issue of slavery and its status in new territories and states, was one of these issues.

Attorney Israel Pickens defeated Dr. Henry Chambers to become Alabama's third governor in 1821. He was reelected in 1823.

To avoid sectional animosity, the legislature determined to choose one senator from north Alabama and one from south Alabama. The Georgia faction proposed two of its own, John Williams Walker and Charles Tait. State senators from south Alabama argued that Tait had not lived long enough in Alabama to merit selection and instead supported attorney William Rufus King of King's Bend in Dallas County. King's selection was a clear renunciation of the Georgia faction and signaled a decline in its political prominence. The resignation and death of John Williams Walker sealed its fate.

When Walker retired from the Senate on November 21, 1822, the Georgia faction proposed John McKinley, an attorney who represented the Planters and Merchants Bank, as his replacement. The opposition, also known as the "Champions of the People" because of their identification with the politics of Andrew Jackson, proposed Huntsville attorney William Kelly to replace Walker. Kelly's candidacy was supported by William B. Long, an attorney originally from Kentucky who had begun publishing a newspaper, the *Huntsville Democrat*, early in 1823. The fiery Long had quickly become known for his opposition to the Georgia faction and was able to stir the electorate sufficiently to compel the legislature to select Kelly over McKinley, who had been regarded as the frontrunner, in an early example of the demagoguery which would appear sporadically in Alabama politics.

Because Alabama's senators were elected by the legislature, not the popular vote of the people, these contests did not clearly define the fortunes of political groups in the state. The election which dates the beginning of definite political alliances and hotly contested issues was the second gubernatorial election involving attorney Israel Pickens and Dr. Henry Chambers in 1823.

The Bank Question

The issue which first triggered this hotly contested statewide election was how to get money circulating in the state. In 1820s Alabama, cash and credit were used to finance the purchase of land and slaves. There was very little cash circulating in the economy to finance other commercial endeavors or to meet the needs of the ordinary citizen. The only sources of legal tender for general circulation were the local banks, which at the time were privately owned. The problem was that there was little money available to provide sufficient capital to underwrite the operation of these banks; therefore, they effectively created money where none existed before, paper which was not backed by solid value in the form of specie. The result had already been evidenced in 1820, when an economic downturn had caused the Merchants and Planters Bank in Huntsville to suspend specie payments, resulting in great hardship and in a political backlash against the Georgia faction, since its

WILLIAM RUFUS KING
1786-1853

Alabama's first senator reached national prominence during his long tenure in public office, ultimately being elected vice president of the United States. King was born in North Carolina in 1786. His father, William King, had been a leader in the American Revolution and served in the North Carolina legislature. William Rufus King graduated from the University of North Carolina and studied law with William Duffy in Fayetteville, North Carolina. He followed his father's example, being elected to the North Carolina legislature in 1808. Shortly thereafter, he was elected to represent his district in the U.S. House of Representatives. He had various positions of service in Washington before moving to Dallas County in the Alabama Territory, where he purchased a large plantation, and soon became one of Alabama's founding fathers.

King was one of the guiding forces in the establishment of Selma, Alabama. He was chosen to represent Dallas County at the 1819 constitutional convention in Huntsville. Shortly thereafter, the Alabama General Assembly elected him to the United States Senate, a position he held consistently until 1844, and then again from 1848 to 1853.

King was a leader in the national political questions that arose during his years of service. He favored a strong federal government, voted for the Missouri Compromise, and supported President Andrew Jackson's fight with the National Bank. He opposed the tariff of 1828, but backed President Jackson's stand against South Carolina, which tried to nullify the tariff act's application to that state, even in the face of a growing sentiment in Alabama which favored the concept of nullification.

King served as president pro tempore of the Senate from 1836 through 1841. In 1844, President Tyler named King minister to France with the task of persuading France not to involve itself in the question of the annexation of Texas to the United States. King was successful, preventing any international involvement in the United States's and Mexico's dispute over the status of Texas. King returned to the Senate after his diplomatic service ended and in Alabama was opposed by the secessionist faction led by William Lowndes Yancey. King supported Henry Clay's Compromise of 1850, the last major effort at compromise over the question of slave and free state issues.

In recognition of his many years of service to the state and nation, the 1852 National Democratic Convention, meeting in Baltimore, nominated him for vice president on the ticket with Franklin Pierce, choosing him over Senator Jefferson Davis of Mississippi. By this time, though, King was suffering from tuberculosis. Shortly after Pierce won the election, making King the only Alabamian to achieve the high office of vice president, King traveled to Cuba for the winter. He was unable to return for the inauguration and became the only major elected American government official to ever assume his office on foreign soil when he was given the oath of office by the United States consul in Havana.

Knowing he was not going to recover, King made his way to his Dallas County home, arriving only two days before his death on April 18, 1853, at the age of 67. King never married; some historians maintain that he was homosexual and that he had an attachment with Pennsylvania senator and later United States President James Buchanan.

most prominent leaders, LeRoy Pope and John Williams Walker, were identified with that bank.

The fragility of the private banking structure in the state resulted in tremendous pressure to create a state bank, underwritten by the resources of state government. The new constitution provided for such an institution and a law had been passed under Governor Thomas Bibb in 1820 to authorize it. The problem was that the 1820 law required a capitalization of $2 million, an amount which would have been impossible to come up with in land-poor Alabama.

The issue of creating an effective state bank brought Israel Pickens to power in Alabama. Ironically, when he was elected for his first term in 1821, he was identified as friendly to the Georgia faction and the interests of the private bankers. At the time, he was president of the Tombeckbee Bank at St. Stephens and an officer of the Bank of Mobile. Yet, Pickens knew first hand that both of these banks were undercapitalized and that the private interests which controlled them were more interested in making a profit than in operating safely and conservatively.

Attorney John Murphy succeeded Israel Pickens as Alabama's fourth governor. Murphy helped promote the establishment of the University of Alabama during his term.

With the help of William Long and his *Democrat*, which made the Royal party the scapegoat of the Panic of 1819, Pickens mounted a challenge to the private banking interests and became the "master of Alabama politics" by acquiring a populist persona and becoming the hero of the common man against "the wealthy, supercilious and crooked" Broad River aristocracy.

When a commission which had been appointed by the legislature during Governor Bibb's term in office attempted to negotiate with the three private banks in the state to become branches of a state bank, and the legislature passed a bill to carry such a plan into action, Pickens vetoed the bill. He justified his action on the basis that, if allowed to become law, this measure would have committed the credit of the state into the hands of a few bankers without careful scrutiny of their affairs. Considering the performance of the private banks up to that point, such a move would have been dangerous, to say the least.

In a move to distance himself from the Royal Party of Pope and Walker, Pickens promoted the establishment of a state bank totally independent of the existing private banks, one capitalized and directed by the state itself. The money to capitalize the bank would come from the sale of lands granted to the state by the federal government for the purpose of founding educational institutions. The bank would be managed by a president and board of directors chosen by the legislature. The issue of implementing the plan put forward by Pickens became the centerpiece of his second campaign for governor in 1823, where Dr. Henry Chambers, a director of the Planters and Merchants bank, again was his opponent.

When Pickens beat Chambers the second time, he broke the power of the Georgia machine and effectively ended its clout in statewide Alabama politics. Shortly after his victory, Pickens guided through legislation which implemented his plan to establish a state bank. In July 1824, the Bank of Alabama opened its doors. The bank's creation was an important step in the development of state government and its power to affect economic development. Further, for many years, the bank's profits underwrote the state's administrative expenses. The presence of the state bank did not end Alabama's currency problems, but within a matter of a few years the bank became "an establishment of portentous possibilities" [1] and Pickens established a place in history as "one of the more successful early governors," and as a man of "exceptional capability, vision, and compassion." [2]

Pickens was followed in office by another attorney, John Murphy, during whose tenure the state capital was moved from Cahaba to Tuscaloosa. Murphy also promoted the establishment of a state university, and his efforts began the process which resulted in the opening of the University of Alabama in Tuscaloosa in 1831. Murphy had been elected by the legislature to the University's board of trustees in 1821. The president of the board at the time was Governor Pickens. Although Pickens supported the creation of a state university, creating a state bank was a

Tuscaloosa became the capital of Alabama in 1826 during the administration of Governor John Murphy. It remained the capital until 1846. The Tuscaloosa capitol building later housed the Alabama Central Female College.

higher priority to him. He redirected the endowment previously earmarked for the educational institution into the capital fund of the state bank instead.

During his time in office, Murphy tried, but failed, to keep a branch of the Bank of the United States from opening in Mobile. The governor feared that the federal bank would undermine the stability of the recently created Bank of Alabama. His fears ultimately were realized.

Gabriel Moore

One of Alabama's founding fathers with a particularly interesting story is Gabriel Moore, Alabama's fifth governor, who also served in both the U.S. House of Representatives and the U.S. Senate. Moore, who was born, educated, and trained as a lawyer in North Carolina, came to Madison County in 1810, at a time when it was the most populous county in the eastern portion of the Mississippi territory. He first served as tax assessor and collector for the county, a position whose duties included supervising the census which determined the apportionment of representatives for the Mississippi Territorial Assembly.

Moore's public career spanned more than 25 years, during which his private life took several twists and turns. In later times of improved communication, this might have ended his public service, but it had little impact during the frontier period in which he lived and served. Moore appealed to the yeoman farmers of Madison County, migrants from Tennessee whose interests conflicted with the Royal party of Broad River aristocrats who had come to Madison County by way of Georgia. Although an affluent attorney as well as a small planter who owned slaves, Moore became identified as the defender of the common man. He was described at the time as "a man of the people, public-spirited, hospitable, and [as] firm in friendship as he was bitter in enmity." [3]

Moore represented Madison County in both the Mississippi and Alabama territorial legislatures, serving as the Alabama Territorial Assembly's speaker during its first session in January and February 1818. He did not seek election as speaker for the second session in November 1818, trying to avoid the notoriety that would come from public attention to the fact that his wife had sought and received a legislative grant of divorce and he, himself, had been involved in a duel with her brother.

Moore's marriage had been brief. He had married the daughter of a politically prominent man who had apparently insisted upon the marriage even though his daughter loved another man. Finding the marriage untenable, Moore's wife soon sought and received one of only three divorces granted during the legislature's second term. Moore's was the only divorce where the wife sought and received the right to return to her maiden name. She shortly remarried, but then died soon thereafter. Moore never remarried. Despite Moore's fears, neither the divorce nor the duel harmed his early political career.

Moore participated in the state's constitutional convention and won election as the first state senator from Madison County, serving as president of the Alabama Senate in 1820. He also served four terms in the U.S. Congress, from 1821 to 1829, where he obtained federal aid for navigation improvements at Muscle Shoals.

In 1829, he resigned his congressional seat to run for governor, a position he won without opposition. Although his legislative programs were popular with the voting public, he did not accomplish passage of most of his agenda, perhaps because almost as soon as he was elected governor he began maneuvering to be elected to the U.S. Senate. He presented himself as a pro-Jackson, anti-U.S.-bank Democrat, spreading rumors that the incumbent senator, attorney John McKinley, was not loyal to Jackson, a litmus test at the time for Alabama officeholders. After a bitter campaign, where his own Jacksonian loyalty was also questioned, Moore was elected by the Alabama legislature to the Senate seat.

Alabama's fifth governor, Gabriel Moore, from Madison County, also served as a U.S. representative and senator, despite a colorful personal life.

Shortly after taking his Senate seat, Moore backpedaled from the staunch pro-Jackson position he had taken during the campaign. He restated his support of Jackson's Indian policy, foreign policy, and fiscal stringency, but then claimed his right to oppose administration positions that he found unwise. Soon he joined the anti-Jackson forces led by John C. Calhoun by voting against Jackson's nominee for minister to Great Britain, Martin Van Buren. This action gained him Jackson's enmity and calls for his resignation from pro-Jackson forces back in Alabama. Even though the Alabama legislature joined the call for his resignation, he refused to do so and served his full term until 1837. He did not run again, knowing that he would be defeated.

Upon his return to Alabama, Moore began to suffer both political and financial reversals, tied in part to the Panic of 1837. Over the course of the next several years, he had to liquidate various assets which had been pledged as collateral on loans, including many of his slaves. In 1843, though, he traveled to Cincinnati, Ohio, with eight of his slaves, where he executed and recorded deeds of emancipation for them. He then moved to Panola County, Mississippi, where he rented and worked a plantation. In 1844, he moved again, to the vicinity of Port Caddo near Soda Lake in Harrison County, Republic of Texas, where he died three months later.

After his death and in the course of litigation over his estate, it was revealed that one of the slaves he had earlier emancipated was his daughter, a young mulatto named Mary Minerva, who had been born while Moore was a congressman during the 1820s. In 1841, during the period of his worst financial reversals, he had made arrangements for Mary Minerva to be educated in Cincinnati and had personally escorted her there, where he boarded her with E. R. Hunter to whom he acknowledged that she was his child. Hunter later testified through interrogatories that both Moore and Mary Minerva claimed their father-daughter relationship.

Many Southern slave owners had children with their slaves, but few treated them with the parental concern and acknowledgement that Gabriel Moore demonstrated, nor did they emancipate them, as Moore did when Mary Minerva was about 14 years old. But because he took these actions in Ohio and failed to communicate the actions to his connections in Alabama and Texas, confusion about the status of the freed slaves who stayed with him until his death (including his daughter) caused them to remain in servitude for at least 12 more years, when litigation resulted in their final freedom.

William Kelly Continues the Politics of Factionalism and Sectionalism

J. Mills Thornton, III, in his book *Politics and Power in a Slave Society: Alabama, 1800-1860*, describes early Alabama politics as "the desperate search for issues with which to authenticate democratic credentials,"[4] an embracing of popular prejudices for political gain. The political career of William Kelly illustrates this point well.

Kelly was born and raised in northeastern South Carolina, where he trained in the law and became a circuit judge. Thereafter, he was known as Judge Kelly, even after he left South Carolina and moved to Huntsville sometime prior to statehood, when he was about 35 years old.

In Huntsville, he soon earned a solid reputation as a trial lawyer. He aligned himself with the "Champions of the People," those settlers who supported Andrew Jackson and fought against the Royal party of the Broad River Georgians. Although he became known as a defender of the common man, he rarely socialized with them outside the courtroom, preferring to spend his free time reading the great classics, especially Horace, the Roman satirist.

Reuben Saffold was one of three Supreme Court justices subjected to impeachment by William Kelly in the "Trial of Judges."

Kelly soon gained political office, serving in the U.S. Congress. After the Panic of 1819, when Senator John Williams Walker resigned due to failing health, the "Champions" supported Kelly against the Royalist candidate John McKinley and were able to gain Kelly's selection due, in part, to the effectiveness of a smear campaign against the Royalist by William B. Long and his *Huntsville Democrat*. Two years later, when Kelly sought a full six-year term, he was defeated by Dr. Henry H. Chambers, a Royalist.

Kelly sought a new issue to challenge the state's "monied interests" and to guarantee his return to state politics. Soon, he was elected to the state legislature on a platform calling for reorganization of the state's judiciary and the impeachment of several state Supreme Court justices.[5] This issue harkened back to the first territorial legislature, which had decided to abolish all limits on the amount of interest which might be charged on loans. That action had proved so unpopular that a usury law was adopted within a year. In the meantime, though, numerous contracts had been entered into where the interest called for ranged from sixty to two hundred and forty percent a year. Many of these contracts provided that a certain sum was to be paid on a certain date, but that if the debt were not discharged as prescribed, it was to bear interest of from five to twenty percent a month until paid. In 1824, the state supreme court had ruled that any additional interest charged after the due date on such contracts could be no more than the statutory rate of eight percent per year. This ruling had been considered a great victory for the common people. But, in 1827, the same court ruled that, for those people who had paid the illegal interest before the 1824 ruling, the statute of limitations prevented them from recovering the illegal interest payment. Suddenly outcries from the Champions transformed the justices into members of the Royal party. Kelly announced a crusade to have certain of the judges impeached and on this platform he was returned to political office generating more animosity against those identified with the Royal Party both in Madison County and in the Black Belt.

Kelly was able to regain political office, but his efforts to impeach three Supreme Court judges failed. In 1828, he petitioned the Alabama Senate to remove judges Anderson Crenshaw, John White, and Reuben Saffold, accusing them of incompetence and neglect of duty and charging they had reversed decisions made while presiding over circuit courts. Kelly himself served as prosecutor in this bizarre "Trial of Judges," which was held before the state senate. The judges were vindicated. Even so, the issue was not allowed to drop and soon a constitutional amendment reducing judicial tenure from the period of good behavior to a term of six years was passed by the legislature and approved by popular vote. This was the first amendment to the Alabama constitution.

Jacksonian Politics and States' Rights

The presidential election of 1824 played a significant role in furthering factionalism in Alabama politics. The Royalists of both north and south Alabama, led by attorney Bolling Hall, a former Georgia congressman who had moved to south Alabama, supported their kinsman William H. Crawford, while Israel Pickens and his followers supported John Quincy Adams. Those who wanted to distance themselves from these two groups, men such as attorneys Clement Comer Clay and John McKinley, gave their support to Andrew Jackson, a favorite among the yeoman farmer class. When Jackson won seventy percent of the vote in Alabama, those who had supported the other candidates quickly moved their support to Jackson in order to guarantee their viability in local and state politics. The Pickens group was able to shift fairly seamlessly, but the Crawford supporters were too closely identified with the planter class that considered itself the elite in the state to garner the support of the "common" folk, who were the voting majority. It seemed their political fortunes were doomed, but then one of their leaders, attorney Dixon Hall Lewis, nephew of Bolling Hall, found an issue which allowed him to win an 1829 election to Congress and gave renewed viability to others of the aristocratic camp who latched on to his rhetoric for their own purposes—that issue was states' rights.

Lewis, after the 1824 election, had shifted allegiance to Andrew Jackson, against John Quincy Adams, who had won the national election in spite of Alabama's overwhelming support of Jackson. It was evident that Jackson would run again in 1828 and, knowing this, Lewis's posturing helped elevate his own political ambitions. Lewis introduced the ideals of states' rights into Alabama's political oratory by using them to attack John Quincy Adams and praise Andrew Jackson during Adams's tenure as president. Lewis preached strict constructionism and laissez-faire economics as the means to preserve farmers' freedom. He proselytized against federal aid to internal improvements, based on the popularly assumed idea that government could easily become despotic if not restrained. He identified farmers' dependence on government as the very definition of slavery. His rhetoric captured the attention of the small Alabama farmer, because, as described by J. Mills Thornton, III, "Southerners knew slavery, and they sought above all else to avoid the condition." [6]

Soon Black Belt politicians observed how appealing Lewis's arguments were to the masses, as did newspaper editors, who set to work propagating the newly packaged doctrine of states' rights. Constant emphasis on the threat which governmental activity posed to liberty and constant reiteration of concern for the preservation of individual autonomy released these politicians from their former identification with aristocracy. Soon an issue arose which broadened their appeal to the masses even more.

Dixon Hall Lewis revived the fortunes of the Royalists when he found the new issue of states' rights to run on during his successful campaign for the U.S. Congress in 1829.

John Gayle and State Sovereignty

An early issue in the growth of the new republic of the United States was the issue of free trade versus protective tariffs. South Carolina had gone so far as to threaten to nullify the application of "The Tariff of Abominations" passed by the federal government in 1828. Many of the states' rightists in south Alabama argued in favor of free trade and the right of nullification. Free trade and nullification as states' rights issues did not grab the attention of large numbers of voters in Alabama, but the arguments concerning the rights of individual states to act on their own behalf were soon put to use on an issue that did grab the popular imagination during the governorship of John Gayle.[7]

John Gayle came to Alabama from South Carolina in 1812 and studied law in the office of Judge Abner Smith Lipscomb in St. Stephens. He soon opened a law office in Claiborne in Monroe County. He was elected governor of Alabama in 1831 as a strong anti-nullification, pro-Jackson candidate, speaking eloquently on behalf of the Union undivided in his first address to the general assembly. He championed internal improvements and was successful in getting Alabama's first railroad built across north Alabama from Tuscumbia to Decatur. He did not seem a likely candidate to champion states' rights, but a champion he became during a crisis which developed during 1831 through 1833 over the issue of lands previously ceded to the United States by the Creek Indians.

The 1832 Creek cession was divided into counties by the state legislature before full surveys were completed. Squatters rushed in and often ventured on to lands the Creeks considered guaranteed to them by federal treaty. Conflicts between whites and Indians occurred and the Indians appealed to Washington for enforcement of the treaty. President Jackson ordered federal troops to remove all white settlers from the Indian cession until surveying could be completed, an ironic turn of events because Jackson's enormous popularity in Alabama came in no small part from his breaking the power of the Creeks at the Battle of Horseshoe Bend.

Governor John Gayle became a champion of state sovereignty during a violent dispute with the Jackson administration over the issue of white settlement of Creek lands.

When troops attempted to remove Hardaman Owens, Russell County commissioner of roads and revenue and a flagrant land grabber, he was killed. A county grand jury indicted the soldier responsible for the death, and Governor Gayle insisted on his surrender to state officials, claiming the state's right to arrest, try, and, perhaps, convict a United States soldier for an act committed as part of his duties. Gayle championed the rights of the settlers, maintained that federal military presence on Alabama soil was an affront to state sovereignty, and ordered that a militia be organized in the counties formed from the cession. It appeared that a confrontation between the state and the federal government was inevitable.

Recognizing the importance of avoiding violent confrontation, President Jackson sent Francis Scott Key to Tuscaloosa to resolve the matter. Key quickly had the land survey completed, required the Indians to select the lands they wanted to keep, and met with Governor Gayle to calm ruffled feathers. The soldier accused of killing Hardaman disappeared, no trial was held, and the army withdrew. Key also arranged for disputed claims to be resolved, stating that only those white settlers on lands expressly reserved for the Creeks would have to vacate. Titles to the lands vacated could be purchased from the Indians. Key's diplomacy succeeded, and a collision between state and federal authority was averted, although the terms of the treaty with the Indians were ignored.

The disruption of Gayle's former close friendship with Jackson and Gayle's conduct in the crisis had a lasting impact on Alabama politics. Jackson's popularity in the state suffered a severe blow, resulting in the realignment of the state's political factions between states' rightists and Unionists. Further, because Alabamians were alarmed by the increasing power of the federal government, the foundation was laid for the states' rights movement in Alabama, which would gain momentum in the 1850s. Gayle himself shifted from support of Jackson's nationalist views within the Democratic Party toward espousing support for states' rights, the foundational issue of the evolving Whig Party. He insisted that the federal government had no legal jurisdiction to negotiate treaties that limited a state's authority over all the citizens and territory within its borders. He claimed that all people within the boundaries of the state, whether Indians, soldiers, whites, or blacks, were subject to the laws of the state.

When Jackson began to promote Vice President Martin Van Buren to succeed him, the Whig Party was born in Alabama and Gayle became a member, running as a Whig presidential elector for Judge Hugh White in 1836 and for William Henry Harrison in 1840. He ran as a Whig candidate in the 1841 race for the U.S. Senate and lost, but was elected to the U.S. House in 1847 as a Whig, and was ultimately appointed as Alabama's federal district judge by Whig president Zachary Taylor in 1849, serving until his death in 1859.

One of the most important politicians in Alabama's early history, Clement Comer Clay chaired the Committee of Fifteen, was the state's first chief justice, speaker of the state house of representatives, its eighth governor, and a U.S. senator.

The Intertwined Careers of Clement Comer Clay and John McKinley

Both Clement Comer Clay and John McKinley were born in Virginia, but soon moved further south, Clay to Tennessee and McKinley to Kentucky. Both were educated as attorneys and both moved to Huntsville while Alabama was a territory. Both aligned themselves with the Broad River Georgians. Clay became a stockholder and director of the Planters and Merchants Bank of LeRoy Pope and McKinley became a member of the powerful Cypress Land Company, which played a significant role in the development of the Tennessee Valley. Other members of the company included LeRoy Pope, President James Madison, Andrew Jackson, and Thomas Bibb.

Clay was instrumental in organizing the territorial legislature when Alabama became an independent territory and joined John Williams Walker in fighting for measures to strengthen the position of the Planters and Merchants Bank, including the removal of limits on interest rates. He also chaired the Committee of Fifteen that drafted the first state constitution. He successfully fought for life terms for judges. Thereafter, the new state legislature elected Clay one of Alabama's five circuit judges, who also jointly constituted the Alabama Supreme Court. He was then chosen by the other judges to serve as the state's first chief justice.

The Panic of 1819 plunged the state into depression, resulting in a spate of cases involving debt collection which ended up before the Supreme Court. Because of the abolition of the territorial usury law, many of these cases involved exorbitant interest payments. Rather than sit in judgment when debtors challenged the validity of the interest rates, Clay resigned his judgeship in 1823 and instead became an attorney for the creditors in the first of what became known as the "big interest" cases. Senator William Kelly represented the victorious debtors, succeeding in convincing the state supreme court to limit the interest payments demanded from them. Thereafter, in 1825, Clay ran for Congress but was defeated by Gabriel Moore, primarily due to Clay's identification with the banking and creditor elements. He then began to alter his public positions in an attempt to broaden his appeal to poorer voters and took on the persona of a Jacksonian Democrat.

John McKinley was elected to serve Madison County in Alabama's second legislature in 1820, and in 1821 was appointed one of 12 trustees to establish the University of Alabama. In 1823, with the support of the Broad River Royalists, he ran for the United States Senate against William Kelly. He was defeated by Kelly, because of Kelly's reputation as a champion of the common man, a reputation gained primarily because of his role in the interest rate cases. After this defeat, McKinley attempted to distance himself from the Royalist faction by publicly becoming an ardent supporter of Andrew Jackson.

Having already served in the Alabama legislature and as a U.S. senator, in 1837 John McKinley became one of only three Alabamians appointed to the United States Supreme Court. He served for 14 years.

In 1826, Clay and McKinley found themselves jointly representing the creditors before the state supreme court in the second of the "big interest" cases where the creditors maintained that the statute of limitations barred debtors from recovery of the usurious interest they had already paid. When Senator Israel Pickens resigned his senate seat due to ill health, both Clay and McKinley sought to replace him.

While both claimed to be ardent Jackson supporters, during a period where such support was a requisite for political advancement, Clay allowed his aristocratic leanings to prevail when he sought the votes of the handful of legislators who admired John Quincy Adams as well. This action alienated a crucial number of Jacksonians, resulting in McKinley's narrow defeat of Clay in a legislative vote of 41-38. McKinley would spend the next six years in Washington.

Clay was elected to the state house of representatives in 1828 and was unanimously chosen its speaker. Although his legislative agenda, staying true to his aristocratic leanings, made him unpopular with small farmers, he was able to win a bid for Congress in 1829 because of the support of voters in Madison County. Once in Congress, Clay began a focused effort to free himself from identification with aristocratic beliefs, taking up the cause of squatters and public land debtors and becoming a consummate supporter of President Jackson's legislative agenda.

In 1835, Alabama Democrats nominated Clay for governor and he defeated the Whig candidate, attorney Enoch Parsons, by nearly two to one. Clay's tenure as governor illustrates the lengths to which he went to maintain political popularity in the face of his natural aristocratic leanings, often to the long-term detriment of the state. As an example, in response to the Panic of 1837, Governor Clay put forth an extreme agenda to the legislature he called into special session in hopes of providing relief to hard-pressed debtors. The legislature enacted the Relief Act of 1837, which required the state bank to suspend immediate collection of debts and provide debtors three additional years to pay. Further, the bill required the issuance of $5 million in bonds that the bank's branches were to sell to raise capital so that they could make additional loans to desperate Alabamians. Historian J. Mills Thornton, III, writing in *Alabama Governors, A Political History of the State*, describes these actions as "extraordinarily foolish acts," which "although they advanced Clay's political career, left the bank with a vast indebtedness and no means to service it."

In the meantime, John McKinley had been defeated for reelection to the Senate in 1831 by Governor Gabriel Moore. He returned to the state and was reelected to the state legislature. In 1833, he returned to Congress but was back in the state legislature in 1836. During that session, he was reelected to the U.S. Senate by his legislative colleagues, but did not claim his seat because President Martin Van Buren appointed him an associate justice of the United States Supreme Court, the first of only three such appointments of an Alabama attorney. McKinley returned to Kentucky in 1842 and died there on July 19, 1852.

McKinley's resignation opened the way for Clement Comer Clay to attain the ultimate political plum to which he aspired. Grateful legislators—many of whom were themselves debtors of the Bank of Alabama—unanimously selected Clay to succeed McKinley in the United States Senate. Clay resigned as governor and took his Senate seat in September 1837. He continued to affect a Jacksonian style during his Senate tenure, but was unable to complete the full term because of a crisis in his personal financial affairs brought on by the deepening depression precipitated by the Panic of 1837.

Upon his return to Alabama, Clay suffered political as well as financial reverses. In the summer of 1843, Governor Fitzpatrick appointed Clay to a vacancy on the state supreme court, but the following December, Whig and Calhounite Democrat legislators joined to defeat Clay's election to the full term. His political reversals might have at least in part stemmed from the fact that once he left elective office, Clay resumed the pro-planter, pro-development attitudes that characterized his early career. It became apparent that he had previously become a Jacksonian almost entirely to advance his political career.

After his retirement from office, Clay returned to his Huntsville law practice which he shared with his two sons, including Clement Claiborne Clay, who had already launched a political career which would take him to both the United States and Confederate senates. During this period, Clay became a strong advocate of the causes of Southern rights and secession.

Clay's support of secession and his son's involvement with the Confederacy made him an object of special hostility when Union troops occupied Huntsville at the end of 1864. Clay was imprisoned as a hostage to force the release of Union leader David C. Humphreys. The time in captivity broke Clay's health, making him an invalid and leading to his death on September 6, 1866.

Arthur P. Bagby and William Lowndes Yancey's General Ticket Bill

Arthur P. Bagby, Alabama's tenth governor, continued the political haggling that defined the framework of the operation of the Bank of Alabama. He served two terms as governor and his contemporaries described him as the quintessential type to fill that office. He looked and acted the part, standing more than six feet tall, with a graceful walk and the demeanor of a gentleman that made him stand out in public. He was a well-read student of law and government, had a voice at once clear and pleasant, and was a gifted orator.

Arthur P. Bagby was elected Alabama's tenth governor during the 1837 financial crisis. After his second term, he served in the U.S. Senate, and briefly, as minister to Russia.

His family migrated to Claiborne, in Monroe County, where he read law and set up a law practice in 1819. His first political office was as state representative from Monroe County in 1821. Soon, he was chosen speaker of the house, at the young age of 28. He served in the state legislature in various capacities for 15 years and was first elected governor in 1837, in the midst of the economic crisis left by the depression in that year. During his tenure as governor, the legislature authorized the issuance of additional state bonds to fund bank operations. Well into Bagby's second term, the Merchants Bank of New York submitted a financial report that disclosed that Alabama owed $11.5 million on state bonds with no apparent way of paying. The state struggled to pay more than $600,000 in annual interest on the bonds and this debilitating debt plagued the state for years.

In 1840, in the wake of Whig candidate William Henry Harrison's election as president, Alabama Democrats found themselves with only a narrow majority in the legislature. In response, attorney William Lowndes Yancey, editor of the *Wetumpka Argus*, proposed that the legislature enact a law requiring the statewide election of congressmen. Such a law was enacted in January 1841 and became known as the General Ticket Bill. The bill, which Bagby signed into law, was clearly a political maneuver designed to strengthen the Alabama Democratic Party at the expense of the Whigs. The Whigs in the state legislature had aggressively fought the bill and were able to force the inclusion of a rider that required a popular referendum on the bill in August 1841. One of their strongest arguments was that the more heavily populated northern counties, which generally voted Democratic, were trying to control the southern counties where the Whig party had its stronghold.

President Harrison called a special session of Congress for May 1841, creating a political dilemma in Alabama. Under then existing law, the terms of Alabama congressmen expired in March and the next regular election was not until August. Governor Bagby was forced to call a special election; the result was the apparent popular election of Democrats in the two northern districts and Whigs in the three southern districts, but the actual election of five Democrats, because the heavily populated northern counties caused an overall majority of votes to be cast for the five Democratic candidates. This outcome supported Whig arguments about disfranchisement and northern control. Thus, when the referendum election on the General Ticket Bill was held in August, enough Democrats joined Whigs to defeat the bill and restore the district system.

Bagby was a strong advocate of slavery. He took the opportunity with his annual message to the legislature in 1840 to publicly defend slavery as a positive good. He maintained that Southern slaves were treated as well as free laborers in other sections of the country, a rationale taken up by many in the years that followed. His was one of the first public speeches in Alabama to maintain this stance.

After his second term as governor, Bagby was chosen by the legislature to fill the vacant U.S. Senate seat left by Clement Comer Clay's resignation. He was elected to a full second term thereafter. He supported Manifest Destiny, the annexation of Texas, and permitting slavery in the territories. In 1848, President James K. Polk appointed him minister to Russia, but he held the position only briefly after Whig candidate Zachary Taylor was elected president later that year.

Benjamin Fitzpatrick, Joshua L. Martin, and the End of the Bank of Alabama

Benjamin Fitzpatrick was Alabama's eleventh governor and eleventh senator. As has been made clear, the story of Alabama's early governors and senators reveals the political history of the early period of Alabama statehood. Of the first 12 governors whose terms comprise this period of Alabama history (1819-1847), ten (every governor except William Wyatt Bibb and his brother Thomas, who between them shared the first two-year term of the governorship) were attorneys. Five of these ten—Israel Pickens, Gabriel Moore, Clement Comer Clay, Arthur P. Bagby, and Benjamin Fitzpatrick—were among the first 11 Alabama senators. Of these first 11 senators, ten were attorneys: John Williams Walker, William Rufus King, William Kelly, Israel Pickens, John McKinley, Gabriel Moore, Clement Comer Clay, Arthur Pendleton Bagby, Dixon Hall Lewis, and Benjamin Fitzpatrick. Only Dr. Henry Chambers was not an attorney. It is clear that attorneys had a defining impact on Alabama's early statehood. Fitzpatrick's term as governor saw a conclusion to an issue that had dominated much of the period of early statehood: the role of the state in the banking system.

Elected Alabama's eleventh governor in 1841, Benjamin Fitzpatrick inherited the banking crisis, and began the process that led ultimately to the demise of the state bank.

Fitzpatrick was a Jacksonian Democrat, but he also led a loosely organized faction of the state party which was sometimes called the "Montgomery Regency," a group that was bound more by family and personal ties than by political ideology. He was born in Greene County, Georgia, in 1802, the son of a Georgia state legislator, and was orphaned at age seven, then raised by his older brothers and sisters. He had little opportunity for a formal education, leading a "knockabout" youth. At age 14, he traveled alone to the newly opened former Creek territory of central Alabama. After working several years as a store clerk in Wetumpka and as a deputy sheriff, he ultimately read law with Montgomery mayor Nimrod E. Benson and was admitted to the bar in 1821 at the age of 19.

In 1827, he was fortunate to marry Sarah Elmore, a member of the wealthy and prominent family for whom Elmore County was named. Their ten-year marriage brought six sons, a large plantation across the Alabama River from Montgomery, and slaveholdings that grew from 24 persons in 1830 to 106 by 1850. After his wife's death in 1837, he turned to politics and was elected governor in 1841. The major issue confronting his administration was the banking crisis.

Not being against corporate capitalism, Fitzpatrick was inclined to take a conservative approach to the crisis, proposing only to liquidate the branch of the bank in Mobile, which was the most troublesome of the bank's branches. He would have merely reformed the bank, but there were more radical forces in the Jacksonian fold who hated all banks. They joined with Whigs who opposed the state ownership of the bank to produce a legislative majority that passed legislation to liquidate all four of the branches and to preserve only the main bank in Tuscaloosa. Fitzpatrick reluctantly signed this legislation into law.

To his surprise, this legislation was well received and led the way to his reelection without opposition. Soon he took a much harsher stance toward the bank. When its charter expired in 1845, he refused to support its renewal and signed a bill eliminating the state's support of the banking system altogether. Others would have had him repudiate the debt that the state had earlier contracted to keep the bank in operation, but this he refused to do. When he left the governorship, the legislature chose him as one of three commissioners to supervise the bank's final liquidation.

Fitzpatrick's successor, Joshua L. Martin, drove the final nail into the bank's coffin. Martin was a descendant of French immigrant Louis Montaigne, who had first settled in South Carolina, after changing his name to Martin, and later migrated to Tennessee, where Joshua was born in 1799. Martin was well educated and showed an aptitude for the law, which he studied in the office of his brother in Russellville, Alabama. He was admitted to the bar, opened a law office in Athens, and in 1822 was elected to the state legislature as a representative from Limestone County.

Joshua L. Martin ran for governor and was elected almost entirely because of his opposition to the state bank. The bank was finally dismantled during his administration.

Martin married twice—to two sisters who were members of the distinguished Mason family of Virginia. These wives gave him seven children, five sons and two daughters.

He was elected governor in 1845, primarily because of his consistent opposition to the state bank. The bank had been chartered in 1823, shortly after his first election to the state legislature. Although the bank had been very popular in its early days, even paying the state's operating expenses through its profits in some years, its popularity had declined due to its imprudent actions following the depression of 1837, resulting in the nonrenewal of its charter in 1845. Even though its charter had not been renewed, there were still powerful forces within both the Whig and Democratic parties who were in favor of renewing the charter and saving the bank. In 1845, a large number of antibank delegates were delayed in arriving at the Democratic convention at Tuscaloosa because their boats could not move through the unusually shallow levels in the Warrior and Tombigbee rivers. In their absence, probank forces were able to hurriedly nominate a candidate who favored renewal of the bank, perhaps owing to the fact that he was a large debtor to the bank.

Martin was incensed by this action and, with the support of the antibank forces, agreed to run for governor

ABOVE: *The state bank building in Decatur still stands, and has recently been restored and reopened as a museum.* RIGHT: *Marengo County attorney Francis S. Lyon oversaw the liquidation of the state bank and is credited with having saved Alabama from bankruptcy.*

as an independent, antibank candidate. There was no Whig candidate. The election was one of the most hotly contested that the young state had so far seen. Perhaps because Martin's opponent had been the author of the general ticket law that had been anathema to Whigs in earlier days, enough of them opposed him that Martin won by a 5,000-vote margin.

As governor, Martin was not popular with many regular Democrats because he had bolted the party. Nevertheless he proceeded to dismantle the bank. The legislature soon appointed attorney Francis S. Lyon of Marengo County as sole commissioner to liquidate the bank and to put the state's financial house in order. Lyon, who served with distinction, saved Alabama from bankruptcy and many of the bank's creditors from ruin.

Martin served only one term because of the fact that he had run as an independent and knew that an effort to run as a Democrat would probably split the party and cause a Whig victory. Therefore, he returned to the practice of law. One other event worthy of note occurred during Martin's term as governor: the capital was moved from Tuscaloosa to the more central location of Montgomery.

As noted by historian Hugh C. Bailey in *Alabama's Governors: A Political History of the State*, "Martin's legacy was one of dedicated public service through the Democratic Party, which ironically reached its zenith when, as an independent governor, he did what other Democrats had feared to do and dismembered the state bank."

Where Alabama Stood as the Early Statehood Period Ended

The men who were Alabama's earliest political leaders, mostly well-educated, experienced, ambitious, and successful men, were not typical of Alabama's early population. The majority of the thousands of people who moved to Alabama from other Southern states during its territorial and early statehood years were young, small farmers without formal education and without slaves. They were people who sought cheap land, economic independence, and individual freedom and were fearful of any impingement upon their rights. As J. Mills Thornton wrote in *Politics and Power in a Slave Society*, "They resented the necessity of dealing in bank-made paper; they resented the necessity of buying their land from the government; they resented the necessity of paying taxes and otherwise encountering the state; they resented the necessity of selling their crops and obtaining supplies from afar. Whenever power impinged upon their lives, they reacted with suspicion and perturbation."

It was this suspicion and these resentments which stoked the fires of division—between classes, between regions, and between parties—that were the hallmarks of Alabama's early statehood and which continue to shape Alabama politics into the twenty-first century. Before 1850, these fires burned primarily within the state, but, during the decade of the 1850s, the issues of slavery and states' rights would cause the flames to spread to a national level and the divisions to encompass the entire South and its feeling of estrangement from the rest of the nation. During this decade Alabama entered a period of crisis which led to civil war.

CHAPTER THREE

THE LEGAL SYSTEM AND PROFESSION IN ANTEBELLUM ALABAMA 1819-1860

With the coming of statehood in 1819, there also came rapid population growth, from 127,000 in 1820 to nearly one million in 1860, including 435,000 slaves. Although the expansion was constant, it was most explosive during the "Flush Times" of the 1830s so eloquently written about by attorney Joseph Glover Baldwin in his book *The Flush Times of Alabama and Mississippi, A Series of Sketches*. During this time, the boundaries of the state filled out as Indians were removed and their lands were added. Seats of government increased as the number of counties grew from 22 at the dawn of statehood to more than 50 in 1860.[1]

As the population grew and boundaries expanded, so did the legal profession in the state. In 1818, there were 200 or so attorneys in the Mississippi Territory. Ninety-eight were licensed in Alabama territorial courts over the next two years. By 1845, there were more than 600 lawyers in Alabama.

Although it might be assumed that members of the profession operated in county seats and towns, available biographical data suggests that many settled in the counties of the Black Belt, the chief plantation district, and the Tennessee Valley. These were men who lived in prosperous small towns or in the country, or who divided their time between town houses and plantation properties. They were following the wealth, power, and social distinction derived from the cotton culture, which increasingly dominated the state's economy during this antebellum period. A much smaller group actually practiced in the larger towns of Mobile, Montgomery, Tuscaloosa, and Huntsville.

Alabama was populated by people seeking land, so it is not surprising that a large portion of the legal business of the territorial and early statehood period involved searching titles, drafting deeds, and litigating land disputes. Another fertile field of litigation was the usury cases which arose during the period when Alabama had no limit on the interest which could be charged by lend-

Opposite Page: *Henry Hitchcock, a native of Vermont and grandson of Ethan Allen, came to the Mississippi Territory in 1816, eventually serving as territorial secretary. From 1820 to 1823 he served as Alabama's first attorney general. In 1835 he was elected to the Alabama Supreme Court, serving as Alabama's fourth chief justice from 1836 to 1837. However, it was as the author of* The Alabama Justice of the Peace, *in 1822 the first book published in Alabama, that he had perhaps his greatest influence on the practice of law in Alabama.*

ers and the debtor-creditor disputes which arose during and after each period of economic panic and downturn. Lawyers both administered and participated in the joint institutions of cotton planting and slaveholding, which came to dominate the public life of the state, as well as supporting the merchant and bank businesses, which were necessary aspects of the cotton economy. And, of course, drawing up wills, assisting in the administration of estates, and participating in the criminal justice system were mainstays of practice then as they are now.

Then, as now, the court system was administered at several levels. The justice courts were administered by justices of the peace, two for each militia district (of which there were several per county) elected by voters of each district. The justices had civil jurisdiction over debts up to $50 and over torts and damages (except slander) up to $20 in value. They had criminal jurisdiction over a variety of minor criminal matters, as well as the responsibility for policing the slave population. Justices of the peace were not required to be lawyers and many of them relied on judge and legal author Henry Hitchcock's *The Alabama Justice of the Peace* (1822), which was the first book published in the state, and Tuscaloosa lawyer and legal author William Russell Smith's *The Justice of the Peace* (1844) to guide their legal reasoning since these authors thoroughly covered basic legal principles and procedures. Although often ridiculed for their lack of sophistication, these justices served an important role and their courts handled a substantial amount of legal business, making their courts a beginning place for many a legal career.

In the antebellum period, cotton was king in Alabama, and many lawyers settled in the Black Belt and the Tennessee Valley to take advantage of the legal business generated by the cotton culture.

The next level of jurisdiction, much of it concurrent with the circuit court, was the county court, which ruled over debt and other civil issues and such minor criminal matters as assault and battery. Up until 1850, this court served as an "Orphans Court" with power to probate wills, oversee administration of estates, decide upon matters of insanity and guardianship, and record real estate conveyances. This area of its jurisdiction was transferred to the Probate Court upon its creation in 1850. County court judges were elected by the legislature and were therefore generally well connected. They often used a county court judgeship as a stepping-stone to the circuit court bench. Still, because the court was only required to be in session for two 12-day terms per year, these judges often continued to practice law while holding office. They tended to be pillars of the local community.

Next in level of jurisdiction, the circuit court was the highest state trial court for civil, criminal, and, until

1839, chancery matters. This court came to the people, as its judges traveled their circuits, comprised of three to six counties, visiting each county at least twice a year on a rigid schedule, for sessions of court usually lasting from one to two weeks. The legislature elected a judge and a solicitor (prosecutor) for each circuit. Young lawyers who wanted to practice before the circuit court also tended to ride the circuit, picking up those clients who, for whatever reason, did not retain local counsel as they entered each new jurisdiction. They had to be prepared to jump into action quickly since often they would find their clients only as they entered a town at the beginning of the court session and would need to be prepared to present their case almost immediately. Because of their importance to local populations, circuit court sessions tended to become social events, attended by large numbers of locals dressed out in their best attire. Legislation passed in January 1839 removed equity jurisdiction from the circuit courts and passed it to a newly created chancery court. Two chancery divisions were created, of three districts each. The first chancery judges, called chancellors, were Elisha Wolsey Peck and Anderson Crenshaw, for the northern and southern divisions respectively. A third "middle" division was created in 1841 and Joshua L. Martin was elected chancellor by the legislature.

In the 1819 constitution, the Alabama Supreme Court was designated as Alabama's only appellate court and was given general supervisory responsibility over the courts below it. The constitution provided that the Supreme Court would be comprised of the judges of the circuit courts. Originally circuit judges were selected by the general assembly and held office during good behavior. The constitution was amended in 1830 to limit the term of office of these judges to six years.

The first term of the Supreme Court began on the first Monday in May 1820, and was held at Cahaba, the state capital at the time. The circuit judges included Clement Comer Clay, Reuben Saffold, Henry Y. Webb, Richard Ellis, and Abner S. Lipscomb. Clay was selected as the first chief justice. Henry Hitchcock was chosen as the first attorney general. In 1821, a sixth circuit was established and Anderson Crenshaw was elected judge. In 1828, a seventh circuit was created and Sion L. Perry was elected judge.

John D. Phelan was elected an associate justice of the Alabama Supreme Court when the number of justices was increased from three to five in 1851. When the number was reduced back to three in 1853, he left the bench and became clerk of the court. He returned to the Supreme Court in 1864, serving until 1866, at which time he again became clerk.

By legislation passed in 1832, the Supreme Court was made an independent entity and the number of judges (only the chief justice was titled "Justice") was set at three. They were elected by both houses of the legislature, with six-year terms. Judges Lipscomb, Saffold, and John M. Taylor were the first to be elected. Taylor resigned in 1834 and was replaced by Henry Hitchcock. From 1851 to 1852, the legislature increased the number of judges from three to five and David G. Ligon and John D. Phelan were elected to the new positions.

These Supreme Court judges generally did not make the judiciary their careers. Of the 24 men who sat as judges from 1832 to 1865, ten served for three years or less, while the average tenure was less than five years. Many of those who left went back to private practice, while others sought other political offices or moved to other states.

In 1849, a referendum was held on the question of popular election of the judges of circuit, probate, and other inferior courts. It decided in favor of popular election of these judges, who had previously been elected by the state legislature. Supreme Court and chancery judges continued to be chosen by the legislature.

Also in 1849, Henry W. Collier left the Supreme Court and was elected governor. He and his colleague on the court, John J. Ormond, had been following the "codification" movement, a loose alliance of lawyers who felt that the civil law tradition of Europe was preferable to

ELIJAH WOLSEY PECK
A LAWYER'S LAWYER

A case which illustrates Peck's skill as an advocate involved a black woman in Tuscaloosa named Milly Walker who asserted her status as a free black in an action against a man who had come to Alabama from Virginia claiming Walker and her children were fugitive slaves. Walker had been born to a free black woman in Virginia about 1800 and was, therefore, free herself. At about age 15, she traveled to Tennessee with a man named William Cook, for whom she worked as a "waiting woman." She became indebted to a local store for $35 and was threatened with incarceration if she did not pay the debt. A man named Moon paid the debt with the understanding that Walker would serve him as an indentured servant. Milly Walker, who was illiterate, was told that the term would be seven years, but the written document upon which she marked her "X" stated the term as 99 years, with the addition that her children would also serve Moon until each reached 21 years of age.

Walker stayed with Moon until 1821, when he sold his "claim" on her and her children for the sum of $250 to Richard Jones of Tuscaloosa County. Jones treated Walker and her children as his slaves and eventually gave one of Milly's children to his son-in-law, who took her to his plantation. At this point, Milly somehow engaged lawyer Eli Shortridge, a brilliant attorney who had previously won a claim of freedom for another black woman

English common law. In response to this movement, an unofficial code was published in 1848 in Mississippi, and Virginia adopted an official code in 1849.

Collier's term coincided with a constitutionally mandated ten-year compilation of statute law and he used this coincidence to urge the state to adopt a code. At his urging, the legislature named Ormond, Circuit Judge George T. Goldthwaite, and Greene County lawyer John Erwin to a commission charged with writing a "code of statutes" and a "code of practice in the courts of this state." This commission worked on the proposed codification for two years, clarifying the law through both reorganization and rewriting. They totally reworked the rules of pleading, replacing common law pleading with pleading based on "a succinct statement of the facts relied on." Their proposed code was approved by a joint legislative committee and it was adopted in February 1852. This code was soon accepted by the legal profession and made the law more certain and logical, results more predictable, and preparation of cases simpler.

Appellate Advocacy

Several lawyers gained reputations for the superior quality of their appellate representation and made names for themselves in the

Left: *Circuit Judge George Goldthwaite was one of three men charged by Governor Henry W. Collier with codifying the laws of Alabama. He was elected to the Alabama Supreme Court in 1852, and was chosen to remain on the court when the number of justices reverted to three. He became chief justice in 1856, but served only 13 days before resigning to return to private practice.* Opposite Page: *Edmund S. Dargan was a leading advocate before the Alabama Supreme Court before eventually joining the court himself.*

in Tuscaloosa, to file a petition for freedom against Jones. Eli Shortridge was the father of George Shortridge, who was a prominent lawyer in his own right, a mayor of Montgomery and a circuit judge, who would be the unsuccessful candidate for governor of Alabama on the American or "Know-Nothing" Party ticket in 1855. The basic law of slavery presumed that every "person of color" was a slave. Therefore, Shortridge had to overcome this legal presumption to gain freedom for Walker and her children. The case was tried in 1833 before a jury in the Tuscaloosa Circuit Court and the jury verdict stated "that Milly Walker and her...children...are *not* slaves and the property of Richard Jones, but are free persons as by their petition is alleged."

Peck entered the life of Milly Walker 15 years after this litigation, when Richard W. Fields of Virginia filed a claim that Walker and three of her children were all his slaves and were fugitives from Virginia. By this time, Shortridge had died (after leaving Tuscaloosa and serving as a circuit judge in Talladega), so Walker somehow retained Peck. Peck first attempted to settle the matter with a non-jury *habeas corpus* proceeding, but the Alabama Supreme Court reversed Peck's victory in that proceeding and required a formal petition for freedom, which called for a jury trial. The trial was held in September 1852 and the jury, for a second time, found that the Walkers were free persons of color and not the slaves of Richard W. Fields. Fields appealed the trial court judgment, but Peck's brief, printed in the appellate reports at *23 Ala. 155* (1853), won the day for his clients when the Alabama Supreme Court affirmed the trial court.

Peck served as chairman of the Reconstruction Constitutional Convention of 1867 and was elected chief justice of the Alabama Supreme Court in the Reconstruction era, earning him criticism for being a "scalawag." Still, he died a wealthy and respected citizen of Tuscaloosa in 1888 and was described in the memoirs of E. A. Powell, a circuit court clerk in west Alabama for many years, as simply the best lawyer he had ever seen in a courtroom. Powell further described Peck's argument to the jury "in a civil case...on the trial of a petition of some Negroes to establish their freedom" as the finest lawyer's argument he had ever heard. It appears that Elisha Wolsey Peck was one of Alabama's early "lawyer's lawyers." [2]

profession as appellate advocates. Edmund S. Dargan of Montgomery and Mobile appeared before the Alabama Supreme Court several times a year and ultimately was elected to serve on the court, becoming chief justice in 1849. Lewis Parsons practiced law in Talladega, but became so highly regarded as an appellate advocate that he regularly argued cases on appeal that had originated in other counties. For example, in the 1847 court term, he handled nine cases originating in Talladega County, as well as cases from Cherokee, St. Clair, Shelby, and Randolph counties. James W. McClung of Madison County appeared before the Supreme Court often and was described as a "dashing orator and bold defender of the right as he saw it." Samuel F. Rice of Talladega was famous for his repartee and was another advocate who was elected to the court and became its chief justice. William Lowndes Yancey of Montgomery had a substantial appellate practice, owing to the power of his oratory. Elisha Wolsey Peck is regarded as one of the state's great appellate pleaders, as well as a great trial lawyer. In 1832, he formed a partnership with Harvey Ellis in Tuscaloosa and, in the June term of 1836, they handled more than 25 appellate cases between them. Later, Peck partnered with Lincoln Clark and by the June term of 1847 he argued appellate cases originating in Covington, Dallas, Lowndes, Marengo, Mobile, Monroe, Perry, Pickens, Russell, Shelby, and Tuscaloosa counties.

Prior to becoming a state, Alabama did not have a federal district court. Therefore, Congress, on April 21, 1820, established a federal district court and extended over the new Alabama judicial district the laws of the United States. In addition a U.S. attorney, clerk, and marshal were provided as staff for the court, which held four terms alternately in Mobile and Cahaba.

Three men were considered for the first federal district judgeship: Harry Toulmin, the former federal territorial

judge, William Crawford, a Mobile attorney, and Charles Tait, the former Georgia senator who had been instrumental in winning Alabama's statehood. Tait was a close ally of Secretary of the Treasury William H. Crawford (no relation to the Mobile attorney also considered), who had also been instrumental in sponsoring Alabama's statehood. His influence with President Monroe helped secure the appointment for Tait, even though Tait's selection was a slight to Harry Toulmin, considered the natural choice for the appointment. Alabama's Crawford was appointed the first U.S. attorney, and was later named to replace Tait when he resigned in 1826. Only two other men served as federal district judge before the Civil War: former governor John Gayle and William Giles Jones, another Mobile attorney.

All four appointments for the one federal district judgeship in Alabama prior to the Civil War were filled by men from south Alabama. Given the fact that Alabama's senators were generally alternated between north and south, it is interesting to note that this alternation

In 1846, during the administration of Governor Joshua L. Martin, the state capital was moved from Tuscaloosa to Montgomery. Likewise, the seat of the newly created Middle District court was also moved from Tuscaloosa to Montgomery.

did not occur in the judgeships, even though sectional politics did enter into the selection process.[3] Probably the most important factor influencing the selection was the fact that the majority of federal cases, which generally involved diversity jurisdiction, arose in the southern part of the state, especially in Mobile, where most of the state's interstate commerce occurred in the form of cotton factoring, insuring, and shipping.

North Alabama citizens regularly complained about the distance that had to be traveled for them to access the federal court. By 1824, Congress addressed these complaints by dividing Alabama into a Northern and a Southern District, with the Northern District sitting in Huntsville. While a different clerk, marshal, and attorney were appointed for the Northern District, the same judge sat in both districts. After Tuscaloosa became the state capital in 1826, the court no longer sat in Cahaba, but it was only in 1839 that court was held in Tuscaloosa, under legislation reorganizing the state into Northern, Middle, and Southern District courts to be held respectively in Huntsville, Tuscaloosa, and Mobile. The seat for the Middle District was changed to Montgomery shortly after that city became the state capital in 1846. Still, Alabama had only one federal district judgeship to handle the litigation from all three districts.

During this antebellum period, each United States Supreme Court justice served also as a circuit appellate judge, riding circuit to hear cases appealed from the federal district courts. Although this appellate function was considered by many to be as important as the justice's service on the supreme court in Washington, it was a burdensome duty that caused a logjam of cases at this juncture in the federal court system, in light of the fact that the responsibilities were considered by some justices as more than one individual could readily handle. (Justice McKinley wrote that "no physical strength could enable one individual to perform the extensive travel in the circuit and attend to the duties of the court.") To ease this logjam, Congress gave district judges in various districts the same appellate jurisdiction as the supreme court judge riding their circuit. In Alabama, this jurisdiction was first assigned to the Northern District and later to both the Northern and Middle Districts. For practical purposes, this meant that when Alabama's one federal judge sat in Huntsville and Montgomery, he had both district and circuit court jurisdiction, whereas in Mobile he had the authority of a district judge only. This situation caused the function and authority of the federal district and circuit courts to be intimately interconnected and gave tremendous power to the district judge.

Two Alabamians served as United States Supreme Court justices during the antebellum period: John McKinley, who rose through the United States Senate to a place on the court and served from 1837 until his death in 1852, and John Archibald Campbell, who replaced McKinley in 1853. Campbell was born in Georgia in 1811, but, after attending both Franklin College and West Point, moved to Montgomery, Alabama, studied law, and entered the bar in 1830. He practiced with the firm of Governor Benjamin Fitzpatrick and Henry Goldthwaite and, later, with George Goldthwaite (whose sister he married) before moving to Mobile in 1837. He built a distinguished practice representing clients in federal court in Mobile and gained a national reputation arguing before the United States Supreme Court. He accepted an appointment to the U.S. Supreme Court in 1853 and served until April 1861, whereupon he resigned and returned South to join the Confederate cause, serving as assistant secretary of war from October 1862 until the war's end. In 1864, he was one of a group of men sent to Hampton Roads to confer with President Lincoln and Secretary Seward on the restoration of peace and the means of reconstruction.

John Archibald Campbell of Mobile was appointed to the U.S. Supreme Court by President Franklin Pierce in 1853, following the death of fellow Alabamian John McKinley. He resigned from the court in 1861, on the eve of the Civil War.

After Richmond was evacuated, Campbell secured from President Lincoln a sort of quasi-recognition of the Confederate government as a basis for reconstruction, but after the death of Lincoln, this plan was discarded. Campbell was imprisoned for six months at war's end and, upon his release, returned to practicing law, soon moving to New Orleans and again becoming distinguished as an appellate advocate who frequently argued cases before the U.S. Supreme Court.

Legal Education and Admission to the Bar

In the early days of Alabama statehood, legal education was a matter of "reading" law under the tutelage of an established lawyer or judge, a system of legal apprenticeship whereby the student paid money, agreed to "write" (clerk) in the office, or both, in exchange for his legal education. Over time, certain lawyers gained reputations as good teachers and regularly attracted would-be students. Nimrod Benson of Montgomery was one of Alabama's most distinguished lawyer-educators, as was William P. Chilton of Tuskegee (who later served as chief justice of the Alabama Supreme Court.) Judge Daniel Coleman of Athens even conducted a law school in his home for a period, having many distinguished attorneys of north Alabama as graduates.

Such treatises as Sir William Blackstone's *Commentaries on the Laws of England* and Sir Edward Coke's *Institutes of the Laws of England* and works by American legal authorities such as James Kent and Joseph Story served as textbooks for would-be lawyers. Harry Toulmin's *Digest of Alabama Laws* localized the students' education. Such reading helped pass on a common law mentality, which views the law as superior to the power of individual people and institutions, and helped train Alabama's early lawyers to defend the individual rights of their clients against the will, the prevailing values, and even the interests of the community, when necessary.

The University of Alabama School of Law traces its history to 1845 when Judge Benjamin Porter was named a legal professor and established a law curriculum at the state's only public university at the time. Judge Porter served as a trustee of the University and was highly regarded as a legal scholar. The legal curriculum never got underway, though, due to a lack of students and to restrictions placed on the "legal department" by the University's regular faculty. It would not become fully operational until 1872, when Judge Henderson Somerville would reorganize it.

Attorney Wade Keyes of Montgomery, a chancery court judge with an academic inclination, attempted to organize the "Montgomery Law School" in late 1860. With the help of former Alabama Supreme Court Chief Justice Samuel F. Rice who was serving in the legislature at the time, Keyes got legislation passed authorizing him to grant degrees and giving his graduates a "diploma privilege" of automatic bar admission. The act placed the Montgomery Law School under the joint supervision of the Supreme Court and the University of Alabama board of trustees. Keyes advertised his school in the spring of 1860, with classes to begin in the fall. He was able to graduate only one class of five or six members before his school fell victim to the furor of secession and civil war.

As late as the 1840s, all a would-be lawyer had to do to gain admission to the bar was to satisfy two circuit court judges that he was morally fit to practice and that he had a basic understanding of legal principles. Given the egalitarian and frontier mentality of the time, judges tended to be liberal in their application of these loose admission standards, taking a generally laissez-faire approach to the admission process. The result was a Darwinian "survival of the fittest" approach to the practice of law, with significant numbers of lawyers being poorly trained, easily licensed, and sent forth to fail or succeed upon their own initiative.

With the adoption of the 1852 code compilation, the practice of law and admission to the bar became subject to uniform regulation. The new code gave power to individual circuit or chancery judges to admit candidates to their bar (while allowing the Supreme Court to retain control over its own bar). The trial court judges were given the duty of enforcing minimum standards of

ABOVE: *The first attempt to establish a school of law at the University of Alabama occured in 1845 when Judge Benjamin Porter tried unsuccessfully to establish a law curriculum.* OPPOSITE PAGE: *William P. Chilton was a highly regarded lawyer-educator during the antebellum period. He was elected to the Alabama Supreme Court in 1848, becoming chief justice in 1852. Chilton County is named in his honor.*

knowledge among admittees, as well as a basic code of ethics among practitioners. Judges were to examine candidates for the bar in each of seven fields—real property, personal property, pleading and evidence, commercial, criminal, and chancery law, and Alabama statutes. This choice of subjects followed national trends, but the code did not define what would be a passing grade. It early became clear that most judges did not want to serve as evaluators, because they soon began to delegate this duty to committees of lawyers. In 1858, the legislature granted the Alabama Supreme Court this same privilege. These committees often performed poorly, but at least the code provided a yardstick against which their performance could be measured.

In the matter of the regulation of legal ethics, the code commissioners were ahead of their times as the Alabama Code was much more detailed in its requirements than other Southern states. Admittees were required to swear an oath to carry out specific obligations such as showing due respect for judges and court officers, and to speak only the truth concerning professional matters. They were to refrain from "offensive personalities" and avoid staining the reputations of witnesses. They were to avoid stirring up legal actions or prolonging them unnecessarily. They were to protect client secrets. Finally, they were forbidden to "reject, for any consideration personal to themselves, the cause of the defenseless or oppressed." A lawyer could be disbarred for violating these rules, disobeying court orders, mishandling money, or being convicted of a crime involving moral turpitude.

CHAPTER FOUR

THE ROAD TO SECESSION

The attention of most Alabamians during the first half of the nineteenth century was focused on the founding of the state and its governmental and constitutional organization. Internal issues of banking, capital liquidity, Indian removal, internal improvements, and internal sectional partisan politics drew the political energy of the state's population, keeping in the background the impact of the power of the federal government and its tariffs, its monster banking system, and its potential threats to the viability of slavery. One man is often credited with bringing these larger national issues to the forefront of Alabama politics and using them to drive a wedge between the state and the Union, which ultimately led to secession. That man is William Lowndes Yancey, who many consider to have been one of the leading attorneys of his era and the "Orator of Secession." [1]

Yancey's life was cut short in 1863 by a kidney infection that resulted in his death at the age of 49. He therefore was spared from living through much of the Civil War which he helped instigate and from its horrific impact on the state, both during and after the fighting. Although short, his life was dramatic and eventful. He came on the public stage in Alabama in 1841 when he was elected as a Democrat to the state house of representatives as a reform candidate against planter domination. In 1843, he was elected to the Alabama Senate. During his tenure in state politics, he was a major leader in the fight in favor of the white basis of apportionment for congressional districts, in bank reform, in the drive for public education, in prison reform and in the right of married women to control their property. These were all issues opposed by the planter-dominated Whig party who were Alabama's slave owners, yet Yancey was able to see many of these reforms become law. It is ironic that Yancey was in favor of many reform movements of the nineteenth century while so adamant in his defense of the South's peculiar institution. This irony extends to his lack of rapport with the planter class, who dominated the Whig party, demonstrated by his opposition to allowing representation on the basis of the slave population.

In 1844, Yancey was elected to the U.S. House of Representatives to fill the seat left vacant by Dixon Hall Lewis's elevation to the Senate. By this time, Yancey was such a partisan of Southern rights that he was unable to make the kinds of compromises that keep the political machinery oiled, even within his own Democratic Party. Although he was elected to a second term in July 1846, he resigned, giving financial reasons but at the same time releasing a public letter in which he impeached the Democratic Party as lacking in principles. Away from elective office, he began a campaign to divorce his fellow Alabamians from allegiance to a national party, on the basis that loyalty to the national political system allowed the chipping away of those rights he felt were unique to Southerners, the rights to hold blacks as property.

In addition to developing a lucrative law practice in Montgomery, he began a career as orator and propa-

Opposite Page: *William Lowndes Yancey was regarded as one of the outstanding public speakers of his generation, able to hold audiences spellbound for hours. At first regarded as a radical, his pro-Southern rights, proslavery, prosecession point of view eventually came to be shared by the majority of Alabamians.*

THE IMPACT OF YANCEY'S YOUTH ON HIS LATER LIFE

WILLIAM LOWNDES YANCEY'S EARLY LIFE may shed some light on the energy that powered his pro-slavery ardor. His father, a South Carolina politician, died when Yancey was three and his mother moved Yancey and his infant brother back to Georgia, where she was from, and where they lived with his maternal grandparents and aunts. The women in the family were known both for being beautiful and also for having hot tempers.

His mother was his first teacher, and she trained him to be an orator and to follow in the footsteps of his father, who had been eulogized as a fountain of "the living waters of eloquence." Later, he attended the Mount Zion Academy, a nearby school with Presbyterian ministers as teachers, where he was taught by Nathan Beman, the school's founder and headmaster. Mr. Beman was a superior academician and a stern disciplinarian, who soon entered into a romance with William's mother and married her when William was seven years old. Thereafter, Beman moved his new family to New York. Before moving, he sold some slaves. Historically, it is not clear whether the slaves belonged to Mr. Beman originally or were part of the estate that Yancey's mother had received upon becoming a widow. (Mr. Beman was later accused of improperly handling this estate, which should have been handled in trust for the Yancey children.) This sale would become an embarrassment to Mr. Beman because, upon returning to the North, he became a well-known abolitionist. He also became a part of the revival movement, which crested with the Great Revival of 1830, the greatest of the modern religious awakenings of the American population up to that time.

There is historical speculation that Mr. Beman and his wife did not get along and became increasingly involved in acrimonious clashes over many issues, including Mr. Beman's ever-growing role in the abolition movement. His mother's displays of uncontrolled temper and his stepfather's coldness, arrogance, and sarcasm which played out in the ministerial surroundings of religious fervor and piety, probably made William Yancey's youth both unstable and unhappy. During this period he developed a temper of his own and was captured by the atmosphere of crusading zeal that surrounded his stepfather.

As he grew to manhood, Yancey grew to resent his stepfather, both for his generally bad treatment of Yancey's mother and for what Yancey conceived of as hypocrisy, especially in Beman's abolitionist fervor. Therefore, rather than following in the abolitionist footsteps of his stepfather, William Yancey became a wild, hot-tempered rebel, the fireeater of secession, who seemed to transfer his specific dislike of his stepfather to a general dislike of all those who supported abolition.

He attended Williams College, where he helped to edit a student literary journal, joined an oratorical society, and studied under a noted teacher of rhetoric, Mark Hopkins. He left Williams College after three years (probably due

gandist for slavery, states' rights, Southern rights, and "principle above party," a career of an unofficial political leader who was not constrained by the need to win an election. The public forum became his specialty; he spoke at hundreds of barbecues, conventions, and public meetings between the years 1846 and 1860.

Henry W. Hilliard, his major Whig protagonist, was quoted as saying about him, "I recall no one who made a greater impression upon me than the Honorable William L. Yancey.... Mr. Yancey's convictions were deep, strong, sincere, and he had the courage of these convictions. It was because he believed that the safety of the South depended upon a vigorous assertion of its rights at all hazards, involving even the subversion of the Union that when he addressed the people, the ardor of his patriotism flamed up with volcanic energy and splendor." [2]

The first issue that fueled Yancey's independent oratory was the introduction of the Wilmot Proviso shortly to financial problems), returning to the South, where he began the study of law in the office of Benjamin F. Perry in Greenville, South Carolina. Perry had been a friend of Yancey's father and was a well-known Unionist who had opposed the theory of nullification during the period when that issue stirred the state (1834-1835). While in Greenville, Yancey became the editor of the *Greenville Mountaineer* and used the paper in his own fight against nullification and the states' rights' activism of John C. Calhoun. When later questioned about his fight against the states' righters in the early part of his career, he would point out that he was only 19 years of age and his ideas were not as yet fully formed. And he needed to make a living.

The decision of William L. Yancey's mother, Caroline Bird Yancey, to marry Nathan Beman had a profound influence on Yancey's life.

In August 1835, Yancey married Sarah Caroline Earle, the daughter of a wealthy Greenville planter. Later in the year, he moved his family and slaves, most of whom he had inherited through his marriage, to a new plantation in Alabama near Cahaba, where he tried out the life of a gentleman planter, while also editing the *Cahaba Democrat*.

Unfortunately he was bankrupted by the panic of 1837 and, before he could recover, most of his slaves died, when the overseer of a neighboring plantation, in a plot to kill Yancey's overseer, poisoned the hillside spring from which the overseer usually drank. In a twist of fate, the whole gang of his slaves took a route they usually did not take and stopped at the spring for a drink the day it was poisoned. Most of them died and Yancey's planting interests were ruined. Thereafter, Yancey moved to Wetumpka and began practicing law and editing the *Wetumpka Argus*, along with his brother, Benjamin C. Yancey.

It was at this point that his political career began and it was during and after this period that a series of incidents illustrated his tempestuous temper. In the late 1830s, on a visit to Greenville, Yancey shot and killed his wife's uncle, pleading self-defense. During his first public speech after being elected to Congress, a Whig congressman from North Carolina challenged him to a duel because the speech was so vitriolic and personal. The duel was halted by the appearance of the police. In 1846, a duel between Alexander Stephens and Yancey was narrowly averted by the mediation of another person. These incidents of violence and near violence have been used by historians to illustrate Yancey's own temper and militancy as well as to argue that the South during the prewar era was generally more militant than any other part of the nation. (Part of this argument is bound up with the ideas of honor and chivalry that captured the imagination of Southern men of that era.)

Yancey's transition from Unionism to states' rights seemed to follow the ever-growing abolitionist clamor from the North, as well as the ever-worsening relationship of his mother and stepfather, which was increasingly fueled by his stepfather's involvement in the abolition movement. One historian has called his stepfather a kind of *bête noir* whom Yancey was fighting all his life.

after he resigned from Congress. Although defeated, this proviso would have kept slavery out of any territory claimed from Mexico after its loss in the Mexican-American War. Conflict over this proposal generally aggravated relations between the North and South and enhanced the stature of states' rights advocates such as John C. Calhoun of South Carolina and those who had been its supporters even as early as the introduction of the ideas of nullification in the early 1830s. Calhounites in Alabama included attorneys James M. Calhoun, a nephew of John, Dixon Hall Lewis, and John Elmore in the Montgomery area; and John A. Campbell, Joseph Lesesne, and Percy Walker in Mobile. Although all were men of stature and enjoyed personal political success, they had never been able to garner significant support behind the ideas of Calhoun and his philosophy that the national political party structure was a threat to the continuation of the "Southern Way of Life."

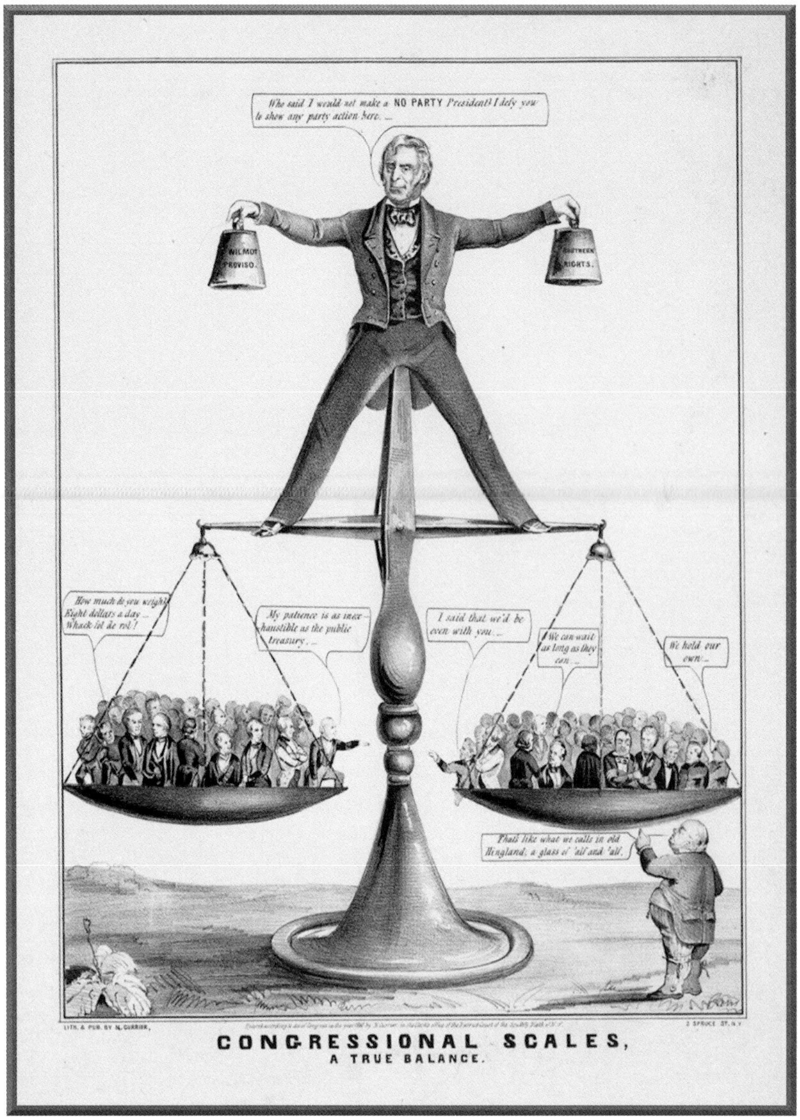

This 1851 cartoon satirizes President Zachary Taylor's efforts to strike a balance between Northern and Southern demands. In one hand he holds a weight labeled "Wilmot Proviso" and in the other a weight labeled "Southern Rights."

Yancey's response to the debate over the proviso was the drafting of the Alabama Platform of 1848, endorsed by the Alabama Democratic Convention. It asserted opposition both to federal interference with slavery in the territories and to "squatter sovereignty," a theory advanced in 1847 by General Lewis Cass of Michigan, which held that early settlers in a territory could decide the slavery question for themselves. Yancey's platform instructed Alabama's delegates to the 1848 Democratic National Convention *"under no political necessity whatever"* to support any candidates not "openly and avowedly" opposed to either form of interference with slavery.

Yancey's platform failed and he walked out of the convention. Still, the platform is considered the first formulation of the position the South ultimately espoused on the issue of popular sovereignty and is seen as a maneuver to forge a Southern political faction unrestrained by national party discipline and bound only to its conception of the proper remedies for the defense of Southern rights.

Yancey opposed the Compromise of 1850 and, thereafter, became more and more a secessionist *per se*. Working with secessionists in other states, he formed Southern rights clubs, the main purpose of which were to unite Southern men to fight for their rights, regardless of party. In 1858, he formed the League of United Southerners to further promote this concept. On June 15, 1858, he wrote what is now known as the Slaughter Letter, in which he declared: "No National Party can save us; no Sectional Party can do it. But if we could do as our fathers did, organize Committees of Safety all over the cotton states...we shall fire the Southern heart, instruct the Southern mind, give courage to each other, and at the proper moment, by one organized, concerted action, we can precipitate the cotton states into a revolution." The disclosure of this letter led many historians to surmise that there was a conspiracy to break up the union among Yancey and the other "fire-eater" proponents of secession that predated the election of Lincoln.

Yancey and his followers nominated attorney Reuben Chapman for governor in 1847. Chapman had served in Congress for six terms as a loyal Democrat representing a north Alabama district with nothing unusual about his service until the debate on the Wilmot Proviso, which he stringently opposed. His energetic defense of states' rights brought him the support of Yancey, who chaired the state Democratic convention and placed his name in nomination.

Yancey continued to support Chapman when he came up for reelection in 1849. In the two years of Chapman's administration, with the aftermath of the Mexican War and the debate over the Wilmot Proviso, party politics

REUBEN CHAPMAN AND THE MANTRA OF "OUTSIDE INTERFERENCE"

Reuben Chapman came to Alabama from Virginia in 1824 at the age of 25. He read law in the office of his brother Samuel. He practiced his profession in Huntsville and prospered to the extent that he was able to acquire a plantation in Black Belt Sumter County, thus forging connections in both sections of the state. He was single until he was 39, whereupon he married a 16-year-old girl with whom he reared two sons and four daughters.

John R. Mayfield in *Alabama Governors: A Political History of the State*, describes Chapman as a transition governor whose administration "served as a transition from Jacksonian-style politics concerned with internal issues such as state banking and Indian removal to politics increasingly dominated by national issues." It was the beginning of the period where state issues became lost in the rhetoric of proslavery and prosecession arguments. Chapman emphasized the external challenges faced by the state, in a pattern that has since become almost a "gubernatorial *sine qua non*" in the state's political arena. He ignored the many real and hard problems of the state, preferring to attack "outside interference," calling on his fellow Alabamians to resist abolitionist attempts to interfere with their rights to take their "property" wherever they pleased.

in Alabama had fractured. The Democratic Party was divided between the states' rights and Unionist factions. Chapman had made a politically fatal mistake toward the end of his term when Alabama's two senate seats became open by ignoring tradition and filling both seats with men from south Alabama (rather than having one senator from the north and one from the south).

The opposition this move created in Unionist north Alabama helped defeat him and brought forth a compromise candidate, Henry Collier, who stepped down from his position as chief justice of the Alabama Supreme Court to serve. Although Collier professed support for states' rights, he had a reputation for being a moderate. Even so, he encouraged the legislature to send delegates to the June 1850 Nashville Convention held to discuss Southern rights and the South's loss of political power within the Union during the intense period of debates surrounding the Compromise of 1850. He refused to call a separate convention to discuss the state's status in the Union, recognizing that the more radical states' righters

THE ILLUSTRIOUS CAREER OF HENRY COLLIER

HENRY WATKINS Collier was born in Virginia on January 17, 1801. He came to Alabama in 1818, settling in Huntsville and reading law with Judge John Haywood of the Tennessee Supreme Court in Nashville. He thereafter moved to Tuscaloosa and entered law practice with Sion L. Perry. In 1827, after Tuscaloosa became the capital city of Alabama, Collier ran for the legislature, serving one term. The legislature elected him a judge of the Third Circuit Court, which had the effect of making Collier a member of the ad hoc Alabama Supreme Court. When the legislature created a separate supreme court, Collier was elevated to that court and served as its chief justice for 12 years.

Henry W. Collier was one of a number of early Alabama lawyers to serve both as governor and as chief justice of the Alabama Supreme Court, a post he held for 12 years.

Collier was a compromise candidate, chosen to enhance the chances of a Democratic win in the gubernatorial election of 1849. Two different groups supported Collier's candidacy: the followers of Clement Claiborne Clay, son of former Governor Clement Comer Clay (the younger Clay having married Virginia Tunstall, one of Collier's nieces by marriage) and followers of William Rufus King, whose nephew and adopted son would marry Collier's daughter in 1856.

During his tenure as governor, Collier promoted educational reform, pushing for a state public education system. In 1850, he proposed the creation of a state superintendent's office to provide leadership and advocated greater funding for education. He spoke out for other liberal causes as well, including judicial reform, creation of a hospital for the mentally ill in Tuscaloosa, and prison reform. He also championed economic diversification and encouraged investment in textile mills.

Collier had a reputation for being a moderate on the issue of Southern rights. When he ran for a second term, he again was the compromise candidate for many, since his only opposition was an extreme Unionist. When William Yancey refused to run as a Southern rights candidate, Collier was the only choice for the Southern rights faction and won handily. Collier's term in office provided a period of moderation before the whirlwind of secessionist fury captured the minds and hearts of Alabamians.

who demanded such a call did not have the support of the majority of Alabama's citizens. Yancey considered running against Collier when the incumbent ran for a second term, but declined, perhaps in recognition that he was ahead of most Alabama citizens in his calls for secession.

The congressional elections of 1851 illustrated dramatically the continued splintering of political parties in the state, with Southern Rights Democrats, Pro-Union Democrats, and Whigs. Among the lawyer candidates representing the Southern rights cause were Judge John Bragg of Mobile, Sydenham Moore of Greensboro,

HENRY W. HILLIARD LAWYER, PROFESSOR, PREACHER, DIPLOMAT, STATESMAN, AND ORATOR EXTRAORDINAIRE

For Henry W. Hilliard, politics was his fourth career. He was born in Fayetteville, North Carolina, in 1808, attended South Carolina College, and then studied law under William C. Preston, a well-known states' rights orator in Columbia, South Carolina. He was admitted to practice in 1829 and set up practice in Athens, Georgia. Hilliard moved to Tuscaloosa, Alabama, in 1831, to serve at the newly formed University of Alabama as a professor of English literature. He stayed at the University until 1834, when he moved to Montgomery to practice law again. At some point, he also became a Methodist lay minister. Soon after moving to Montgomery, he stepped forward as a Whig candidate for office, first serving in the Alabama House of Representatives in 1938. Soon, he was involved in the national Whig Party and was appointed charge d'affaires to Belgium by President Tyler from 1842 to 1844. Thereafter, he was elected to Congress for three terms. While in Congress, he served as a regent for the Smithsonian Institution. He supported the Compromise of 1850. At the end of his third term in 1851, he decided to return to the practice of law, although he continued his involvement in Whig national party politics.

As the leading Whig politician in Alabama, and an outstanding speaker in his own right, Henry W. Hilliard used his eloquence to oppose William Lowndes Yancey and the secessionists.

Highly regarded throughout his career as an orator, he used his skills throughout the 1850s in an effort to defeat the calls for secession by William Lowndes Yancey and his followers. He fought to maintain the Union until Alabama seceded. At that point, he served the state as a brigadier general, raised Hilliard's Legion of about 3,000 men, and fought with General Bragg in the West. He resigned his commission after some months.

After the war, he moved to Georgia and practiced law there. He also authored several books during his career, including an 1865 novel entitled *De Vane, A Story of Plebeians and Patricians,* which adapted Sir Walter Scott's *Ivanhoe* to college life on the grounds of the University of Virginia. Following Scott's lead, Hilliard's book focused on the cult of manners, the cult of women, the cult of the gallant knight, and the loyalty of caste, themes that had dominated Southern culture before the war and remained influences in its postwar society as well. Hilliard returned to diplomatic service in 1877, when he was appointed United States Minister to Brazil by President Hayes.

WILLIAM RUSSELL SMITH LAWYER, WRITER, UNIVERSITY PRESIDENT, AND KNOW-NOTHING CONGRESSMAN

WILLIAM R. SMITH was born in Kentucky in 1815, but moved to Tuscaloosa, Alabama, with his widowed mother and siblings. His mother died in 1823, leaving him and his siblings in dire circumstances. The children were placed among several Tuscaloosa families. General George W. Crabb, realizing the boy's genius, eagerly assisted him with his education. When the University of Alabama opened its doors in 1831, he was among its first students. There he was positively influenced by Professor Henry Hilliard, developing a lifelong love of writing, especially poetry. He left the University in 1834 to study in the law office of General Crabb and was admitted to practice the next year, establishing a practice in Greensboro in 1835.

He served as a captain of Alabama troops in the second Creek War, remaining in Mobile when his company was disbanded there. He devoted himself to literature for a year while there, establishing a monthly periodical entitled *The Bachelor's Button*. He continued publishing the magazine after he returned to Tuscaloosa, although the publication lasted little more than a year. He returned to the practice of law, began editing *The Monitor*, a Whig newspaper, and in 1839 was elected mayor of Tuscaloosa. In 1844, he moved to Fayette, was elected brigadier general of the militia, and continued to practice law. In 1850, he was elected judge of the circuit court, but resigned in 1851 because he was elected to Congress in the 1850 congressional election as a Unionist Democrat. He was reelected twice (the second time as an independent candidate and the last time as a Know-Nothing candidate), but finally was defeated by Judge Sydenham Moore in 1856. He was invited by the Alabama Phi Beta Kappa Society to read a poem at the commencement of the University in 1860. The poem, *The Uses of Solitude,* was considered by critics at the time, and even later, to be one of the great American poems.

He attended the 1861 secession convention and published *History and Debates of the Convention*. After secession, he served in the Confederate congresses from 1861 to 1865. Thereafter, he served as the fourth president of the University of Alabama in 1870 and 1871. Under a joint resolution of the legislature, he began a consolidation of the *Alabama Reports*, which were published in ten volumes, the first in 1870 and the tenth in 1879. In 1879, he moved his family to Washington, D.C., where he practiced law and devoted himself to literary pursuits for the remainder of his life.

Samuel F. Rice of Talladega County, and John Cochran of Eufaula. Judge William S. Mudd of Jefferson County and lawyers William Russell Smith of Tuscaloosa, Stephen Hale of Eutaw, Alexander White of Talladega, and James Abercrombie of Montgomery were pro-Union Democrat or Whig candidates. Yet, the most interesting feature of this congressional election did not involve candidates. For years after this election, Alabama voters talked about the contest in the second district as being one of the most memorable in the state's history because of the participation of orators William Yancey and Henry Hilliard, the state's most popular Whig politician, in debating the issues, even though neither was a candidate for office. It was called "the battle of giants" by contemporaries, even "Armageddon" between the Democrats and the Whigs.

TOP: *Samuel F. Rice ran unsuccessfully for Congress as a Southern Rights Democrat in 1851. In 1855 he was appointed to the Alabama Supreme Court, becoming chief justice a year later.* ABOVE: *Judge Andrew B. Moore became Alabama's sixteenth governor in 1857.*

Even with the participation of Yancey in his prime, the Union Democrat candidates won in most congressional districts in 1851 because most Alabama voters did not favor secession. But as events occurred, minds began to change. Even with the participation of its effective spokesman, Henry Hilliard, the Whig Party began to disintegrate after the 1851 election because the party became identified with abolitionists in the North, and thereby lost its appeal in the South. Soon, though, the American, or Know-Nothing, Party, known primarily for its antiimmigration and anti-Catholic platform, began to draw former Whigs and strong Unionist voters. In the 1855 gubernatorial election, the party fielded candidate Judge George D. Shortridge of Montgomery County against the incumbent Democrat John A. Winston, who won by nearly 12,000 votes. Even in losing, Shortridge polled the largest vote ever before polled against a Democratic candidate for governor in the state. In addition, the American Party elected two congressmen, attorney Percy Walker (son of John Williams Walker) in the first district and attorney William Russell Smith in the fifth district, and won a large representation in the legislature, especially in the lower house.

In the period after the 1851 congressional contest, William Yancey returned to practicing law and stayed out of politics. It was the entry of the Know-Nothing Party into competition with the Democratic Party in the 1856 presidential election, where Know-Nothing Millard Fillmore faced Democrat James Buchanan, that drew him back into the fray. The compromises reached in 1850 and 1851 began to erode with the passage of the Kansas-Nebraska Act and with the increase of antislavery sentiment in the North, strengthening the Republican Party. Yancey traveled the state debating with Know-Nothings and his old Whig enemies, including attorneys Henry Hilliard, Jeremiah Clemens, and Lewis Parsons,[3] continuing to assert his Southern rights' message and to attack the Know-Nothings in Alabama and the Republicans in the North. Crowds appeared from all around the state at each of his debates and his ideas began to convince his listeners of the validity of his principles of states' rights and the reasonableness of possible secession from the Union. After this election, the Know-Nothing Party disintegrated and the Democratic Party, with no other opposition, dominated state politics for the next four years, electing its gubernatorial candidate Judge Andrew B. Moore of Perry County in 1857. By 1860, the Southern Rights wing of the Democratic Party dominated state politics, with William Lowndes Yancey as its invincible leader.

JEREMIAH CLEMENS LAWYER, AUTHOR, U.S. SENATOR, AND VICTIM OF "SIR WALTER DISEASE"

Mark Twain, who was Jeremiah Clemens's cousin, had a theory about what caused the Civil War: "Sir Walter Scott had so large a hand in making Southern character, as it existed before the War, that he is in great measure responsible for the war." To Twain, "Sir Walter disease" was a profound sensitivity to slights against honor created by the "grotesque chivalry" of Scott's heroes. Twain experienced the "cult of chivalry" while in the Missouri-based Confederate band "The Marion Rangers," encountering young Southern men full of romance and love of rank, caste, and "bogus" decorations.

At least one professor of history described Jeremiah Clemens's public career as an example of the "damage that the cult of chivalry could do to southern men."[4] Clemens was born in Huntsville in 1814, and seemed destined for greatness as a lawyer, politician, military leader, and writer, but his early promise turned to frustration in later years as his vacillations over slavery and states' rights versus Unionism, particularly in the United States Senate to which he was elected in 1849 (at age 35), brought him censure and reelection defeat.

To Clemens and others with "Sir Walter disease," chivalric honor for a statesman meant political independence from both popular influence and personal ambition and a willingness to resort even to murderous violence in defense of principle or reputation. Personal autonomy and independence of judgment were important values in the Southern mind, tied up with ideas of manhood and personal worth.

Clemens became a victim of these ideas after he first sought the defeat of the Compromise of 1850 then became an avid supporter of the Compromise when it proved to be popular in North Alabama after its passage. This turnaround appeared too opportunistic to the minds of voters and also reinforced suspicions that he had made a political deal to support Zachary Taylor's Whig administration in return for Whig support for his original

Yancey Splits the National Democratic Party and Secession Follows

When the Alabama Democratic Party met in convention at Montgomery in January, 1860, Yancey's Alabama Platform was resurrected and its doctrine of federal protection of the rights of slaveholders in the territories, validated by the U.S. Supreme Court in the *Dred Scott* decision, was adopted. Delegates were instructed to withdraw if the national convention, to be held in Charleston in April, did not incorporate this view into the Democratic national platform. Thus, Yancey's arguments finally carried Alabama and, subsequently, the South. The emphasis he placed on Southern rights, as against party loyalty, set the stage to make party insurgency for the sake of rights seem proper.

Yancey was the acknowledged spokesman for Southern rights in an Alabama delegation that included attorneys Francis S. Lyon, Reuben Chapman, LeRoy Pope Walker, and Alexander Beaufort Meek. He spoke on behalf of the South in defense of the Southern Rights plank of the platform reported to the convention. The convention ultimately adopted a platform that did not conform to the one supported by Yancey. After the vote was announced, LeRoy Pope Walker read a protest, and the Alabama delegation rose and walked out of the convention, fol-

election as a U.S. senator. These suspicions, and his failure to challenge any of his accusers to a duel, undermined Clemens's reputation and tarnished his integrity, resulting in the disintegration of his political career.

Some say that he left office a broken man, retreating to his plantation to focus on writing novels. Between 1856 and 1860, he wrote three historical novels but he did not have the talents of his cousin Samuel and his writing exposed an unrelenting racism, which makes it disconcerting to the modern reader. But his work still is noteworthy for its illustration of the Southern mind and its ideals of honor.

Clemens returned to the political arena to oppose disunion during the secession crisis of 1861. Clemens's stand against secession drew further attacks on his honor. He rejected the proposition that states had the right to secede, as opposed to merely seeking to delay secession until a convention of all slaveholding states could be held to coordinate their actions, as most other opponents sought. When the articles of secession passed, Clemens at first determined to fight on the Confederate side, but he soon left the Confederate army because he was not given a position commensurate with his military experience (due, it is said, to enmity toward him by the Confederate secretary of war, LeRoy Pope Walker.) He crossed over to the union side in 1862 and became the most prominent Alabamian to oppose the Confederacy, but only after he was savagely caned by a Confederate officer on a Huntsville street. Caning was a further affront to his honor since one caned a person beneath one in rank or caste, while dueling was the method of challenging an equal, under Sir Walter's code of chivalry.

Between 1862 and 1865, he divided his time between Huntsville, the center of north Alabama's general opposition to the war, and the North and during 1863 and 1864, he wrote a novel entitled *Tobias Wilson*, a fictionalized account of guerilla fighting in the north Alabama upcountry. In the book, he clearly rejects the ideals of chivalry, which had pervaded his earlier works, arguing that honor was irrelevant in a warring society where community standards have broken down. Nearly blind and broken in health and spirit, Clemens died in Huntsville on May 21, 1865.

lowed by other Deep South delegations. The convention subsequently adjourned without a nominee, agreeing to meet again in early summer in Baltimore. The Baltimore convention failed to reach unity on a candidate.

By midsummer, there were four candidates for the presidency: Stephen A. Douglas, nominated on a Northern Democratic ticket favoring popular sovereignty in the territories; John C. Breckinridge, nominated by Southern Democrats on the Alabama Platform; John Bell, nominated by a group of Whigs on the Constitutional Union ticket with a compromise platform; and Abraham Lincoln, nominated by the Republican party, with a platform that would prohibit slavery in the territories.

Yancey supported Breckinridge and toured the North speaking on his behalf. Although Yancey drew large crowds, Breckenridge garnered few votes in the North. He did carry the state of Alabama and his vote totals were seen as an indication that Alabama voters would want to secede if Abraham Lincoln was elected president, because Breckenridge was the only candidate whose supporters argued outright that the election of a Republican would be sufficient grounds for secession. Yancey called the election a referendum on secession and called for a secession convention to be organized upon Lincoln's election.

Governor Andrew B. Moore issued the summons for a convention on December 24, 1860. Immediately, candidates who wanted to be convention delegates began organizing. Yancey and his followers favored immediate secession and were called "straight-out secessionists." Another group was called "cooperationists" because they favored a coordinated withdrawal of all the Southern states. There were Unionists who wished the North to address Southern grievances; and Ultra-Unionists who were adamantly opposed to secession.

The campaign for delegates was spirited. Yancey spoke out for immediate secession. The election results followed the traditional sectional division within the state, with north Alabama generally electing cooperationist candidates and south Alabama choosing immediate secessionists. Although the issue of secession was never presented to voters directly, the delegate selection resulted in a slim majority (54-46) for the immediate secessionists. The delegates were mostly lawyers and planters. Among the lawyers were John T. Morgan, John Bragg, William L. Yancey, Thomas H. Watts, Edmund S. Dargan, David P. Lewis, Lyman Gibbons, William M. Brooks, Edward Courtney Bullock, Alpheus Baker, James D. Webb, Nicholas Davis, Jr., Jeremiah Clemens, and William R. Smith. Seventy-nine of the 100 members owned slaves. The convention was convened on January 7.

Attorney William M. Brooks, a secessionist, was selected as permanent chairman of the convention. His election foretold the convention outcome. When the vote on the ordinance of secession was taken on January 11, 61 votes favored and 39 opposed secession. On this vote, Alabama became a "free, sovereign, and independent state."

TOP: *John C. Breckenridge of Kentucky was the Southern Democrat nominee for president in the election of 1860. William Lowndes Yancey campaigned vigorously on his behalf.* ABOVE: *Most of the delegates to the secession convention were planters or lawyers, and some, like former Alabama Supreme Court Justice Lyman Gibbons, were both.*

William Yancey had demanded immediate secession, believing that the North would not interfere with Alabama's peaceful and orderly withdrawal from the Union. Most Alabamians hoped for peace, since the state was not well situated to fight a war. Governor Moore, though, began quietly to prepare in the event war was declared. He sent agents north to purchase arms and pressured state banks to stop redeeming notes with specie in order to have funds to finance munitions. He sent commissioners to other Southern states, stating that he needed to stay informed, but the real purpose was to encourage the states to join Alabama in secession.

On January 3, 1861, Governor Moore activated six companies of the Volunteer Corps of Alabama, which had been created the previous year, and the next day he ordered the troops to seize federal installations in the state before it seceded. By January 5, Fort Morgan, Fort Gaines, and the United States Arsenal at Mount Vernon were controlled by Alabama. The governor appointed attorney George T. Goldthwaite adjutant general for the army, a position that the secession convention empowered him to create for the defense of the state. The governor's quick response to secession made Alabama more prepared for independence and for defending itself than any other Southern state.

The secession convention worked for two months, assuming extensive powers to

revise the Alabama constitution to reflect elimination of federal control and to establish institutions to replace functions previously held by the federal government within the state. The convention also debated whether to reopen the African slave trade but determined not to.

While the convention was in session, the state responded to a suggestion of South Carolina and invited representatives of all the seceding states to convene in Montgomery to discuss the formation of a confederate government. Ironically, although one reason for choosing to establish the Confederate government in Montgomery was the presence of secessionist leader William Yancey, the Alabama convention failed to include him in its delegation to the Confederate Congress. Nor was Yancey seriously considered for the presidency of the new government. Alabama did provide several important officers, including attorney LeRoy Pope Walker, who was named secretary of war for a time, and attorney Johnson Jones Hooper, who served as secretary of the Confederate Congress. Thomas H. Watts served as attorney general and Yancey served in the Confederate Senate and was later appointed as commissioner of the Confederacy to England and France. Francis S. Lyon, James Phelan, James L. Pugh, and David Clopton were other Alabama attorneys who served in the Confederate Congress.

Shortly after the formation of the Confederate government, war was precipitated when President Lincoln refused to order the evacuation of Fort Sumter upon demand by the South. In response, the fort was fired upon and war began.

TOP: *This engraving from* Frank Leslie's Illustrated Newspaper *shows the Confederate Senate meeting in the Alabama state capitol.* ABOVE: *LeRoy Pope Walker was the son of John Williams Walker and the grandson of LeRoy Pope. As secretary of war in the Confederate cabinet, he issued the fateful order to fire on Fort Sumter.*

CHAPTER FIVE

WAR AND RECONSTRUCTION

In 1860, there were 748 attorneys engaged in the practice of their profession in 131 Alabama towns. When the war started in 1861, a number of Alabama attorneys took leadership roles in the Confederate military. Two attorneys served as major generals during the conflict. Henry D. Clayton, an attorney who practiced in Eufaula, was chairman of the military committee of the Alabama legislature at the onset of the war. He commanded a regiment in Braxton Bragg's Kentucky campaign and rose to the rank of major general by the end of the war. In 1867, he was elected judge of the Third Judicial Circuit of Alabama, serving in this position until he resigned in 1886 to become the ninth president of the University of Alabama. Jones M. Withers, an 1835 graduate of West Point, who had fought in the Seminole Indian and Mexican wars, was an attorney who was mayor of Mobile at the war's outbreak. He commanded the "Army of Mobile" from 1861 to 1862 and was made a major general in August 1862. After the war, he returned to Mobile and became the editor of the *Mobile Tribune*.

Alabama commissioned 36 brigadier generals. Among these were attorneys Edmund W. Pettus, Edward O'Neal, John Tyler Morgan, John Norwood, John Reid, Sterling Wood, Isham Garrott, LeRoy Pope Walker, James Holtzclaw, Cullen Battle, James Clanton, Alpheus Baker, Moses Hannon, George Johnston, Tennent Lomax, Edward Tracy, and William Henry Forney. Two other well-known attorney heroes were Lieutenant General Joseph "Fighting Joe" Wheeler (who was later named a major general of volunteers in the Spanish-American War) and Raphael Semmes, who had the unusual distinction of serving as an admiral in the Confederate navy and also being named a brigadier general of the Confederate States Army. Semmes captained the Confederate raiding cruisers *Sumter* and *Alabama*, and his vessels inflicted a total loss to Union shipping of $6 million. He practiced law in Mobile both before and after the war.

Opposite Page: *A lawyer before and after the war, Raphael Semmes attained renown as the commander of the CSS* Alabama, *which wreaked havoc on Union shipping during the Civil War. When the war was over, the United States sued Great Britain for damages for allowing the* Alabama *and two other raiders, the* Florida *and the* Shenandoah, *to be built and sold to the Confederacy. The so-called "Alabama Claims" set a precedent for international arbitration, resulting in a settlement of $15.5 million for the United States.* Above: *Eufaula attorney Henry D. Clayton attained the rank of major general in the Confederate army.*

HOW GENERAL "FIGHTING" JOE WHEELER BECAME A LAWYER

After the Civil War, General Joe Wheeler became a prosperous planter, successful businessman, and lawyer, United States congressman and, finally, major general of volunteers during the Spanish-American War. Few people know of the murder trial that inspired his becoming a lawyer, which in turn led to his political career.[1] The facts of the murder have been described as follows:

"Late in the afternoon of May 3, 1871, several shots rang out from within a small blacksmith's shop on the Lawrence County, Alabama, plantation of the former Confederate cavalry commander General Joseph Wheeler. The shop was occupied by blacksmith Dandrige T. Galey and his son, Elam. Moments before the shooting began, Wheeler and his brother-in-law Thomas Jones had approached the shop armed with pistols. When the shooting stopped, the elder Galey lay dead with a bullet lodged in his brain and his son was seriously wounded by a shot to his back. Joe Wheeler and Tom Jones were charged with murder and assault with intent to murder. After one of the most unusual and irregular trials in the history of Alabama jurisprudence, Jones, by then the sole defendant, was found 'not guilty.'"[2]

Alabama's Wartime Governors—All Attorneys

Andrew B. Moore (1857-1861) was originally elected as a moderate Unionist, but he is remembered in Alabama history as the governor who called together the secession convention that took Alabama out of the Union. Throughout his first term and well into his second term, which began in 1859, his actions were cautiously aimed at preserving the Union. It was John Brown's raid at Harper's Ferry that made him a forceful advocate of Southern rights. Even before secession, he worked with the legislature to prepare the state for war. On his recommendation, the legislature passed a military bill providing for a volunteer corps in every county and a $200,000 appropriation to equip troops. Two scholarships were funded for each county to send students to military schools. He worked to expedite the construction of the South and North Railroad and to develop Alabama's mineral district.[3] He remained hopeful that the Union would be preserved by the election of a Democrat as president. When Republican Abraham Lincoln, who advocated prohibiting slavery in U.S. territories, was elected, Moore finally agreed to call a secession convention. Moore's second term as governor ended on December 2, 1861, but he continued to support the war effort as a special aide to the new governor, John Gill Shorter, by traveling to north Alabama to recruit troops and purchase supplies. He also worked to supply salt and food to the state's

The Wheelers and the Joneses were sufficiently powerful in Lawrence County that no mention of the murder or indictments appeared in the local newspapers of the day, even though the parties involved were among the region's most prominent citizens. Most of the information available was found in Wheeler's personal materials left with the Alabama Department of Archives after his death. Even the volume of the Lawrence County criminal court proceedings of 1871 to 1872, during the period when Wheeler was dismissed as a defendant and somehow maneuvered to have his name as a defendant expunged from the proceedings, is missing.

It is known that after Wheeler was released as a defendant, his brother-in-law dismissed his attorneys, who included Richard Walker, a Mr. Robinson of Huntsville, and Colonel Luke Pryor of Limestone County, because of supposed disagreements over legal strategy and fees. (The attorneys' $10,000 fee was the largest ever charged in Lawrence County up to that time and they subsequently sued Jones to collect their fees.) The dismissal allowed Jones to gain a six-month continuance, during which time, Wheeler studied law, got himself admitted to the bar, and became Jones's defense attorney. He then obtained a change of venue to a part of the county friendlier to Wheeler-Jones interests. And by the time the trial was to start, the state's only eyewitness, Elam Galey, son of the victim, had left the state with his mother and siblings and moved to Texas. (A Galey descendant told the story that Jones, after a trip to Huntsville where the Wheelers banked, brought a black satchel to the home where the Galeys were living and handed it to Mrs. Galey, after saying something to her. She turned and went back into her house and a day or so later she and her children caught the train right at Wheeler Station and went to Texas.) With the change of venue and the loss of its eyewitness, the state's case was in shambles and it was a simple matter for Wheeler to secure a "not guilty" verdict for Jones, claiming self-defense.

Wheeler may have won his first case as an attorney by adroit manipulation of the legal system, regardless of the actual guilt or innocence of the defendant. The victory constituted a turning point in Wheeler's life, marking the beginning of a successful legal practice (subsequently shared with Thomas Jones as his partner) that had begun as a necessary remedy to a very pressing family matter but ended launching him on a congressional career that lasted almost two decades.

In 1871, former Confederate General Joe Wheeler, opposite page, used a six-month continuance to become a lawyer, and then proceeded to successfully defend his brother-in-law Thomas Jones, above, on a murder charge.

indigent population and to the widows and wives of Confederate soldiers throughout Shorter's administration.

John Gill Shorter was a member of a prominent Barbour County family. At the time of his election as governor, he was a former circuit judge who was serving in the Confederate Congress in Richmond. Prior to his appointment as a judge in 1851, he had practiced law with his brother Eli Sims Shorter, who, from 1855 to 1859, was the U.S. congressman from his area of the state and who served as a colonel in the military forces of the Confederacy. Among the several candidates that John Gill Shorter defeated when he was elected in August 1861 was Thomas H. Watts, who would soon defeat Shorter in his bid for reelection.

Shorter entered office just as the hardships of war began to be felt by the populace. He spent his time overseeing an enormous expansion of power to both the state government and the Confederate government, which had originally met in Montgomery but had moved to Richmond in April 1861. This expansion of governmental power was resented by the independent-minded voters of Alabama, including Shorter, who only participated out of wartime necessity.

In December 1861, the Confederate government enacted a highly unpopular conscription law which Shorter assisted in enforcing, even though it resulted in the decimation of Alabama's home-front militia. Voters, particularly Democrats from north Alabama (where Union troop invasions caused great suffering), remembered his support, albeit reluctant, for this act when he stood for reelection and held him accountable. He became unpopular with planters because he gained authority to impress slaves into forced labor for the state, particularly to construct defenses to protect Mobile from naval attack. The planters complained bitterly that their slaves received ill treatment and were poorly cared for while laboring for the state. Shorter was confronted with a growing problem of indigency among the families of soldiers. Many were on starvation diets and were without salt to preserve food. It became evident that suffering families at home were the major cause for the ever-increasing desertion of Alabama troops, many of whom placed loyalty to family above loyalty to the state. In October 1862, Governor Shorter called a special session of the legislature for the purpose of appropriating aid to indigent families of soldiers. The legislature appropriated $2 million to be disbursed through the probate judges of all counties, who then distributed the relief under the supervision of the county commissioner courts. In November 1863, the number of indigents had grown sufficiently that $3 million had to be appropriated. This relief was funded through an issuance of treasury notes, which resulted in increased inflation and a commensurate decline in the value of the funds appropriated. Therefore, Shorter put an emphasis on the purchase of supplies by state agents in order to thwart speculators, but a poor transportation system often made in-kind supplies impractical.

It fell upon Shorter to address the problems of providing food for the total population, which involved keeping prices reasonable and discouraging extortion and speculation. It even involved controlling the distillation of liquor, since distillation used up important grain supplies. Further, finding salt supplies became a serious issue, since salt was the main means of preserving food and before the war the primary source of salt was that used as ballast for European ships coming into Mobile to transport cotton back to Europe. War disrupted access to this source when shipping was barricaded.

With the introduction of conscription came an ever-increasing problem of desertion and "draft dodging." Some historians maintain that the strong antiwar sentiments of north Alabama and the wiregrass region of southeast Alabama caused Alabama to have a greater problem with deserters than any other Confederate state. And because it was a crime, deserters tended to hide out in packs and to show organized resistance to those who were sent to deal with them. Stories of violence, rape, and pillage began to be heard, inducing other, loyal soldiers to desert in order to protect their vulnerable families. Therefore, as the war continued, the presence of large bands of deserters became an ever-growing problem.

As governor from 1861 to 1863, John Gill Shorter had to deal with all the domestic problems brought on by the war, including providing aid to the families of soldiers, and dealing with roaming bands of deserters.

When it was time for Shorter's reelection, he found himself the target of the wartime frustration of the voters. He lost overwhelmingly to Thomas Hill Watts by a three to one margin. Shorter had been an able and energetic governor who earnestly addressed the problems that confronted the state, and his defeat can be seen to be in part a protest against the secessionists of 1861, who led the state into war, and their Democratic party. John Gill Shorter had been one of them.

Thomas H. Watts had been a Unionist Whig during the 1850s, and became a Know-Nothing when the Whig Party collapsed. He ran for Congress but was defeated by his Democratic opponent over the ongoing crisis in "bleeding" Kansas, where conflict between proslavery and antislavery forces had openly erupted. As late as 1860, Watts continued to hold a moderate position on the issue of Southern rights, supporting the Constitutional Unionist candidate John Bell for president. After Lincoln and the Republicans won, Watts began advocating immediate secession and was elected as a secessionist delegate from Montgomery (actually garnering more votes than

Montgomery's second elected delegate, William Yancey).

Soon after secession, Watts entered the gubernatorial election that Shorter won. He also lost a bid for the Confederate Senate to Clement Claiborne Clay (who had left his position as Alabama's United States senator when Alabama seceded.) During both campaigns, opponents raised questions about Watts's loyalty and devotion to the Confederate cause based on his previous Unionist tendencies.

Watts helped to organize the Seventeenth Alabama Regiment and served in the military until he was called upon by President Jefferson Davis to serve as the Confederacy's attorney general. While serving in that position, he participated in the organization of the Confederate court system and also wrote opinions defending centralization of government authority in the Richmond-based Confederacy. He wrote an opinion allowing the Confederate president to appoint officers from within state regiments to Confederate positions, a controversial position that was tantamount to legalized impressment of state soldiers into Confederate service. Watts also upheld the constitutionality of the Confederate Conscription Act of 1862.

LEFT: *Clement Claiborne Clay, the son of Clement Comer Clay, defeated Thomas Hill Watts for the Confederate Senate. Clay's portrait appeared on the Confederate $1 bill.* ABOVE: *Watts won the governorship from John Gill Shorter in 1863.*

These positions came back to haunt Watts when he was elected governor in 1863. The very authorities that Watts had supported as attorney general of the Confederacy soon plagued his administration as governor of a Confederate state. He was elected by war-weary voters who thought he shared their desire for a quick end to the war, but he soon revealed a deep commitment to the Confederate cause, spending great energy struggling with an obstructionist "Peace Party" clique within the legislature. His conflict with this group interfered with his ability to address pressing problems such as adequately defending Mobile and finding food and supplies to address the deteriorating economic and social conditions in Alabama.

ABOVE: *This* Harper's Weekly *illustration shows Huntsville under Union occupation in 1864.* OPPOSITE PAGE: *State Senator R. S. Heflin was an attorney and court clerk prior to his election to the state legislature. During the war, he was part of the secret "Peace Society." In 1869, he was elected to the U.S. Congress, starting a family tradition that includes two U.S. senators, Tom Heflin, his nephew, and Howell Heflin, his grandnephew.*

By 1864, Watts had issued an executive proclamation suspending state taxes in nine enemy-occupied counties in north Alabama, hoping to relieve some of the burden that came from the "in-kind" taxation imposed by both the state and the Confederate governments (since Confederate money was worthless). But this did not relieve the terrible conditions wrought by Confederate impressments agents who came into the state to secure foodstuffs (and often paid with counterfeit Confederate dollars) and Confederate cavalry who foraged for food, as well as the bands of Confederate and Union deserters who roamed and plundered the countryside and attacked vulnerable targets. As time went on, civil order no longer existed in Alabama, and there was little Watts could do to restore it. Confederate conscription policy allowed the Confederate government to deplete the ranks of the state militia, leaving Watts little manpower to control the bands of deserters or to properly defend the port of Mobile.

In April 1865, when Union general James H. Wilson entered Montgomery, Watts fled to Union Springs and the city of Montgomery gave up with no resistance. In May 1865, Union troops arrested Governor Watts, as well as Moore and Shorter, along with other state and Confederate officials. Watts was sent briefly to a Union prison and while he was there his plantation home, his slave houses, and his entire cotton crop were burned. He lost much of the land he had owned prior to the war and was forced into bankruptcy.

Watts lived for 27 years after the war, practicing his profession in Montgomery. He served as part of the force that "redeemed" the state from Radical Republicans and became a prominent figure in the renamed Democratic and Conservative Party, which dominated postwar politics after Reconstruction.[3]

PRESIDENTIAL RECONSTRUCTION FOLLOWS THE WAR'S END

Throughout Alabama's nineteenth-century history, geography had been a significant influence in its unfolding. The Black Belt, which bisects the state, the fertile coastal plain in southwest Alabama, and the Tennessee Valley, which rests behind the foothills of the Appalachian Mountains, were the regions where the plantation economy based on cotton and slaves thrived. The wiregrass region of southeast Alabama and the hilly areas of north Alabama sustained a white population which developed a small-farm economy using family labor.

Before the Civil War, because of lack of efficient transportation and few common interests, there was generally little interaction between these different geographical regions. Politicians had tried to create interest in con-

necting the areas through the development of internal improvements, but those in power had generally resisted using public funds to improve transportation, thereby fostering a resentful sectionalism that saw political and economic power primarily reside in south Alabama. This domination was evident in 1860 and 1861, when south and central Alabama pushed secession upon the state even in the face of strong Unionist sentiments in north Alabama.

Once war began, it was north Alabama which suffered invasion of federal troops and both north and southeast Alabama which had increasing problems with deserters from both federal and Confederate armies. There was a strong feeling that the plantation elite were able to buy their way out of the fighting, sending replacement troops in their stead. This feeling led to further disillusionment with the war and increasing disillusionment of hill country whites toward the planter aristocracy. North Alabama even saw men volunteer for the First Alabama Cavalry, a Union regiment. And, beginning in 1862, some former Unionist leaders, including former U.S. Senator Jeremiah Clemens and future Republican governors William H. Smith and David P. Lewis, as well as Colonel J. J. Seibels of Montgomery and R. S. Heflin, a state senator from Randolph County, organized a secret peace group known as the "Peace Society," which had greater and greater impact on home-front elections as the war continued, bringing more moderates into both the state and Confederate governments. Many Alabamians who held anti-Confederate feelings and desired to evade conscription took local civil and judicial positions that allowed them to stay at home and provide some protection to themselves, their families, and their property.

In the spring of 1865, as the war concluded, Alabama was quietly awaiting news as to what would happen next. Most Alabamians were relieved that the war was over and were ready to accept whatever peace was forthcoming from the North, and were prepared to cooperate with their restoration to the Union. At the time, there was little arrogance concerning their "lost cause" and there was acceptance of the abolition of slavery. Even with acceptance of the end of slavery, though, there was also a prejudice that believed in the inferiority of the black race when it came to the responsibilities of citizenship, especially suffrage and office-holding. There was a decided distinction made between granting former slaves their freedom and granting them political privileges.

Andrew Johnson Appoints Lewis E. Parsons Provisional Governor

Those Alabama leaders who had opposed secession and war expected to lead the state back into the Union when war ended, considering themselves the "better element" to return the state to the civil authority of the United

Lewis E. Parsons was a Unionist in the period leading up to secession. In 1865, President Andrew Johnson appointed him provisional governor of Alabama, a post he held until 1867.

States government. They organized in order to be able to provide nominations for a provisional governor when presented the opportunity. Among those suggested were attorneys David C. Humphreys of Madison, William H. Smith of Randolph, Lewis E. Parsons of Talladega, and Thomas M. Peters of Lawrence.

After the death of Abraham Lincoln, Andrew Johnson asserted his authority to devise and supervise a presidential reconstruction. He appointed Lewis Parsons provisional governor in June 1865. Parsons had been politically active as a Whig and then a Know-Nothing before the Civil War and he had been one of those who debated on behalf of the Union against William Yancey prior to secession. During the war, he neither fled the state nor fought in the Confederate army, the choices made by many other of the Unionists when confronted with secession. Instead, he continued practicing law in Talladega, being too old to be captured by the Confederate draft. He had two sons who fought for the Confederacy. In 1863, as opposition to the war mounted in the state, voters elected a governor and legislature that they thought would end Alabama's participation in the war. Parsons was one of those elected.

Johnson selected Parsons provisional governor because of his reputation as a moderate Unionist. Parsons served until December 20, 1865, and during his governorship he declared all Alabama laws enacted before January 11, 1861, except those regarding slavery, to be in force. He retained all current officeholders and called for an election of delegates to a constitutional convention. Veterans had to take a loyalty oath to the federal government to regain their citizenship and right to vote, with those who were disfranchised having to apply for a presidential pardon.

Under the terms of Johnson's plan of reconstruction, a constitutional convention was called in September 1865, with former governor Benjamin Fitzpatrick as its president. The convention abolished slavery, repealed the ordinance of secession, and repudiated the state's $20 million wartime debt, leaving the state with only its 1861 debt of less than $3.5 million. The issue presenting the greatest controversy was legislative reapportionment, the effort by northern white counties to gain control through having the basis of reapportionment be the white male population. If freed blacks had been included, then south Alabama would have continued its prewar domination of state politics. Thus, sectional politics set the stage for the rights of the newly freed blacks to be ignored in the reestablishment of the government and ultimately served as an excuse for the rejection of the reconstruction plan implemented by President Johnson in the state.

The constitutional convention adopted the new constitution by proclamation and called an election for governor, legislature, and congressmen for November. Robert Miller Patton, a merchant and planter, won the governor's office, again provisionally, and the legislature elected Lewis Parsons to the U.S. Senate. He was never seated because Congress rejected all representatives elected from the South.

Parsons returned to his law practice in Talladega, although he remained active in postwar politics. His first efforts were to work to defeat proposed congressional reconstruction, which everyone recognized would be much more punitive than Andrew Johnson's presidential reconstruction plan. These efforts failed when, early in 1867, Congress passed three acts that took control of reconstruction away from the president. The new congressional plan abolished all that had been previously done to reestablish Alabama's statehood. A new constitutional convention was called in November 1867, under which blacks were enfranchised, and significant numbers of whites were disenfranchised, with no pardon available. The state was reapportioned on the basis of the total population. In one of the state's most interesting historical ironies, dominance in the legislature now returned to the Black Belt counties of the state.

In September 1867, Parsons had joined and became a party leader in the Democratic and Conservative Party, the Alabama Democratic Party which had been reorganized to confront the Republican party beginning to operate in the state and to resist congressional reconstruction and the passage of the radical 1867 constitution. The party's efforts only resulted in the delay of Alabama's readmission to the Union until July 1868.

When the Republicans were victorious in the state elections in November 1868, Parsons determined that further opposition to that party and to congressional reconstruction was futile. He then changed parties and joined the Republicans. Because he was considered a native white Republican leader, he was also considered a leading "scalawag." Soon, Republican scalawags were engaged in factional infighting to control the state Republican Party, opposing outside "carpetbaggers" and black politicians. Parsons was elected to the Alabama House of Representatives in 1872, where he served as speaker and assisted in defeating proposed civil rights bills. Also in 1872, Parsons represented Alabama as a delegate to the Republican National Convention, was chairman of the convention's platform committee, and was a presidential elector for Ulysses S. Grant.

Alabama Democrats "redeemed" the state from Republican rule in the 1874 election. Still, Parsons continued in the Republican Party, although many other white Alabama Republicans rejoined the Democrats. Parsons attempted to receive an appointment as U.S. attorney for the Northern District of Alabama, but was frustrated by the opposition of his political enemies. He returned to Talladega and continued to practice law until his death on June 8, 1895.

General Wager T. Swayne came to Alabama as the Assistant Commissioner of the Freedmen's Bureau. When Congress took charge of Reconstruction in 1867, Swayne was appointed military governor of Alabama.

Wager Swayne and the Freedmen's Bureau

When Congress took over Reconstruction in March 1867, General Wager T. Swayne, trained as an attorney, became governor in everything but name. He was the assistant commissioner of the Freedmen's Bureau for Alabama, under both Governors Parsons and Patton. He was a graduate of Yale University and Cincinnati Law School and his father was appointed a member of the U.S. Supreme Court by Abraham Lincoln. Young Swayne had practiced law with his father for a short period before the outbreak of the war. He joined the army and commanded the Forty-third Ohio Volunteer Regiment through much of the war. He rose to the rank of brigadier general and eventually won the Congressional Medal of Honor. Late in the war, Swayne lost his right leg in battle at Rivers Bridge in South Carolina. His conduct as an officer had impressed his superior officer, General Oliver O. Howard, who was appointed to head the national Freedmen's Bureau at war's end and Howard appointed his convalescing subordinate to the post of assistant commissioner for Alabama.[4]

Swayne came to Alabama shortly after Lewis Parsons was appointed governor. It was Swayne's responsibility to protect the interests of the newly freed black population under bureau labor codes. In his early days in Alabama,

In this symbolic A. R. Waud illustration from Harper's Weekly, *General Oliver O. Howard, head of the Freedmen's Bureau, stands between armed groups of blacks and whites.*

Swayne garnered a reputation for being moderate and even conciliatory toward the former Unionists who were trying to govern the state and lead it back to statehood. Swayne worked well with Governor Parsons and Governor Robert Patton, the two governors who steered Alabama through presidential reconstruction. Still, as time passed, it became evident that Swayne's conciliatory approach would not work, as violence against blacks soon became commonplace, with little response from the conservative white civil authorities. When Congress seized control of Reconstruction from the president, enacting its military reconstruction in March 1867, Swayne was appointed military commander as well as bureau chief. He outlawed the use of chain gangs by local governments and released those who had been jailed as "vagrants" under Alabama's black codes. He also worked to open up educational opportunities for blacks.

Swayne became active in organizing black voters and was a founder of the Republican Party of Alabama at a convention held in June 1867. The bureau soon became overtly partisan, with one of its employees organizing the state Republican Party's Union League. William H. Smith, who became Alabama's first Republican governor, was Swayne's superintendent of voter registration. Three of the six Alabama congressmen elected during the period were bureau agents. After Swayne's active intervention at the constitutional convention of November 1867, he was ordered removed from his position by President Johnson and was replaced by General Julius Hayden. Even though the constitution drawn up by the Republicans was never officially ratified, Congress, nevertheless, admitted Alabama back to statehood under the constitution in July 1868.

Swayne as an historical figure has had disparate treatment, with his early conciliatory advances being held up as evidence that he failed to sufficiently protect the rights of emancipated slaves. But when his career in Alabama is reviewed as a whole, it is apparent that he moved toward more drastic means of enforcing bureau policies as his conciliatory efforts failed to give adequate results. Throughout his tenure, he had actively sought to provide a foundation for the public education of black children and, from the base he established, educational opportunities for blacks expanded as the years passed.

Governor William Hugh Smith and the Railroad Scandals

Attorney William Hugh Smith was an anomaly. Before the war, he had owned slaves and opposed secession on the grounds that it would imperil slave property. He had been a states' rights Democrat as late as 1859 but gradually evolved into a strong Union man. After war was underway, he fled the state and lived behind Union lines in Nashville. He spent his time recruiting soldiers for the First Alabama Cavalry, and he accompanied that regiment during General William Sherman's march to the sea. After the war, he was a contender for appointment as provisional governor, but was not successful. He developed interests in mining and railroad promotion, after a short stint as a circuit judge.

With military reconstruction, Smith became a leading Republican, having chaired the first statewide Republican convention. His service as head of the voter registration bureau, established to implement the Military Reconstruction Acts, paved the way for his election as governor. His tenure was marked by violence perpetrated by the Ku Klux Klan. Smith failed to organize a militia to meet this threat, because such a militia would be overwhelmingly composed of newly freed black men, and Smith feared their presence in a militia could lead to a racial bloodbath. His reaction to the Klan led to disillusionment with his administration among freedmen and white Republicans to whom he owed his office.

The Republican administration of Governor William Hugh Smith was marred by corruption and increased Ku Klux Klan violence.

Smith's major goal was the economic development of the state, and he drew on his own prior business experience to promote the development of railroads, using public funding. The legislature had already passed a general subsidy act for railroad building in the state as early as the period of presidential reconstruction. With Smith's support, public funding was expanded and local support was encouraged, which resulted in a dramatic increase in railroad mileage in the state but also in potential government liability.

Backers of the strategic Alabama & Chattanooga line, which was to go through the mineral district which would soon become the new city of Birmingham, contributed substantial sums to the governor and reportedly financed Smith's own separate railroad corporation, as well as paying bribes to legislators. The result was a $2 million direct aid bill primarily benefiting the Alabama & Chattanooga line. The governor endorsed bonds in amounts well above those authorized by law, leaving his successors with a financial quagmire that ultimately resulted in insolvency for the state.

When it came time for reelection, Smith had little support, having alienated his freedman constituency with his lack of performance in the area of civil rights and with his lukewarm treatment of the Ku Klux Klan. Further, Smith had alienated whites by his financial mismanagement of the railroads. He was also the victim of political contrivances by Alabama's Radical Republican senator, George Eliphaz Spencer, who had continually undermined Smith's political effectiveness in order to wrest from him any claim to federal patronage authority he might have based on being the state's governor.

Governor Robert B. Lindsay, 1870-1872

Robert Lindsay was born in Loch Maben, Scotland, on July 4, 1824, and was well educated there, receiving academic prizes from the University of St. Andrews, prior to coming to America in 1844.

In 1849, he migrated to Tuscumbia, Alabama, where he read law and was admitted to the bar in 1852. He quickly entered state politics, and married Sarah Miller Winston, the half-sister of then-governor John Winston in 1854. This marriage furthered his political career. Still, in 1860, he vehemently opposed secession and did little to support the Confederacy. At the war's conclusion, he returned to state politics.

He remained in the Democratic Party and was selected as the nominee for governor in 1870 because of his moderate position toward Reconstruction. He won

GEORGE ELIPHAZ SPENCER THE WORST EXAMPLE OF "CARPETBAG" INFLUENCE

Attorney George E. Spencer was one of Alabama's United States senators from 1868 through 1879. Alabama regained statehood in 1868, so that its choice for senator was finally accepted by the national legislature, after three years of not being seated. Spencer was a "carpetbagger," having come to Alabama in 1863 to recruit troops for the First Alabama Cavalry from among its unionist populace. He led a cavalry brigade in William Tecumseh Sherman's 1864 Georgia campaign and march to the sea. He was brevetted a brigadier general for his bravery in that campaign and when the war ended he returned to Alabama to set up a law practice in Decatur.

In 1868, the radically controlled state legislature chose him and planter Willard Warner to its vacant seats in the Senate. Spencer was a close personal friend of President Ulysses S. Grant and was able to trade upon this friendship over the course of time to control all federal patronage in Alabama. In the meantime, he did all he could to damage the political standing of both Senator Warner and Governor William Hugh Smith, all for his own personal gain. One "trick" he used was to foment racial animosity and then call for federal troops to intervene when violence erupted. He successfully maintained his seat even in the face of a Democratic resurgence in 1872 by using these racial tactics and confusing the outcome of the general election, so that Alabama ended up with two legislatures. The one under Republican control reelected Spencer and even though the Democratic winner challenged Spencer's election, the challenge was never acted upon by the Senate Committee on Privileges and Elections and Spencer was permitted to retain his seat for six years, even though the legitimacy of his reelection was questionable.

Finally with the election of Rutherford B. Hayes, who was a friend of Willard Warner, whose career Spencer had ruined, Spencer's patronage influence was eliminated. He left the Senate in 1877.

by a narrow margin in an outcome that was disputed by Republican William Hugh Smith. He finally took office in December 1870 and was immediately faced with the consequences of his predecessor's corrupt action of issuing unauthorized railroad bonds as the Alabama & Chattanooga Railroad was unable to pay interest on its bonds on January 1, 1871. Lindsay decided on what he believed was an honorable course of action by promising to honor all bona fide bonds but delaying payment because of Governor Smith's failure to maintain adequate records of the number of bonds issued. He called for a legislative investigation into the prior administration's conduct and sought instruction on determining which bond claims were legitimate.

Although a seemingly reasonable course of action, the state's delay in paying on the bonds sent shock waves through Wall Street, not only drying up financing for the Alabama & Chattanooga Railroad but also imperiling several other uncompleted railroad projects throughout the state. Because of the delays in payment while the legislature studied the situation, all railroad bonds issued by the state and even local governments within the state were impaired. Several railroad companies halted construction and ultimately went bankrupt during the Panic of 1873, causing the state to be unable to pay other obligations as well.

Lindsay was forced to seize control of the Alabama & Chattanooga Railroad under state law upon its default. The state lacked the legal authority and the expertise to complete its railroad construction, resulting in the railroad running at a ruinous loss. Since it could not be sold until completed, the state was left in a very difficult position. Then it was revealed that the corrupt board of directors of the railroad had paid large sums of money to one of Lindsay's friends, who promised the directors that they would retain control of the railroad. This apparent bribery, in which Lindsay's personal role was unclear, permanently damaged the governor's reputation.

Elected in 1870, Governor Robert Lindsay, a native of Scotland, inherited the financial crisis caused by the railroad scandal. His solution seemed honorable, but it pleased no one, and actually made matters worse.

Lindsay's standing was further damaged by the impact of funding problems in the efforts of the state to support public education. Because of the railroad scandals, cuts were made that closed schools prematurely. Editorials attacked Lindsay for diverting tax dollars to "Wall Street gamblers" and foreign speculators for the benefit of private corporations and at the expense of Alabama children.

Because of his growing unpopularity, Lindsay did not run for reelection. His replacement as the Democratic Party's candidate, attorney Thomas H. Herndon of Mobile, ran poorly and was beaten by attorney David P. Lewis, who won resoundingly when eight previously Democratic north Alabama counties voted Republican.

Governor David P. Lewis, and Alabama's Two Legislatures

The administration of Republican governor David P. Lewis set the stage for the end of the Reconstruction period in Alabama and the reestablishment of the Democratic Party as the wielder of political power in Alabama. Lewis had been born in Virginia around 1820 and came to Alabama shortly after his birth when his family moved to Madison County. He studied law in Huntsville with Judge Robert C. Brickell, Judge Daniel Coleman, and attorney Luke Pryor, as well as attending lectures in law at the University of Virginia. He moved to Lawrence County in 1843 and successfully practiced law, so that by 1860 he was a wealthy man and the owner of 34 slaves.

He represented Lawrence County in the 1861 Alabama convention that voted to take Alabama out of the Union. He personally opposed secession but signed the ordinance of secession based on instructions from his constituents who had held a public meeting on the subject. Although he served briefly both in the Confederate government and the Confederate army, by 1862 he had returned to north Alabama and participated in the organization of a secret peace society which advocated seeking ways for Alabama to end its involvement in the war and return to the Union. He also served as a judge of the Fourth Judicial Circuit until January 1, 1864. He should have been exempt from conscription because he owned a public mill, but he was ordered to report for military service in the fall of 1864. He refused to serve and crossed through the federal lines to Nashville, where he remained until the end of the war.

After the war, he returned to Huntsville and opened up his law practice. Under the presidential plan of reconstruction, he was required to take a loyalty oath and to seek a presidential pardon in order to regain the right to vote. He applied and was certified as a voter. Between 1865 and 1868, he remained outside of politics, focusing on rebuilding his law practice.

A north Alabama Unionist, David P. Lewis switched to the Republican Party in 1869, becoming its candidate for governor in 1872, and winning an easy victory.

In 1868, Lewis attended the Democratic National Convention as a delegate. But in 1869, he decided to become a Republican. In the newly formed Alabama Republican Party, southern white Republicans (scalawags) were able to control political action, even though they were outnumbered by newcomers (carpetbaggers) and blacks. Yet these "scalawags" suffered under congressional reconstruction, when radical congressmen imposed upon them the same political disabilities imposed on those who had actively supported secession, even though most of the "scalawags" were former Unionists who had fought secession until it was an accomplished fact. Lewis became an active spokesman in favor of congressional removal of these disabilities. This issue was the main focus of his political involvement prior to 1872. He was not personally involved in the competition for power between the natives and the newcomers and blacks within the Republican Party during that period.

Republicans realized that in order to regain the governorship in 1872, they needed major support from the prewar Unionists. They decided to come up with a ticket composed entirely of native Unionists, especially those from north Alabama, and selected David P. Lewis as their candidate for governor because he was a well-known north Alabama Unionist with few political enemies. He won the governorship easily.

The legislative races were thrown into controversy when conflicting returns were reported in many of these contests. Both parties claimed victory, and each organized a separate legislature on November 18, 1872. The Democratic-controlled body met in the state capitol while the Republican-controlled body met at the federal courthouse. Lewis recognized the Republican-controlled legislature and sought federal troops to protect them.

Lewis sent a delegation to report on the situation to President Grant, who referred them to his attorney general, who directed Lewis to allow the legislatures to meet separately until he could forge a compromise. The attorney general's plan organized a fusion legislature which met on December 17, 1872. This fusion legislature was almost evenly divided between Democrats and Republicans and was soon deadlocked.

During Lewis's time in office, the Panic of 1873 further disrupted the state's economic situation, already in trouble because of reckless railroad development in the two previous administrations. Lewis was blamed for the state's near-bankrupt condition by 1874, even though the situation was just the culmination of conduct that predated his term.

In 1873, a black representative introduced a civil rights bill in the Alabama House of Representatives, which forbade discrimination on common carriers and

White and black members of the Reconstruction legislature stand shoulder to shoulder on the steps of the Alabama State Capitol in this group photograph taken in 1872.

in hotels, schools, and theaters. The "scalawag" chairman of the Judiciary Committee permitted no action on the bill until black legislators on the house floor moved to force committee action, resulting in a bill being reported which provided for separate first-class accommodations on common carriers and integrated second-class accommodations. The reported bill did not mention hotels, schools, or theaters; the committee adversely reported the original bill. After stormy debate, the original bill died as the full house concurred with the adverse report and no action was taken on the substitute.

The Senate also confronted a similar civil rights bill introduced by a black senator and its Judiciary Committee reported a substitute, stating that all citizens were entitled to equal accommodations in hotels and on common carriers. The substitute passed but the legislature adjourned before the House acted on the Senate bill. The action and acrimonious debate on these bills offended the Republican Party's black constituency, especially since the house had a Republican majority and did not pass a bill, while the Senate, with a Democratic majority, did pass a bill. These bills demonstrated that racial issues were undermining the Republican Party in the state because it became clear for all to see that the endorsement of any civil rights bill would lose the votes of north Alabama whites, whose racial attitudes differed little from the planters of south Alabama, while opposing a civil rights bill alienated black Republicans.

When David Lewis sought a second term as governor, race became the dominant issue in the election. Black Republicans were still feeling betrayed by the party and blamed the governor because he did not involve himself in the legislative debate over civil rights. The Democrats used the consideration of civil rights legislation in Congress as the basis for making race the leading issue of the campaign, promoting the theme of white supremacy. Whites deserted the Republican Party in droves and the Democrats reclaimed power at all levels of state government. This election ended Reconstruction.

Although Reconstruction was a trying period for all involved, very little was accomplished to secure the rights of the freedmen. The stage was set for an effective return of the black population to an agricultural system tying them to land they did not own. Although they were not slaves, their conditions of life would soon have the same effect.

CHAPTER SIX

BOURBON DEMOCRACY 1874-1900

THE ELECTION OF 1874, WHICH IS REMEMbered as the election that "redeemed" the state from Radical Reconstruction, ushered in the period in Alabama history commonly referred to as the "Bourbon" era. The term began as a pejorative term used by Republicans to label their Democratic opponents as reactionary and unenlightened, the reference being to the return of the royal house in France after the French Revolution and the Napoleonic wars. For Democrats, the term represented conservatism, limited government, frugality, and white supremacy at any cost.

Several themes run throughout the period: the struggle to ensure white control of the electoral process and the political realm as well as social control of the freedmen; the search for ways to keep blacks and poor whites available as sources of cheap labor for both an expanding industrial base and the traditional agricultural economy of the state; and the elimination of the Republican Party as a threat to Democratic dominance. Bourbon democracy also refers to the continuing disproportionate influence of the Black Belt in Alabama politics and its gradual affiliation with the industrial bosses of north Alabama to create a stranglehold on the political process that lasted well into the twentieth century.

To understand the impetus behind the call for white supremacy, it is noteworthy to realize that, in 1870, roughly forty-five percent of the total voting population in the state was black. White voters, who had a majority of only about 23,000, were divided by geographic sections and by political factions, with former Democrats and Whigs, Republicans, and Unionists each vying for political strength. Thus, during Radical Reconstruction, recently freed blacks controlled many elections, even though they had little education and no experience with government. Newly enfranchised black voters were in a majority in 24 counties, particularly those that made up the Black Belt, the stronghold of the cotton planters prior to the Civil War. In three of these counties, Dallas, Greene, and Hale, blacks outnumbered whites nearly five to one, and in most of the others there were from two to four times as many blacks as whites. Thus, the call for white supremacy was actually a call to white voters to ignore their sectional, factional, and party differences and become a united front of white voters to take back political control of the state.

One man masterminded the winning election strategy that brought Democrat George S. Houston to the gover-

OPPOSITE PAGE: *Although he never held elective office, attorney Walter L. Bragg was one of the most influential politicians of the postwar period. As chairman of the Democratic State Executive Committee, he engineered the election of George S. Houston, ushering in the "Bourbon" era. In 1878, he was a leader of the movement to create the Alabama State Bar Association, and served as its first president. In 1887, President Grover Cleveland appointed him to the newly created Interstate Commerce Commission, on which he served until his death in 1891.*

norship in 1874 and ended Reconstruction, a young man named Walter Lawrence Bragg. Born in 1835 in Lowndes County, he attended Harvard Law School for three terms and was admitted to the practice of law in Arkansas in 1856. After serving as a captain in the Civil War, he returned to Alabama, first setting up practice in Marion and then moving to Montgomery in 1871 where he entered a law partnership with General John Tyler Morgan and William S. Thorington. Morgan would become Alabama's United States senator in 1876, serving until 1907, and Thorington, who had been admitted to the practice of law in 1867 and was a highly regarded practitioner, later served as an associate justice on the Alabama Supreme Court and as chairman of the University of Alabama Department of Law. Within three years, Bragg was chosen chairman of the Democratic State Executive Committee at the state convention of the Democratic and Conservative Party and was given unlimited powers to manage and conduct the 1874 campaign. The ensuing Democratic victory has been attributed largely to Bragg's organizational abilities, getting white voters to rally around the call for white supremacy, overlooking any other issues that might otherwise divide them, and turning out in large numbers to vote.

The election of Governor George Houston marked the end of Reconstruction in Alabama. The "Bourbon" Democrats would dominate Alabama politics for the next 25 years.

The result was the election of attorney George Houston as governor. He was a candidate acceptable to both former Whigs and more traditional Democrats. His two administrations set the agenda for the Bourbon Democrats. An important issue that he addressed, which would continue to be confronted by Bourbon governors throughout the '70s and '80s, was the huge indebtedness of the state, in large part from the railroad bond program that had run amuck under the previous Republican governors. Houston established a three-man commission, which included attorney T. B. Bethea of Montgomery, to study the bonded debt issue and to recommend a program for retiring it. Then, in a move that became typical of government conduct during this era, he named himself chairman of the debt commission without regard to his personal conflict of interest arising from the fact that he had been a director of the Louisville & Nashville Railroad, whose interests would be affected by the outcome of the commission's work. Another appointee to the commission, businessman Levi Lawler, had also served as a railroad director. As one would assume, the commission's work inured to the benefit of the powerful L&N Railroad, whose presence as a dominant regional corporation would have a tremendous impact on the state in general ways and on the legal profession and its growth in specific ways throughout the Bourbon period.

During Houston's term, the practice of leasing prisoners to business concerns and having the state receive pay for their labor was expanded. Leasing of convict labor by both state and counties, although always controversial, would continue well into the twentieth century and would be felt by many to be a blight upon the state's honor.

Houston won a second term and set a precedent of two-term administrations for subsequent Bourbon governors. After he left the governorship, he was elected to the United States Senate, serving for less than a year before his death.

The Constitution of 1875

During Houston's tenure, a committee headed by attorney Peter Hamilton of Mobile was organized to consider the possibility of revising the 1868 state constitution. The committee recommended that a convention be held and Walter Bragg, then chairman of the Democratic State Executive Committee, managed the campaign for the convention, stressing the goals of adjusting the state debt, making possible economy in government, eliminating unnecessary offices and boards, and forbidding state and local aid to internal improvements, especially to railroads and other corporations.

The delegates elected to the convention, half of whom were attorneys, read like a roster of the political leaders who would dominate the Bourbon era, including attorneys Rufus W. Cobb of Shelby County; Edward A. O'Neal of Lauderdale County; William C. Oates of

Barbour County; William J. Samford of Lee County; Thomas H. Herndon of Mobile; William S. Mudd of Jefferson County; and James L. Pugh of Barbour County, all of whom were Civil War veterans. Also elected were Leroy Pope Walker, whose service as president of the convention was his last public service to the state; Francis S. Lyon, who had liquidated the state bank in 1845; Samuel F. Rice, who had served on the Alabama Supreme Court and was the most important Republican of the convention; and attorney Lewis Maxwell Stone of Carrollton who had had an active legislative career prior to the convention. Robert A. McClellan, brother of Thomas N. McClellan, future attorney general and chief justice of the Alabama Supreme Court, and father of Thomas Cowan McClellan, who would serve as an associate justice of the Alabama Supreme Court during the early part of the twentieth century, represented Limestone County. Alberto Martin, who was instrumental in the founding of the city of Birmingham, represented Jefferson County. Wiley Coleman, uncle of Thomas W. Coleman, who had been a delegate at the 1865 constitutional convention and would be a dominating force at the future 1901 constitutional convention, represented Greene County. George P. Harrison, another future powerhouse at the 1901 constitutional convention, represented Lee County in 1875. William Manning Lowe, delegate from Madison

ABOVE: *LeRoy Pope Walker served as president of the 1875 Constitutional Convention.* BELOW: *Half of the delegates to the convention were attorneys.*

County, would be elected to Congress as the most important representative of the "Greenback" movement in the Alabama Democratic Party in 1879 and would successfully contest the election of Joseph Wheeler in 1882 to replace him, serving until his death on October 12, 1882. Elbert Decatur Willett represented Greene and Pickens counties at the convention. His son, Elbert Decatur, would represent Pickens County at the 1901 convention. Richard H. Powell of Union Springs represented the Sixteenth District. (Another Richard H. Powell of nearby Tuskegee would serve as president of the Alabama State Bar from 1926 to 1927.)

The new constitution set rigid limits on the ability of not only the state, but also counties and cities, to tax; prohibited state and county aid to railroads and other corporations; and abolished the office of lieutenant governor (and a few other offices) and the Board of Education introduced during Reconstruction; it also limited other state officeholders to two two-year terms, and reduced many salaries. Legislative sessions went from being annual to biennial, and were limited to 50 days per session. Separate schools for blacks and whites were required. Popular election of judicial offices, which had been introduced in the 1868 document, was continued. The convention attempted to limit the impact of local legislation on the work of the legislature, but failed to provide for home rule on the county or local level. This 1875 constitution was submitted to the voters and won approval throughout the state, even though many thought it was overly legislative and conservative.

The Founding of The Alabama State Bar Association

Walter Bragg, besides leading the "redemption" of the state from Reconstruction and the campaign for a new constitution, also helped lead the movement to form a state bar association, in association with Daniel S. Troy, who had attended an organizational meeting of the American Bar Association in early 1878. In a call dated December 13, 1878, over 50 lawyers[1] sent out a request to the bar of each county to appoint at least one delegate to attend a "Convention of the Bar of the State" on January 15, 1879, to be held in the hall of the House of Representatives. Edmund Pettus and William Brooks of Selma and Walter Bragg of Montgomery were chosen to prepare a plan of organization to be submitted to the convention. (A foundation had been laid for a state organization by the incorporation of the Mobile Bar on April 12, 1869, whose primary purpose was to provide for, and maintain, a library for the use of the lawyers in that area.)

Alexander Troy of Montgomery was elected the first secretary and treasurer of the new Alabama State Bar Association, a post he held for more than 40 years.

At the meeting, LeRoy Pope Walker of Huntsville was elected chairman and George W. Taylor of Choctaw was elected secretary pro tem. Bragg, reporting for the committee organizing the association, submitted a constitution and by-laws, which were adopted, subject to amendment by conference. Joseph Wheeler of Lawrence County nominated Alexander Troy of Montgomery to be secretary and treasurer of the Alabama State Bar Association. Troy was elected and filled that position for over 40 years. Walter Bragg, William G. Little, Jr., of Sumter County, and Gaylord B. Clark of Mobile were appointed to prepare the act of incorporation for the organization. The named incorporators included Edmund W. Pettus; LeRoy Pope Walker; Peter Hamilton; James L. Pugh; William M. Brooks; William G. Little, Jr.; and John Little Smith. Walter L. Bragg, Daniel S. Troy, John Little Smith, and H. A. Woolf of Linden, Marengo County, were appointed to nominate a president and five vice presidents for the association's first year. This committee nominated the following, who were unanimously elected: President, Walter L. Bragg, Montgomery; Vice Presidents, Peter Hamilton, Mobile; Edmund Pettus, Selma; LeRoy Pope Walker, Huntsville; H. M. Somerville, Tuscaloosa; and James L. Pugh, Eufaula.

PILLARS OF THE LEGAL COMMUNITY

Of the more than 50 prominent lawyers who put out the call for the formation of the Bar Association, 14 would serve the bar as president, including Walter L. Bragg of Montgomery; Edmund W. Pettus of Selma; John Little Smith and Thomas H. Watts of Mobile; M. L. Stansel of Pickens County; Henry C. Semple of Montgomery; William M. Brooks of Dallas County; H. C. Tompkins of Montgomery; Milton Humes of Madison County; A. C. Hargrove of Tuscaloosa; Daniel S. Troy, John D. Roquemore, Thomas G. Jones, and William S. Thorington of Montgomery; and George P. Harrison of Lee County.

James L. Pugh served 16 years as a U.S. senator, and was a founding member of the Alabama State Bar Association.

Among the first officers was Peter Hamilton, whose practice dated back to 1838. That practice, which can be traced through several members of his family to 1982, still continues in the Mobile firm of Hamilton, Butler, Riddick, Tarlton, & Sullivan, making it the oldest known continuously operating law firm in the state. Henderson M. Somerville of Tuscaloosa founded the University of Alabama School of Law in 1873 and was its first head, although at that time in its history it was considered a department of the university. Somerville also served as a justice of the Alabama Supreme Court for ten years. James L. Pugh of Eufaula served as Alabama's U.S. senator from 1880 to 1896. Ironically, Edmund Pettus, who was a brigadier general in the Civil War, won Pugh's senate seat in 1897, at the age of 75. Founder Joseph Wheeler, "Fighting Joe" of Civil War fame, served as a U.S. congressman from 1885 to 1890, served as a major general of volunteers in the Spanish-American War, and was memorialized by one of the two statues of Alabama citizens placed in Statuary Hall in the U.S. Capitol at the turn of the century. Thomas Goode Jones served as governor of the state and also as a United States district judge.

The Protection of Property and the Advancement of Wealth: Governors Rufus W. Cobb, Edward O'Neal, and Thomas Seay

Rufus W. Cobb, governor from 1878 to 1882, was from the coal mining area of the state and represented the industrial interests who joined forces with the Black Belt planters to control political power in the state during the Bourbon period. Their common goals were the protection of property and the advancement of wealth. Cobb and his successors, Edward O'Neal and Thomas Seay, were staunch supporters of these goals.

During his years of law practice, Cobb served as president of Central Iron Works in Helena, Alabama, and represented the powerful Louisville & Nashville Railroad (L&N). During the 1875 constitutional convention, he led the fight to oppose repudiation of the railroad debt generated by earlier Republican administrations and to structure the terms of a debt settlement that was favorable to the L&N Railroad.

During Cobb's tenure, he appointed John Hollis Bankhead as warden of the prison system. Bankhead, who would later become a United States senator and sire two attorney sons who would also become important political leaders in the U.S. Congress, used his position as warden to grant Pratt Consolidated Mines an exclusive right to lease all state prisoners in their coalmines.

In recognition of growing public agitation against abuses, Cobb sponsored the establishment of a railroad commission to regulate the powerful railroad industry in the state. Among the first appointees to the commission was Walter Bragg, who served as the commission's first president and subsequently served on the national Interstate Commerce Commission. Alabama's railroad commission was the predecessor of today's Public Service Commission, but in its early days had only limited power to regulate.

Attorney Edward O'Neal was Cobb's successor (1882-1886). During his early years of public service, he was a states' rights Democrat who had favored secession and ultimately was made a brigadier general by the state of Alabama in recognition of his military service in the Civil War. His tenure as governor caused little stir, maintaining a safe status quo. In sympathy for the small farmer, O'Neal's administration did see the establishment of Alabama's State Department of Agriculture, appointing Judge E. C. Betts of Huntsville as its first commissioner.

O'Neal was the first, and so far the only, governor in Alabama history to have his son (attorney Emmet O'Neal) also elected governor. (Governor Jim Folsom's son would serve as governor upon the felony conviction of the incumbent governor during his term as lieutenant governor.) O'Neal served as president of the Alabama State Bar Assocaition in 1881 and 1882, the year before his election as governor. His son, Emmet, served as state bar president in 1909 and 1910 and served as governor from 1911 to 1915. There have been other father-son teams who have served as state bar presidents, including Thomas Goode Jones (1900-1901) and his son Walter B. Jones (1954-1955), and Robert B. Albritton (1971-1972) and his son W. Harold Albritton, III (1990-1991).

TOP: *Governor Rufus W. Cobb represented the industrial faction of the Bourbon coalition.* ABOVE: *Governor Edward O'Neal had previously served as president of the Alabama State Bar Association.*

Edward O'Neal was followed in office by attorney Thomas Seay in 1886. During Seay's four years in office, anger at Bourbon rule became aroused, particularly among Alabama's small farmers, who were suffering from a depressed agricultural economy, a crop lien system which more or less left many of them in peonage, and a general lack of means to advance their own well-being. Seay appointed Reuben F. Kolb as his state commissioner of agriculture. Although unintentional on Seay's part, as Seay was not a particular friend of the small farmer, Kolb was able to use this appointment to build his own power base and influence among this constituency. Kolb would soon become Alabama's leading Populist and the major threat to continued Bourbon rule.

Kolb was not an attorney, but he was the grandnephew of former governor and attorney John Gill Shorter. He was one of the most successful farmers in Alabama because he had moved away from growing cotton and had developed his own brand of watermelon, the Kolb Gem, on his Barbour County farm and built his enterprise and his wealth by selling his watermelon seeds nationally. As commissioner of agriculture, he went around the state urging Alabama farmers to use more scientific methods of farming and, in the process, became a spokesman for the aspirations of the farmers in the state. He was a pioneer leader of the Farmers' Alliance, which was a membership organization of farmers whose activities were gradually becoming more politically oriented. Soon the Alliance, with Kolb as its candidate, would enter a struggle to take control of the Democratic Party from the conservative Bourbon machine that had controlled it for almost two decades. Reuben Kolb's chief antagonist in this struggle would be attorney Thomas Goode Jones.

Bourbon Governor Thomas Seay, top, appointed Reuben F. Kolb, above, Commissioner of Agriculture. Ironically, the appointment gave Kolb, a Populist, a platform from which to oppose the Bourbons.

Thomas Goode Jones versus the Farmers' Alliance and its Populist Leader

Thomas Goode Jones was considered a committed Bourbon Democrat, but he had friendships with Radical Republicans and held "liberal" attitudes on race issues, being an opponent of the convict lease system and the peonage system that flourished under the state's contract labor laws, as well as an active foe of lynching. His professional life was committed to public service and he is remembered for writing a code of professional ethics for the Alabama State Bar Association that was used as a model by the American Bar Association, for his service as president of the Alabama State Bar, and for his service as a federal district judge in Alabama's Middle District. Yet, his elections to the governorship in 1890 and 1892 followed contests in the Democratic primary that were among the most fraudulent, scurrilous, and racist in Alabama's history. His role as the defender of the Bourbon Democracy put him in a position that seems in contradiction to many of the values he espoused.

There were four touted candidates at the 1890 Democratic convention besides Jones: Joseph F. Johnston of Jefferson County; James Crook of Calhoun County; Judge William Richardson of Madison County; and Populist Reuben Kolb of Barbour County. Johnston, Crook, Richardson, and Jones all represented the Bourbon status quo, all were lawyers, all had honorable war records, and all were conservative and successful. Reuben Kolb ran against these four essentially as the challenger to the status quo. At the convention, the first round of voting showed Kolb at the front of the pack and his lead continued through 33 ballots, although he never had a majority. On the thirty-fourth ballot, his opponents combined against him and nominated Jones, the vote being Jones, 269, Kolb, 256.

Throughout the campaign for delegates leading up to the convention, Kolb had been attacked in the press as a bolter from the Democratic Party, out to destroy it. As instruments of the Bourbon machine, various newspapers, particularly the Montgomery *Advertiser* and its editor, attorney William Wallace Screws, worked to convert a contest that was based on fundamental social and economic questions into one based upon the need to protect the Democratic Party and its role in maintaining white supremacy. Kolb's run for the governorship was compared to a political rebellion against the party that had saved the state from "the political hell" of Reconstruction and would lead to the return to power of the black electorate within the Republican Party at the expense of white Democrats.

This kind of demagoguery continued as Kolb worked to succeed Jones in the 1892 election. As described by

"THE END OF NOWHERE"

YOUNG EDGAR THOMAS ALBRITTON WAS IN the depths of despair when he left Snow Hill, North Carolina, on a train bound for Mobile, Alabama, in 1886. He had lost his wife of four years to typhoid fever and his infant daughter to diphtheria and had almost died himself of the fever that had killed his wife. His infant son, William, was staying with a maiden aunt in Washington, D.C. until Edgar could situate himself. Edgar left his law practice in Snow Hill, planning on joining his younger brother, who was working for the United Fruit Company out of Mobile. They would go by boat to pick up fruit from various countries in South America. Edgar hoped this diversion would help him recover his enthusiasm for life.

On the way to Mobile, the train stopped in Greenville, Alabama, to unload a circus on its way to winter quarters in Florida. While visiting the circus, Edgar met a local lawyer named Dempsey Powell who had just been admitted to the bar and begun his practice in Greenville. Edgar told Dempsey his sad story, adding that what he really wanted to do was to go to a place at the "end of nowhere" and start a new life. Dempsey Powell suggested that Edgar go to Andalusia, Alabama, telling him that it was the best place he knew that would fit that description. Edgar followed Dempsey's advice, going to Andalusia, which was, to Edgar, "the end of the road, the end of the railroad, and the end of nowhere." By January 12, 1887, Edgar was admitted to practice law in Alabama and began a practice which continues today, and which has had Albritton family members as partners throughout its more than 120-year history, now into the fifth generation, including a father and son who served as presidents of the Alabama State Bar. This firm is the oldest known in the state continually in practice with descendants of its founder still active in the firm. And the firm has been instrumental in the growth of the city of Andalusia, which no one would call the "end of nowhere" today.

A chance meeting with attorney Dempsey Powell in Greenville, sent Edgar T. Albritton, above, to Andalusia, where he established a law firm that is still active today.

Dempsey Powell made his own mark on the profession. He read law in the office of his uncle J.S. Powell at Greenville and was admitted to the bar in 1886. He associated in his practice with the firms of Powell, Hamilton & Steinhart of Greenville; Powell, Hamilton & Middleton of Hayneville; Sentell, Hamilton & Powell of Luverne, and Powell & Albritton of Andalusia, having an impact as an outstanding trial lawyer throughout South Alabama. He worked with three generations of Albrittons in Andalusia as well as maintaining connections with other lawyers in Greenville and Luverne throughout his career.

Previously known as a moderate who had written the code of ethics for the Alabama State Bar Association, Thomas Goode Jones used every method to defeat Reuben Kolb for the governorship in 1890 and 1892, including massive voter fraud.

Albert B. Moore in his *History of Alabama and Her People*, "A campaign ensued that was notorious for its popular interest, heat, and muckraking. Political cunning, sophistry, oratory, slander, and press diatribes and canards were prominent features. The scandals of the preceding campaign were told again and new ones were spread abroad with brutal zest. It was a still tongue that retailed no scandal or calumny, and most tongues were wagging." [2] Throughout the campaign, voters were warned of the dangers of the "return to Negro rule." Bourbon leaders tried to keep the voters in line by arguing that the Alliance movement (which had as many black members as white) was a Republican conspiracy to break up the Democratic Party in the South. Traditional Bourbon leaders such as U.S. senator, attorney and Civil War general John Tyler Morgan and congressman, attorney and former Civil War general William Henry Forney and other "big guns" were brought into the fight.

Jones won the 1892 Democratic nomination, although historians agree that there is little doubt that Kolb would have won in a fair election, but that he lost due to massive fraud perpetrated either by excluding black votes or stuffing ballot boxes as needed. Bourbon Democrats were willing to do whatever it took to stay in power. But this time Kolb did not acquiesce. Instead, he and his followers established a separate Democratic Party wing, the Jeffersonian Democrats, which held its own convention and put forth a state ticket with Kolb at the head. Kolb's campaign was managed by Birmingham attorney Peyton G. Bowman, a "stump speaker extraordinary." Kolb and Bowman demanded a "free ballot and a fair count" and argued that "the time had come in politics when all thievery and ballot-box stuffing should be stopped." In the August 1 general election, Jones received 11,425 more votes than Kolb out of the 243,033 votes cast. Again, there were claims of voting fraud and even threats of armed rebellion among the Kolb supporters, since the law did not provide a means to challenge the results of an election. Much agitation followed the election and many threats were made, but Jones's election remained in place, since there was no way to contest it. Still, Jones's position as Kolb's opponent and head of the Bourbon machine during this period of election chicanery cast a shadow over his long record of public service.

The "Magical Process"—The Sayre Election Law of 1893 and the 1894 Governor's Election

"In the Black Belt there was a magical process by which Negroes who walked into the polling place to vote Republican, plus those who stayed at home, and even a few who were dead, were all counted in the Democratic column." [3]

Several names besides Thomas Goode Jones are linked with Bourbon Democratic control of the election machinery in the 1890s, including attorneys John Barnard Knox of Talladega (who served as chairman of the Democratic Executive Committee), Francis L. Pettus (speaker of the Alabama House of Representatives), Willis Brewer (state legislator), and William C. Oates (who followed Thomas Jones as governor). Because the Populist Party was comprised primarily of white and black farmers and laborers, few lawyers were identified with it. Among those who were are Peyton Bowman (Reuben Kolb's campaign manager); Frank Baltzell (defeated candidate for Congress in 1892 who challenged the election in court); Junius P. Oliver (who served as secretary of the Farmers' Alliance for several years and was a member of the Kolb state executive committee); and Adolphus P. Longshore (who served in the legislature during the 1890s.)

One prominent Bourbon Democrat, attorney Anthony D. Sayre, will forever be associated with the party's manipulation of elections in Alabama. He was chairman of the Alabama Legislature's Committee on Privileges and Elections in 1893, during a period when there was much discussion of a proposed bill put forward by Francis L. Pettus calling for a constitutional convention to address the franchise. Rather than reporting Pettus's bill, which was controversial because of Populist fears of the impact of constitutional "reform" on the vote of small farmers, Sayre drafted his own bill to control the franchise. With passage of his bill, the conservatives could ensure that when a constitutional convention was called, they would control it.[4]

The Sayre act's disfranchisement was not obvious, because to directly prohibit the freedman's right to vote would have invited intervention by the federal government. Instead, the bill placed great power in the hands of electoral officials through the use of "adjustments" tothe current political machinery. One "adjustment" was that election officials, who had previously been locally appointed, would thereafter be appointed by the governor, who could thereby heavily influence the manipulation of votes. Another "adjustment" was the use of the Australian ballot, which listed all names alphabetically, without being divided by party affiliation. A voter who could not read would be unable to vote a straight party ticket and would be at the mercy of election officials to "help" him vote. This category of voter was comprised predominantly of blacks and poor whites. Finally, voter registration was limited to the month of May, the busiest month of the year for the state's agricultural workers, both blacks and poor white farmers, and could only take place in the precinct where the vote was to be cast.

This bill was not one that disfranchised voters directly; it just made their

TOP: *Governor William C. Oates, here in the uniform of a brigadier general in the Spanish-American War, defeated Reuben Kolb in the 1894 election for governor, the first to demonstrate the effect of the Sayre Election Law.* LEFT: *Anthony D. Sayre was the author of the Sayre election law., which had the intended effect of disenfranchising blacks and poor whites.* OPPOSITE PAGE: *This 1894 election cartoon in favor of Reuben Kolb depicts the People's Party attempting to awaken sleeping Democrats and Republicans to the oncoming dangers of plutocracy and monopoly.*

WAKING UP THE SLEEPERS.

votes easier to manipulate. As described by David Bagwell in his *Alabama Review* article, "It was a cool, deliberate move toward election fraud"[5] with its impenetrable barriers which (1) gave the voter a printed card explaining the voting process; (2) provided the Australian ballot; and (3) limited the voter to five minutes in the voting booth. Illiterate voters had no choice but to submit to the election official or an aide for help, both of whom would have been appointed by the governor. (An amendment before passage of the bill added election inspectors and justices of the peace to the list that the illiterate could turn to, but the effect was not much different since these officials would most likely represent the status quo as well.)

Thomas Goode Jones was the governor who was empowered to appoint all election officials for the 1894 election. Since he was in his second term at the time, he could not run again. Reuben Kolb would again be the opposition candidate. In his search for a successor, Jones decided to cast his support behind attorney and congressman William C. Oates, a conservative ex-Confederate officer who had lost an arm to a Yankee bullet (a political badge of honor) and who was one of the architects of the system by which Bourbon Democrats had been able to produce majorities sufficient to overcome any opposition since 1874.

The difference between the 1892 election and the 1894 election can largely be attributed to the impact of the Sayre law. The total number of votes cast fell, from 242,483 in 1892 to 192,554 in 1894, with most of the change occurring in the Black Belt. Further, conservative election officials often marked and handled votes for Kolb in such a way as to invalidate them or actually switched the votes of illiterate voters intending to vote for Kolb to votes for Oates. Historians such as David Bagwell and Sheldon Hackney have little doubt that there was substantial voter fraud that was carried to extremes in the Black Belt. Kolb ascribed his loss to fraud, issuing a statement on election night that the fraud was worse than in 1892. It was so apparent that even some Democratic-leaning newspapers protested its magnitude.

In response to voter outrage about the lack of fairness to opposition parties, the legislature made several changes to the Sayre law in February 1895. It was willing to make changes because it recognized that the surge of Populism had crested in 1894 and there would be little effective opposition from that source in the future. Further, the fraud was so great in 1894 that there was a genuine revulsion to this disparagement of the democratic process. Finally, even though as a party Populists were in decline, Populist ideas had begun to influence the mainline Democratic Party, especially with the triumph of the Free Silver movement at the national Democratic convention. The 1896 Democratic gubernatorial nominee would be prosilver, nearly-Populist candidate attorney Joseph Forney Johnston of Birmingham and Reuben Kolb would be a mainline Democrat, while Thomas Goode Jones and his followers would join the defecting "Gold Democrats." Times were changing and the Sayre law would end up being a temporary expedient leading up to the even more successful disfranchisement of black and poor voters by the 1901 constitution.

ABOVE: *Governor Joseph Forney Johnston was considered a reform candidate when he first won the governorship in 1896, by a margin that made fraud unnecessary.* OPPOSITE PAGE: *Johnston's opponent in the 1896 election was Congressman Richard H. Clarke, who subsequently served as president of the Alabama State Bar Association from 1896 to 1897.*

Joseph Forney Johnston and Constitutional Reform

In his election for governor in 1896, Joseph Forney Johnston did not have to face Reuben Kolb and his Farmers' Alliance as reformer opponents. He himself was considered a reform candidate, a prosilver man who worked to bring the Populists and the Jeffersonians back to the mainstream Democratic Party and to incorporate many of their desired reforms into the party's platform.

Johnston was a lawyer who had practiced law in the Black Belt city of Selma for 17 years before moving to the young city of Birmingham in 1884 and serving as president of the Alabama National Bank and then of Sloss Iron and Steel Company. Pursuing an involvement in politics, Johnston was able to capitalize on his contacts in the Black Belt and his contacts within the industrial and financial communities in Birmingham to work his way up the ladder of the Bourbon Democratic Party. He was a leading figure in the 1890 defeat of Reuben Kolb, being one of the candidates for the Democratic nomination who swung his support to Thomas Jones and deprived Kolb of the nomination. In 1892, Johnston was chairman of the platform committee, which, through its thirteenth plank, directed the legislature to enact a law to secure "the government of the State in the hands of the intelligent and the virtuous." From this direction, came the Sayre law of 1893.

In 1894, Johnston challenged William C. Oates for the party's nomination. Oates was extremely conservative and combative, characteristics the party considered necessary to again meet the challenge of Reuben Kolb and the Populists. Johnston, by that time, was leader of an emerging element in the party that advocated free silver and called upon the party to consider reforms that would appeal to its opponents within the Democratic ranks.

In 1896, Populists were fusing with Democrats on the national level to nominate prosilver candidate William Jennings Bryan. Johnston ran again as a reform, free silver candidate and this time defeated "goldbug" congressman Richard H. Clarke (who also served as president of the Alabama State Bar Association from 1896 to 1897). Johnston won the election by a margin that demonstrated he did not need the Black Belt machine to manipulate votes for him. He came into office as the head of a broad coalition that included Birmingham industrialists, reform-minded regular Democrats, former Kolb supporters, and farmers from the white counties of north Alabama.

To recognize the interests of the various segments of his coalition, Governor Johnston proposed substantial reforms. He encouraged northern capital to enter the state and offered tax exemptions to manufacturing firms to promote industrial development. To ensure that this development would be orderly, he proposed that the railroad commission be elected and be given power to set freight rates and to punish noncompliance. He advocated the establishment of a state tax commission to bring assessment and collection under more centralized control and to ensure that large landowners as well as corporations were appropriately evaluated and their taxes properly levied. In addition, corporations would be subject to a franchise tax on both their property and the market value of their stock. Johnston further planned to investigate the convict lease system, to build more roads, and to increase the budget for the state's public schools by adding more than $100,000 and an extra one mill ad valorem tax. Johnston encountered opposition to his proposals from the railroads and from the conservative element of the party that continued to advocate for the status quo and therefore his reform efforts had only modest success.

Johnston took on one "reform" issue that backfired and subsequently destroyed his efforts to take the Democratic Party in a new direction. That issue was constitutional reform. For Johnston, the 1875 constitution represented a roadblock to progress, one that "crippled and dwarfed enterprise, education and progress." For example, it restricted government aid to industry and to internal improvements while its limitations on taxation prevented such growing cities as Birmingham and Anniston from raising funds needed to finance development and expansion.

To most of its advocates, the most important reason for constitutional reform was to restrict the right of suffrage, a topic which had been swirling around state politics since at least 1892. Eliminating black voters did not bother Johnston, who questioned their qualifications for the suffrage, as disfranchisement would contribute to more "pure elections" where fraud would not be needed, since the electorate under reformed suffrage laws would be limited to the "intelligent and the virtuous."

This issue proved, however, to be the downfall of Johnston's attempt to redirect the Democratic Party because opposition to the plan for a new constitution came primarily from within his own coalition. Former Kolbites and Populists voted against the convention bill presented in the 1896-1897 legislature because they feared poor and illiterate whites would become victims of disfranchisement. When Johnston realized his supporters did not favor constitutional revision, he backed off from his support. But a convention bill passed by an 18-11 vote in the Senate and by 52-41 in the House.

Although Johnston signed the bill into law, he still was alarmed at the turn of events, especially when it became clear that the conservative wing of the party was winning many of the nominations for delegates at large and seemed likely to win significant influence in the convention. Then, against Johnston's opposition, the Democratic Party at its state convention in March 1899, made support of the call for a constitutional convention a party loyalty issue.

At this turn of events, Johnston followed a risky course by calling a special session of the legislature and demanding that the convention bill be repealed, thereby breaking with the traditional party leadership on an issue it had made a litmus test of loyalty. Although Johnston had made sure he had a majority in favor of repeal before he made the special session call, he and his supporters still faced the opposition of every Alabama congressman except one,

JOHN TYLER MORGAN AND ALABAMA'S POST "REDEMPTION" SENATORS

JOHN TYLER MORGAN WAS ELECTED IN 1877 TO replace Senator George Thomas Goldthwaite, who had served in the U.S. Senate during the frustrating period from 1871 to 1877, when Reconstruction policies resulted in disfranchisement of the South. Goldthwaite had been considered one of the most learned lawyers in the state and had had a successful practice in Montgomery as well as service on the circuit court bench and the Alabama Supreme Court before the Civil War. His term as a U.S. senator accomplished little because of its timing. The same cannot be said for John Tyler Morgan, a brigadier general in the Civil War with a distinguished military career and a successful law practice in Selma both prior to and after the war's conclusion. He served as U.S. senator from Alabama for 30 years in a national

RIGHT: *John Tyler Morgan, one of the architects of the Bourbon ascendancy, served in the U.S. Senate for 30 years.* OPPOSITE PAGE: *With the election to the U.S. Senate of Edmund W. Pettus in 1896, at the age of 75, Selma gained the distinction of being home to both of Alabama's U.S. senators.*

two ex-governors (William Oates and Thomas Jones), and both United States senators (John Morgan and Edmund Pettus). The Democratic State Executive Committee met and organized a campaign committee to work against repeal. It called for a rally for the night before the special session was to meet and Morgan, Pettus, Oates, and Jones addressed those in attendance. After four days of debate, the legislature followed Johnston's wishes and repealed the call for a convention.

The Black Belt press, which had never liked the governor, now denounced him with vehemence. The Selma *Times* wrote: "Joe Johnston hails from Dallas. We speak of it with shame. He knows that the people of the Black Belt held up the hands of the party when Republicanism was rampant and the people were being led into the mistake of populism. He knows that the people of this section of the state ask to be relieved of the burden of the black man, and the people in the northern part of the state wish to relieve them, and he calls an extra session of the legislature to defeat the will of the people. We call him Judas because he betrays his friends that made him; we call him Judas because he bargains with the enemy for our undoing, and for his own selfish ends, and we call him Judas because the only thing left for him to do is to hang himself on the first tree and thus rid the state of its chief trickster who disgraces its highest executive office."[6]

career where he was most noted for supporting America's expansionist vision. He is mainly remembered for his support of the building of a canal to connect the Atlantic and Pacific oceans, although he worked tirelessly for a route through Nicaragua rather than Panama. Other expansionist proposals he supported included an inter-American railway plan, annexation of the Hawaiian Islands, and acquisition of Puerto Rico and the Philippines.

In January 1880, attorney Luke Pryor was chosen to complete Senator George Houston's vacant term when Houston died after only one year of service. Pryor resigned the office in November of the same year and did not seek election. Pryor is remembered in Alabama history for his efforts in the 1850s to promote the building of a railway system in the state. His election to the legislature in 1855 gave him a platform from which to promote these views. Under his persistent prodding, lawmakers passed a bill to underwrite the subscription of $200,000 of capital stock of the Tennessee and Alabama Central Railroad Company. The act was vetoed by Governor John A. Winston, but he was overridden. From this beginning, the railroad system of Alabama got underway. The magic city of Birmingham might not have appeared so soon after the Civil War had Pryor's efforts not succeeded.

Pryor was succeeded by attorney James L. Pugh, who was chosen by the legislature to complete the four years remaining of Houston's term. Pugh was a prosilver Democrat who served as chairman of the Senate Judiciary Committee. President Cleveland offered him a seat on the U.S. Supreme Court, but he declined. He served in the Senate for 16 years, but lost his reelection bid in 1896 in a four-way race where he was opposed by noted attorney and former Confederate general Edmund Winston Pettus, John Hollis Bankhead, Sr., and Governor William Oates. Pettus was the victor.

Edmund Pettus was an influential leader of the state Democratic Party (having served as chairman of the state delegation to each national convention from 1872 through 1896) but he had never sought political office until 1896 when he was 75 years old. (He served as the second president of the Alabama State Bar Association from 1879 to 1880.) He might not have run if Pugh, who was 76, had not told him he was too old. Being a stubborn old warrior, Pettus took those as fighting words, being particularly sensitive since President Cleveland had declined his bid for appointment to the U.S. Supreme Court because of his age.

With his win, Pettus gave Selma the unique honor of being the home of two U.S. senators at the same time. During these years, the two former generals were bound together by the character of their service, both being remembered for their tenacity and their composure, even in the midst of volatile political controversy.

Convention advocates did not accept defeat and instead determined to make the call for a convention an issue in the 1900 elections for the legislature and U.S. Senate. Since Joseph Johnston had served two terms as governor and could not succeed himself, he intended to oppose Senator John T. Morgan. He presented himself to voters as the leader who had defeated a convention that might have arbitrarily taken away the rights of the common man. Senator Morgan declared that a vote for legislative candidates supporting him was a vote for the convention and denounced Johnston as a traitor to the Democratic Party. Morgan was assured of reelection when, in April 1900, a majority of legislators partial to him was nominated in Democratic county primaries and conventions around the state (senators still being elected by the legislature at that time.)

Morgan's campaign manager, attorney Frank S. White (who would later serve as Alabama State Bar Association president from 1912 to 1913 and as a U.S. senator himself from 1914 to 1915), issued the following statement: "Morgan's victory is a triumph for better politics in Alabama. It means a constitutional convention. The state can no longer do without it. Alabama cannot exist with a foundation under it of corruption at the polls. The constitutional convention and the elimination of fraudulent elections are bound to be the results."

CHAPTER SEVEN

BENCH AND BAR 1861-1901

DURING THE CIVIL WAR, BUSINESS in Alabama's trial courts was close to a standstill, as continuances were granted in those cases where parties, attorneys, or even judges were not available because of war service. Gradually the caseload of the Alabama Supreme Court also fell off. Chief Justice A. J. Walker and his colleagues issued more than 80 opinions for the June 1861 term with more than 100 lawyers taking part. By January 1863, the numbers were down to 55 cases argued by about 80 lawyers. Two years later, 37 lawyers participated in 21 cases. Many of the cases that were heard forecast things to come since the parties often were corporations, especially railroad corporations, who would produce a growing proportion of the cases that would come before the courts after the war's conclusion, when industrialization in the state expanded. Other issues the court faced involved state sovereignty versus Confederate conscription, where, following the lead of Associate Justice (later Chief Justice) George W. Stone, the court usually ruled in favor of Confederate war powers.[1]

At war's end, the state supreme court briefly ceased to function until presidential reconstruction was established and the court was revived in the fall of 1865, still headed by A. J. Walker. Then, under Radical Reconstruction and the Constitution of 1868, Republicans were appointed to the court. Two of the three justices were prewar Unionists, Chief Justice Elisha Wolsey Peck (who chaired the 1868 constitutional revision commission which introduced popular election of all judges for six-year terms) and Associate Justice Thomas Minott Peters, both of whom had well-established law practices prior to the war, had supported remaining in the Union, and had left the state and then returned during Reconstruction to support the Republican Party's efforts to reorganize state government. The third justice was Associate Justice Benjamin F. Saffold, son of Reuben Saffold, a member and former chief justice of Alabama's first Supreme Court.

The court was increased by two more justices, in response to increasingly heavy caseloads generated during the Bourbon period. Thomas N. McClellan, Alabama's attorney general at the time, filled a position created in 1889 and Richard W. Walker, Jr. (whose father, a brother of LeRoy Pope Walker, had also served on the court in earlier years) filled a position created in 1891. Walker became presiding judge of the Alabama Court of Appeals, when it was established in 1911, and later a U.S. circuit judge for the Fifth Judicial Circuit in 1914.

On the trial court level, the economy-minded constitution of 1875 reduced the number of circuits from 12 to eight, but the increasing caseload generated by postwar growth and social change resulted in an increase

OPPOSITE PAGE: *When the Alabama Supreme Court was increased from three justices to five in 1889, attorney general Thomas N. McClellan was appointed to one of the new positions. In 1898 he became chief justice, serving until his death in 1906.* ABOVE: *These tracks outside Montgomery demonstrate the boom in railroad building following the Civil War, with a corresponding boom in employment for the new breed of corporate lawyers.*

of circuits to 16 by 1907 (with Jefferson County constituting a circuit by itself). A phenomenon generated by constitutional restrictions and local ambitions as another response to increasing caseloads was the creation of numerous "special" courts throughout the state, which operated alongside the traditional circuit courts, including city courts, criminal courts, and court of quarter sessions. Each was created by a special act of the legislature and, as such, was subject to sudden changes, giving state justice the look and feel of a patchwork quilt.

Chancery courts, which had been separated from the circuit courts in 1839, had a more modest growth during this period, from three "divisions" in the 1840s to five in the 1890s. Although an important area of practice, the equity courts were often seen as an unnecessary expense whose equity function could be merged back into the law courts with little problem. Merger of these courts became a subject of frequent debate at meetings of the Alabama State Bar Association, even as their flexible powers to set aside fraudulent conveyances, settle trusts and partnership accounts, grant divorces, enforce mechanics and vendors' liens, appoint receivers, and remove clouds on titles became even more in demand as life became more complicated in both the business and personal realms.

LAWYER DEMOGRAPHICS, 1860-1920

The most important postwar demographic change in the population of lawyers took place in Jefferson County, where the creation of the city of Birmingham and its development as a center of business and industry saw an increase in its population of attorneys from seven in 1860 to over 100 in 1887, comprising nearly 14 percent of the lawyers in the state in that year. A similar growth took place in smaller industrial cities like Gadsden and Anniston. At the same time, numbers in the profession declined dramatically in the Black Belt, the center of legal prestige before the Civil War. In Dallas County, once a magnet for practitioners, the number of attorneys dropped from 67 in 1860 to 23 in 1887. Corresponding numbers in Marengo County were 23 to nine, in Wilcox County 26 to 11, and in Sumter County, 26 to nine. In east Alabama's Barbour County, there was a drop from 25 to 14. The decline in the Black Belt probably came about because there was little growth or change in the nature of the legal issues that arose there after the war. The money to be made from the practice of law after the war was in the cities, and especially in the new and quickly growing city of Birmingham, which fast became the center of industrialization with its many mills, mines, and factories. A perusal of the roster of the Birmingham Bar in 1887 shows that most of its members were born and even practiced in other parts of the state before migrating to the city. By 1920, the city had a population of close to 200,000, with over 200 lawyers.[2]

Phillip Phillips, a prominent Jewish attorney, was known for producing the first digest of state supreme court decisions and for serving as U.S. congressman for the Mobile district from 1854 to 1855. He remained in Washington D.C. and built a well-recognized practice before the U.S. Supreme Court. He has been called "probably the most accomplished and respected American Jew of the first half of the nineteenth century."

Lawyers and Alabama's Postwar Corporate Development

After the Civil War ended, there was an explosion of railroad building and business organization throughout the state. At the same time, the most important feature in the development of law practice during the postwar period was the development of firms that specialized in corporate practice. Railroad companies were the main corporations that inspired this specialization and the lawyers who represented them dominated the profession during their heyday.[3]

Lawyers were involved in efforts both before and after the Civil War to establish railroads. Without their foundational efforts, the growth of Alabama's railroad system would have been even slower than it was. First among the early pioneers was attorney David Hubbard of Tuscumbia, who organized one of the first railroads in the United States. Completed in 1832, the Tuscumbia Railroad ran from Tuscumbia to Decatur on wooden rails. The inspiration for building this railroad was to circumvent the shoals at Muscle Shoals.

Attorney Phillip Phillips also played an important role in promoting the building of railroads during his term of service in the state House of Representatives representing Mobile. Elected in 1851, he became chairman of the Committee on Internal Improvement, which he used as a platform to promote state involvement in internal improvement projects. He had served as chairman of a railroad convention the year before his election and gave a speech advocating connecting north and south Alabama, using both river and rail transportation. In the speech and in reports as committee chairman, he noted that Alabama was split commercially, with north Alabama having to transport goods to New Orleans via the Tennessee, Ohio, and Mississippi rivers, while south Alabama shipped its goods on rivers whose outlet was Mobile.

The dream of uniting the two sections of the state had been around since the beginning of statehood, and Phillips thought the time was right for realizing the dream. Although his efforts were widely supported and several railroads were chartered, Alabama's governor at the time was John A. Winston, who was elected by those who rejected the concept of state aid to internal improvements.

Winston and his followers thought such improvements should be funded through private enterprise without state involvement. So, while the state chartered 73 railroad companies during the 1850s and even approved state funding for many, Winston continually blocked state aid during his terms in office (1853-1857) and little track was actually laid during the decade leading up to the Civil War.

In 1849, Phillip Phillips chaired an organizational meeting of the Alabama & Tennessee River Railroad Company. Over the course of time, this railroad, which was chartered to go from Selma to the Tennessee River, did receive state funding, perhaps because one of its main proponents (and ultimately its president for six years) was Thomas A. Walker, a lawyer, circuit judge, and legislator who was president of the senate as well as president of the railroad company. The company was able to complete the laying of track to Blue Mountain in Calhoun County before the war broke out.

University of Alabama professor (with a legal education) Landon C. Garland, who first was chair of English literature, rhetoric, and history, then chair of mathematics, and finally president of the University in 1854, was also president of the North East & South West Railroad Company, which was chartered in 1853 to connect Meridian, Mississippi, with Chattanooga. Although only 27 miles of this railroad's track was built (from Meridian to York) when the war broke out, it survived the war and became part of Alabama's railroad system (being renamed the Alabama & Chattanooga Railroad Company.)

Hurieosco Austill, who practiced law and served in the Alabama legislature from Mobile, was one of the organizers, and served as president for a time, of the Mobile & West Alabama Railroad. He devoted much of his later years to railroad development, promoting the Mobile, Jackson, & Kansas City Railroad, among others. Edward L. Russell was admitted to practice law in Mississippi in 1871, and in 1875 began representing the Mobile & Ohio Railroad. Thereafter, he progressed to become the railroad's general solicitor, general counsel, vice president, general manager, and finally president from 1898 until 1911. The railroad was headquartered in Mobile, so Russell moved to Mobile and became active in Alabama affairs, even serving as president of the Alabama State Bar Association from 1901 to 1902 and as a trustee of the University of Alabama. John Daniel Rather of Tuscumbia served as vice president and then president of the Memphis & Charleston Railroad, during a career which saw him serve as a circuit judge, state senator, and founding member of the firm Kirk, Rather & Hughston, which survived in Tuscumbia into the 1990s as Hughston, Hughston, & Hughston.

Attorney Thomas J. Judge, a legislator at the time, was elected president of the Alabama & Florida Railroad at its stockholders' meeting

TOP: *Landon C. Garland became president of the University of Alabama in 1854, serving through the Civil War. He also served as president of the North East & South West Railroad Company. After the war, he became the first chancellor of Vanderbilt University.* ABOVE: *Mobile attorney Edward L. Russell spent the greater part of his career with the Mobile & Ohio Railroad, eventually rising to become its president in 1898.*

on May 3, 1853. John Turner Milner was hired by this company to survey its ultimate route, the same John Milner who would survey the route for the Alabama Central Railroad (later changed to the South & North Alabama Railroad), whose crossing point with the North East and South West Railroad (which later became the Alabama & Chattanooga Railroad) would become the site for the city of Birmingham. The Alabama Central Railroad was chartered in 1854. When attorney Andrew B. Moore was elected governor after John Winston, Moore appreciated and supported the idea of state-financed improvements and saw that $10,000 was appropriated to pay Milner for surveying the route.

Milner's survey report was submitted to the legislature in 1859. There was a faction in the legislature, led by Judge Thomas Walker, which supported the Alabama & Tennessee River Railway and saw the proposed Alabama Central Railroad as a threat. Walker, along with attorney Senator J. M. Calhoun of Dallas County, worked to defeat acceptance of Milner's report. But future governors Robert M. Patton and George S. Houston (an attorney who was a U.S. congressman at the time) came to Milner's aid in support of the report. Through their efforts, sufficient votes were secured to have the state sanction the report and have it

LEFT: *Robert Jemison of Tuscaloosa was a wealthy planter, as well as an attorney and politician. As a member of the state legislature before the war, he was one of the leading opponents of secession. An early industrialist, he was president of the railroad that became the Alabama & Chattanooga.* BELOW: *The new city of Birmingham acted as a magnet to lawyers around the state. Within 15 years of its founding, 14 percent of the lawyers in Alabama were practicing in Birmingham.*

printed. Milner later said about Houston's support, "I have never ceased to thank him. That was the turning point of my life, and then and there was the beginning of the city of Birmingham."

The building of the South & North Alabama Railroad and its intersection with the Alabama & Chattanooga Railroad would not come about until after the Civil War. Milner's dream of a workshop town where Jefferson County's mineral resources could be mined and manufactured would begin to turn into reality with the founding of the city of Birmingham in 1871. Many men would have a part in the establishment of the town and the industrial base it would provide the state of Alabama, including lawyer-entrepreneur Robert Jemison, who was president of the railroad that would become the Alabama & Chattanooga; Bolling Hall, Jr., an Elmore County lawyer-planter-legislator who promoted both the South & North Alabama Railroad as a director and the city of Birmingham as one of the organizers and a director of the Elyton Land Company; and Judge William Swearingen Mudd, also an organizer and director of the Elyton Land Company, which was the creator of the city. Daniel Shipman Troy of Montgomery (who served as the Alabama State Bar Association president from 1895 to 1896) served as attorney for the land company, as well as holding stock, and had substantial influence over its plans to grow the city. Troy's nephew, Alexander Troy London, who practiced law with his uncle and Henry C. Tompkins in Montgomery (state bar president from 1886 to 1887), moved to Birmingham in 1890 to serve the company as counsel, joining forces with John London to establish the firm of London & London, today's London, Yancey & Elliott, LLC. John London served as Alabama State Bar Association president from 1910 to 1911.

TOP: *Daniel Shipman Troy was an attorney and stockholder of the Elyton Land Company and had great influence on its plans for the new city. He served as president of the Alabama State Bar Association from 1895 to 1896.* ABOVE: *Daniel Troy's nephew Alexander Troy London came to Birmingham in 1890 to serve as counsel to the Elyton Land Company.*

Because of the precarious financial position of the South & North Alabama Railroad, the Louisville & Nashville Railroad entered the state. As one of the strongest railroads in the country, it was able to absorb the South & North Alabama Railroad and make it an important part of the L&N system. Before long, it was involved in the purchase or creation of other railroad lines to make connections among and between important population centers both within and without the state. As its land holdings and railroad assets grew, so did its power.

In the legal profession, this power manifested itself in a whole new type of practice—the corporate specialty—and practices representing corporations (which expanded to include banks, insurers, mines, mills, and manufacturers and other corporate businesses, in addition to railroads) grew into firms with multiple attorneys who themselves became specialists. The large corporate firms could be found primarily in the major cities of Mobile, Montgomery, and Birmingham. Business practices which dominated in smaller towns tended to be more general in scope and have fewer attorneys. The shift toward firms that primarily represented corporations and other business entities began as the nineteenth century drew to a close.

The L&N Railroad was one of the first corporations in Alabama with its own law department. Charles Pollard Jones, younger brother of Thomas Goode Jones, entered its law department in

1882, as tax representative, and then was appointed assistant district attorney for the railroad in 1890. Later, he served as division counsel for the Central of Georgia Railway. (He also practiced with his brother until Thomas Goode Jones was appointed a federal judge in 1901.)

An early example of a successful "railroad" practice was that shared by George Goldthwaite, Samuel F. Rice, and Henry C. Semple, who were prominent both before the war and during the early days of Reconstruction. Located in Montgomery, much of their business involved appellate work before the Alabama Supreme Court. These lawyers were highly regarded in the profession (Goldthwaite had been on the first committee to codify Alabama's laws and had served both on the Alabama Supreme Court and in the United States Senate; Rice served as a legislator and as chief justice of the Alabama Supreme Court; and Semple was one of the early presidents of the Alabama State Bar Association). Prominence and attainment became hallmarks of the successful railroad lawyers, especially those named as "district attorneys" (such as for the Birmingham district) who oversaw legal work that might be delegated to a more general practitioner who practiced in the court where an individual case would be tried.

When Goldthwaite left the practice upon his election in 1870 to the U.S. Senate, Rice joined with young lawyers Thomas Goode Jones and Ariosto A. Wiley, themselves becoming well connected through public service (Jones would serve as governor, Alabama State Bar Association president, and a federal judge and Wiley would become a highly regarded U.S. congressman after years of service in the Alabama legislature.) Then Jones went into practice with Jefferson Falkner, perhaps the most eminent of Alabama's early corporate lawyers and they practiced together as skilled railroad lawyers, troubleshooters, and "political fixers" for more than ten years, until Jones was appointed to the federal bench.

TOP: *Preeminent corporate attorney Jefferson Falkner joined with Thomas Goode Jones to form the firm of Jones & Falkner.* ABOVE: *Montgomery attorney Robert E. Steiner served in the state legislature and, with Benjamin Crum and Leon Weil, founded the firm known today as Steiner, Crum & Byars.*

Ray Rushton studied law in the Jones & Falkner firm and entered practice in 1890. He became prominent in Democratic politics, even serving as a candidate for the U.S. Senate twice in the early years of the twentieth century. He also served as president of the Alabama State Bar Association from 1914 to 1915. Rushton's practice evolved and continues today as Rushton, Stakely, Johnston & Garrett, P.A., one of the major corporate law firms in Montgomery.

In 1884, Robert E. Steiner entered the practice of law in Montgomery. Soon, he was a member of the state legislature and then the state senate. In 1894, Benjamin P. Crum began practicing in Montgomery with Tennent Lomax (son of the attorney and Confederate general) and Leon Weil after having practiced with George R. Farnham of Evergreen for a number of years. Lomax had been practicing since 1879 and was heavily involved in business endeavors, as well as serving as county solicitor. Soon after Lomax's death, Crum and Weil became partners with Robert Steiner as Steiner, Crum & Weil, later Steiner, Crum & Baker. This practice survives today as Steiner, Crum & Byars, P.C., still a highly regarded corporate firm.

Fred S. Ball studied law under Henry C. Tompkins, who had served as attorney general of Alabama from

1878 to 1884 as well as chairman of the state Democratic Executive Committee, beginning in 1886, and president of the Alabama State Bar Association from 1886 to 1887. Tompkins had an active practice as a legal adviser for a number of corporations throughout the state. Fred Ball's practice soon also included corporations and continues today as the Montgomery firm of Ball, Ball, Matthews, & Novak, P.A. John Dupree Roquemore (president of the state bar from 1898 to 1899) represented the Central Railroad and Banking Company of Georgia in a number of precedent-setting cases before the Alabama Supreme Court in a firm that included Joseph M. White and S. H. Dent, Jr., of Montgomery and Barbour County.

Mobile attorney Joseph H. Lyons began his practice in 1900, specializing in corporate law. Presidents Woodrow Wilson, in 1918, and Franklin Roosevelt, in 1933, appointed him collector of customs for the Port of Mobile. The firm he founded continues today as Lyons, Pipes & Cook, P.C.

The success of Montgomery firms has always been closely tied to the presence of state government. Thus, appellate work and administrative work have always been important areas of specialization for those representing corporations in Montgomery. The firm description in the 2006 edition of the Martindale-Hubbell legal directory for the firm of Steiner, Crum & Byars, for example, reads in part, "Administrative Law, including Health Care, Utility Regulation, Intrastate Transportation Regulation, Banking, Financial Institution and Regulatory Law, Corporate, Commercial, Communication, Railroad, Alabama State Taxation, Alcoholic Beverages Law, Legislation, Constitutional Law." (This firm has produced four presidents of the Alabama State Bar, more than any other firm in the history of the bar, including B. P. Crum (1922-1923); Robert E. Steiner, III (1966-1967); M. R. Nachman (1973-1974); and Walter R. Byars (1984-1985)).

In Mobile, brothers Gaylord Blair Clark and Francis Bernard Clark, Jr., (both of whom had been organizers of the Alabama State Bar Association) formed a practice that ultimately represented such corporate clients as Western Union and L&N Railroad. Gaylord practiced before the supreme courts of Alabama, Mississippi, Florida, and Louisiana. Francis was known for his legal scholarship as well, authoring Clark's *Manual of Criminal Law*, which was used as a text at The University of Alabama Law School. He also developed a widely used legal form book and helped revise the Alabama Code, published in 1886.

Harry Pillans, who served as mayor of Mobile, began a practice in 1870 that at one time or another included Hurieosco Austill, George N. Steward, Charles Torrey, Henry Hanaw and Palmer Pillans (his son) before the turn of the century. That practice continues in the modern-day firm of Reams, Brooks, Schell, & Gaston in Mobile.

Thomas McCorvey Stevens came to Mobile in 1896 and began a practice that continues today as Johnstone, Adams, Bailey, Gordon & Harris, L.L.C., established 1897, one of Mobile's large corporate firms. Stevens was president of the Alabama State Bar Association from 1913 to 1914. Gessner T. McCorvey of the Johnstone firm was president of the state bar from 1948 to 1949. Joseph H. Lyons, a Harvard law graduate, began his practice in Mobile in 1900, which has evolved into today's corporate firm of Lyons, Pipes & Cook, P.C., another substantial corporate firm in south Alabama. Sam W. Pipes of that firm served as president of the Alabama State Bar from 1968 to 1969.

Firms operating in Mobile have always needed attorneys who specialize in admiralty law, since the port of Mobile has generated admiralty cases from the city's earliest history. Of course, railroads bringing goods to the port have also needed corporate representation. These two types of corporations, as well as the insurance companies who cover their liabilities, have been major sources of business to corporate attorneys in Mobile throughout the years.

TOP: *As an organizer of the Elyton Land Company, William S. Mudd was one of the founding fathers of Birmingham. He also served in the state legislature and as a delegate to the 1875 constitutional convention.* ABOVE: *Attorney Alexander O. Lane served twice as mayor of Birmingham.*

In Huntsville, Milton Humes, who read law in the law office of LeRoy Pope Walker and served as president of the Alabama State Bar Association from 1888 to 1889, had a large railroad practice, representing the Memphis & Chattanooga Railroad, the East Tennessee, Virginia & Georgia Railroad, and the Nashville, Chattanooga & St. Louis Railway, among other corporations.

Edward C. Betts, who was Alabama's first commissioner of agriculture, and Tancred Betts, his son, practiced together during this period and their practice, with the later addition of Robert K. Bell and Schuyler H. Richardson, originated the firm of Bell, Richardson P.A., a major corporate firm in modern Huntsville (with whom Patrick W. Richardson, president of the Alabama State Bar from 1969 to 1970, practiced).

In Selma, Phillip Henry Pitts entered practice with N. H. R. Dawson (president of the Alabama State Bar Association in 1884) and later practiced with his son Arthur M. Pitts in a general practice that continues to represent CSX Transportation and many national insurers under the firm name of Pitts, Pitts, & Thompson. Another Selma attorney who became president of the Alabama State Bar Association (1907-1908) was H. S. D. Mallory, whose practice began in 1869. He also served as Selma's mayor. His practice is the predecessor of today's Reeves & Stewart, P.C., which represents both individual and corporate clients in Dallas, Bibb, Hale, Perry, and Wilcox counties.

In Tuscaloosa, J. Manly Foster began practicing law in 1886. He served as a legislator, county solicitor, and delegate to the 1901 constitutional convention. He also served in the district counsel's office of the L&N Railroad in Montgomery for a time. Later, he would practice with Charles B. Verner and Fleetwood Rice as well as his son Richard Foster and serve as president of the Alabama State Bar Association from 1918 to 1919.

The Birmingham Bar

Birmingham had been a city for eight years when the Alabama State Bar Association was established in 1879. During its first decade, the city experienced both a cholera epidemic and a financial panic, which had driven many of its early settlers away. Its growth did not accelerate until the early part of the 1880s.

Most of its early attorneys, including William Swearingen Mudd, Alberto Martin, John C. Morrow, M. T. Porter, Goldsmith Hewitt, and William A. Walker, Jr., had well-established practices in the county seat of Elyton before Birmingham was founded. Others, including John T. Terry, E. T. Taliaferro, B. H. Tabor, H. A. Sharpe, James E. Webb, James Weatherly, Alexander Troy London, Edward K. Campbell, Alexander O. Lane, John T. Heflin, and Joseph Forney Johnston, migrated from other Alabama and out-of-state towns and cities and established significant practices, becoming important members of the bar and leaders in the business community of Birmingham. Many young lawyers came to Birmingham during its real estate boom in the 1880s, but did not necessarily stay after the boom ended. In 1887, there were about 60 lawyers practicing in Birmingham.

One important newcomer was John P. Tillman, who began practicing law in 1871, the year of the city's founding. He was born in Perry County in 1849, was educated in Selma, attended Howard College and the University of Kentucky at Lexington, and studied law in the Selma office of Edmund Pettus and N. H. R. Dawson (both of whom served as presidents of the Alabama State Bar Association in its early days.) He practiced with Pettus and Dawson and with Joseph Forney Johnston in Selma. In 1883, he moved to Montgomery to serve as special reporter of supreme court decisions, but left to come to Birmingham in October 1884, where he practiced at different times in partnership with James E. Webb (who practiced in Greensboro for about 20 years before coming to Birmingham in 1885 and who served as president of the Alabama State Bar Association from 1894 to 1895); Alexander Troy London; Edward K. Campbell; and William A. Walker, Jr. In 1884, he was appointed by Chief Judge Robert C. Brickell of the Alabama Supreme Court as one of two assistant commissioners to codify the laws of the state, and after the work was adopted by the legislature, he was selected as sole commissioner to supervise the printing.

In 1871, William A. Walker, Jr., top, was one of the founders of the firm which has evolved into Bradley Arant Boult Cummings, Alabama's largest law firm. One of the early partners was John P. Tillman, above, the first president of the Birmingham Bar Association, founded in 1885.

With so many connections, it was natural for Tillman to be the inspiration behind the founding of the Birmingham Bar Association in 1885, serving as its first president. In 1897, he would be the first member of the Birmingham Bar to serve as president of the Alabama State Bar Association. Tillman was also among the early partners in the first major corporate law firm in Birmingham. In 1871, Goldsmith Hewitt and William A. Walker, Jr., had formed a partnership, which also included John C. Morrow for a time. Besides being an accomplished trial lawyer, Walker was one of the first corporate lawyers in the city, representing a number of streetcar and dummy rail lines, which later became the Birmingham Railway Light and Power Company, the firm's major corporate client. In the late 1880s, M. A. Porter became a partner, as did John Tillman shortly thereafter. Tillman, an experienced appellate attorney, represented Sloss-Sheffield Steel and Iron Company (predecessor of Jim Walter Resources, Inc., Sloss Industries Corporation, and U.S. Pipe and Foundry Company), another significant corporate client of the firm. Over the course of time, the firm founded by Hewitt and Walker evolved into the largest firm in the state today, Bradley Arant Boult Cummings LLP.

Edward H. Cabaniss was admitted to practice law in Union Springs, Alabama, in 1878, after studying law at Harvard University. He and J. J. Banks came to Birmingham from Union Springs in 1887 and established a law practice that would include important Birmingham lawyers Samuel Weakley and Sydney J. Bowie, as well as his son, E. H. Cabaniss, Jr. The firm would later be joined by Forney Johnston, son of Joseph Forney Johnston, and become the predecessor of today's Cabaniss, Johnston, Gardner, Dumas & O'Neal LLP, another

important corporate firm in Birmingham.

Walker Percy moved to Birmingham in 1886. He would become an important corporate specialist and, after the turn of the century, would join with Augustus Benners and Borden H. Burr to found the firm that continues today as Burr & Forman, LLP. Borden Burr served as president of the Alabama State Bar from 1931 to 1932.

Just as the railroads encouraged attorneys to specialize in corporate representation, they also caused a need for specialists who would represent individuals injured by them. Most parties injured by corporate defendants were represented by firms with general practices that had litigators who knew how to persuade juries. One such litigator was former governor Thomas Hill Watts, who practiced with his sons Thomas Henry and John Wade Watts and his son-in-law Daniel S. Troy in Montgomery in the 1870s. (Watts served as president of the Alabama State Bar from 1889 to 1890.) One Birmingham firm from its beginning built a reputation as a "personal injury firm." It still survives today as Hare, Wynn, Newell, and Newton, LLP. Peyton G. Bowman (who is remembered for managing Reuben Kolb's campaign to become the Farmers' Alliance governor) and Griffith Harsh established the firm in 1890, shortly after Bowman weathered an attempt by the Birmingham Bar Association to have him disbarred for his willingness to represent unpopular clients. Soon, Charles P. Beddow joined the firm. (He would later develop a separate practice with his son, Roderick Beddow, who would become one of Alabama's most famous criminal attorneys and serve as president of the Alabama State Bar from 1944 to 1945). In the 1920s, the firm became Harsh, Harsh, and Hare when Griffith Harsh was joined by his son Griffith Harsh, Jr., and young Francis Hare in the practice. From there, the Hare, Wynn firm evolved. Francis Hare would serve as president of the Alabama State Bar from 1949 to 1950 and firm member Alva C. Caine would be president from 1989 to 1990.

Edward H. Cabaniss, left, and his partner J. J. Banks came to Birmingham in 1887. The photograph above shows a very young Forney Johnston, on the left, meeting with a Mr. Fitzgerald in the offices of Cabaniss and Banks in 1905.

ALABAMA LAWYERS AS WRITERS, EDUCATORS, SUPPORTERS OF EDUCATION, JOURNALISTS, HISTORIANS, ARCHIVISTS, AND IDEOLOGUES

Two lawyers recognized by literary critics for their contributions to American literature were humorist writers Johnson Jones Hooper and Joseph Glover Baldwin. Hooper came from North Carolina, practiced law in Lafayette, and edited the *East Alabamian*. In 1844, Hooper began writing stories about fictional Captain Simon Suggs, whose motto was, "It is good to be shifty in a new country." In 1845, he published *Some Adventures of Captain Simon Suggs,* a major contribution to the popular genre of realistic humor about the Old Southwest, full of scoundrels, swindlers, con artists and other men on the make whose likes were common in early Alabama, illustrating the contrasts between the more settled society from which he came and the one emerging from the Alabama frontier. Baldwin's humor was similar, but his audience was a more sophisticated one than Johnson's. His best-known work, published in 1853, was *The Flush Times of Alabama and Mississippi.*

Alexander B. Meek, attorney and writer (he was editor and a contributor to the *Southron*, a literary magazine, from 1839 through 1842; editor of the *Flag of the Union* at Tuscaloosa from 1835 to 1839; and associate editor of the *Mobile Daily Register* from 1851 to 1858) represented Mobile in the legislature during Governor John A. Winston's first term. He sponsored the first legislation to address state funding for free public schools in Alabama—the Education Act of 1854, fashioned after Mobile's county school financing system. The act provided for the state to divide $100,000 a year among the counties and allowed counties to collect real estate and personal property taxes for educational purposes. The act also created a state superintendent of education and was later amended to establish county superintendents. The timing of the act, though, was unfortunate because the Civil War began before much could be accomplished to create a system of public education.

Governor Andrew B. Moore supported increased appropriations to Alabama schools and saw the completion of the school for the deaf and blind in Talladega just before the state withdrew from the Union. The Civil War stifled further efforts toward building a public system of education.

After the war ended, the state was in such dire financial straits that there were few funds to direct toward education. The Freedmen's Bureau, under the direction of Wager Swayne, made education for the emancipated slaves a major concern. Swayne approached northern benevolent societies and churches for support, and even expended money from the Freedmen's Bureau's own budget to cover expenses. His activist policies laid the groundwork for expansion of public education for black children.

Governor William Hugh Smith's administration, 1868 to 1870, oversaw creation of a free school system that for the first time included Alabama's black children, but the railroad bond scandals that occurred during his adminis-

Mobile attorney, editor, and legislator Alexander B. Meek was the first person to sponsor a bill to fund public education in Alabama. Unfortunately, the Civil War intervened before his proposals could be implemented.

WILLIS GAYLORD CLARK
LAWYER, AUTHOR, NEWSMAN, PUBLIC OFFICIAL

THE MOBILE EDUCATION PLAN THAT ALEXANDER Meek used as a model was first proposed in the pages of the *Mobile Daily Register* by Willis Gaylord Clark, a lawyer originally trained in his home state of New York who migrated to Mobile in 1849 after spending several months traveling throughout the South and writing about his travels in the form of letters to *The Picayune* in New Orleans. These letters were widely copied and attracted much attention. He submitted articles to other newspapers, including the *Mobile Daily Register.* Clark was admitted to the Alabama Bar in 1850 and opened a practice in Mobile. In his early days in Mobile, he accepted the position of editor of *The Southern Magazine.*

In 1852, he took editorial charge of *The Daily Advertiser* in Mobile, when its editor had to take a leave of absence due to illness. It was during this period that Clark proposed his education plan for Mobile. The plan was subsequently adopted and Clark became a member and sometime president of the Board of School Commissioners of Mobile County. He soon bought *The Daily Advertiser* from its owner C. C. Langdon, who had served as mayor of Mobile. When the *Advertiser* and the *Register* became affiliated, he coedited the *Mobile Advertiser and Register* with John Forsyth, another attorney who also practiced journalism. (Forsyth also served as mayor of Mobile and, in 1856, had served as minister to Mexico under President Pierce.)

Clark left the practice of law and headed up several manufacturing enterprises after the Civil War. He also served as a trustee of the University of Alabama both before and after the war. When, in 1884, the Congress of the United States donated 46,000 acres of public land to the University, Clark was made chairman of the committee of three appointed for the management of the land. In 1888, he prepared, on request of the federal commissioner of education, a monograph on *The History of Education in Alabama*, which was published by the United States Bureau of Education in 1889. He also was a member of the State Democratic Executive Committee. In the spring of 1885, he was appointed by President Cleveland as collector of the Port of Mobile and served during the Cleveland administration. Clark was author of chapters on "Progress of Education" and "State Industrial Interests," in the *Memorial Record of Alabama* (1893). He was made an honorary vice president of the Alabama Historical Society because of his historical writings.

tration forced cuts in education and premature closing of schools during Governor Robert Lindsay's administration because of the financial crisis that resulted. In 1881, during Governor Rufus Cobb's administration, the Tuskegee Normal and Industrial School (later known as Tuskegee Institute) was established, with a student body of twenty-five. During Governor Edward O'Neal's governorship, state normal schools for the training of white teachers opened in Jacksonville and Livingston. The number of elementary and secondary public schools increased, yet in 1883 the total state budget for education was $130,000. Governor Thomas Seay, in 1886, publicly endorsed the Blair Education Bill, a controversial proposal in the U.S. Congress to grant federal funds for education on the basis of the illiteracy rates within the states. (Alabama's well-known and highly regarded senator, John T. Morgan, opposed the proposal because he feared that it was the first step towards federal control of education). Seay further supported an appropriation "to introduce technical teaching of agriculture at the State Agricultural and Mechanical College (Auburn)"; urged the founding of a black school for the deaf, which the legislature approved in 1891; and oversaw the establishment of the Normal School at Troy (Troy State University) and the Normal School for Colored Students in Montgomery (Alabama State University).

Governor Thomas G. Jones opposed a bill passed by the legislature in 1891, which allowed local officials to arbitrarily apportion school funds among schools, effectively allowing them to channel their small education budgets to white schools in greater amounts than to black schools. Although education generally was underfunded in the state, education for blacks began to fall further and further behind after passage of the 1891 act.

The late nineteenth century governors of Alabama whose administrations saw the creation of a dual public school system and the establishment of several public colleges and universities, both black and white, were all attorneys trying to administer government during a period of political upheaval, social chaos, and financial restraint. Their involvement came about primarily because of their political position. Several other prominent attorneys were involved in education for other reasons.

Jabez Lamar Monroe (J. L. M.) Curry, born in 1825 in Georgia, came to Alabama in 1837, and received his legal education from the Dane Law School of Harvard University in 1845. He read law for a short time in Talladega with Samuel F. Rice and served in the state legislature, representing Talladega County during the 1850s, and showed a particular interest in legislation dealing with education. He was elected to the U.S. Congress in 1857 and 1859, resigning in 1861 to return to the Confederacy, where he served in its congress for two years, before serving as a lieutenant colonel in the 5th Alabama Cavalry regiment until war's end. After the war, he was elected presiding officer of the Alabama Baptist Convention and also served as president of Howard College, then at Marion, Alabama, until 1868. Thereafter, he taught at Richmond College in Virginia for several years, as an English professor and later as a professor of philosophy. He also lectured on constitutional and international law.

In 1881, Curry was elected general agent of the Peabody Fund,[4] an important private charitable fund which had been established in 1867 by George Peabody,

Under the leadership of a former slave, Booker T. Washington, Tuskegee Institute emphasized the teaching of practical skills in addition to academics. This photograph from the early twentieth century shows a carpentry class.

Jabez Lamar Monroe Curry was an attorney and educational reformer. As general agent for the Peabody Fund, he travelled widely, promoting the idea of free public education. In 1903, he was honored with a statue in the U.S. Capitol.

a wealthy Boston merchant and financier, to be used "for the promotion and encouragement of intellectual, moral, and industrial education among the young of the more destitute portions of the Southern and Southeastern States of our Union." The fund became well known during its time as an alternative source of funds to support public education. The Peabody Board of Trustees was composed of prominent men from the North and South, with the former always being in the majority. Attorney and judge Henderson M. Somerville (founder of the law school at the University of Alabama) was the only Alabamian to serve on the Peabody Board of Trustees. He served from 1889 until the fund was dissolved in 1914. The trust funds, although coming from a private source, were used to promote free public education and the establishment of teacher training schools. Cities and towns were offered financial aid if they would raise local money to fund schools which were free and open to all students. Alabama received a total of $79,200 from the Peabody Fund to support and encourage the establishment of public schools and normal schools during the life of the fund.

As the fund's agent, Curry traveled extensively and wrote copiously for newspapers and magazines promoting public education and the ideal that the states owed a free public education to the children of its citizens. This principle helped overcome the notion that education was a private concern and that public schools were primarily charitable institutions aimed at the poor. This indirect philosophical "aid" from the Peabody Fund was perhaps even more substantial in promoting the cause of public education than the actual funds expended. Because of his efforts on behalf of education, Dr. Curry was designated as one of Alabama's representatives in Statuary Hall in the U.S. Capitol in Washington by legislative action in 1903, the year of his death.

Another Alabama attorney, Nathaniel Henry Rhodes (N. H. R.) Dawson,[5] who served as Alabama State Bar president in 1884 and practiced law for many years in Selma, while also serving in various political positions, including chairman of the Democratic Executive Committee from 1884 to 1886, was appointed in 1886 as United States Commissioner of Education during the administration of President Grover Cleveland. His tenure in this position was marked by the production of a series of historical studies, including one in 1887 entitled "Contributions to American Educational History, No. 1" (a history of the College of William and Mary), followed shortly thereafter by both *The Study of History in American Colleges and Universities,* and *Thomas Jefferson and the University of Virginia.* In recognition of his contributions to education and its history during this period of service, he was awarded the degree of doctor of letters by Columbia College. Another contribution he made during his tenure as commissioner was his promotion of the establishment of a public school system in the Territory of Alaska, to which he traveled during the summer of 1887. He took copious notes on all that he saw and then commented fully in the press and in subsequent writings about the forests, the animals, and the great mineral richness of the territory. He even speculated about the future of Alaska as a tourist attraction.

Attorney Hugh Shepperd Darby (H. S. D.) Mallory, an early president of the Alabama State Bar Association (1907-1908), was also very involved in educational matters, serving at different times as a member of the

Selma city board of education; as president of the board of trustees of the Dallas Male and Female Academy; as a member of the board of trustees of the Alabama Girls' Technical Institute; as a member of the board of trustees of the state normal school in Montgomery (now Alabama State University); and as a trustee of the Southern Baptist Theological Seminary. He also served as Selma's mayor and as president of the Alabama State Baptist Convention and the Alabama State Sunday School Association. In 1910, he was an unsuccessful candidate for governor against Emmet O'Neal. In 1911, Howard College conferred upon him the honorary degree of doctor of laws.

John Martin McKleroy, who practiced law in Eufaula for many years, was elected state superintendent of public instruction in 1874, serving for one term. He was an unsuccessful candidate for governor in both 1882 and 1886.

Charles S. McDowell, Jr., of Barbour County, who was admitted to the bar in 1896, served as superintendent of education in Barbour County from 1897 to 1906, then became mayor of Eufaula in 1908. He was a member of the State Democratic Executive Committee from 1898 to 1900, served as a trustee of the Alabama normal schools from 1911 to 1917, and served as a trustee of Auburn University. He was president of the Alabama State Bar Association from 1915 to 1916.

John William Abercrombie graduated from Oxford College, Oxford, Alabama with a bachelor of arts degree, in 1886 and from the University of Alabama, with a bachelor of laws degree in 1888. Thereafter, he was continuously interested in educational matters, serving as president of Ashland College (1886-1887); as principal of Cleburne Institute (1888-1889); as president of Bowdon College, Georgia (1890-1891); as superintendent of public schools in Anniston (1891-1897); and as president of Anniston College for Young Ladies (1897-1898). He also served as mayor of Edwardsville from 1889 to 1890; was a member of the state senate from Calhoun and Cleburne counties from 1896 to 1897 and 1898 to 1899; and was elected State Superintendent of Education in 1898, serving until 1902, when he became president of the University of Alabama, serving until 1911. In 1906, under his direction, the University celebrated its seventy-fifth anniversary. In 1912, he was elected at large to Congress and served until 1917. He served on the Alabama Textbook Commission; was chairman of the Alabama Rhodes Scholarship Selection Committee; was organizer and president of the Alabama Association of Colleges; and served on a multitude of other education-oriented bodies. He also acted as solicitor of the U.S. Department of Labor under President Woodrow Wilson.

John William Abercrombie earned a law degree at the University of Alabama, but spent most of his career in higher education, eventually serving as president of the University of Alabama. In 1912, he was elected to Congress, serving until 1917.

Attorney Richard Channing Jones practiced both before and after the Civil War at Camden, serving as a brigadier general of the state militia from 1876 until 1890. From 1882 to 1886, he was a member of the state senate. In 1890, he was appointed by the University of Alabama Board of Trustees to serve as president of the University upon the death of Henry D. Clayton, Sr., who died in office. Jones served as president for seven years, during which time he was also professor of international and constitutional law. In 1896, he served as president of the Alabama State Bar Association.

Henderson M. Somerville of Tuscaloosa founded the University of Alabama Department of Law in 1873 and was its first chair. He later served as a justice on the Alabama Supreme Court. His son, Ormond Somerville, served as professor of law at the University from 1896

ABOVE: *Henderson M. Somerville founded, and was the first chair of, the University of Alabama Department of Law. He was appointed an associate justice of the Alabama Supreme Court in 1880.* RIGHT: *A law professor at the University of Alabama, Andrew C. Hargrove served as president of the Alabama State Bar Association from 1892 to 1893.*

to 1909, and then also served as a justice of the Alabama Supreme Court, being elected in 1910 and in 1916. John Mason Martin, who served in both the state legislature and the U.S. Congress during his years of practice, also served as a professor of equity jurisprudence at the University of Alabama from 1875 until 1886. Burwell Boykin Lewis, who served as a state at-large congressman in the 1870s, resigned from Congress before his last term ended to accept the presidency of the University of Alabama and to teach constitutional and international law until his death in 1885. His law partner, Andrew C. Hargrove (president of the Alabama State Bar Association from 1892 to 1893) was a law professor at the University from 1888 until 1895. William S. Thorington, who had earlier practiced law in Montgomery with Walter L. Bragg and John T. Morgan, among others, served as dean of the law department at the University of Alabama from 1897 until 1915, serving as president of the Alabama State Bar Association from 1908 to 1909.

Hannis Taylor[6] was born in 1851 in North Carolina and attended college at the University of North Carolina at Chapel Hill before family financial reverses ended his formal education after only one year. At the age of 17, he began the study of law with an attorney in his hometown. In 1869, he left his family and moved to Mobile where he continued his legal studies in the office of Anderson and Bond. He was admitted to practice law in 1872 and gained admission to the U.S. Supreme Court bar in 1885. Even without university training and by private instruction in law, he achieved a reputation throughout the world as one of the most eminent authorities on constitutional history and constitutional law of his day. He began early in his career writing and lecturing on his ideas about American foreign policy, especially as it pertained to the United States's role in Cuba's efforts to free itself from Spanish rule and on ideas of American expansionism generally. He authored such works as *The Origin and Growth of the English Constitution, A Treatise on International Public Law, The Science of Jurisprudence,* and *The Jurisdiction and Procedure of the Supreme Court of the United States.* In 1892, he

became a professor of constitutional and institutional law at what is today George Washington University. He served as minister to Spain during President Grover Cleveland's administration, from 1893 until 1897, during the period that led up to the Spanish-American War. He maintained an active correspondence with other international law scholars and also with political leaders of his time. He received honorary degrees of doctor of laws from seven universities, including Dublin and Edinburgh. He also served as president of the Alabama State Bar Association from 1890 to 1891.

John Little Smith, president of the Alabama State Bar Association from 1880 to 1881, was born in 1822 in North Carolina and came to Alabama at the age of fifteen. He received both undergraduate and master's degrees from the University of Alabama and attended Harvard Law School before being admitted to practice law in 1849. He set up his practice in Sumter and adjoining counties and practiced for almost four years. Then, in 1852, he went to France to study international law at L'Academie de Droit at Paris, from which he graduated in 1854. He then continued his legal studies at the University of Paris until 1857, when he was graduated and received the diploma "de Licencie en Droit," an honor never previously conferred upon an American. In 1858, he returned to the United States and was admitted to the bar of the U.S. Supreme Court. He then returned to Alabama and established a law practice in Mobile. Although not an educator, he certainly was an unusually committed student of the law.

ABOVE: *Mobile attorney Hannis Taylor, despite the lack of a formal education, became a law professor, author, and diplomat, serving as minister to Spain under President Grover Cleveland.* LEFT: *William S. Thorington was the first dean of the University of Alabama Department of Law. He was president of the Alabama State Bar Association from 1908 to 1909.*

Thomas McAdory Owen was a lawyer, historian, and founder and director of the Alabama Department of Archives and History. He authored *History of Alabama and Dictionary of Alabama Biography*, published in four volumes in 1921. He was born outside Bessemer near Jonesboro in Jefferson County in December 1866, and received bachelor of arts and bachelor of laws degrees from the University of Alabama. He practiced law in Bessemer from 1887 to 1894, in Carrollton, from 1897 to 1900, and in Birmingham, from 1900 to 1901. Because of his

Attorney Thomas McAdory Owen was the founder and first director of the Alabama Department of Archives and History, the first state-funded entity of its kind. After his death, his work was carried on by his wife, Marie Bankhead Owen.

efforts, the Department of Archives and History was established by legislative act on February 27, 1901, being the first recognition by a state of the principle of public support of archive preservation and history work through a department of the state designated for that purpose. He was named its first director and continued in that position until his death in 1920, whereupon the Board of Trustees elected his wife, Marie Bankhead Owen, to continue as director of the department. Owen was active in founding or supporting historical organizations of all sorts, including, among others, the Southern History Association, the Alabama Historical Society, the Bartram Natural History Society of Alabama, the Mississippi Valley Historical Society, the Confederate History Club of Montgomery, and the Alabama Conference Historical Society (Methodist). He was a charter member of the Iberville Historical Society in Mobile, as well as being active in several national historical organizations.

Hilary Herbert[7] was born in South Carolina, came to Alabama in 1852 to attend the University of Alabama, and read law under the supervision of Judge J. K. Henry at Greenville. He was admitted to practice law in Alabama in 1856 and began practice in 1857, but it was soon interrupted by service in the Confederate army. After the war, he practiced law in Montgomery and worked diligently to regain political control for the Democratic Party. In 1877, he was elected to Congress from the second district and remained a congressman until 1893. His service on the Committee on Naval Affairs, which he served as chairman through three congressional sessions, culminated in his being named secretary of the navy by President Grover Cleveland in 1893. Twenty-two ships were commissioned while he was secretary, all having been authorized during his service on the committee.

Herbert is considered by some contemporary historians as a leading apologist of the "Redeemer" or "Bourbon" regimes of the post-Reconstructionist South. This reputation rests, for the most part, on his books, *Why the Solid South?* (1890) and *The Abolition Crusade and Its Consequences* (1912) in which he proposed a theory of history which made the South the defender of the Constitution, which had been corrupted by the conduct of the North. In Herbert's writings, though, the country had passed through a period of sectional reconciliation and was at the point of a reestablished constitutional union of coequal states more perfect than at any time since the adoption of the U.S. Constitution. But he named threats to this perfection, including the racial situation that had been created by Reconstruction. He defended the South's efforts to defeat racial equality by arguing that Negroes were naturally inferior to whites. In developing his case, he used Edmund Burke's theory of an ethnic "natural aristocracy" of color which elevated and ennobled whites and fitted them to rule. Furthermore, he argued that God willed a structured society in which Negroes were fixed in the present, as in the past, in the lowest class, with whites having paternalistic dominion over them. He acknowledged his conservatism and his belief in "the old ways" of strict constitutionalism, sectionalism tempered with reconciliation, and race paternalism as the answer to racial problems in the South. His writings helped frame the mindset of Alabamians as the state entered the twentieth century.

Another attorney who greatly influenced Southern history contemporary to the post-Civil War period and thereafter was Alabama Senator John Tyler Morgan.[8] His ideas regarding race relations influenced the conduct of the state toward its black citizens well into the 1960s. After Reconstruction ended, the attention of the federal government shifted to matters other than race issues, until 1889, with the election of Republican president Benjamin Harrison together with a Republican-dominated Congress, which returned national political attention to what was alternately called the "Negro question," the "Southern question," or the "race problem." The Republicans hoped to reinstate full suffrage rights for black southerners by passing a strong federal elections law, which had been proposed by Massachusetts congressman Henry Cabot Lodge. Southern Democrats wanted to avert Northern intrusion into matters that Southerners felt were not their concern. John Tyler Morgan was a leader among the Southern forces. His congressional speeches and published writings reveal his leadership in forging the ideology of white supremacy that dominated American race relations from the 1890s to the 1960s. Morgan "emerged as the most prominent and notorious racist ideologue of his day, a man who, as much as any other individual, set the tone for the coming Jim Crow era."[9] Morgan, who was first elected to the Senate in 1876, soon distinguished himself by his hard work, long hours, and extensive knowledge of the public issues of the day. He rose to prominence as a leading Democrat and, more importantly, as an adamant defender of the South. He defended the Southern cause and its philosophy throughout his tenure on Capitol Hill. Primary among these rights, he maintained, was the right of states to establish their own racial mores and laws. By 1890, he was "one of the most virulent race ideologues of his generation, a man extraordinary in his ability to articulate what the masses of white southerners were thinking." He capitalized on every opportunity to promote and justify white supremacy in his native region. "Although he has received little recognition as an important historical figure outside his home state, his racist oratory and publications garnered a national and even international audience at the time, giving him a degree of influence over the course of American race relations that was greater than that of most of his peers." [10]

Hilary Herbert's views on the superiority of the white race as expressed in his books reflected the philosophy of the Bourbon Democrats. An eleven-term congressman, he was appointed secretary of the navy by President Grover Cleveland in 1893.

In response to the proposed Federal Election Bill, which mandated federal monitoring of Southern elections, Morgan proposed the adoption of literacy tests for voting instead. This idea gained favor, and Mississippi soon introduced literacy testing, resulting in approximately 90 percent of the state's black voters and 50 percent of its white voters being disenfranchised. Morgan's later role in the 1901 constitutional revision in Alabama would bring a similar result to his own state. Morgan also led a debate on the floor of the Senate that served the same purpose as a filibuster, keeping it going until Democratic forces were able to sway sufficient Republicans to their cause to result in the Republican leadership withdrawing the election bill.

CHAPTER EIGHT

THE 1901 CONSTITUTION: LETTING THE PAST CONTROL THE FUTURE

DURING THE DECADE THAT preceded the end of the century, a movement began across the nation that has been called Progressivism. This movement was contemporary with Populism, but had a broadly reformist aspect. One of the earliest proponents of its tenets in Alabama was attorney Samuel Williamson John, who was born in 1845 in Perry County, son of attorney Joseph Reid John. Sam Will John was admitted to the bar shortly after the Civil War ended and entered upon a career as a lawyer and legislator in Selma and, later, in Birmingham. During the 1890s, he introduced several pieces of humanitarian reform legislation such as a revenue bill designed to shift more of the tax burden from ordinary citizens to railroads and corporations by placing an excise tax on bank deposits and intangible assets. He attempted to lead reform of the convict lease system and of child labor laws. When he saw little accomplished by his legislative efforts, he joined forces with Joseph Forney Johnston in his race to become governor because of Johnston's announced purpose of bringing about progressive reforms.

There was great elation among other reform-minded Democrats, such as attorney Daniel S. Troy and attorney and journalist Chappell Cory, when Johnston won because of their interest in reforming corrupt election practices. Braxton Bragg Comer (an industrialist who would soon become governor himself) supported Johnston because of his desire to see reform of the Railroad Commission by giving it more power to effectively regulate rates. Attorney-legislators William J. Boykin, William W. Brandon (a future

ABOVE: *Jefferson County representative Sam Will John had little success in the state legislature with his attempts to reform the convict lease system and child labor laws.* OPPOSITE PAGE: *From May 21 to September 3, 1901, the Alabama House of Representatives was the scene of Alabama's sixth constitutional convention.*

governor), and Reid Barnes also supported this regulatory effort, although the bill they sponsored was defeated by railroad interests in the House of Representatives.

Lawyer-legislator John J. Mitchell of Lauderdale County hailed Johnston's efforts to equalize tax assessments through the creation of a state tax commission to oversee local tax assessors, authoring the bill establishing the commission and guiding its way through the legislature. Mitchell would serve as chairman of the commission from 1907 to 1911. But efforts to tax the fair market value of the capital stock of corporations, as well as their real and personal property (i.e., a franchise tax), was defeated, when Edward L. Russell, attorney-president of the Mobile and Ohio Railroad and Governor Johnston's friend (and president of the state bar from 1901 to1902) spoke against the provision before the Judiciary Committee. The same fate befell Johnston's financial program in the subsequent session when the governor wanted to increase levies for licenses and fees. This bill was emasculated by the myriad business interests which

The convict leasing system not only saved Alabama the expense of imprisoning convicts, but actually earned the state money. This photograph shows the prison camp at the Pratt Consolidated Coal Company Banner Mine. An explosion at the mine on April 8, 1911, killed 128 miners, of whom 125 were convicts.

would have been affected. In the 1898 session, the House passed a measure that would have placed a tax for the first time on the gross income of corporations, but it was defeated in the Senate. As with the other major thrust for equity—railroad reform—"the Progressive spirit was willing, but the legislature was…weak."[1]

Johnston's tenure as governor demonstrated his persistent effort at reform. Success depended on the power of the interests that would be affected. Business interests were very powerful and those interests favored the status quo that favored them. Thus, where they were concerned, little change occurred.

One demonstration of this fact was Johnston's effort to abolish the convict leasing system, a humanitarian effort

ARIOSTO A. WILEY— TRAINED BY THOMAS G. JONES

ARIOSTO WILEY DIED IN 1908 AT THE AGE OF sixty. He was born in Clayton in Barbour County, to Judge James McCaleb Wiley, who had practiced both as a physician and a lawyer during his career and had been elected to Congress after the Civil War, but was not allowed to take his seat. Ariosto Wiley graduated from the law department of Emory and Henry College, Virginia in 1871 and began the practice of law in Montgomery in 1872, where he later entered into partnership with ex-Chief Justice Samuel Rice and Thomas G. Jones in their successful corporate and railroad practice. He served on the Montgomery city council for 15 years. In 1882, he was elected to the legislature from Montgomery County, and served continuously until his election to Congress in 1900, effectively representing the business interests of his firm's clientele.

He served in the Spanish-American War as a lieutenant colonel, was legal adviser and chief of staff of Henry W. Lawton at Santiago, and assisted General Leonard Wood in the establishment of civil government in the eastern provinces of Cuba. This service brought his name before the constituency of his congressional district, from which he was elected for eight years, until his death in 1908. He was an active legislator, and it is said that his crowning achievement was in securing the enactment of a law for the relief of certain homesteaders in Alabama, who had entered on lands that were part of a land grant to the Mobile, Coosa, and Tennessee Railroad. He saved the homes of "many hundred poor but deserving people." He also introduced a bill conferring upon federal courts jurisdiction concurrent with state courts to apprehend, try, and punish railroad marauders in certain cases.

that threatened both the coal industry and the railroad companies that depended on their freight. Russell M. Cunningham, a state legislator, had been the physician for the Tennessee Coal, Iron and Railroad Company. Joining with Johnston, he convinced the legislature to appoint a joint committee to investigate the deplorable conditions in which convict laborers worked. This committee learned that the death rate for convict miners was four times the rate for free black miners and ten times the rate for free white miners in the same county. They also learned that mine operators were quite happy with the system, especially as a check against strikes. The committee recommended abolition of convict leasing and the institution of a penal system that would pay for itself and yet would aim at reformation rather than the punishment of convicts. Cunningham's proposed bill would have accomplished this goal and he skillfully managed his bill through the Senate, but he was thwarted in the House by attorney-legislator Ariosto A. Wiley, a railroad lawyer, who got his own version of a "reform" bill passed which essentially left the convict leasing system intact. The conference committee appointed to reconcile the two bills accepted the Wiley version. (Wiley had also arranged the defeat of Johnson's revenue bill.)

Governor Thomas Seay became the first prominent Alabamian to propose a constitutional convention in 1890 in response to the perceived threat to the Democratic Party caused by the alignment of the Grange, the Wheel, and the Farmers' Alliance with the Populist Party. As the Democratic traditionalists fought the power of Reuben Kolb and his efforts to dominate the party, they used fraud and corruption at the polls to accomplish their goals, primarily through manipulating the votes of blacks. As the nineties progressed, more and more calls were heard to insure that the "virtuous and the intelligent" controlled political power in Alabama. For most Bourbon Democrats, that meant themselves, and the remedy was disenfranchisement. Their excuse was to protect "white supremacy" but their hidden agenda was to rid themselves of the threat they saw from poor white voters as well.

Most of Alabama's elites saw nothing wrong with black disenfranchisement, a movement that started in Mississippi in the 1890s and was moving throughout the South. Joseph F. Johnston, as Alabama's leading Progressive, saw other reasons for calling a constitutional convention, reasons that traced back to the contents of the 1875 constitution, reasons which compelled action from the reform-minded. Current conditions cried out for authority to levy special local taxes for education, expand the borrowing capacity of municipalities (such as Birmingham, Gadsden, and Anniston, which were having problems funding infrastructure to support their current rapid growth), and to use state funds for internal improvements (such as roads). The continued need for a stronger state railroad commission, abolition of the convict lease system, provisions for statewide primaries, reorganization of the overworked state judicial system, and changes in the tenure and method of choosing various public officials could also be addressed by such a convention. Johnston thought his coalition of Progressives, Populists, former Republicans, and friendly industrialists could accomplish these reforms and bring Alabama out from under the heavy burden of the 1875 constitution, which had been written in a period of postwar trauma that had now passed.

Johnston's desertion by those who feared disenfranchisement of poor whites threatened the enactment of reforms. His loss to John Tyler Morgan in the Senate election of 1900 guaranteed a legislature that would support the call for a convention whose only real goal would be disenfranchisement. Reform was not on the agenda of those who won control: the railroad and corporate interests of north Alabama and the planters of the Black Belt. The choices made would determine whether Alabama would be able to step into a brighter future or would remain in the straitjacket of its tainted past. And things did not work out well for the future.

The Lawyers Who Were Convention Advocates

By 1899, the humanitarian reformers who had earlier advocated for a constitutional convention were no longer in control. Such men as attorneys George L. Comer, John B. Knox, Sydney J. Bowie, and George P. Harrison were the new movement leaders. And who were they? George L. Comer was the brother of Braxton Bragg Comer and a lawyer in Eufaula who had served as its mayor for 12 years. He was division counsel for the Central of Georgia Railway Company, vice president of the Bank of Eufaula, a director of the Eufaula Cotton Mills, owner and proprietor of the New St. Julian Hotel, and had an ownership interest in the Bluff City Mills. He was a deacon in the Baptist Church and had served as president of the Alabama Baptist State Convention, was a Master Mason, an Odd Fellow, a Knight of Pythias, an Elk, a Knight of Honor, and a Democrat.

Attorney Sydney J. Bowie practiced in Talladega before moving to Birmingham, where he joined with Edward H. Cabaniss. In 1901, he was elected to Congress.

John B. Knox was an Anniston attorney who had served as chairman of the State Democratic Executive Committee and had managed Johnston's first gubernatorial campaign. He practiced in the firm of Knox, Acker, Dixon and Sterne that represented railroad and other corporate clients in Calhoun County. He was a Presbyterian, a Knight of Pythias, and an Elk. He was popular among both Black Belt planters and North Alabama industrialists. Sydney Bowie practiced law in Talladega from 1885 to 1899, when he moved to Birmingham and practiced law with Edward H. Cabaniss, representing corporate clients. He was elected to Congress from the fourth congressional district and took his seat in 1901.

George Harrison had ended military service in the Civil War as a brigadier general and entered the legal profession in Opelika shortly thereafter. His practice took him throughout the Black Belt counties. He had been a part of the political movement that "redeemed" the state

Anniston attorney John B. Knox had served as chairman of the State Democratic Executive Committee and campaign manager for Joseph Forney Johnston. When the constitutional convention met in Montgomery in May 1901, he was chosen as president of the convention and chairman of the powerful Rules Committee.

in 1874, serving as a delegate to the 1875 constitutional convention. He had been a member of Congress from the third district in 1894 and 1896 and had served in the Alabama legislature through several terms. He was a mason, serving as chairman on the committee on Masonic jurisprudence, and was twice grand master of the Grand Lodge of Alabama; he was elected major general of the Alabama Division, United Confederate Veterans, four times; and he was a Methodist. He was one of the originators of the Alabama State Bar Association, being vice president in 1884, again from 1897 to 1898, and from 1904 to 1905, before serving as president from 1905 to 1906. Harrison's family was descended from Benjamin Harrison, a signer of the Declaration of Independence.

All of these men were linked to the interests of railroads and industrial corporations as well as being part of the faction known as gold Democrats. They represented interests that many of the people in the state feared (which is one reason that Joe Johnston was able to repeal the first act authorizing a convention). These interests did not want to see change, other than disenfranchisement of those they believed unworthy to vote, and their advocates worked to see that disenfranchisement would be the only result of the convention.

Attorney Alfred M. Tunstall, who practiced law in Greensboro, was a member of the legislature in the late 1890s, and served as speaker pro tem during the session of 1900 to 1901, was instrumental in getting legislation authorizing a convention passed a second and last time. Attorney John V. Smith was chosen to lead the referendum campaign to get voter approval of the convention and to elect delegates. He would become president of the railroad commission in 1901.

Attorney Frank S. White was a speaker at political rallies on behalf of the convention. The *Montgomery Advertiser* issue of March 15, 1901, quoted White as stating the purpose of the convention: "Time has demonstrated that the Negro has no capacity to rule, but a great capacity to ruin. The Negro...was disfranchised years ago by fraud and the purpose now [is] to do it by constitutional enactment." Ironically, it was the vote in the Black Belt that provided a majority in favor of the convention. As stated by historian Malcolm Cook McMillan, "Black Belt counties gave such large majorities for the convention that it is safe to conclude that even on an issue so vital to the Negro as his franchise, the Black Belt leaders could still manipulate the Negro vote."[2]

The Lawyer-Delegates at the 1901 Constitutional Convention

Although no one man controlled the convention, the person in a position to have the most influence was the convention president. John B. Knox was chosen convention president and also was named chairman of the Rules Committee, which allowed him to establish committees and name committee chairmen and members.

The committee that "tower[ed] above all others" was the Suffrage and Elections Committee. Thomas Wilkes Coleman of Greene County was named chairman. Twenty-one of the 25 members of his committee were attorneys, among the most important being: George P. Harrison of Lee County; former governor William C. Oates; future senator Frank S. White; future governor Emmet O'Neal; Gregory Little Smith of Mobile (nephew of 1880-1881 state bar president John Little Smith); James Weatherly (later appointed by Governor O'Neal to serve on the three-member Birmingham City Commission when that form of government was adopted in 1911); and Richard Channing Jones (from Wilcox County, former president of the University of Alabama and president of the state bar from 1895 to 1896, whose family can be traced back to Colonel John Jones, a member of the Virginia House of Burgesses from 1775 to 1776, and to John Paul Jones.) The last three were important railroad and corporate lawyers.

Historians say that those representing the Black Belt and business interests who dominated the committee were interested in disenfranchising Negroes and illiterate and non-propertied whites in order to legally create a conservative electorate which would keep the Bourbon oligarchy in power. These men, considering their lineage and accomplishments, felt comfortable that they and their like were the "virtuous and intelligent" who should control political life in Alabama.

Lawyer-Delegates to the Convention—A Survey

Of the 155 delegates elected to the constitutional convention, 96 were attorneys and it is often referred to as "the lawyer's convention." Who were these lawyers? In his book, *Populism to Progressivism in Alabama*, Sheldon Hackney broke the delegates down into four groups, the Bosses, the Planters, the Progressives, and the Agrarians. From his perspective, the Bosses and Planters controlled the convention and the constitution that the convention produced. The Progressives were those who hoped to accomplish some of the reforms for which Joseph F. Johnston had fought (and who would have more success when Braxton Bragg Comer became governor in 1907), and the Agrarians were the vestiges of the political movement that had been led by Reuben Kolb. Attorneys can be found in each group. Looking at these lawyer-delegates, their families, partners, and circumstances gives us a snapshot of the legal professionals who were guiding the state into the twenty-first century, many of whom would influence its political life for years to come.

The Bosses

David C. Almon was born in 1867 into an extended family of lawyers who have been important members of the profession in northwest Alabama, including Lauderdale, Limestone, Colbert, Franklin, and Lawrence counties, since the arrival of George W. Almon in the early years of statehood. George Almon had seven children, three of them sons who were all lawyers. One of the sons was Edward B. Almon, who served as a legislator, a circuit judge, and a congressman. Another was George C. Almon, a lawyer and probate judge in Franklin County. The third was William M. Almon, father of David C. Almon, the delegate to the 1901 constitution who was also solicitor for the Eighth Judicial Circuit. David Almon's brother, Charles Pomeroy Almon, became a circuit judge for the Eleventh Judicial Circuit and resided in Florence. From this extended family would come Clopper Almon, president of the Alabama State Bar from 1960 to 1961, and

Ninety-six of the 155 delegates to the 1901 convention were attorneys, including Gregory Little Smith, opposite page, who was a member of the Suffrage and Elections Committee.

Reneau Almon, who served on the Alabama Supreme Court in later years.

Cecil Browne read law with Judge John T. Heflin at Talladega, and was admitted to practice there in 1878, serving as a legislator and state senator from Talladega County for many years. He was the chairman of the Taxation Committee at the convention and made the committee's report to the convention. (The committee's recommendation that the 7.5 mills limit on property taxes of the 1875 constitution be reduced to 6.5 mills was adopted by the convention, thereby weakening the state's ability to fund government services.) Cecil's brother, William B. Browne, was a highly regarded lawyer in Columbiana in Shelby County.

John F. Burns, born in Dallas County, studied law in the offices of Thomas Watts and William Lowndes Yancey, and was a veteran, a planter, a justice of the peace, and a legislator. He was a delegate to the 1875 constitutional convention and was involved in local Democratic politics, serving as a delegate to five national Democratic conventions.

Two delegates were members of the Carmichael family, another extended family that has given the state many lawyers, including Archibald Hill Carmichael from Tuscumbia, Colbert County, and his half-brother, Malcolm Smith Carmichael, from Elba, Coffee County, the youngest delegate at the convention. Their father, Jesse Malcolm Carmichael (state auditor, judge, lawyer, and planter) of Ozark, Alabama, had a third son, attorney Charles D. Carmichael, who lived in Geneva, in Dale County, and served as its mayor.

George Hays Carnation, who represented Choctaw County at the convention, practiced law and also farmed. He served as county solicitor from 1880 through 1886 and as county administrator from 1890 to 1904. James Edward Cobb, a delegate from Macon County, practiced in Tuskegee, was a judge from the Ninth Judicial Circuit and in 1886 was elected to Congress, serving for nine years.

Tuskegee attorney James E. Cobb was a Confederate veteran of the Battle of Gettysburg. After the war he was a circuit judge, and served in Congress from 1887 to 1895.

Thomas Coleman, who represented Greene County, was a leading force at the convention as chairman of the Suffrage and Elections Committee. He traced his lineage back to the Scottish branch of Hamiltons which produced Alexander Hamilton. He was a graduate of Princeton, an ex-slaveholder, a veteran, a legislator, and former associate justice of the Alabama Supreme Court. He served in the Greensboro Guards during the Civil War and was the only member to have served as a delegate to the 1865 convention. He was president of the Merchant and Farmers Bank in Eutaw and chairman of the executive committee of the Board of Trustees of the University of Alabama. His son, Ezra Wilson Coleman, practiced law in Jasper, in the firm of Coleman & Sowell. He also served as a delegate to the convention, representing the twelfth senatorial district, and was a stockholder in several coal companies. (His law partner, Thomas Lamar Sowell, would serve as register in chancery, a legislative representative, a solicitor, and a state senator, as well as state auditor from 1900 to 1905, and circuit judge for the Fourteenth Judicial Circuit.)

Joseph Brown Duke of Lafayette in Chambers County served as mayor and register in chancery. He was a vice president of the Alabama State Bar Association from 1899 to 1900 and was a delegate to the convention from Chambers County. John Charles Eyster of Morgan County was register in chancery for Lawrence County for several years, but represented Morgan County at the convention. He founded a law practice in Decatur which continues as Eyster, Key, Tubb, Weaver & Roth, LLP. Two other Eyster family members, Charles H. Eyster, Sr., and Williams B. Eyster, practiced in the firm until late in the twentieth century.

Charles Wesley Ferguson, who represented Jefferson County at the convention, was a solicitor of the Tenth Judicial Circuit and city court judge during his career. He was the younger brother of Frederick Summerfield Ferguson, who was a veteran, a legislator, and an attorney.

John Manly Foster, who represented Tuscaloosa at the convention, was a member of the legislature, a railroad lawyer, and a county solicitor during his career. He was state bar president from 1918 to 1919. His brother, James Henry Foster, was a lawyer who served as superintendent of city schools in Tuscaloosa. His son, Richard Foster, practiced law with his father in Tuscaloosa and later became president of the University of Alabama. Henry Bacon Foster, a member of the extended Foster family, was a county court judge and member of the Alabama legislature from Tuscaloosa. John Arthur Foster, another family member and a delegate to the 1875 convention, was one of the members of the bar who called for the founding of the Alabama State Bar Association. He was from Clayton in Barbour County. His son, John Webb Foster, practiced law in Abbeville in Henry County, serving as register in chancery, county superintendent of education, and as a legislator. (Another family of Fosters, probably not related to the Tuscaloosa Fosters, came from Macon County. One, Wilbur F. Foster, served as president of the state bar from 1887 to 1888, and was also speaker of the Alabama House of Representatives from 1882 to 1883.)

Edward A. Graham from Montgomery was one of four delegates from Montgomery to the 1901 convention, had served as Montgomery's mayor and city attorney (during which period he prepared the city code in 1895), and as a legislator, as well as being vice president of the state bar from 1897 to 1898. Leonidas W. Grant, from Jacksonville in Calhoun County, was a Civil War veteran who surrendered with Robert E. Lee at Appomattox. He was admitted to practice law in 1866. In 1867, he established the *Gadsden Evening Times* and by 1870 owned a one-half interest in the *Jacksonville Republican*. He served in both the Alabama House and Senate and represented the fourth congressional district as delegate to the convention.

George P. Harrison, as chairman of the Committee on Corporations and a member of both the Committee on Suffrage and Elections and the Committee on Taxation, was in a powerful position to influence the constitution. He was an influential legislator and former congressman from the Black Belt. He represented the twenty-seventh senatorial district at the convention.

Two delegates, brothers John T. Heflin and James Thomas Heflin, were members of the extended Heflin family founded in Randolph County by their grandfather Wyatt Heflin, a lawyer and Indian trader, who served in the Alabama legislature in the 1840s. Wyatt was the father of Judge John T. Heflin, who read law in Chambers County in the office of Steiner & Phillips and was admitted to practice in 1841. Heflin practiced law for nearly 50 years, serving as a circuit judge during the Civil War, as a delegate at the 1875 constitutional convention, and practicing in Birmingham after 1882, in the firm Heflin, Bowdon, & Knox. He was a candidate for the Alabama Supreme Court in 1886 and considered himself a Bourbon Democrat of the old school. (Some say that the town of Heflin, Alabama, was named for him.) Another son of Wyatt Heflin was Robert Stell Heflin, also a lawyer, who served as both a representative and a senator in the state legislature, as well as a congressman in the U.S. House of Representatives.

Wyatt Heflin was also the grandfather of Harrington P. Heflin, who read law with his uncle, Judge John T. Heflin, was admitted to the bar in 1887, and practiced law in Birmingham with Colonel W. D. Bulger before becoming a circuit judge. Harrington's brother, John T. Heflin was a lawyer, planter, and merchant who represented the fifth legislative district at the 1901 convention. Another brother, James Thomas Heflin, was an attorney who began practicing law in Lafayette in 1893, and served as its mayor, as Chambers County register-in-chancery, and as a legislator. He was delegate to the 1901 constitutional convention, representing Chambers County, before entering national politics as a congressman and later as a United States senator. Harrington's brother, Howell T. Heflin, was a graduate of the University of Maryland, who practiced as a doctor in Roanoke, and whose later namesake, Howell T. Heflin, would become a lawyer after World War II and serve as president of the Alabama State Bar from 1965 to 1966, as chief justice of the Alabama Supreme Court, and as a United States senator. Currently Senator Heflin's son, H. Thomas Heflin, continues to practice law in Tuscumbia.

Jefferson County delegate Charles Wesley Ferguson studied law at the University of Alabama. In 1903, he was appointed judge to the city court by Governor Jelks.

Evans Hinson, solicitor and general administrator of Lowndes County, represented the county at the convention. Samuel Calhoun Jenkins, convention delegate for the second congressional district, was admitted to practice law in 1894, while he was serving as superintendent of education for Wilcox County. He also represented the county in the legislature from 1896 to 1900.

William Bullock Inge, Jr., represented Hale County at the convention. He was a planter who had been born at "Tishaba" plantation in Greene County. His lineage in Alabama traces back to Richard Inge, Sr., a Revolutionary soldier and planter born in Virginia who immigrated to Alabama, settling in Tuscaloosa County. Richard Inge had two wives, who had seven children each. From these 14 children and their descendants came many planters, physicians, and lawyers. The lawyers included William Marshall Inge (who represented Tennessee in Congress from 1833 to 1835, and later came to Alabama and formed a law partnership with Robert H. Smith in Sumter County); Robert Sturdivant Inge (who served as mayor of Tuscaloosa, then moved to Livingston in Sumter County); Samuel Williams Inge (who practiced law in Eutaw and Livingston, represented Sumter County in the legislature, and was elected to Congress in 1847); William Murphy Inge (brother of Samuel who practiced in Mississippi); Richard Freer Inge (a lawyer and state legislator who practiced in Eutaw with J. D. Webb and Thomas H. Herndon until he fought in the Civil War and died at Chickamauga); Zebulon Montgomery Pike Inge, Jr. (a lawyer and state legislator who studied law at the University of Virginia and practiced in Mobile); and Francis James Inge, Jr. (born in Hale County, practiced law in Mobile, served as president of the state bar from 1934 to 1935, and practiced with his brother, Richard H. Inge. His son Francis H. Inge was state bar president from 1955 to 1956.) In a recent directory of the Alabama State Bar can be found some of the descendants of this great family, including Herndon Inge, Jr. (admitted in 1948); Herndon Inge, III, (admitted in 1974), of Mobile; Samuel Williams Inge, (admitted in 1956), of Fairhope; William Bullock Inge, (admitted in 1959), of Point Clear; and Zebulon M. P. Inge, (admitted in 1974), of Mobile.

Emmet O'Neal was elected governor of Alabama in 1911, the only son of a governor to be elected in his own right. He also served as president of the Alabama State Bar Association.

Richard Channing Jones was born in Virginia and traced his roots to members of the Jones family who served in the Virginia House of Burgesses from 1772 to 1775, and whose relative was John Paul Jones. Jones served on the Committee on Suffrage and Elections and the Committee on Education, and represented the twenty-second senatorial district, which included Wilcox County.

James Thomas Kirk, a delegate from Colbert County, practiced law with E. B. Almon in Tuscumbia during part of his career and was a vice president of the Alabama State Bar from 1901 to 1902. William Washington Kirkland who represented Dale County at the convention, began his law practice in 1891 and served as mayor of Ozark from 1897 until 1899. Tennent Lomax of Montgomery, president of the Auditorium Company of Montgomery and a director of the Capitol City Bank and the People's Cotton Factory, was elected to the convention as a delegate at-large. Before John B. Knox was chosen as president of the convention, Lomax was considered for the position. He had earlier served for ten years on the State Democratic Executive Committee and was chairman of the Committee on the Preamble and Declaration of Rights.

Gordon MacDonald was a Montgomery County delegate to the convention. His father was killed in 1855 by one of his slaves who in turn was burned at the stake by infuriated neighbors. MacDonald was admitted to practice law in 1874. John Thomas Martin represented Calhoun County at the convention. He practiced law in Jacksonville and Anniston and was elected solicitor of the Seventh Judicial Circuit in 1880 and reelected in 1886. Christopher Nesmith, who represented Lamar County, was admitted to the bar in 1894. He had served as deputy solicitor and register in chancery in Lamar County, before moving to Birmingham in 1903 to practice with Jesse Stallings and Judge Zell Gaston.

Emmet O'Neal, son of former Governor Edward O'Neal and a future state bar president as well as future governor of the state, represented the eighth congressional district at the convention. He was a member of the Rules Committee and the Suffrage Committee, and chaired the Committee on Local Legislation, which made a thorough study of the problems that result from excessive local legislation. The committee recommended that the convention follow the lead of 27 states and absolutely prohibit certain enumerated local or private laws. The conservative convention majority failed to follow the committee's recommendation, deeming it an innovation they were unwilling to accept. This failure to provide for even a limited home rule for local government has continued to limit the legislative branch's ability to govern efficiently and has placed too much power in the hands of each locality's legislative delegation, who often have little contact with or knowledge of local governments' needs.

Henry Opp, who represented Covington County at the convention, served as county solicitor and also as mayor of Andalusia. George Henderson Parker, who represented Cullman County, was admitted to practice law in 1875 and was in the banking business. He had been Cullman's mayor from 1889 to 1897. At the convention he chaired the Committee on State and County Boundaries and was a member of the Committee on Suffrage and Elections. John Franklin Proctor, who was born in Scottsboro and represented Jackson Country at the convention, received his law degree in 1893. He served as assistant clerk of the Alabama House of Representatives from 1892 to 1895 and as secretary of the Senate from 1896 to 1899. He was serving as solicitor for Jackson County at the time of the convention.

Henry Fontaine Reese represented Dallas County as one of its three delegates and served on the committees on education, legislative department, and state and county boundaries. James Oscar Sentell represented Crenshaw County. He taught school and was in the mercantile business before becoming a lawyer in 1892. He was elected the first mayor of Luverne in 1889, being reelected in 1892 and 1897, and was a legislator at the time of the convention. James Harvey Stewart represented Perry Country at the convention and was a member of the Suffrage Committee. He fought in the Civil War and, after the war, was admitted to practice law in 1866. He joined the firm Christian, Lovelace and Stewart in Uniontown, before serving as probate judge for several years.

Watkins Mabry Vaughan, who represented the fourth legislative district at the convention and was a member of the committees on militia and local legislation, came from Dallas County, was admitted to practice law at Selma in 1895, and was a member of the legislature from 1898 to 1899. He was elected recorder of the police court at Selma in 1907 and was reelected for three terms. He wrote *Vaughan's Complete Alabama Form Book*, published in 1902. Boswell deGraffenreid Waddell, who represented Russell County at the convention, was admitted to the bar in 1887 and practiced at Seale. He served in the legislature from 1902 to 1903.

James M. Weatherly, who represented Jefferson County at the convention, was a highly regarded railroad and corporate lawyer, admitted to practice law in 1879. He first practiced in Montgomery in the firm of Clopton, Herbert & Chambers, then moved to Birmingham in 1882 and practiced with H. A. Sharpe until 1885, when Sharpe became a judge. Thereafter, he practiced in the firm of Weatherly, Underwood and Thach, where he represented Southern Railway, Southern Bell Telephone & Telegraph Company, and Maryland Casualty Company among other corporate clients. Later, during the administration of Emmett O'Neal, he was appointed one of the first commissioners when Birmingham adopted the commission form of government in 1911.

James M. Weatherly served with Emmet O'Neal on the Suffrage and Elections Committee. As governor, O'Neal appointed Weatherly to the newly created Birmingham City Commission.

Pickens County delegate Elbert Decatur Willett, Jr., of Carrollton was the son of Elbert Decatur Willett, an attorney who came to Alabama from Tennessee in 1854 and who was a delegate to the 1875 constitutional convention. There were two other sons who were attorneys: Joseph Jackson Willett, who served as president of the Alabama State Bar Association from 1899 to 1900, and Archibald M. Willett, who got his law degree from Georgetown University in 1895 and practiced at Carrollton. Delegate Elbert Decatur Willett, Jr., practiced with his brother J. J. Willett in Anniston for a few years, but returned to Carrollton and practiced with another brother A. M. Willett after 1897. He was a member of the state legislature and editor of the *West Alabamian*, a weekly newspaper published at Carrollton from 1898 to 1901.

Arthur Ellis Williams, who represented Elmore County at the convention, was a lawyer and planter who was admitted to practice law in 1891 at Wetumpka. He served as city clerk from 1891 to 1894, and as a member of the Wetumpka City Council in 1894. He edited the *Times Democrat* at Wetumpka in 1890. Gesner Williams represented Marengo County at the convention. He began his law practice at Demopolis in 1891 and served the town as mayor from 1895 to 1897 and city attorney from 1899 to 1901. Jeremiah Norman Williams represented the second legislative district, which included his home county of Barbour, at the convention. A veteran of the Civil War, he was elected to Congress in 1874 and reelected in 1876. In 1893, he was appointed chancellor. His son, Judge Sterling Williams, read law with his father, served as mayor of Clayton for nine years, and became a circuit judge in 1915.

Massey Wilson who represented Clarke County at the convention, was engrossing clerk of the Alabama House of Representatives from 1890 to 1891, clerk of the house from 1892 to 1898, a legislator in 1900, and in 1902 was elected attorney general.

The Planters

William A. Altman was a planter and merchant who represented Sumter County at the convention. He was not a lawyer, but his brother was John Jasper Altman, who was a lawyer. John J. graduated from the University of Virginia Law School in 1871 and migrated to Birmingham in 1886 and practiced there with William D. Bulger (whose brother was a delegate to the convention as well) and, later, with his son, John W. Altman. John J. became an alderman, a legislator, and a chancellor.

David Bethune represented the twenty-sixth senatorial district, including his home county of Bullock, at the convention. He was a Civil War veteran, practiced at Union Springs, and served as a state senator. Thomas Lafayette Bulger, a delegate to the convention from Tallapoosa County, was the son of Michael Jefferson Bulger, a Black Belt planter who was elevated to brigadier general during the Civil War. Thomas Bulger was educated at Roanoke College in Virginia and attended West Point, but did not graduate from there. He entered law practice at Dadeville in 1877, and served in both the House and Senate. His brother, William Douglas Bulger, was a veteran who practiced both in Dadeville and in Birmingham, where he was in practice with John T. Heflin, John J. Altman, and Harrington Heflin.

Reuben Chapman, who represented Sumter County at the convention, was the son of Judge Samuel Chapman, the brother of ex-Governor Reuben Chapman (1847-1849). Chapman was a veteran, but fought only one year due to ill health. He was admitted to practice law in 1856, and practiced in Livingston, where his father had been appointed circuit judge, and also served as mayor of Livingston from 1887 to 1892. He was also county solicitor and a member of the legislature, from 1900 to 1901.

At the convention, Thomas L. Bulger introduced a measure calling for segregated elementary schools, with black schools funded only by black taxes. The measure was defeated.

Benjamin Hogan Craig, who represented Dallas County at the convention, was one of three attorney sons of James D. Craig, an attorney who had come to Alabama shortly after statehood. James Craig had served as probate judge and mayor of Cahaba for several years, practiced in Selma, and ultimately moved to San Francisco, as did his attorney son, William Craig. Benjamin Craig studied law at Cahaba in the firm of Gayle and Williams, being admitted to practice in 1857. He was a Civil War veteran and moved to Selma after the war, where he served as register in chancery from 1863 to 1898, being a Democrat retained in office even during the Radical Reconstruction period. After 1887, he also practiced with his brother, George Henry Craig. George served as a circuit judge in Selma before being elected to Congress from the fourth district in 1882 as a Republican, although he was not able to take his seat until two years after the election because his election was contested. He was appointed U.S. attorney for northern and middle Alabama by President Chester Arthur. Both brothers had sons who also became lawyers. George Craig's son, William Benjamin, practiced with his father's firm of Craig and Craig and ultimately was elected as a member of Congress himself.

Thomas Marion Espy, who represented Henry County at the convention, was admitted to the bar in 1885 and practiced in Dothan. His brother was John Jolly Espy, who was admitted to practice in 1899, then practiced at Dothan and at Headland, where he engaged in the mercantile banking, livestock, agriculture, and fertilizer businesses. He served as mayor of Headland and as a legislator. Algernon Sydney Fletcher, another Civil War veteran, represented Madison County. He was admitted to practice law in 1858, served as an alderman and councilman for Huntsville for 15 years, and was in the legislature off and on over several years. He was a member of the Municipal Corporations Committee and chaired the Committee on Banks and Banking. Augustus Clayton Howze represented the ninth legislative district, which included Jefferson County. He fought in the Civil War, graduated from the University of Georgia, and studied law in the law office of Governor Andrew B. Moore in Marion. He practiced law in Marion and Birmingham, and served as a probate judge in Perry County and as a special criminal judge in Birmingham.

James McLean Jones was born in Greensboro, Hale County, in 1872, got his law degree from the University of Alabama, and began practicing in Greensboro in 1892. He represented Hale County at the convention and also served as chairman of the Hale County Democratic Executive Committee. Norvelle Robertson Leigh, Jr., represented Escambia County at the convention. He obtained his law degree at the University of Alabama. His brother, John David Leigh, served as county chairman of the Democratic Executive Committee for 24 years, was solicitor for 14 years, and served as circuit judge for the Twenty-first Judicial Circuit, composed of Monroe, Conecuh, Escambia, and Baldwin counties.

Augustus C. Howze, a Civil War veteran, practiced in Perry County, where he was a probate judge, and in Birmingham, where he was a special criminal judge.

William Thomas Lowe of Lawrence County began practicing at Moulton in 1887 after reading law with Judge W. P. Chitwood there. He served as a legislator after the convention. Allen Hunter Merrill was the son of lawyer Allen Kent Merrill and had a lawyer son named Allen Kent Merrill. Allen Hunter Merrill was a Civil War veteran, studied law in the offices of U.S. Senator James L. Pugh, and was admitted to the bar in 1869. He was president of the East Alabama National Bank of Eufaula, and served as a legislator, and as a member of both the Barbour County Democratic Executive Committee and the State Democratic Executive Committee. His son also represented Barbour County in the state legislature.

Joseph Neeley Miller who represented Wilcox County at the convention read law under General Edmund Pettus of Selma and Judge S. C. Cochran of Camden and was admitted to practice in 1873. He was the older brother of Benjamin Meek Miller, who would serve as governor in the 1930s, and was United States district attorney for the southern district from 1893 to 1897. John Henry Parker was born in 1853 in Elmore County. He read law with Oliver & Garrett in Dadeville, and was admitted to practice in 1877. He practiced in Rockford, Coosa County, and founded and edited the Rockford *Enterprise* newspaper from 1879 through 1888. He served as state senator for the eighteenth senatorial district in 1892, then moved to Wetumpka and practiced there, serving as delegate from the fifteenth senatorial district at the 1901 convention.

Erle Pettus represented Limestone County at the convention. He attended the University of Alabama, where he was editor-in-chief of *The Crimson White* and a debater. He attended both Cumberland Law School (in Lebanon, Tennessee) and the University of Alabama School of Law, graduating in 1899. He served as a legislator from 1898 through 1901, and introduced a resolution that passed, favoring the direct election of U.S. senators. He also authored the first primary election law ever placed on the Alabama statute books. In 1906, he moved to Birmingham and practiced with Zell Gaston.

Phillip Henry Pitts was born in Uniontown, Perry County, served in the Civil War, was admitted to the bar in 1874, and practiced in Uniontown with Colonel J. W. Bush. He served as solicitor of Perry County for 14 years, before moving to Selma, where he practiced with the firm of Dawson and Pitts. He served as a member of the legislature from 1896 to 1897, and was chairman of the Committee on Representation at the 1901 convention, representing the thirtieth senatorial district. He served as probate judge in Dallas County until his death. His younger brother, Alexander, also trained as an attorney and moved to Selma in 1893 to practice for a time with his brother, in the firm of Pitts & Pitts.

James Jefferson Robinson represented the ninth senatorial district at the convention, which included his home county of Chambers. He was a Civil War veteran, suffering the amputation of his right arm at the battle of Chancellorsville. He was admitted to practice in 1865 and served as a legislator from 1872 through 1882, when he became probate judge for Chambers County in 1883 and served through 1892. Thereafter he practiced in the firm of Robinson and Duke.

William Hodges Samford was the son of William James Samford, who was governor for six months in 1901 (dying on June 11, 1901). He attended what would become Auburn University for two years, withdrawing because of ill health. He worked as a civil engineer for a few years before studying law with his father. He was admitted to the bar in 1894 and practiced in Troy, Alabama with A. B. Foster and J. S. Carroll until 1909. He served as solicitor of Pike County, and later as city attorney of Troy. At the 1901 convention, he represented the twenty-sixth senatorial district and served on the committees on the judiciary and executive departments. William Hodges was the grandson of William Flewellen Samford, an attorney who greatly influenced political thinking in Alabama during the 1850s as a writer and editorialist, promoting secession in conjunction with William Lowndes Yancey and called by at least one historian "penman of Southern Rights."[3] He also wrote articles about Reconstruction that were published in the North after the end of the war, and were said to present "the most reliable data of that period." William H. also had a brother, Thomas Drake, who was an attorney who served as a U.S. district attorney after having practiced with his father and having served as his private secretary while he was governor. Both William Hodges and Thomas Drake had sons who became attorneys, creating an extended family with multiple generations of lawyers, many of whom have given significant service to the state.

William J. Samford was governor of Alabama when the convention began, dying in office on June 11, 1901, while his son, William H. Samford, was serving as a delegate.

William Thomas Sanders, representing the first senatorial district, was from Athens in Limestone County. He was admitted to practice law in 1889. He served on the committees on local legislation and militia at the convention and would later serve on the Railroad Commission from 1903 to 1907.

John William Augustine (J. W. A.) Sanford represented Montgomery County at the convention. Originally from Georgia, he was admitted to the bar in 1852 and moved to Montgomery to practice. He was a Civil War veteran and a Democrat who supported Breckenridge in the 1860 election. After the war, he was elected attorney general of Alabama, but was forced to resign at the beginning of Radical Reconstruction. He wrote a letter of protest to General Meade, the commander of the military district, asserting the right of Alabama to establish a government for itself. This letter was widely published and inspired his election as attorney general again in 1870, in which office he remained until 1878, when he declined further nomination. Thereafter, he became clerk of the Alabama Supreme Court until 1892. As a member of the tax committee, he argued for reducing the limit of taxation of property, stating, "The more you limit power, the more you expand liberty; the more you curtail authority, the better it is for freedom, and therefore, I am for limiting the Legislature in its power of taxation to the utmost point that can safely be done." (*Official Proceedings II,* 1359.) This quote expresses well the underlying attitude toward government of those in power in Alabama throughout the period that followed Reconstruction.

Gregory Little Smith of Mobile, who represented the thirty-third senatorial district as its delegate to the convention, was the nephew of John Little Smith, an early president of the Alabama state bar. The Smith family was another extended family of lawyers. Gregory's father, Robert Hardy Smith, had three sons who were attorneys, including Richard Inge Smith, who served as an officer in the Civil War, and Harry T. Smith, who practiced law with his brother, Gregory, in Mobile. John Little Smith's son, Thomas Herndon Smith, served Mobile as a legislator and as a chancellor. Gregory joined the bar in 1875 and practiced with his brothers. In 1878, he was appointed chief attorney for the Mobile and Montgomery Railway Company, which was absorbed by the L&N Railroad. Thereafter, he was an important corporate attorney, representing major banks and other significant corporations. At the convention he chaired the Judiciary Committee and the Committee on Credentials.

Malcolm Alexander Smith represented Autauga County at the convention and was a Civil War veteran who studied law with W. H. Northington of Prattville. He was mayor of Prattville for three terms and state legislator and state senator during the 1880s and 1890s. Michael Sollie of Dale County represented the third senatorial district. He was a lawyer, circuit judge, and farmer, who practiced law in Eufaula, Abbeville, and Ozark. Robert E. Spragins, who began practice in Huntsville in 1883, represented Madison County. At the convention, he served on the militia, and order, consistency, and harmony committees. After 1901, he served several terms in the legislature.

William Henry Tayloe of Uniontown represented Perry County at the convention. He attended Washington & Lee University during the period that Robert E. Lee was president, and practiced in Demopolis, Linden, and finally Uniontown. He was a state senator from 1886 to 1890, served as an equity court chancellor from 1898 to 1903, and was a vice president of the state bar from 1897 to 1898.

Richard Wilde Walker, Jr., of Madison County, was the grandson of John Williams Walker, Alabama's second United States senator. His father was a judge on the Alabama Supreme Court, as well as a senator in the senate of the Confederacy. Walker, Jr., also served as an associate justice of the Alabama Supreme Court. He practiced outside the state, but returned to Alabama to practice in Huntsville. He became presiding judge of the Alabama Court of Appeals from 1911 (when it was created) to 1914, and then became U.S. circuit judge for the Fifth Judicial Circuit.

The Progressives

John Thomas Ashcraft, born in 1859, represented Lauderdale County, where he had practiced law since 1889, serving as alderman of Florence for two terms and as secretary of the Board of Education. He served as president of the board of Florence University for Women and was a member of the Board of Trustees of Howard College. He was a strong supporter of prohibition.

Charles Peter Beddow, who represented Jefferson County at the convention, was born in Tennessee and was admitted to the Tennessee Bar in 1881. He came to Alabama in 1890 after serving as superintendent of various Tennessee coal companies. In Birmingham, he was superintendent of the Sloss Iron and Steel Company in Coalburg. In 1895, Beddow began practicing law in the firm of Bowman, Harsh & Beddow. He was recognized as a spokesman for Birmingham labor when he proposed an amendment which would have eliminated the convict labor system. This amendment was tabled by a voice vote. Beddow was vice president of the state bar from 1916 to 1917 and from 1922 to 1923. He was the father of Roderick Beddow, a celebrated criminal lawyer and state bar president from 1944 to 1945.

Charles P. Beddow began his legal career in the coal industry, coming to Alabama in 1890. At the convention, he proposed an amendment to abolish the convict lease system.

Leslie Everitt Brooks, who represented Mobile County at the convention, was born in Mobile before the Civil War, graduating from the University of Virginia in 1856. He read and practiced law before the war, of which he was a veteran, and became a merchandiser in Mobile after the war. He also was a legislator in the 1890s and postmaster of Mobile in 1885. He was among a number of lawyer-delegates, including John W. A. Sanford of Montgomery and Frank S. White of Birmingham, who supported providing for state control of the railroads in the new constitution, one of the major issues to come before the convention. Because of the conservative nature of the majority of delegates and the power of the railroad companies among that majority, railroad regulation did not become part of the constitution.

Stouten Hubert Dent was born in Maryland and came to Alabama to teach in Eufaula in Barbour County. He read law in the firm of Pugh and Bullock and was admitted to practice in 1856. He was a Civil War veteran and, after the war, returned to the practice of law. In 1879, he was elected president of the Eufaula National Bank. He served on the State Democratic Executive Committee and signed the minority report of the Suffrage and Elections Committee, along with William C. Oates, Frank S. White, and George P. Harrison. This report was a vigorous dissent against the descendants clause which would allow any descendant of a veteran of various listed wars to register to vote under a temporary plan without having to meet rigorous literacy and property requirements. The dissenters felt the clause was an indirect violation of the Fifteenth Amendment.

Edward deGraffenreid of Hale County was born in 1861 and studied law under Governor Thomas Seay, being admitted to practice in 1882. He represented the sixth congressional district at the convention. He became president of the state bar from 1903 to 1904 and later served as legal advisor to Governor Emmett O'Neal, who appointed him to be associate judge on the Alabama Court of Civil Appeals, created in 1911. Thereafter, he served as an associate justice of the Alabama Supreme Court. His son, Edward, Jr., born 1899, was an attorney. Edward, Jr.'s sons, William Ryan and Edward W., both became attorneys, as did William Ryan's son and grandson. Political service was a hallmark of this family as well.

William Cochrane Fitts, who represented Tuscaloosa County at the convention, was an 1886 graduate of the University of Alabama Law Department and practiced law in Tuscaloosa until 1894, when he was elected Alabama attorney general. He served as vice president of the state bar from 1912 to 1913.

Joseph Brown Graham, who represented the eighth senatorial district, was named chairman of the Committee on Education at the convention. He had taught school and served as superintendent of the Talladega city schools from 1887 to 1893. He read law with Charles Whitson at Talladega and was admitted to the bar in 1893, although he continued his involvement in education administration, serving in the Alabama Education Association in various capacities, including president, throughout the 1890s. He also served as president of the county superintendents organization from 1899 to 1900 and on the State Democratic Executive Committee as vice-president in 1900. He was a highly regarded educator whose presence as a delegate reflected the efforts of the education establishment in the state to get a constitution that would provide more stable funding for public education in Alabama. They were partially successful in this effort in that a 3 mill tax allocation for education was included in the constitution, guaranteeing some stability. But the convention failed to provide for special municipal or district taxation for schools, used by other states to provide adequate education funding. This failure worked a substantial continuing hardship on Alabama public schools.

Robert J. Lowe was the nephew of a congressman and served in the state legislature. At the time of the convention he was chairman of the State Democratic Executive Committee.

Oliver Roland Hood of Etowah County who represented the seventh congressional district at the convention was admitted to the bar in 1890. He practiced in Gadsden where he was an alderman from 1893 to 1895.

Thomas Goode Jones represented the second congressional district and was named chairman of the Committee on the Executive Department, which made few recommendations for change, and what changes were made increased the power of the executive. This committee recommended that the position of lieutenant governor be reestablished. Terms for executive offices were extended from two to four years and provisions were made for gubernatorial succession. (Gubernatorial succession was an issue because Governor-elect William J. Samford was deathly ill prior to the time of taking office and there was no president of the new senate to take his place if he should die before the new legislature was organized.) Jones played an active role on many other issues and represented, along with William C. Oates, a paternalistic approach to the suffrage issue and Negro rights, defending the rights of blacks to an education and to have at least the possibility of the right to vote, particularly for the "intelligent and thrifty." In comments concerning the conduct of the convention majority towards the rights of blacks, he stated, "We come in contact with [blacks] everywhere. If we do not lift them up, they will drag us down." He had Progressive leanings in his support of child labor laws, his opposition to more severe tax limits than those found in the 1875 constitution, and his opposition to lynching. His views did not carry the convention.

Robert Joseph Lowe, elected a delegate from the state at-large, was the nephew of William Manning Lowe, a former congressman from Huntsville, who was elected as a Greenback Democrat to the Forty-sixth Congress (1879-1881), and successfully contested the election of

Joseph Wheeler to the Forty-seventh Congress in 1882. Robert J. Lowe graduated from the University of Alabama Law Department in 1881 and practiced in Birmingham, where he became associated with William H. Smith, former governor of Alabama, and David D. Smith, his son. Lowe was a state legislator and involved in state Democratic politics, including serving as chairman of the State Democratic Executive Committee from 1898 through 1902.

James Dean Norman of Bullock County studied law in the Union Springs office of his father, James Talmadge Norman, and was admitted to practice in 1879. He served as mayor of Union Springs for several years and represented Bullock County at the convention.

William Calvin Oates of Montgomery was elected as a state at-large delegate to the convention and served as chairman of the Committee on the Legislative Department. He had been a delegate at the 1875 constitutional convention, as well as serving as governor of the state. He, like Thomas Goode Jones, opposed disenfranchisement of the whole Negro race and opposed the grandfather clause. He voted against the suffrage article as written and supported education for blacks. His legislative committee reported recommendations that reflected the general distrust of legislative bodies that was a nationwide trend. Most importantly, the committee recommended that the legislature meet only quadrennially for 50 legislative days, instead of either annually or biennially as it had under previous constitutions. Although this was an innovation found in no other state, the recommendation was adopted. Other restrictions on the legislature were adopted as well, further limiting its ability to be effective.

Harry Pillans of Mobile was born in 1847 and served in the Civil War. He studied law in the offices of Peter Hamilton in 1866 and in the office of Smith and Henderson from 1868 to 1870. He entered the practice in 1870 with Hurieosco Austill, then established his own firm which survived under different names for over 125 years and included his son, Palmer Pillans. He served as a vice president of the state bar from 1898 to 1899 and also served as a commissioner of the city of Mobile for several years.

Mobile attorney Harry Pillans established the firm that survives today as Reams, Brooks, Schell, & Gaston. He also served as mayor of Mobile from 1916 to 1917.

Henry Clay Selheimer came to Birmingham from Pennsylvania in 1885, shortly after completing his undergraduate education at Princeton and reading law in a Philadelphia law firm. He represented Jefferson County at the convention. Jasper Fritz Thompson, who represented the ninth congressional district, received his bachelor of laws degree from the University of Alabama in 1896, was admitted to practice in Texas, but returned in 1897 to Centreville where he was elected a member of the legislature and served as solicitor for the Fourth Judicial Circuit. He served on the committees on state and county boundaries and impeachments at the convention.

Thomas Henry Watts of Montgomery, who represented Montgomery County at the convention, was the son of Governor Thomas Hill Watts. He served as assistant secretary at the 1875 constitutional convention and practiced law with his father and brother, John W. Watts, and Colonel Daniel S. Troy (who was married to his sister Florence), Henry C. Tompkins, Alexander Troy (who was married to his sister Alice), and Frank S. Caffey. He was a member of Montgomery's city council, serving as president and acting mayor. His son, Edward Seabrook Watts, was also a Montgomery attorney, admitted to the bar in 1904.

John Bedford Weakley, Jr., was born in Lauderdale County, where he read law in the offices of Judge R. T. Simpson and was admitted to the bar in 1884. He practiced in Lauderdale County until 1902, when he moved to Birmingham for a time. He served as mayor of Florence in 1907 for two years, and also as a member of the Florence Board of Education. He was president of the League of Alabama Municipalities and was named chairman of the Committee on Municipalities at the constitutional convention. He worked hard to report a well-designed article on municipalities similar to those found in other states, but it was largely set aside by the General Assembly of the convention, which was much more conservative in its thinking than his committee. Only limited improvements to the approach of the 1875 constitution were made at the convention. John B. Weakley's brother, Samuel D. Weakley, was a Birmingham attorney after locating there in 1887. In 1889, he served as city attorney and compiled the code of city ordinances. He practiced with Edward H. Cabaniss until he was appointed chief justice of the Alabama Supreme Court in 1906 for a brief term. Upon returning to Birmingham after his tenure concluded, he practiced law with his brother and became very involved in the temperance movement and authored the first statewide prohibition bill in 1907.

Frank S. White of Jefferson County, a Civil War veteran who already had had a political career in Mississippi, where he was born, before coming to Birmingham in 1886, was a state at-large delegate to the convention, and a member of the Committee on Harmony and Consistency and the Suffrage Committee. Together with John W. A. Sanford of Montgomery and Leslie Brooks of Mobile, White worked actively to bring up the issue of regulating railroads through an elective railroad commission, proposing an amendment to that effect, which was defeated when opposed by the influential delegates representing railroad interests. White had served as campaign manager for Senator John T. Morgan in the campaign in which Joseph F. Johnston had sought his senate seat. He later served as statewide campaign manager of the campaign that would bring B. B. Comer to the governorship in 1907, a campaign that again focused on the state regulation of railroads. White served as president of the state bar from 1912 to 1913 and also chaired an association formed for the purpose of removing convict labor from coalmines. He was the first Alabamian elected to the United States Senate by direct popular vote in 1914. Two of his sons, William T. and Frank S., Jr., were also attorneys.

A former mayor, John B. Weakley, was named chairman of the Committee on Municipalities at the convention.

The Agrarians

John Robert Beavers, who represented Shelby County as a convention delegate, was a high school principal, educated at Oxford College and Southern University, who read law and was admitted to the bar in 1892. He practiced law in Columbiana.

Hugh Walker Cardon, who represented Cherokee County at the convention, was born in Tennessee, attended Cumberland University in Lebanon, Tennessee, studied law, and was admitted to the bar. He practiced law in Cherokee County, beginning in 1873, and represented the county in the Alabama House of Representatives from 1877 to 1878.

William Thomas Cofer was born in Mississippi and came to Alabama after studying two years at the University of Mississippi. He was admitted to the bar in 1876 and opened a law practice in Cullman, where he was elected several times to the legislature. He represented Cullman County as an independent Democrat at the 1901 convention.

Hubert Trevelyan Davis, born in Tuskegee, entered the practice of law in Gadsden in 1890, was solicitor of the city court from 1895 to 1901, and served several years as a trustee of the University of Alabama. He represented the sixth congressional district as a convention delegate and was a member of the committees on order, consistency and harmony and on representation.

Milo Moody, who represented Jackson County at the convention, was born in Georgia, came with his family to Jackson County, Alabama in 1867, and attended the University of Alabama. He studied law and was admitted to the bar at Scottsboro in 1889. He served as a constable, as a county tax commissioner, and in the Alabama House of Representatives. (He would later be involved in the famous Scottsboro boys trial.)

William Oscar Mulkey, born in Pike County, was a Republican as late as 1896, when he was an elector on the McKinley ticket. Thereafter, he became a Democrat. He represented Geneva County at the convention and, later, in the Alabama legislature. In 1914, he was elected to Congress from the third district to fill the vacancy caused by the resignation of Henry D. Clayton, Jr. He was state bar president from 1921 to 1922.

James Bartley Sloan was born near Warrior in Jefferson County. He studied law in the office of M. L. Ward of Oneonta and was admitted to the bar there in 1897. He served as an alderman and as mayor of Oneonta and represented Blount County at the 1901 convention. He was a Republican, serving as chairman of the executive committee of Blount County for five years.

George Andrew Sorrell, who represented Tallapoosa County at the convention, was originally from Chambers County. He studied law under Colonel W. D. Bulger in Dadeville and was admitted to the bar in 1887. He set up his practice in Alexander City, where he spent his legal career, later serving in the legislature.

Napoleon Bonaparte Spears was born in Tennessee, educated in Virginia, and practiced law after his admission to the bar, in 1869, in Tennessee, Georgia and Alabama. He served in the legislatures of both Tennessee (1874-1875) and Alabama (1898-1901), and was a delegate to the convention representing St. Clair County. He was a Republican who lived in Pell City.

William Wallace Whiteside was born in Calhoun County and received his legal education at Cumberland University in Lebanon, Tennessee, graduating in 1881. He began his practice at Oxford, Alabama, and remained in private practice until 1904 when he was elected chancellor of the northeastern chancery division for two terms. He was a legislator from Calhoun County from 1884 to 1885, and represented the county at the constitutional convention. He was a member of the Oxford school board for a number of years and served on the Calhoun County Democratic executive committee from 1882 to 1896.

Joseph F. Johnston, who as governor had first proposed a new constitution, became its most vocal opponent.

Ratification of the 1901 Constitution

Attorney and Congressman Oscar W. Underwood led a 14-member committee to carry out the Democratic State Executive Committee's campaign for ratification of the 1901 constitution. Their principal argument was that a vote for the constitution was a vote for "white supremacy." They disingenuously maintained that the vote of white men would not be affected. The state's most prominent political figures (other than those who supported Joseph F. Johnston, who was the constitution's main opponent) spoke in its favor. At the end of election day, November 11, 1901, almost 200,000 voters cast their votes. The constitution was adopted by a majority of 26,879 votes. As in the elections which had preceded it in the last decade of the nineteenth century, there was substantial evidence of fraud and it was the Black Belt vote that carried the constitution to victory.

Malcolm McMillan, in his book *Constitutional Development in Alabama, 1798-1901: A Study in Politics, the Negro, and Sectionalism,* stated, "In its general revision of the constitution, the convention of 1901 acted with the utmost conservatism for two reasons. In the first place it was dominated by...conservatives. And in the second place, these conservatives were able to convince other delegates that any change of a controversial nature would endanger ratification of the suffrage decision. It was the old story of using the Negro issue to prevent change or reform. The convention refused to provide for an elective railroad commission with mandatory powers, discarded all except a fragment of the progressive report on municipalities, made no reforms in regard to child labor or convict leasing, provided for a more severe state tax limit, and gave counties and municipalities little relief from tax limits. The convention made some progress in education and refused to adopt the unjust and unconstitutional proviso for division of the schools funds according to the amount of taxes paid by each race [a proviso supported by delegates Erle Pettus and J. Thomas Heflin].... It provided for infrequent elections and embarked the state on a new and untried course in regard to quadrennial sessions. It strengthened the power of the governor and continued the process begun in 1875 of putting the legislature in a straitjacket. Fundamentally, except in regard to the suffrage, the Constitution of 1901 was a readoption of that of 1875."[4]

In 1914, Governor Emmet O'Neal, a delegate at the 1901 convention, would seek a new constitution by arguing, "The Constitutional Convention of 1901 was called for a paramount purpose of reforming the suffrage and removing from our electorate the menace of an ignorant and purchasable vote. Little consideration was given to matters of reform, and hence the Constitution of 1875 which had been framed to meet conditions which can never again exist, was practically readopted."[5] Governor O'Neal's efforts would fail, and the 1901 constitution, as amended several hundred times, still comprised the fundamental law of Alabama as late as 2009.

CHAPTER NINE

PROGRESS BEGINS SLOWLY

GOVERNOR JOSEPH F. JOHNSTON in the 1890s introduced Alabama to some of the ideas of the progressive movement, but there were reasons that the state was not immediately prepared to follow the governor's lead. Coming out of the Civil War, Alabama faced poverty, both materially and spiritually. Before 1874, when Radical Reconstruction effectively ended, the power to reconstruct their communal lives was not in the hands of those who had been the antebellum leaders of the state. Much of the energy of this constituency was spent trying to wrest back political and economic control from those they regarded as "carpetbaggers" and "scalawags" in any way they could. After they succeeded in ending Reconstruction, their focus was on maintaining the political and economic power they had acquired by whatever means were necessary. They were busy constructing a New South and reconstructing vestiges of the South that had been devastated by war. In the process, they corrupted the political process through their manipulation of the votes of black freedmen.

Their energy was focused on what their relationships would be with the freed blacks, whom they had previously held as property. Would their attitude be one of paternalism or hostility? Would they aid black aspirations to full citizenship or be adversarial to those aspirations? Would they promote education for freed blacks and poor whites or deny them equal opportunity?

Another theme that state leaders and the emerging developers of Birmingham responded to immediately after the Civil War was industrialization. The North was years ahead of the South in industrial development. What little had been accomplished in Alabama before and during the war was in ruins at war's end. With the founding of Birmingham in 1871, and the growth of Gadsden and Anniston as industrial centers, state leaders wanted to create an environment that promoted business expansion. Railroad building statewide was part of this vision. Little thought was given to the negative effects of laissez-faire economic growth and to the fact that much of the entrepreneurial talent and financing were coming from outside the state, effectively making Alabama's centers of industry colonial holdings of larger firms headquartered in the North.

Postwar circumstances resulted in other developments that might not otherwise have occurred. With the elimination of the institution of slavery, where blacks had been controlled within the plantation system, and the disruption of agriculture, all of a sudden the state, whose coffers were empty, had to come up with something to do with freed blacks and dislocated whites who committed crimes or who were vagrants. Out of this need,

Crusading photographer Lewis Hine travelled the country documenting on film the living and working conditions of factory laborers, particularly children. He photographed many places in Alabama, including the Adelaide Mill village in Anniston, above, and a group of young boys working at the Barker Mills in Mobile, opposite page, where he praised the working conditions.

the convict leasing system developed. Instead of spending money building prisons, the leasing of convicts actually brought money into the state treasury and also took the burden of caring and feeding of the convicts away from the state. It was a system, though, that soon became corrupted as sheriffs, judges, and others representing the state conspired with "lessors" to maximize the number of convicts available to work in the system, whether the "convicts" were guilty of a crime or not. Out of this system developed local political "machines" which thrived on the fees and fines charged to those in the criminal "justice" system.

Another circumstance involved the control of labor. In effect, a system of peonage developed because of the inability of blacks and poor whites to buy land and implements and seed to farm, or to buy food and pay rent with cash. They became sharecroppers or tenant farmers who paid their landlords and the merchants who supplied them with the tools of their trade after the fact with the money made from their crops. Blacks and poor whites, as well as foreign immigrants, who came into the cities became miners or mill workers who had to buy or rent on credit from landlords or owner merchants in company towns. Once in debt, they were rarely able to escape, since crops failed and wages were low. Whole families had to work to provide themselves a living, resulting in many children going to work at a young age with no way to attain an education and in unsafe and unhealthy conditions. Since their labor was the backbone of the industries that were developing in Alabama, there was no momentum to come to the aid of these downtrodden. Nor was there a preexisting political philosophy that looked to the state for such aid. Further, reform threatened interests that had political control of the state and that had created a social structure and a power system over which they were determined to maintain control.

With the turn of the century, calls for reform were being heard nationwide. Progressives, like the Populists before them, pressured politicians to cure social ills and purify corrupted governmental systems. In Alabama, reform began to come in small doses as more and more Alabamians experienced the impact of unrestrained capitalism and institutional corruption and called on the state and federal governments to impose their powers on behalf of the downtrodden. Lawyers were involved on both sides of the struggles that ensued.

Direct Primaries and Judge Thomas Goode Jones and Railroad Rate Regulation

Joseph Johnston attempted to become governor again in 1902 on the issue of introducing a whites-only statewide direct primary to replace the party convention process that he argued was controlled by a limited, but powerful few. This reform, which was being considered and adopted in many other states, was endorsed by the incumbent governor, newspaper owner William D. Jelks, and did not gain Johnston the reform "spotlight" that he sought. Nor did it gain him the election although direct primaries did soon replace the convention system.

During the 1902 election contest, industrialist Braxton Bragg Comer pushed for an elected railroad commission and Jelks committed to signing such a reform bill if it were to pass. A bill did pass and Comer became the first elected president of the Railroad Commission in 1903 (beating attorney John V. Smith for the position), but the legislature postponed its application to two Jelks appointees until 1906, effectively preventing Comer from gaining any substantive reform of railroad rate regulations through the commission. In response to his frustration with the commission, Comer entered the 1906 gubernatorial election, working not only to gain the governorship but also control of the legislature itself so that he could succeed in regulating the railroad industry in the state. His subsequent victory was the beginning of four years of progressive government in Alabama.

Comer was not an attorney, but one of his advisers, Frank Shelley White of Birmingham, was, as were the constitutional officers who helped him enact his legislative agenda. White had chaired an organization started in 1903 and called the Farmers', Merchants', and Laborers' Association, which had successfully worked to elect legislators sympathetic to railroad regulation. Attorneys C.C. Whitson of Talladega, Thomas M. Stevens of Mobile, William H. Samford (son of ex-Governor William J. Samford) of Opelika, Edward B. Almon of Tuscumbia, and Jefferson Falkner of Montgomery, most of whom had

Industrialist Braxton Bragg Comer became the first elected president of the Railroad Commission in 1903. Frustration with road blocks to reform set up by the legislature motivated him to seek, and win, the governorship in 1906.

ties to the railroad industry, led the opposition to reform. They cast the opposition argument to railroad reform as one of public power versus property rights, arguing that regulation of railroads would interfere with the right of the owners to do with their private property what they would.

Attorney Alexander London, who had become prominent as a crusader against county political rings and the fee system which they tended to abuse, argued that for almost two decades the state had been run by a machine comprised of Black Belt politicians and the appointed Railroad Commission, controlled by what Comer termed "railroad bossism." In this way, London linked the drive to reform corrupt government with the campaign for an elected railroad commission and railroad rate reform. The political argument was that the railroad industry was quasi-public because of its impact on the public good and that rate discrimination was detrimental to the whole community. Regulation on behalf of the public was required.

THE DEAD SHOE PRIMARY OF 1906 AND THE DIRECT ELECTION OF SENATORS

As part of the primary process for the 1906 gubernatorial election, the State Democratic Executive Committee succumbed to agitation for a senatorial primary whereby voters could indicate to the legislature their choices for United States senator as appointments became necessary. Part of this primary included the nomination of senatorial alternates in recognition of the advanced age of Alabama's two incumbent senators at the time, John T. Morgan (born 1824) and Edmund Pettus (born 1821). This feature became known as the "Dead Shoe Primary."

The result of this unique primary was that John T. Morgan received 81,705 votes, Edmund Pettus received 78,343 votes, Congressman John Hollis Bankhead received 48,362 votes, and ex-Governor Joseph F. Johnston received 36,107 votes. Thereafter, Bankhead and Johnston came to be called "Senatorial pallbearers" and each soon became a senator, with Morgan's death on June 11, 1907, and Pettus's death on July 25, 1907.

Bankhead would serve until 1920 while Johnston, whose term was to run until March 1915, died suddenly of a heart attack in August 1913, and was replaced by attorney Frank White in a 1914 election. White was the first United States senator in Alabama to be elected by a direct vote of the people under the terms of the Seventeenth Amendment to the U.S. Constitution.

Congressman John Hollis Bankhead came in a distant third in the "Dead Shoe Primary," but only had to wait a year to become a senator, following the death of John Tyler Morgan.

This type of argument, with variation, was being made in many contexts throughout the nation during the early part of the century as reformers tried to combat the economic power and impact of monopolies and trusts.

Before Comer won the governorship, the speaker of the Alabama House had been attorney Alfred M. Tunstall of Hale County, whose most important client in his Greensboro practice was Southern Railway, and whose

William Logan Martin, Sr., who had a private practice with attorney Virgil Bouldin of Scottsboro until 1902, was chosen speaker of the House at the beginning of Comer's term and served through most of the first legislative session until his death on May 7, 1907. Martin had served as Alabama's attorney general from 1889 to 1894 and was part of the Johnston reform wing of the Democratic Party. Archibald H. Carmichael, from Tuscumbia in Colbert County, served as speaker of the House after Martin's death and through special sessions called by Comer. He was again selected speaker during the governorship of Charles Henderson, another businessman who served as governor from 1915 to 1919. During the administration of Governor Emmett O'Neal (1911-1915), another attorney from Colbert County, Edward B. Almon, served as speaker. Remarkably, Almon would later represent the eighth congressional district, elected in late 1914, and Carmichael would assume his seat upon Almon's death in 1933. Carmichael served as a state senator from 1919 to 1923. He served as chairman of the committee on education, helping to enact the educational code of the state and being largely responsible for the passage of the general health laws of Alabama. His nephew, Albert A. Carmichael, served as attorney general from 1935 to 1939 and lieutenant governor from 1939 to 1943.

ABOVE: *Frank S. White was one of the most influential progressive politicians in Alabama during the late nineteenth and early twentieth centuries. He was campaign manager for Governors Johnston and Comer, was a delegate to the constitutional convention, and in 1914 became the first U.S. senator from Alabama elected by direct popular vote.* RIGHT: *Joel Goldsby of Mobile served as president pro tem of the Senate during the Jelks administration and later as a judge of the Thirteenth Judicial Circuit.*

father, Wiley C. Tunstall, was a Jelks appointee to the Railroad Commission. (Wiley C. Tunstall, Jr., was an Anniston attorney who also represented railroads.) The president pro tem of the Senate was Joel Goldsby of Mobile, a railroad attorney as well.

Because of the success of Frank White's group in electing supportive legislators, Comer had little trouble getting railroad reform legislation adopted in the early days of his administration. He secured the passage of a series of railroad acts, commonly called the railway code, which, among other things, reduced passenger fares on intrastate traffic from three to two and one-half cents per mile, and fixed the freight rates on 110 commodities at approximately the same rate charged in the state of

Georgia (which had already passed reform legislation). The act provided for the forfeiture of the charter of any railroad that challenged the law in federal court. This threatened forfeiture did not prevent a challenge to the law in federal court.

The federal district judge who heard the case was ex-governor Thomas Goode Jones, former counsel for the L&N Railroad, the leading plaintiff in the challenge case. What ensued became a prolonged and bitter battle between Milton Smith, president of the L&N, and Governor Comer, with Judge Jones supporting Smith at every opportunity. Both men had been bitter enemies of Comer in the struggle to create an elected railroad commission. Jones felt no qualms that his position as a former railroad lawyer created a conflict of interest that would require him to step down from the case. The federal Interstate Commerce Commission was in place and required that all rates for interstate transportation were to be reasonable and just; however, a United States Supreme Court decision created an almost unusable constitutional test for whether rates were reasonable or confiscatory.

Birmingham attorneys Samuel D. Weakley, top, and Henry C. Selheimer, above, acted as special counsels for the state during the "railroad war." Selheimer had been a delegate to the constitutional convention. Weakley would later serve on the Alabama Supreme Court.

Although ostensibly the Alabama case involved the issue of the justness of the state rates, it really represented Milton Smith's effort to defeat any state regulation of his railroad. And although Jones's decisions against the state ostensibly involved the evaluation of the constitutionality of the state's system of regulation, it seemed to involve even more a personal vendetta against Governor Comer for his insults to Jones's character, to which Jones was overly sensitive. Comer and his supporters portrayed Judge Jones's decisions favoring the railroad as a miscarriage of justice influenced by his long and intimate association with the railroad industry and called him "railroad environed" and a puppet of Milton Smith. The judge was quoted as saying that it was a "wicked thing" for the governor to "excite the passions of the people against the authority of the courts."[1] This railroad war was the first notorious instance of an Alabama governor railing against a federal judge for interference with the state's ability to control its own affairs. It went on for seven years before a settlement was reached during the administration of Governor Emmet O'Neal.

Alexander M. Garber and Robert C. Brickell, Jr., (whose father Robert C. Brickell had served as chief justice of the Alabama Supreme Court from 1880 to 1884 and then again under then-Governor Thomas Jones from 1894 to 1898) served as Alabama's attorneys general during the period of this litigation and represented the state in the case. Special counsels were hired as well, including Birmingham attorneys Henry C. Selheimer and Samuel D. Weakley (who would later serve as a justice of the Alabama Supreme Court). Robert E. Steiner and George W. Jones, both Montgomery corporate attorneys, represented the L&N.

Ex-governor Comer resented the settlement of the cases by Governor O'Neal, because federal appellate courts had ruled in favor of the state and he thought a decisive victory was possible. Still, other pressing matters made the railroad litigation slip in importance and made settlement very attractive, including what to do about liquor and the saloon society of the times.

Progressivism, Public Morality, and the Administration of Governor Emmet O'Neal

One strain of the Progressive Movement was a focus on public morality and the impact of alcohol abuse in the many saloons that peppered the emerging industrial towns and cities and the brothels that accompanied them. On one side of these issues were the Anti-Saloon League and the Women's Christian Temperance unions while on the other side was the Safe and Sane League, organized by attorney Leon C. McCord of Albertville (who from January 1911 to January 1915, served on the railroad commission and who was appointed a judge of the Fifth Circuit Court of Appeals by President Franklin D. Roosevelt in 1938.) The Safe and Sane League promoted the power of local government to control these issues while the other organizations sought total prohibition by constitutional amendment.

As early as 1909, an amendment was proposed to the Alabama constitution that would prohibit the sale of liquor (a precursor of the eighteenth amendment to the U.S. Constitution). This issue, like others, split the Alabama Democratic Party along the same conservative versus progressive lines that seemed inherent in what otherwise was a one-party state. Progressives who wanted to reform public morality, including attorneys Hugh S. D. Mallory of Selma, Samuel D. Weakley of Birmingham, and A. H. Carmichael (who was speaker of the house at the time) favored prohibition, with the resultant elimination of saloons and the prostitution that seemed to go hand in hand with them. Samuel Weakley, who practiced law with his brother John B. Weakley in Birmingham, not only drafted the amendment but also authored the first statewide bill on the subject that had passed the legislature in 1907, which was described as one of the most drastic antiliquor codes in the country at the time. The conservatives, or old-line party members, including attorneys Emmet O'Neal, William Oates, Hilary Herbert, Frank Moody (lawyer, banker, and state senator from Tuscaloosa), John Knox, Ray Rushton, Sydney Bowie, the two U.S. senators, and most of the state's congressmen, opposed the amendment, as much to defeat Comer as to express principle. They favored "local option," which would allow local governments to decide for themselves their approach to alcohol distribution and consumption.

The amendment lost, but this did not stop the forces for regulation of alcohol. Out of the contest came gubernatorial candidates for the 1910 contest: for the old-line forces, Emmet O'Neal of Florence, and for the Progressives, Hugh S. D. Mallory, Samuel Weakley and A. H. Carmichael, who were Comerites considering a run to replace him. Mallory became the progressive candidate. Both O'Neal and Mallory were prominent lawyers; both had been recent presidents of the Alabama State Bar Association; and both had similar positions on other issues in the race, such as educational progress, moderate regulation of public service institutions, and improved road building programs. The primary difference was on the issue of prohibition. O'Neal won the election and shortly saw to it that the 1907 antiliquor law was repealed and replaced by a local option law. (Statewide prohibition would be enacted again during the administration of Governor Charles Henderson and Alabama would

Governor Emmett O'Neal's administration saw the passage of a number of laws promoting Progressive reforms. The first state court of appeals was created during his administration.

be a dry state even before enactment of the Eighteenth Amendment.)

Although O'Neal never considered himself a Progressive, his administration saw strides made in the regulation of child labor, improved protection for mine workers, and the promotion of agriculture. Also while he was in office, the first court of appeals was created to handle many of the increasing number of appeals that had caused the Alabama Supreme Court to become bogged down with a backlog of cases. His administration reacted to the Progressive call for reform of local forms of government by passing legislation that allowed cities to adopt the commission form of government. He appointed Birmingham attorney James M. Weatherly, a prominent corporate attorney who had practiced law with Oscar W. Underwood before his election to Congress, as the first commissioner under the first commission form of government in Alabama, which was adopted in Birmingham.

O'Neal's administration was marred by thefts and rumors of theft among state employees. Two major embezzlements occurred, one in the state convict department and one in the Department of Agriculture and Industries, highlighting a deficient system of public accounting and audit. Although honest himself, O'Neal's apparent mismanagement tarnished his reputation as governor even though he was one of the most highly educated and intellectual men to have occupied the governorship.

RIGHT: *Attorney Leon McCord headed the Safe and Sane League, which opposed statewide prohibition.* BELOW: *Demonstrators in Birmingham march in favor of an amendment to the Alabama constitution banning the sale of alcohol in this photograph taken in 1909.*

ALABAMA LAWYERS AND NATIONAL ISSUES

TWO MAJOR NATIONAL ISSUES that were fomenting during the Progressive period were regulation of monopolies and trusts and the erection of tariff barriers to protect American business against imports. With industrial development under the laissez-faire philosophy of the Republican administrations in post-Civil War America, there had been a general trend toward concentration of economic power through large corporate monopolies, trusts, and syndicates. With their large concentration of economic power, some of the "industrial magnates" and "robber barons" were able to make demands on both labor and government that turned out to be injurious to the public good. Over the course of years, and as the century turned, the spirit of reform gave impetus to increased regulatory involvement by the federal government. The Interstate Commerce Act and Commission, Federal Trade Commission, the Sherman Anti-trust Act, and the Department of Commerce and Labor were created to provide a basis for governmental action.

Henry DeLamar Clayton, Jr., the son of Confederate general Henry D. Clayton, was an influential congressman on antitrust and tariff issues.

One Alabama congressman, Henry DeLamar Clayton, Jr., of Barbour County (he served in Congress from 1897 to 1914), was involved in the evolution of legislation to empower government to oversee trusts and monopolies. His name was associated with the antitrust philosophy of the time when a statute he sponsored to strengthen the government's power

Regulation of the Legal Profession

Another movement which accompanied progressivism was a nationwide effort to make more rigorous the standards by which one entered and maintained one's membership in the "learned professions" in the United States, including the law. For Alabama's legal profession, this movement began in 1907 with the legislature's creation of a Board of Bar Examiners and culminated in 1923 with the passage of an act creating an integrated bar (i.e., a bar integrated into the regulatory system of state government and giving the Alabama State Bar the power to police the profession).

When the Alabama State Bar Association was established in 1879, it was created as a voluntary association and its membership continued to be a relatively small percentage of practicing lawyers throughout the early years of its existence, dominated by the bar's best known and most successful practitioners. Members met annually in convention, presenting papers on the legal issues of the day. The president gave an annual address which included a review of the state of the law throughout the country. The standing committees of the bar during its early years, appointed annually with five members each, included committees on Jurisprudence and Law Reform, Judicial Administration and Remedial Procedure, Legal Education and Admission to the Bar, Publication, Correspondence, Legislation, and Local Bar Associations

Under the organization's constitution, the Executive Committee was authorized to nominate and/or accept applications for membership. Members had to accept membership once elected by a letter written to the to prosecute and dismantle trusts was enacted as the Clayton Antitrust Act. Clayton was the son of lawyer and Civil War Major General Henry DeLamar Clayton who in June 1886 became president and professor of international law at the University of Alabama. Congressman Clayton resigned his seat in 1914 to accept appointment as a federal district judge for the Middle District of Alabama and served until 1929. His brothers, Jeff Davis Clayton and Lee Johnston Clayton, both practiced law in Barbour County.

Another issue of concern to Progressives was reform of America's protective tariff system. From the progressive perspective, protective tariffs merely enhanced the power of corporate America, which progressives perceived as too concentrated and influential. Thus, for years, they worked to lower tariffs to encourage more competition and lower prices.

Congressman Oscar W. Underwood was a Birmingham attorney who was first elected to Congress in 1894. During his years there, he served on the committees on judiciary, on rules, arid lands, appropriations, and on ways and means (of which he was chairman for four years; this position carried with it floor leadership of the majority Democratic Party when they were swept into power in 1910.) One of the issues that Democrats had won on was to revise tariffs downward to a revenue basis (as opposed to a trade barrier). This issue, among others, was to serve as the foundation for an effort to elect a Democratic president in 1912. Underwood's House leadership proved so successful, with the passage of the Underwood-Simmons Tariff Act and other promised reforms, that he became the first Southerner since the Civil War seriously considered for the presidential nomination at the 1912 Democratic convention in Baltimore.

Oscar W. Underwood was a serious candidate for the Democratic presidential nomination in 1912 and 1924.

His name was placed in nomination by attorney-delegate William B. Bankhead (Alabama Senator Bankhead's son), who would himself become an important congressman in succeeding years. Woodrow Wilson was ultimately selected and elected as president. Underwood ran in 1914 for an open Senate seat and defeated fellow congressman Richmond Pearson Hobson. He was reelected in 1920, defeating, among others, attorney Samuel D. Weakley. He was subsequently elected minority leader of the Senate (the Republicans having returned to majority status) and thus became one of the few Democrats to that time to serve as his party's leader in both houses of Congress. Both he and Congressman Clayton were considered among the most important congressmen of their day.

secretary of the association and by payment of dues. The constitution originally stated that any member of the legal profession who was a member of the bar of the state of Alabama and in good standing could become a member of the association on open nomination at any meeting, or by vote of the Executive Committee at any meeting of that committee held between meetings of the association. It was amended in 1913 to read "any white member" of the bar could become a member of the association.

A report of the standing Committee on Legal Education and Admission to the Bar, chaired by W. R. Walker of Athens, made recommendations at the 1911 annual convention to upgrade the requirements for qualification to enter the practice of law. At that time, once the bar association agreed, the leadership was then required to work with the legislature, since the legislature, in effect, regulated the bar through the statutes it enacted. The committee's recommendations included that no one should be permitted to be examined by the Board of Examiners unless he had at least a high school education and either three years of law school attendance or an equivalent period of time studying in "the office of some reputable lawyer." The applicant who wished to study or read law should be required to register with the chairman of the Board of Examiners his intent to study law. Also recommended was a review of the character of the applicant taking the examination.

The Central Council consisting of five members was created to supervise the ethics and the professional conduct of the bar. The Association adopted a Code of Ethics in 1887 and used it as the basis for evaluating professional conduct. Under a statute enacted in 1903, the bar association or its Central Council could bring actions to have attorneys prosecuted in order to suspend or disbar them from the practice of law. The prosecution had to be handled through the office of the solicitor in the circuit where the attorney resided. Prior to an amendment enacted in 1915, the action had to begin within one year of the unethical or illegal act; the limitation was extended to three years under the 1915 amendment.

Review of the proceedings of state bar conventions after the turn of the century illustrates the kind of conduct that association members considered unethical. Often the conduct complained of involved the solicitation of cases directly or by using "runners" or, in criminal cases, deputy sheriffs and wardens to get referrals (with a fee paid for the referral). At the 1912 annual convention, a special committee chaired by Alexander M. Garber of Birmingham, reported on its investigation of unethical and improper practices in Jefferson County on both sides of personal injury litigation. Included were the following highlights:

1. The term "rake-off" was used to describe the pay that nonlawyers expected if they referred a case to a personal injury attorney, including elevator boys, preachers, etc.

2. It was impossible to get damage suits without either active solicitation of a potential plaintiff or the use of "runners" who expected a percentage of the recovery.

3. There existed "agencies" in Birmingham that siphoned off cases to firms in Georgia if jurisdictional requirements could be met, because Georgia juries were more generous and Georgia appellate courts tended to uphold jury verdicts where in Alabama this was often not the case.

4. Plaintiff lawyers and defense lawyers through their runners and claims agents did battle to either get a suit filed or settled until the very moment that the bottom line was signed one way or the other by the plaintiff.

5. Even after the suit was filed, the defendant's claims agents would often attempt to settle the case without consultation with the plaintiff lawyer.

6. The defense would use "jury selectors" who had such intimate knowledge of the jury list, acquired during years of helping defense counsel, that the plaintiff would often end up with little chance of anything save a compromise verdict or a mistrial.

George Huddleston, Sr., was a native of Tennessee and a graduate of the Cumberland School of Law before it moved to Birmingham. He practiced law in Birmingham, and served in the U.S. House of Representatives for eleven terms. His son, George Huddleston, Jr., was a five-term congressman from 1955 to 1965.

7. Defendants even acted in concert with certain hospitals to secure settlements while preventing runners from approaching injured plaintiffs, who often were misled by corporate agents who would misrepresent the magnitude of the injury they had suffered.

8. In cases where multiple deaths occurred, there were instances where someone would apply to the probate court to serve as administrator for all the dead in order to be in a position to negotiate a settlement of the case with the defendant. The committee also described and denounced as unethical the defense practices of delaying cases to the detriment of the plaintiff so that witnesses might become scattered or the plaintiff be forced by "the stress of poverty" to make a detrimental settlement; the practice of fighting the case through all the courts on every technicality in order to intimidate or coerce the plaintiff into an unfair

settlement; and the use of claim agents to obtain distorted ex parte affidavits with which the witness would be confronted and his testimony affected at the trial.

The report concluded, "It may be safely stated that every unfair practice indulged in by the plaintiff or his representatives has its equally reprehensible counterpart on the other side of the case. These practices, whether upon one side or the other, we regard, as not only harmful to professional standards, but as resulting in nearly every case in a contest for a verdict without regard to the *administration of justice*." The committee recommended that the association denounce the described practices as unethical and unprofessional and forbid attorneys to "consciously remain a part of a system, any essential member of which resorts to unjust practices, or practices tending to obstruct justice. Attorneys should be held responsible where they knowingly act as general advisers to clients who make it a practice to corrupt or obstruct justice."

The committee further recommended that a committee be appointed to draft a "working man's compensation act" for the benefit of all employees. Other legislation was recommended which the committee had prepared and appended to its original report.

Other members of this special committee included Henry U. Sims of Birmingham, who served as president of the state bar from 1917 to 1918 and as president of the American Bar Association from 1929 to 1930, George Huddleston, Sr., James A. Mitchell, and Edmund H. Dryer.

TOP: *Birmingham attorney Henry U. Sims served as president of the Alabama State Bar Association, and was the first Alabamian to serve as president of the American Bar Association.* ABOVE: *John London joined with Alexander Troy London to form London & London, today's London, Yancey & Elliott, LLC.*

Another special committee served that year, for the purpose of preparing a bill to establish a court of appeals. That committee consisted of C. P. McIntyre of Montgomery; Thomas M. Stevens of Mobile (president of the state bar, 1913-1914); Joseph N. Nathan of Colbert (president of the state bar, 1916-1917); James Weatherly of Jefferson; and John Pelham of Calhoun (president of the state bar, 1911-1912). The bill, drafted after close discussion with members of the Alabama Supreme Court, was supported by Governor Emmet O'Neal and was enacted during his administration. It created a court whose jurisdiction in civil cases involved matters worth a maximum of $1,000 and criminal cases involving misdemeanors and felonies where punishment did not exceed 20 years. It was estimated that these limits would capture 95 per cent of criminal cases and about 50 percent of civil cases.

In his presidential address in 1912, John London encouraged the bar to be active in seeking reform measures to make justice more efficient. He stated his belief that people were restive and dissatisfied because "of an inefficient administration and lax and delayed enforcement of the laws, due in a great measure to a cumbersome and antiquated procedure that is out of joint with the people and the times." The next proceeding, in 1913, reported that the legislature had granted the Supreme Court of Alabama limited rule-making authority and the court had adopted some new rules for itself and for the circuit courts as well. Of particular note was Rule 45, which changed the previous rule that error carried with it a presumption of injury. The new rule required that the record affirmatively demonstrate injury arising from error at a trial, thereby redressing numerous stories of reversals on "technicalities."

The association adopted a resolution in 1911 to create a body of commissioners to promote uniformity of laws. With this action, it provided official representation to the National Commission of Uniform State Laws.

Papers presented at the annual meetings during this period show the issues that were of concern and that were being addressed by various bar committees. Many times, in association with the presentation of a paper, came the formation of a committee to propose legislation to remedy the problem. Legal education would often be the subject of presentations as well. Some examples of the presentations during the era leading up to integration of the bar follow: In 1902, Daniel Coleman of Limestone County discussed jury reform. In 1903, Judge Paul Speake of Huntsville presented "Wantonness in Personal Injury Cases." C. P. McIntyre of Montgomery talked about civil procedure in 1904, while H. E. Gipson of Prattville addressed "Delay in the Law as an Excuse for Lynching." F. M. Purifoy of Tuscaloosa addressed the issue of "Growth and Development of the Scope and Power of Trust Companies." In 1905, Huntsville's Lawrence Cooper's subject was "Our Railroad Commission," while Thomas G. Jones discussed the question "Has the Citizen of the United States in the Custody of the State's officers, upon accusation of Crime against its Laws any Immunity or Right which may be protected by the United States against Mob Violence?" Charles B. Verner of Tuscaloosa presented a paper in 1910 entitled "Administration of the Criminal Laws of Alabama." Thomas M. Stevens of Mobile gave one entitled "The Alabama Supreme Court is overworked and should have relief." In 1911, Sam Will John of Birmingham presented his paper, "Our Imperative Duty to Procure a Judicious Reform of the Judicial Procedure in the Courts of Alabama," and in 1912, Governor O'Neal presented a paper entitled "Law Reform."

In 1914, Sam Will John presented "Do the Bench and Bar really desire a genuine reformation of the Practice and Procedure in our Courts." In 1917, ex-governor O'Neal presented "The State Constitution." Also in 1921, Thomas E. Orr presented "Does Alabama Need a New Constitution?" and, in 1922, Charles A. Calhoun read "The Progress of the State is being Retarded by Our Present State Constitution—Some Suggested Changes." In 1923, Henry U. Sims read "The Importance of Adopting in Alabama more of the Uniform State Laws Prepared by the National Conference" and Marvin Woodall of Birmingham presented "Professionalism Against Commercialism in the Practice of Law." If the number of presentations of papers indicated activity and influence within the bar itself, Sam Will John, an influential legislator during this era, would be considered the most influential, since he presented nine papers between 1885 and 1920, on such subjects as local legislation, jury law, judicial procedure reform, necessity of a workers' compensation law, and a law for registration and insurance of land titles. Governor O'Neal would also be considered very influential with his six presentations on subjects ranging from the state constitution to quadrennial sessions of the legislature.

R. Tyler Goodwyn, seen here with his wife and six children, served for five years in the state legislature and from 1910 to 1915 as chairman of the State Democratic Executive Committee.

During the Progressive Era in Alabama history, primarily the years 1900 through 1920, only two governors were lawyers: William J. Samford, who served only six months before his death on June 11, 1901, and Emmet O'Neal, who served from 1911 to 1915. Thus, much of the impact of the bar in the political realm came through the work of the committees of the Alabama State Bar Association, many of whose members were legislators, judges, and politically influential practitioners. Some of these, whose names show up in legal realms throughout the first half of the twentieth century, include brothers Hugh D. Merrill and Walter B. Merrill of Cleburne County; J. Kelly Dixon of Anniston (who served as Federal Prohibition director in Alabama once the federal Prohibition era began and whose son was Birmingham attorney Brewer Dixon); Allen K. Merrill of Eufaula; Robert C. Brickell, Jr. (Alabama's attorney general during the administration of Emmet O'Neal, 1911-1915, and son of two-time Chief Justice Robert C. Brickell of the Alabama Supreme Court); R. Tyler Goodwyn (chairman of the State Democratic Executive Committee from 1910 to 1915, a member of the Alabama legislature from 1902 to 1907, and an "organization man," having memberships in the Elks, Woodmen of the World, Red Men, Eagles, and Odd Fellows); John R. Sample of Hartselle; Joseph N. Nathan of Colbert County (a circuit judge who served as president of the state bar from 1916 to 1917); R. C. Hunt, solicitor, of DeKalb County; William C. Davis of Jasper; Dempsey M. Powell of Greenville; Nimrod Denson of Opelika (who practiced with his son Nimrod, Jr., and his brother John V. Denson); brothers Gaston Gunter and William A. Gunter, who both served as legislators and city fathers of Montgomery (Gaston served as an alderman while William served as a commissioner after a change in the form of government; they both served as mayors of Montgomery); Oscar S. Lewis of Tuskegee; W. H. Mitchell of Florence (who became president of the state bar from 1953 to 1954), Fleetwood Rice of Tuscaloosa; Walker Percy of Birmingham; Seybourn A. Lynne of Decatur; James N. Granade of Chatom; and R. B. Evins of Greensboro (the last president of the state bar from 1923 to 1924 before it became the integrated bar and legal advisor to Governor O'Neal from 1911 to 1915).

TOP: *William A. Gunter was active in Montgomery city politics serving as an alderman and as mayor.* ABOVE: *Walker Percy was at the forefront of the movement to change Birmingham's form of government to a city commission, which occured in 1911.*

The movement to create a unified bar began in 1921 when Alexander Garber gave a report of the Committee on Local Bar Associations, announcing that there were 20 local bars throughout the state. It was resolved by the organization that the officers would travel throughout the various counties to try to organize more local bars as a way to encourage increased interest and membership in the state organization. John H. Peach of Sheffield (who served as president from 1925 to 1926) proposed that a plan should be formulated to coordinate the local bars with the state organization "as to make the organization compact, so that they can always be in immediate touch with each other." Borden Burr of Birmingham responded by pointing out that the state bar association "purport[ed] to represent the lawyers of Alabama" but its membership was "a minority of the number of lawyers of Alabama" and had no organized strength. He called it a "debating society or social

Borden Burr, seen here representing the Tennessee Coal, Iron and Railroad Company at a congressional hearing in the 1930s, first broached the idea of integrating the Alabama State Bar Association into the state government, and chaired the special committee appointed to craft the necessary legislation.

club," and then he pointed out that the issue of the status of bar associations was being seriously discussed by state bars all over the United States and that a number of states had already acted "along progressive lines in reference to it."

Burr presented a pamphlet of the American Judicature Society, which addressed the issue of the organization of bar associations with a proposed bill. The goal of the proposed bill was to integrate the bar association into state government so that it would be the governmental entity which would regulate the legal profession in the state. Burr discussed a bill then pending before the Ohio legislature which he described as being aimed at requiring every lawyer who was admitted to practice to become a member of the association, thus giving the association power to represent the interests of the bar. The bill also delegated to the bar the authority to police the ethics of the profession. Burr proposed that a committee should investigate the Ohio bill more thoroughly and draft a comparable one to be presented to the Alabama legislature. After discussion, the matter was turned over to the Executive Committee for further study and proposed action.

In 1922, little had been done, but there was much discussion of the same issue, with Borden Burr, Henry U. Sims and W. H. Mitchell of Florence leading the discussion. At this meeting, with Judge W. O. Mulkey of Geneva presiding as president, a resolution passed to create a committee of 25 members who would have the responsibility of developing a report and proposed law to be presented to a convention of the Democratic Party already set to discuss several issues concerning the election, tenure, and salary of judges. Burr proposed that the issue of the authority of the state bar association should be made a part of the convention call.

A special committee was then appointed under the chairmanship of Borden Burr of Birmingham, with five members of the committee being appointed as a subcommittee, to put together legislation to be presented, including chairman H. F. Reese, W. P. Acker, C. P. Beddow, A. F. Fite, and J. T. Stokely, with Borden Burr and B. P. Crum (that year's state bar president) as ex officio members. A bill was drafted and presented to the Democratic State Convention, whose judiciary committee reviewed and approved it unanimously. The bill then was introduced in the Senate by Senator Boswell D. Waddell and ultimately was passed by a vote of 24-10.

The bill received opposition in the House, where several criticisms were made and addressed, and it failed to pass out of the House Judiciary Committee. During discussion at the 1923 convention, it was alleged that there were legislators who fought the bill because they would have been prime objects of the bar's proposed disbarment powers. It also became clear that much of the unethical activity that was occurring in Birmingham was directly related to the power being wielded by the resurrected Ku Klux Klan and that corruption of many public officials was suspected. Several lawyers noted that younger members of the bar actually "crave protection against some of the older members of the Bar." There was discussion that the

SPECIAL COMMITTEE APPOINTED TO RECOMMEND LEGISLATION

THE SPECIAL COMMITTEE; in addition to chairman Borden Burr of Birmingham (state bar president, 1931-1932) consisted of the following members: J.T. Stokely of Birmingham (state bar president, 1919-1920); C. P. Beddow of Birmingham (whose son Roderick Beddow would be state bar president from 1944 to 1945); Norville R. Leigh, Jr., of Mobile (state bar president, 1927-1928); Thomas M. Stevens of Mobile (state bar president, 1913-1914); Ray Rushton of Montgomery (state bar president, 1914-1915); Henry U. Sims of Birmingham (state bar president, 1917-1918); George W. Jones of Montgomery; Lawrence Cooper of Huntsville (state bar president, 1902-1903); W. H. Mitchell (state bar president, 1953-1954); Seybourn A. Lynne of Decatur (a member of the legislature and future federal district judge); R. B. Evins of Greensboro (state bar president, 1923-1924); H. F. Reese of Selma; E. W. Pettus, II of Selma; J. Kelly Dixon of Talladega (state bar president, 1920-1921); C. E. Hamilton of Greenville (first president of the integrated state bar, 1924-1925); W. O. Mulkey of Geneva (state bar president, 1921-1922); Boswell D. Waddell of Seale; William P. Acker of Anniston; Arthur F. Fite of Jasper; B. G. Farmer of Dothan; Bernard Harwood of Tuscaloosa (state bar president, 1929-1930); Hugh M. Caffey, Jr., of Brewton; John V. Denson of Opelika; and Henry McDaniel of Demopolis.

Ray Rushton was one of 12 members of the committee to serve as president of the Alabama State Bar Association.

special committee's membership should be reviewed and that Mr. Burr should be replaced as chairman, since one of the arguments against the bill was that his chairmanship evidenced that it was being sponsored at the behest and for the benefit of corporations (Mr. Burr making the suggestion for his removal himself.)

Mr. Robert B. Evins was elected president of the bar based on his stature as a legislator and former legal advisor to Governor O'Neal, with the fight for passage of the "lawyer's bill" in mind. He did revise the committee of 25, but he kept Borden Burr as chairman. He took off the committee several of the other members who were well-known corporate lawyers, such as Thomas M. Stevens, Ray Rushton, Henry Upson Sims, Lawrence Cooper, and George W. Jones and added House members R. Tyler Goodwyn of Montgomery and Finis St. John of Cullman, as well as Francis W. Hare of Monroeville, J. Fritz Thompson of Birmingham, Jerome T. Fuller of Centreville, Malcolm S. Carmichael of Montgomery, Albert A. Carmichael of Geneva, and Chauncey Sparks of Eufaula. He removed A. F. Fite of Hamilton and John V. Denson of Opelika. Although Fite had been on the committee that drafted the legislation, his brother, Fred Fite, was one of the leaders of the opposition to the bill in the House. When it was passed later in 1923, Fred Fite was one of only two lawyers who voted against the bill. He was also one of the first lawyers whose disbarment was attempted when the Alabama State Bar was organized sufficiently to begin policing the profession. (Fite was disbarred in the early 1930s for improperly handling personal injury cases, but was later reinstated and practiced in Hamilton, Alabama.)

CHAPTER TEN

THE INVISIBLE EMPIRE BECOMES VISIBLE AGAIN

When the century turned, change confronted the state of Alabama, the pace of which gradually sped up and caused reaction. At the time, Alabama's white population, which controlled both government and popular culture, was virtually homogeneous, being close to ninety-nine percent native born and ninety-six percent Protestant. A conservative population with a high resistance to change, Alabamians had chosen intolerant racism in its relationship to the state's black population, which existed under the oppressive legal principle of "separate but equal."[1]

There was extensive immigration nationwide from such countries as Italy, Lebanon, and Greece, of people whose skin was darker than Northern Europeans, whose religions were not Protestant, and who did not neces-

sarily come from democratic traditions. Birmingham boosters had recruited such immigrants as part of their plans for growth and industrialization, but all of a sudden the city was confronted with a Catholic cathedral in its center (surrounded by the predominant Protestant churches), and with people whose cultures saw nothing wrong with drinking wine as part of their meal (when the community at large was clamoring for prohibition); whose work brought them in regular contact with the black laboring community (when the community at large was segregating itself); and whose foreign languages and Catholic-oriented traditions tended to keep them segregated from the greater white community and its conservative Protestant mores.

Then, early in the new century, as war on European soil seemed inevitable, there appeared a number of preparedness organizations that created an upsurge in patriotism and nativism and advocated conformity and traditionalism. At the same time, many women nationwide were struggling to gain the vote. For many Alabama traditionalists, the advent of the vote and the activities of women outside the home, in their own clubs and organizations, were seen as threats.

In response to all of these trends, various fraternal societies were organized to promote "100% American values," civic pride, business networking, charity, and fraternalism. Lawyers, along with their clients, joined the Masons, the Shriners, the Odd Fellows, the Woodmen of the World, the Rotary Club, the Elks, and the Knights of Pythias, many of them becoming almost professional "fraternalists," since membership brought them contacts and clients. These organizations promoted a sense of unity and tradition and aid to members and to their communities.

On Thanksgiving night in 1915, a new organization appeared. A small group of men who had attended the Atlanta premiere of D.W. Griffith's silent movie *Birth of a Nation*, based on the Reverend Thomas Dixon's romantic account of the Reconstruction-era Ku Klux Klan (KKK), climbed Georgia's Stone Mountain and lit a cross to summon the "invisible empire" back into existence after a hiatus of 40 years. There were various aspects to the resurrected KKK which appealed to different seg-

This 1923 Ku Klux Klan rally at East Lake in Birmingham yielded 2,100 new members. Although on the surface it shared characteristics with more mainstream fraternal organizations, the increasing use of threats and violence to enforce its views soon separated the Klan from the others. As the state headquarters of the Klan, and with the largest membership, Birmingham felt the influence of the Klan more than any other city in Alabama. By 1925, the Klan effectively controlled the city's government.

ments of the population, including charitable work, fraternal meetings, promotion of civic-mindedness, expanded education, and progressive government. There was also an aspect which promoted conformity to conservative, Protestant morality and to white supremacy. Gradually, the drive for conformity generated a tendency toward the use of violence.

This newly constituted version of the Klan soon outstripped any of the other active fraternal organizations in Alabama in membership. The growth in membership has been attributed, in large part, to the energetic efforts of Birmingham attorney James W. Esdale, a consummate fraternal promoter who would become the state Klan's Grand Dragon as it expanded in size and political clout. As it grew in power, it created a list of enemies that also grew to include not only African Americans but also Catholics and other immigrants, political radicals, labor unions, women suffragists, "wets," Jews, and anyone who deviated from what the Klan deemed "one hundred percent Americanism."

The Klan was a secret society, so it is unknown how many lawyers were members statewide. Some members who were attorneys are known and include Birmingham lawyer-politicians George Frey (who was Esdale's law partner); Hugh Locke (the founder of the Birmingham School of Law and a circuit judge); and Horace Wilkinson (who served as Grand Cyclop of the powerful Nathan Bedford Forrest Klan Klavern in Woodlawn and as a Klan lawyer and political strategist.) Two other Klan-affiliated lawyers were law partners Crampton Harris (who became Cyclops of the Robert E. Lee Klavern in Birmingham, the oldest and largest of the klaverns of the resurrected Klan), and Hugo Black (whose affiliation with the Klan provided the votes he needed in 1926 to become a U.S. senator from Alabama). Being the Klan headquarters and having the greatest Klan membership (approximately 18,000 members at its height), Birmingham felt the impact of the Klan more than any other place in the state during the first half of 1920s. By 1925, the Klan's slate had won a bitterly contested election and the Klan controlled the government of Alabama's largest city.

TOP: *Birmingham attorney James W. Esdale is credited with the rapid growth in Klan membership in Alabama.* ABOVE: *George P. Bondurant urged passage of legislation to outlaw Ku Klux Klan tactics through both the Birmingham and state bar associations.*

The Klan Gains Political Control of the State

The Klan revealed a penchant toward violence soon after its organization in 1915. The pace of violence picked up with uneven reaction by state and local law enforcement officers (who were often themselves Klan members). An incident involving the flogging of Birmingham's public health officer in May 1922 inspired the Birmingham Bar Association to attempt to get the city commission to adopt a local ordinance forbidding parades of masked persons and making abduction a criminal offense. Leadership was provided by state senator and attorney George P. Bondurant and former U.S. Senator Frank White. These efforts failed when a large contingent of Klan members attended the commission meeting where it was proposed and made their opposition known.

The state bar association at its annual meeting in 1923 adopted a resolution proposed by its legislative committee, headed by Bondurant, to submit a comparable proposal to the state legislature. The act read:

Be it enacted by the Legislature of Alabama:

1. It shall be a felony for any person or persons to wear any mask or other disguise in order to escape identification while engaged in or about menacing, intimidating, frightening, assaulting, or otherwise harming or making an overt demonstration of force against any person or

ATTORNEY WILLIAM W. BRANDON GOVERNOR, 1923-1927

THE KLAN'S POLITICAL POWER GREW RAPIDLY, but it was not until the statewide election of 1926 that it had an impact on the governor's office. Attorney William W. Brandon, the third attorney to win the governor's office in the twentieth century, was carried into office in 1923 on the personal popularity he had achieved prior to the advent of the Klan. Known as "Plain Bill," he was born in Talladega, received his early education at Cedar Bluff Institute in Cherokee County, and graduated from high school in Tuscaloosa. He took a law course at the University of Alabama in 1891 and opened a law practice in Tuscaloosa in 1892. Brandon was a member of the National Guard and, in 1899, was appointed state adjutant general by Governor Joseph F. Johnston and reappointed by Governors Samford and Jelks, serving until 1907.

His political career began in 1891 when he was elected Tuscaloosa's city clerk, serving for three terms. He also was a justice of the peace and a state legislator, and served as reading clerk at the 1901 constitutional convention. He was state auditor and Tuscaloosa's probate judge. He made his first run for governor in 1918, against Thomas Kilby, coming in second to Kilby in the Democratic primary. He continued campaigning throughout Kilby's term in office, laying the foundation for success in 1922 against Bibb Graves. His winning platform was economy in government, no new taxes, and defense of the convict lease system. He was no progressive, and little new in social or governmental reform was accomplished during his administration. He inherited a substantial debt from Kilby's administration, where money had been spent on building a new state prison (named for Kilby) and expanding services to the mentally ill at Bryce Hospital and to children through the creation of the Child Welfare Department, which began enforcing laws regulating child labor and supervising institutions that cared for children. Kilby had also increased funding for education (from $3,750,000 in 1919 to $8,269,596 in 1922) and guided the passage of a new school code through the legislature (with the help of House speaker, attorney A. H. Carmichael).

A fiscal conservative, William W. Brandon turned the deficits inherited from Governor Kilby into a modest surplus.

Because the state prospered during his administration, Brandon was able, through financial restraint and good economic fortunes, to pass on a small surplus to the next governor. He also used bond money authorized during the Kilby administration to improve roads, which was important because of the increasing use of automobiles in the state. A major accomplishment of the Brandon administration was the creation of the Alabama State Docks Commission and construction of the docks in Mobile. The State Docks opened on June 25, 1928, with Governor Bibb Graves, Congressman John McDuffie, and U.S. Senator Hugo Black in attendance, all of whom were attorneys.

persons, or doing injury to any property, or while engaged in the doing of any unlawful act.

2. The wearing of any mask or disguise in any public place, or by any trespasser, shall be *prima facie* evidence of a violation of the preceding section. It shall be a felony for any person or persons to enforce or conspire with other persons, or endeavor to enforce any rule or order of conduct upon any other person or persons by means of physical force, or to endeavor or threaten to inflict physical punishment upon any person or persons for any cause whatsoever; provided, however, that this act shall not apply to parents, school teachers, or to officers of the law in the discharge of their respective duties.

3. Any two or more persons who jointly, or with others, participate in the same violation of any of the foregoing provisions may be tried jointly without the right to severance and separate trial, and the court may fix upon each one such punishment, if convicted, as in the judgment of the court shall seem just.

Klan influence defeated the proposal.

In fact, there were more and more examples of Klan political power as time went by. One of the first dramatic examples involved the 1924 Democratic National Convention, where Alabama Senator Oscar Underwood was again vying to become the Democratic candidate for president. Underwood had no ties to the Klan and chose to denounce the Klan in order to distinguish himself from his rival, William Gibbs McAdoo of Georgia, who identified himself as affiliated with the Klan. Underwood had sufficient clout to control the Alabama delegation, whose chairman Governor William Brandon became a fixture of political lore for his support of Underwood. Standing on a chair to be seen, given his five-foot, one-inch frame, he blasted out as the first votes were cast through 103 ballots, in a voice that did not need amplification to carry to the radio audience, "Alabama casts twenty-four votes for Oscar W. Underwood."

Brandon's voice and votes were remembered and talked about for years. His loyalty to Underwood did not prevent a ruckus from occurring when Underwood's campaign manager Forney Johnston (son of former Governor Joseph F. Johnston and a prominent Birmingham corporate attorney) called upon the convention to censure the Ku Klux Klan during his speech nominating Underwood. Johnston's nominating speech touched off fistfights, parades, and demonstrations between Klan supporters and opponents which threatened to tear the convention apart. Underwood failed to win the nomination and totally alienated himself from the group soon to be the most powerful political force in his home state, resulting in his withdrawing from politics in 1926 when it was time for him to run for the Senate again.

ABOVE: *Basing his candidacy for the Democratic nomination for president on opposition to the Ku Klux Klan proved to be the undoing of Oscar W. Underwood, and ended his political career.* OPPOSITE PAGE: *Hugo Black, by unobtrusively resigning from the Ku Klux Klan, was able to exploit both pro- and anti-Klan support to win a surprise victory in the 1926 U.S. Senate race.*

Hugo Black, a self-described "jiner" of fraternal organizations, had joined Birmingham's Robert E. Lee Klan No. 1 Klavern in 1923, both to build the client base for his criminal and personal injury practice and to position himself to become a serious politician. He entered the 1926 Senate race even before Underwood bowed out. There were eventually five candidates to fill Underwood's seat: Former governor Thomas E. Kilby; James J. Mayfield, a former state supreme court justice; John H. Bankhead, II, attorney son of Senator John H. Bankhead, Sr.; Breckenridge Musgrove of Jasper who had run for the Senate in 1920 and almost beat Underwood at that time; and Black, who was considered the least likely to win since it was his first time to run for statewide office.

Within a month of announcing his candidacy, Hugo Black wrote a letter to James Esdale resigning his Klan membership. No public notice was given of the resignation, but it was a deliberate act of political strategy. There was little public awareness outside Birmingham of the fact that he had been a Klan member. He was better known for his work in the Baptist church, where he was a popular Sunday school teacher. He also had a reputation for his work enforcing prohibition as both a special assistant state attorney general and also, at times, as a special assistant U.S. attorney. Labor organizations were aware of his work as state president of the Alabama Prison Reform Association in 1923, when he had fought the use of convict labor in state coalmines. By quietly resigning his Klan membership, Black kept the advantages of Klan support while relieving himself of the disadvantages that membership would bring if he became a U.S. senator. Grand Dragon Esdale made sure that Black spoke at klavern meetings throughout the state on subjects of general interest. Black was also given the opportunity to speak on Sundays and Wednesday nights at Protestant church meetings, being described as a "noted Bible student." Although businessman Breckenridge Musgrove had had Klan support when he ran against Underwood in 1920, Esdale remained loyal to Black even after Musgrove entered the race, perhaps because they were both Birmingham attorneys.

While the other candidates and the political establishment paid him little notice, Black traveled the state daily, speaking in all 67 Alabama counties at least twice before primary election day. When the votes were counted, the state's traditional political establishment was surprised to find that Hugo Black had won the election with his down-home eloquence and his ability to relate to the common folks who came out in large numbers to vote.

The 1926 election also carried two other popular Klan members into statewide office: Bibb Graves and Charles C. McCall, both Montgomery attorneys and members of Montgomery's Klan No. 3, which was known for its civic-minded activities and which Graves had served as Grand Cyclops. Graves, a University of Alabama graduate with a civil engineering undergraduate degree and a membership in Phi Beta Kappa, had studied law for two years at the University of Texas before transferring and graduating from Yale's law school in 1893. He served in Alabama's legislature as early as 1898 and joined Joseph Johnston in opposing Alabama's 1901 constitution.

Graves served as chairman of the State Democratic Executive Committee in 1914, being elected as part of the statewide primary. In that election, B. B. Comer had sought a second term as governor and lost in the primary runoff. Graves, a Comer supporter, collaborated with the Anti-Saloon League in writing a new election law that abolished runoffs and provided that, in races with three or more candidates, each voter could, but was not required to, cast a first- and a second-choice vote. Candidates with a majority of first-choice votes were

THE GOVERNORSHIP OF BIBB GRAVES, 1927-1931

HISTORIANS MAINTAIN THAT BIBB GRAVES WAS an important governor because of his reform policies, especially in education. He was the first governor to serve two four-year terms in office. His alliance with the Klan was responsible for his election, since he had virtually no other organized support, whereas Charles McDowell, endorsed by Governor William Brandon, was the candidate of the traditional Bourbon elite and the supposed front-runner. A. H. Carmichael was the candidate of the small business, education, and prohibition forces, and A.G. Patterson, president of the state public service commission, attracted those who favored a "pay-as-you-go" approach to highway construction. The Klan's alliances with labor and temperance groups helped counter the electoral power of the Black Belt planters and corporate elites who made up the conservative forces that had traditionally controlled the Democratic Party.

During World War I, Graves commanded an Alabama regiment that saw action in France, reaching the rank of colonel and being known as Colonel Graves thereafter. He was active in veterans' affairs after the war, helping organize the American Legion in Alabama. His first run for the governorship was against William W. Brandon, who had soundly beaten him in 1922. That loss caused many to write him off when he ran again in 1926, but the election demonstrated the political power of the resurrected Ku Klux Klan. It also demonstrated the impact of the double-choice primary system he had helped introduce in 1915. He received less than thirty percent of first-choice votes, but had more combined first- and second-choice votes than any other candidate and thus became the Democratic nominee.

Once in office, he entered upon a course of progressive government which included the abolition of the convict lease system and an aggressive highway and bridge construction program, funded by $30 million in state bonds financed by driver's license fees and gasoline taxes and matched by federal highway monies. He also

nominated, but if no candidate secured a majority, the nomination went to the one receiving the largest combination of first- and second-choice votes. This new system remained in effect during the 1918, 1922, 1926, and 1930 gubernatorial elections, and Graves became its major beneficiary. He won the 1926 election against attorney candidates A. H. Carmichael (former speaker of the House) and Charles S. McDowell (Governor Brandon's lieutenant governor who represented the interests of the traditional Democratic machine) by receiving the largest combination of first- and second-choice votes.

Charley McCall was the son of Charles E. McCall, who had served as chief examiner of public accounts and as a Montgomery circuit judge. He studied law at Georgetown and American Universities in Washington, D.C. and served as a JAG (Judge Advocate General) in World War I. Upon his return to Alabama, he joined Klan No. 3 in Montgomery for political reasons, riding its popularity to the office of attorney general in 1926.

Ironically, McCall, the state's chief law enforcement officer, soon became an adversary of the Klan when he was confronted with Klan violence throughout the state in 1927. One notorious incident involved Jeff Calloway, an illiterate 19-year-old white orphan, who was flogged with an automobile fan belt for being intoxicated at a Sunday night service at Antioch Baptist Church. Public outcry caused Governor Graves to order an investigation and McCall was able to get a conviction of two of the floggers, inspiring several others to plead guilty and pay fines. Birmingham attorney Horace Wilkinson was the defense attorney for the Klansmen. This incident is remembered as the cause of a precipitous decline in Klan membership (dropping from an estimated 94,000 statewide in 1926 to 10,500 by the end of 1927.)

Although elected with Klan backing, Bibb Graves's first term was marked by a number of reforms, including the abolition of the convict lease system, and major increases in spending on education and highway and bridge construction.

kept his campaign promise of providing adequate funding for education and expanding the annual school term to seven months statewide (44 counties had shorter terms in 1926.) The legislature (many members of which were also elected with Klan backing) passed the largest appropriation for education thus far in Alabama's history, going from a $9.9 million dollar budget under Governor Brandon to $25 million during Graves's first administration. Additional sources of funding were directed to education through taxes on tobacco products and corporations.

Graves also oversaw the rewriting of Alabama's education codes, including the addition of a Division of Negro Education with an African-American director and staff member. In 1929, the normal schools at Florence, Jacksonville, Livingston, and Troy were designated as state teachers' colleges, which could grant bachelor of science degrees. Although still behind in most respects when compared with other states, Alabama's educational system saw tremendous advances under Graves when compared with its own past. Public and mental health services, as well as child welfare services, also benefited from Graves's attention, increasing appropriations and decreasing the number of employed children.

The Klan supported Graves's reformist efforts, but required payment. The price was ignoring Klan violence or interfering with the prosecution of Klan perpetrators. Historians debate whether the price was too high, and Graves's reputation as a liberal was tarnished by his Klan association during his first administration.

Violence erupted throughout the state during 1927 and floggings became epidemic. Concerted efforts to prosecute Klansmen usually failed, because of intimidation of witnesses, recalcitrance of defendants, and jury venires sympathetic to the Klan. McCall and other prosecutors, such as Bart B. Chamberlain of Mobile and Jim Davis of Birmingham, who helped McCall prosecute throughout the state, were frustrated by the legal maneuvers of Horace Wilkinson, who became well known for his ability to devise legal strategies to defeat the prosecutors. Frustration arose because the prosecutors were aware that Wilkinson was one of Governor Graves's chief political advisors.

In one Klan-controlled county, Crenshaw County, McCall was able to convince the grand jury to hand down over 100 indictments involving at least 44 members of the Klan. McCall presented evidence of at least 20 acts of flogging, including such outrageous incidents as the savage beating of a husband and wife who had both had previous marriages. The Klan member who led the group of floggers in this incident was the Baptist preacher who had performed the couple's marriage. Another victim was a 17-year-old divorcee who was beaten for dating a farmer. The "Cyclops" of the Crenshaw County Luverne Klavern was Ira Thompson, an attorney who was active in several fraternal organizations, his church, and Democratic politics. (He would later serve as legal counsel to Governor Jim Folsom during his first administration.) He later maintained that a rogue element of undisciplined and violent men was able to subvert the klavern and use it for their own violent ends, as they planned and executed several outrageous floggings while he was so busy with his legal practice and other organizations that he lost control over the klavern.

Attorney General Charles C. McCall, above, served as a JAG during World War I. When he took on the Klan, his legal antagonist was Horace Wilkinson, right, also a veteran of the war, and a Klan member. Wilkinson had a valuable ally in Governor Graves, who was suspected of undermining McCall's efforts.

Evidence presented by McCall to the grand jury suggested though that it was the Klan's state and local leadership that actually authorized the floggings. Soon, Klan leaders began pressuring Governor Graves to quiet McCall, and Graves did this by reducing the attorney general's budget and pulling the support of his office for McCall's anti-Klan activities. McCall even found evidence in a search of Ira Thompson's home that suggested that the governor's office and the state police were actually trying to actively undermine McCall's prosecutorial efforts.

At the time of this prosecution, there were less than ten attorneys in Crenshaw County, one of them being the local Klan leader. McCall employed another, F. B. Bricken, to help him prosecute. Even with local help, McCall was unable to gain one guilty verdict and, to make matters worse, Wilkinson was able to get the Calloway prosecutions overturned upon appeal on technicalities. The Klan did in fact control state government.

The Traditionalists Fight Back

As the Klan grew in political power, more and more of the state's newspapers used their editorial pages to fight it. These newspapers represented the traditional Bourbon oligarchy that had for so long controlled state Democratic politics. Historian Glenn Feldman suggests that much of the opposition to Klan violence was actually rooted in the oligarchy's desire to regain control of the state's political machinery. The 1928 presidential contest gave them that opportunity.[2]

In 1928, the National Democratic Convention nominated Al Smith, the governor of New York, as its presidential candidate. Herbert Hoover was the Republican candidate. For Alabama's conservative Democrats, Smith represented all the national issues that repelled them. He was a Catholic with an immigrant background, an anti-Prohibition stand, and a membership in Tammany Hall, which for many was the supreme example of a corrupt political machine. For Klansmen, especially, his candidacy caused a quick, negative reaction. The anti-Smith force was led by U.S. Senator J. Thomas Heflin and Birmingham lawyers Hugh Locke and Horace Wilkinson. Racism

which was automatically part of the campaign, added to the national issues of "rum, Romanism, and nativism," giving a decidedly Southern flavor to the campaign in Alabama. Wilkinson introduced the "hate sheet" campaign tactic, viciously attacking Smith and his supporters with vulgar race-baiting handouts distributed throughout the state. Heflin became an anti-Smith speaker throughout the country, ranting against the Catholic Church and its pope.

As the campaign progressed, the Klan contingent encouraged Alabama Democrats to vote for Hoover, even entering an agreement with the state's Republican party boss, Guntersville attorney Oliver D. Street, to list 12 Democrats as Hoover electors, thereby allowing voters to vote for anti-Smith Democrats rather than voting for Republicans. This maneuver threatened the regular Democrats, who deemed party loyalty and regularity as the state party's most important political principles. The reaction of the State Democratic Executive Committee (SDEC) was to label those who supported Hoover as "bolters" from the party. The committee particularly condemned Heflin, who had been an elected Democratic official for many years. He reacted by publicly vowing to "vote against Al Smith, so help me God!"

Race-baiting became a part of the SDEC's campaign strategy to maintain the status quo. They called to voters' minds Republican Reconstruction and federal interference in state affairs, playing upon what one historian has described as "Reconstruction Syndrome," the continuing fear, hatred, and mistrust of the federal government that had been aroused after the Civil War ended. They raised the image of ignorant black voters taking control of state and county offices, which they argued would be the result of a Hoover victory. "White supremacy" required that voters maintain the one-party politics that had been the hallmark of Alabama politics since the "Redemption" in 1874.

William B. "Buck" Oliver, top, and John McDuffie were Alabama congressmen who stumped for Al Smith during the 1928 Presidential campaign. Oliver was Smith's campaign manager in the state. Mobile's John McDuffie served eight terms in Congress.

The party regulars who covered the state in favor of Al Smith included all of Alabama's congressmen: William B. Bankhead, George Huddleston, Henry Steagall, E. B. Almon, Lister Hill, John McDuffie, and William B. "Buck" Oliver, all of whom were attorneys. "Buck" Oliver, who represented Tuscaloosa and its surroundings in Congress, was in charge of Smith's Alabama campaign. Other Democratic heavyweights supporting Smith included attorneys John Bankhead, II, of Jasper; Judge Leon McCord of Marshall County; Mayor William A. Gunter of Montgomery; Wilcox County judge Benjamin M. Miller (who became governor in 1931); Edmund W. Pettus, II, of Selma (who was the chairman of the SDEC and grandson of Senator Edmund Pettus); Thomas Samford of Opelika (son of ex-governor William J. Samford); and state representatives R. Tyler Goodwyn of Montgomery and Samuel Hobbs of Selma. Birmingham attorneys F. D. McArthur (who had managed Governor William Brandon's gubernatorial campaign) and Frank Dixon (who became governor in 1939), Attorney General Charley

McCall, and former house speaker A. H. Carmichael as well as former attorney general Major Harwell G. Davis, also promoted Smith. Two important Alabama politicians who did not take part in the contest were Governor Bibb Graves and Senator Hugo Black. They kept faith with the regular Democratic Party, understanding that it would ultimately seek revenge on the bolters and that the KKK was only a shell of the political force that it had been when they were elected into office in 1926. They did not publicly rebuke the bolters.

When Smith carried the state, the political capital of Heflin, Locke, and Wilkinson plummeted. Wilkinson redirected his energies to Birmingham, where he continued to control political patronage in city government. Locke wanted to run for governor in 1930, while Tom Heflin would face a reelection campaign. Heflin had embarrassed the regular Democratic Party and undermined its position in the national political arena by his demagogic conduct during the 1928 campaign. The party was prepared to do

Their unwavering opposition to Al Smith in the 1928 election led to the political downfall of both U.S. Senator Tom Heflin, above, who faced reelection in 1930, and Hugh Locke, opposite page above, who had gubernatorial aspirations. When the state Democratic party moved to expel both men, attorney Ben Ray, opposite page below, was among those to speak out unsuccessfully in their favor. Heflin and Locke were forced to run as independents.

what it took to prevent his return to the U.S. Senate. A proposal was made that the bolters be expelled from the party and not allowed to conduct their 1930 campaigns as candidates of the Democratic Party.

At a December 1929 meeting, Decatur attorney Seybourn Lynne, a former speaker of the Alabama House of Representatives, made the motion for expulsion. Tuscaloosa attorney John D. McQueen, a future chairman of the party and president of the Alabama State Bar (from 1932 to 1933), seconded the motion. Birmingham attorneys Ben Ray and Horace Wilkinson, as well as

Hamilton attorney Arthur F. Fite, spoke against expulsion, but the motion passed by a margin of six votes (27-21). Other attorneys on the committee at the time included Birmingham attorneys Borden Burr and Frank Dominick and Selma attorney Samuel Hobbs.

Soon the expelled candidates brought suit against the SDEC. Wilkinson and Crampton Harris of Birmingham represented the bolters, who won at the Court of Appeals level, arguing that they were treated unlawfully since voters who had supported Hoover were not being expelled from the party. The SDEC, represented by Forney Johnston, appealed to the Alabama Supreme Court, which found in the committee's favor, holding that the expulsion was a party matter over which the committee had absolute power.

Locke and Heflin then determined to run as independent "Jeffersonian Democrats," with Wilkinson as their unofficial campaign manager. Attorney Dempsey Powell of Greenville ran as their candidate for lieutenant governor. The Republicans agreed not to run candidates for the offices they were seeking in the general election.

Jasper attorney John H. Bankhead, II, ran for the U.S. Senate in the Democratic primary, beating Frederick Thompson, a newspaper publisher. Bankhead had previously managed the congressional campaigns of his father (who was in the U.S. Congress for a total of 33 years, 20 years in the House and 13 years in the Senate) and his younger brother, attorney William Bankhead, who was first elected to Congress in 1917. John H. Bankhead, II, beat Tom Heflin and joined his brother in Washington in time for them to become important supporters of Franklin Roosevelt's New Deal during the Depression.

Benjamin M. Miller, a circuit judge from Wilcox County and a die-hard fiscal conservative, who made opposition to the KKK the keystone of his campaign, was the gubernatorial candidate supported by the regular Democrats. Attorneys Charley McCall, Jeff Carnley of Coffee County, and William C. Davis, who had been Graves's lieutenant governor, also ran in the Democratic primary. Miller won the primary and beat Hugh Locke as well. Hugh D. Merrill, who had served as speaker of the House during William Brandon's administration, was the Democratic nominee for lieutenant governor and beat Dempsey Powell in the general election.

Tom Heflin contested his lost election before the U.S. Senate, with Horace Wilkinson directing the contest. Hugo Black, in an obvious split with the KKK, voted against holding the hearing on alleged voter fraud that Heflin requested, but other senators supported Heflin, and the hearing was held. The contest was considered a huge embarrassment by many Alabamians and effectively ended Tom Heflin's political career when the decision went against him. It was also the end of the political power of the 1920s version of the Ku Klux Klan.

CHAPTER ELEVEN

THE NEW DEAL AND WORLD WAR II YEARS

The U.S. Labor Department described Birmingham as the American city hardest hit by the Depression and people all across the state suffered as well. Alabama entered the Depression already in debt due to Governor Bibb Graves's spending to promote education and other social services during his first administration. Benjamin Miller was a fiscal conservative proud to have it known that he still used oil lamps instead of electricity on his Wilcox County plantation to save money (even though Miller's family had huge land holdings in Wilcox County, he had a substantial law practice, as well as having been a circuit judge, and even an associate justice of the Alabama Supreme Court before becoming governor). He campaigned as an advocate of strict fiscal responsibility and no new taxes, and he held to this promise in the early days of his administration. Miller even brought his own favorite cow to the governor's mansion to provide milk and butter for his family.

But, in the face of the human suffering from the Depression, Miller borrowed $500,000 to keep the state's social service agencies functioning and proposed to increase its borrowing limits. He commissioned a study by the Brookings Institution to evaluate Alabama's finances and governmental systems, but the legislature failed to pass any of the reforms the study proposed.

In an attempt to balance the state's budget, Miller eliminated hundreds of state jobs and restricted the use of state automobiles. As time passed, he moved away from his "no new taxes" pledge, seeking a two-cent hike in the gasoline tax, which eventually passed as a one-cent increase. Refusing to push for a sales tax, because it was regressive and hurt the very people who were already suffering the most, Miller proposed a state income tax instead. It took three attempts to get a constitutional amendment authorizing such a tax, but it finally passed when it was matched with an amendment previously passed by the legislature as the "Budget Control Act of 1932," guaranteeing that money could only be spent if it was already in the state's treasury. This promise of a balanced budget inspired voter approval of an income tax measure. At around the same time, the Twenty-first Amendment repealing Prohibition was also ratified by state voters. In the midst of Miller's term, Franklin Delano Roosevelt was elected president and soon his New Deal programming began bringing much needed revenues to the state.

Even though one theme of Miller's campaign for governor had been his opposition to the Ku Klux Klan, he did little in the face of several violent episodes of vigilantism during his term.

It was during this period that the famous Scottsboro boys were tried, convicted, retried, and began their stay trapped for years in the Alabama legal system, even though it was apparent to many (mostly outside the state) that they were innocent of the alleged rape of two white girls who were caught "riding the rails" on the same train as they were. Many commentators consider this case the first success in the long battle of African Americans to gain civil rights, since from it came two major U.S. Supreme Court cases, one granting blacks the right to have African Americans on grand jury and petit jury venires, and the other granting a right to adequate appointed counsel.

OPPOSITE PAGE: *Governor Benjamin Miller cultivated a frugal image somewhat at odds with his wealth and political influence.* BELOW: *The Historic American Building Survey, a New Deal program, photographed Miller's Camden law office in 1937.*

LAWYERS AND THE SCOTTSBORO BOYS TRIALS

Alabama lawyers primarily played the roles of jurists and prosecutors in the Scottsboro boys' trials. The nine were first tried before Circuit Judge Alfred E. Hawkins in Scottsboro, with circuit solicitor H. G. Bailey prosecuting. Hawkins originally assigned all seven members of the Scottsboro Bar to represent the boys, but soon all but one withdrew. Three—John Franklin Proctor, James Moody Proctor, and John Milton Snodgrass (the mayor's son)—were hired by locals to help the prosecutor. D. P. Wimberly, a corporate attorney who represented Alabama Power Company, requested and received permission to

withdraw. Finally, only Milo C. Moody and Ernest Parks remained. Moody was just about to turn seventy. He was a Jackson County delegate to the 1901 Constitutional Convention with an agrarian political philosophy and was described by one who met him at the time as a "doddering, extremely unreliable, senile individual who is losing whatever ability he once had." A Chattanooga attorney, Stephen R. Roddy, who represented unpopular causes, but who also had a drinking problem, was retained by a black ministers' group to investigate a possible defense for the boys. Although the judge had appointed Ernest Parks as counsel, he was allowed to withdraw when Moody and Roddy agreed to represent the boys on the day the trials began.[1]

The case of the Scottsboro boys was an early battle in the civil rights war. Twice the guilty verdicts were appealed to the United States Supreme Court, and twice the convictions were overturned, with important precedents being set regarding the composition of juries and the right to legal counsel.

Because the trials took place within days of the boys' arrest, the lawyers had no time for preparation and only a brief interview with the defendants. In this first trial series, eight of the boys were found guilty and given the death penalty. There was a mistrial in the case of the 13-year-old defendant because seven of the jurors insisted on the death penalty even though the state had only asked for life imprisonment.

Within days of the convictions, both the International Labor Defense organization (ILD) (the legal arm of the American Communist Party) and the National Association for the Advancement of Colored People (NAACP) had decided to intervene in the case. The organizations struggled for months to get the defendants and their parents (since they were all minors) to authorize representation for an appeal by one or the other of the organizations. The NAACP was able to gain a commitment from the Birmingham firm of William E. Fort, Roderick Beddow, and Ben Ray (with Roderick Beddow, who many considered to be Alabama's foremost criminal lawyer, to conduct the representation) to defend the boys if the parents and defendants agreed. Beddow interviewed the defendants several times, but finally the ILD was able to get the necessary authorizations to take charge of the defense and the NAACP had no alternative but to withdraw. Therefore, the Scottsboro boys were represented by George W. Chamlee, Sr., a member of a prominent Tennessee family from Chattanooga, retained on the boys' behalf by the ILD, and Joseph Brodsky, ILD's chief counsel from New York, as their case continued through the appellate process.

The case raised several issues for white Alabamians. For even those who were moderate where race was concerned (moderate, because at the time there were few who could truly be described as liberal in the state), the fact that the case was tried seemed a huge step in the right direction, since a mass lynching could have easily occurred. Also, when rape was the charge, white Alabamians always believed the white woman over the black man as a matter of tradition, the idea being that white Southern womanhood was placed on a pedestal, regardless of the social status or the previous moral conduct of the woman. Therefore, the guilty verdict based on the testimony of the white "victims" seemed justified. Outside intervention was unacceptable to a society that still rankled from the memory of Radical Reconstruction and the mythology of the "Lost Cause." Added to that was the fact that the outsiders were communists, or, in the case of Chamblee, willing to be retained by a communist organization on the boys' behalf, aggravating fears of radicalism. Further, the communists added insult to injury by opening an office in Birmingham and openly recruiting membership in Birmingham's black community, which was suffering from the Depression, as well as planting an organizer in rural Tallapoosa County. Anti-Semitism became an issue because the ILD's chief counsel, who participated in the trial, was Jewish. And, finally, at the foundation of the Southern response was a strongly held belief that the black race was inferior to the white race and that blacks had to be controlled, because radical outsiders, black or white, could possibly organize a black revolt. Alabamians accused of prejudice were certain that their prejudices were justified and the times insured that fairness and justice would be difficult to come by, since there were differing versions of what fairness and justice would entail, especially when the American Communist Party was using the case as a propaganda tool to recruit new members.

On appeal to the Alabama Supreme Court, the state's case was argued by Attorney General Thomas E. Knight, Jr., who was the 34-year-old son of a sitting associate justice. Chief Justice John C. Anderson opened the court by noting the number of letters and telegrams received by the court, which he described as "highly improper, inflammatory, and revolutionary in their nature." Although Brodsky and Chamblee eloquently presented several reasonable arguments for why the cases should be overturned, the decision went against the defendants. The Communist Party's use of the case as a vehicle for raising the "class consciousness of the proletariat" only increased the prejudice against their cause among Alabamians, including members of the court. The court's decision was written by Thomas E. Knight, Sr., the attorney general's father.

Thomas E. Knight, Sr., was an associate justice on the Alabama Supreme Court when his son, Attorney General Thomas E. Knight, Jr., argued the case for the state in the first Scottsboro boys' appeal. Judge Knight also wrote the opinion.

The case was appealed to the U.S. Supreme Court, with the ILD retaining Walter Pollak, considered one of the nation's preeminent constitutional attorneys, to represent the defendants. The Court agreed to hear the appeal. Again Knight represented the state, rebutting Pollak's arguments that the defendants were not given adequate counsel or a jury of their peers and that there was an overall lack of fairness in the circumstances of their trial. After deliberating for a month, the court delivered its decision on November 7, 1932, holding that Judge Hawkins had been unacceptably casual in providing the defendants with legal representation, thereby violating the defendants' due process rights to adequate counsel, which the Court concluded were provided by the Fourteenth Amendment.[2] The cases were remanded for retrial.

On retrial, the ILD employed New York attorney Samuel Leibowitz to represent the boys. Considered by many to have taken the retired Clarence Darrow's place as America's leading criminal trial attorney, he would finish his career as a justice of the New York Supreme Court. The first action of the defense was to move for a change of venue. The motion was granted by Judge Hawkins, who transferred the case to Decatur, with Judge James Edwin Horton, Jr., presiding. Attorney General Thomas Knight, Jr., along with Morgan County solicitor Wade Wright and Jackson County solicitor H. G. Bailey, represented the prosecution.

At the opening of the trial, Wright read the indictment, which the defense immediately moved be quashed because there were no blacks on the Jackson County venire from which the grand jury had been selected. After testimony was presented, Judge Horton denied the motion. Then, Leibowitz challenged Morgan County's jury venire as well, on the basis that there were no blacks on the roll from which the jury in the current case would be drawn. Again Judge Horton denied the motion, but he did rule that the defense had established a *prima facie* case of exclusion. He lectured those in attendance, and, through them the whole county that he had heard rumors of possible violence planned against the defense attorney and he stated sternly that "only by obeying all the laws of the land could a free people enjoy the benefits of liberty. No other course is open to you…and let no one think they can act otherwise than in this manner."

The state offered as witness only one of the two doctors who had examined the alleged rape victims, stating that the testimony of the second doctor would be duplicative. According to an interview given by Judge Horton many years later, the second doctor, Dr. Marvin Lynch, asked to talk to the judge privately. In that private meeting, the doctor told the judge that he firmly believed that the girls had not been raped at all. He is quoted as telling the judge, "Judge, I looked at both the women and told them they were lying, that they knew they had not been raped and they just laughed at me." The doctor then told the judge that if he were to testify, he knew that he would not be able to practice again in Scottsboro and he did not want to have to start over.[3] This news left the judge stunned and shaken in his prior belief that the defendants were probably guilty, a conviction already weakened because the testimony of the state's primary witness, Victoria Price, had been evasive and contradictory. He contemplated requiring Dr. Lynch to testify or ending the trial himself. He decided to put his faith in the jury, since he knew more than half of them and trusted they would do justice.

John C. Anderson was the chief justice of the Alabama Supreme Court at the time of the Scottsboro boys case. When Judge James E. Horton vacated the verdict in the second trial, Attorney General Knight pressured Anderson to remove Judge Horton from the case.

But his faith was not borne out, even though witnesses Lester Carter, who had ridden the train with the girls, and Ruby Bates, the other alleged victim, appeared after having been in New York, and testified that there had been no rape. Morgan County solicitor Wade Wright gave the state's summation, giving voice to all the prejudices of the area residents, including anti-Semitic slurs toward defense counsel, and ended his statement by saying, "Show them, show them that Alabama justice cannot be bought and sold with Jew money from New York." The first defendant who was retried, Haywood Patterson, was found guilty and given the death sentence.

Observers commented at the time that, even though evidence which suggested innocence was presented, the jurors, like the community at large, suspected that the witnesses for the defense had been paid money and coached in giving their evidence, because local residents distrusted the ILD and the intrusion of outside lawyers and outside money. Thus, the case against the defendants, already prejudiced by their race and the fact that their alleged victims were white, was furthered prejudiced by the latent anti-Semitic "Shylock" image evoked by Wade Wright's chants of "Jew money" and the image of radical "outside interference" in a local matter. As historian Dan T. Carter summed it up, the "jury's loyalty to its white caste could only be proved unequivocally by a guilty verdict. Whether Haywood Patterson was guilty or innocent was, at most, a peripheral question."

The verdict was handed down on April 10, 1933. On June 22, 1933, Judge Horton convened court in his hometown, Athens, to hear a defense motion for a new trial. Prior to that date, Judge Horton had quietly communicated with state officials concerning the future of the case and had even proposed to Attorney General Knight that the state *nol pros* the remainder of the proceedings and then pardon Haywood Patterson. Although Knight agreed to consider the judge's suggestion, he ultimately rejected it, perhaps because he knew it would kill any chances he had of fulfilling his aspirations to be elected governor of Alabama. Therefore, on June 23, Judge Horton took matters into his own hands and immediately began reading from his already prepared opinion, "Social order is based on law and its perpetuity on its fair and impartial administration." He noted that although the victim of deliberate injustice died quickly, and his suffering ceased, "the teachings of Christianity and the uniform lessons of all history illustrate without exception that its perpetrators not only pay the penalty themselves, but their children through endless generations." After carefully reviewing the evidence in elaborate detail, especially the evidence which failed to corroborate the fact that there had been a rape at all, he granted the defendant's motion for a new trial, finding that there was insufficient evidence to support the verdict. It was his hope that his reasoned and deliberate opinion, and perhaps his stature in the community, might inspire the state to stop pursuing the prosecution of the Scottsboro boys, but it did not. Attorney General Knight quickly and angrily avowed that a new trial would be pursued as soon as possible.

Chief Justice Charles Evans Hughes of the U.S. Supreme Court delivered the opinion in the second appeal stemming from the Scottsboro boys trials. The court overturned the convictions holding that the exclusion of blacks from the jury pool was a violation of the Fourteenth Amendment.

Thereafter, Knight was able to bring pressure on Chief Justice Anderson to have Horton removed from the case. Anderson wrote Horton requesting that he voluntarily withdraw to which Horton reluctantly acquiesced, even though he had supporters, including Leo Oberdorfer, incoming president of the Alabama State Bar (1933-1934). His detractors accused Horton of being a coward, kowtowing to outside agitators and seeking notoriety; today, he is considered the hero of the whole affair. In the May 1934 Democratic primary in which Horton sought reelection, he ran second in a field of three candidates (after having no opposition in the 1928 primary) and although he campaigned actively throughout the circuit, he lost in the runoff, 9,416-6,856. Attorney General Knight, on the other hand, was elected lieutenant governor.

Horton, who was a member of one of north Alabama's pioneer families, thereafter served as an attorney for the Tennessee Valley Authority, dealing specifically with land acquisitions for the New Deal project. After 1940, he spent most of his time running his family's 1,440-acre farm which was described as "one of the most progressive and highly improved agricultural establishments in north Alabama," raising prize-winning pure-bred Angus cattle. He moved his "beautiful antebellum mansion" which had been in his family since the 1840s from the city of Athens to his farm. In conversations over 32 years after the trial, he insisted to Dan T. Carter that he had no regrets, saying that there was a motto in the Horton family best expressed in the Latin phrase he had learned as a child—*fiat justitia ruat coelum*—let justice be done though the heavens may fall.

Although Judge Horton had hoped to forestall further damage to the reputation of the state and its judicial system by his actions, the prosecution of the Scottsboro boys continued. This time, they were tried in Decatur by Judge William Washington Callahan, who was born in Lawrence County in 1863, and was 70 years old when he took charge of the case. After two trials, in which both verdicts were guilty with the death sentence, the rest of the trials were postponed so that these two cases could be appealed, on the theory that blacks had been systematically excluded from the jury rolls. The verdicts were again upheld by the Alabama Supreme Court. But this time, on appeal to the U.S. Supreme Court, the court, with Chief Justice Charles Evans Hughes delivering the opinion, held that exclusion of all blacks from jury service deprived a black defendant of his right to the equal protection of the law guaranteed by the Fourteenth Amendment.[4] The Court also found that sufficient evidence of such exclusion had been presented. The case was again remanded to the Alabama Supreme Court for further action, and it quashed the indictments.

By this time, Bibb Graves had been elected governor for a second term. He was given high marks when he instructed all circuit courts to insure that blacks were included on their venires. A new grand jury convened in Jackson County, with one black member, and issued a new indictment against the nine Scottsboro boys. They were returned to Decatur for trial before Judge Callahan. Thomas Knight was now lieutenant governor, but newly elected Attorney

General Albert A. Carmichael retained him to continue with the prosecutions. The ILD retained Huntsville attorney Clarence Watts for the defense, with Leibowitz behind the scenes.

In the first trial, against Haywood Patterson, the sentence was 75 years in prison, not the death penalty, even though there was a guilty verdict. The jury foreman, a young, prosperous farmer who believed that there had been no rape, would not agree to the death penalty, but could not convince the other jurors to acquit. Historian Dan Carter suggests that that verdict may have been a turning point in the prosecution and some movement toward a compromise soon began.

Future Alabama Supreme Court justice Thomas S. Lawson, then assistant attorney general, took over prosecution of the Scottsboro boys trials following the unexpected death of Lieutenant Governor Thomas E. Knight, Jr.

Five days before resumption of the trials, Thomas Knight, Jr., died suddenly and the case was taken over by Assistant Attorney General Thomas Lawson (who would soon be elected to the Alabama Supreme Court). This case involved Clarence Norris, who was found guilty and given the death penalty. In the next three cases, the death penalty was not sought. Andy Wright was found guilty and given 99 years. Charley Weems was found guilty and given 75 years, and Ozie Powell was prosecuted only for assault and given 20 years. Then, the cases of the remaining four defendants were *nol prossed*: They were Willie Roberson, who was crippled with venereal disease at the time of the original arrest; Olen Montgomery, who was almost blind at the time of the original arrest; and Eugene Williams and Leroy Wright, who were 12 and 13 years old at the time of the original arrest. Thus, after six years of being held in prison, four of the prisoners were released.

The Alabama legislature created a Pardon and Parole Board in 1939, which was given full authority to grant pardons and paroles. (Birmingham's state senator, attorney James Simpson, was a primary force behind the creation of the board.) The first board was comprised of Judge Alex Smith, Judge Robert M. Hill (who had been judge of Lauderdale County's law and equity court), and Edwina D. Mitchell (an attorney who served as an assistant attorney general, wrote the legislation establishing the Pardon and Parole Board, and who later became superintendent of the Julia Tutwiler Prison). They were approached by the Scottsboro Defense Committee (a group which had been established in 1935 to support the defense of the boys) concerning a parole. Beginning on November 17, 1943, the board began to quietly release the remaining boys, with Charley Weems being the first. Finally, on October 25, 1976, Governor George Wallace, with the sponsorship of Attorney General Bill Baxley, signed a full and unconditional pardon for Clarence Norris, the last of the boys still alive, restoring his civil rights.

The story of the Scottsboro boys is a long story which continued to stir many prejudices throughout the period of the thirties and forties. Its impact on the attitudes of Alabamians should be recognized when one considers the political climate confronting African Americans who would begin struggling against "Jim Crowism" in the 1950s.

Alabama's Attorney Congressmen and the New Deal

President Franklin Roosevelt found several of the strongest advocates for his New Deal among Alabama's congressional delegation, considered the South's most liberal (on issues other than race) during the 1930s and 1940s. Congressman William B. Bankhead was in the House of Representatives from 1917 to 1940 and held many powerful positions, including majority leader in 1935 and speaker of the House from 1936 to 1940. He was a loyal supporter of Roosevelt, even on his most unpopular proposals. He was particularly interested in agricultural matters, his best known legislation being the Bankhead Cotton Control Act of 1934, named for both himself and his brother, John Hollis Bankhead, II, who was elected senator from Alabama in 1930. This act established the principle of adjusting the supply of an agricultural commodity to fit the market demands by compulsory control of acreage or marketing.

Senator Bankhead is known for the Bankhead-Jones Farm Tenancy Act, which established a federal loan program to help farm tenants buy farm land and get

Alabama's congressional delegation in 1938 consisted of, seated, left to right, Senator John H. Bankhead, II, Speaker of the House William B. Bankhead, and Senator Lister Hill; and standing, left to right, U.S. Representatives Pete Jarman, Frank W. Boykin, Henry Bascom Steagall, Joe Starnes, John J. Sparkman, Sam Hobbs, and Luther Patrick. Of the ten, only Frank Boykin, a businessman, and Pete Jarman, who had held several statewide offices including secretary of state, were not attorneys.

rehabilitation and subsistence loans to help them survive the Depression. Another Bankhead-Jones Act appropriated funds for Extension and Experiment Station work and Land Grant College support. It funded a regional agricultural experiment station at Auburn University. Although a loyal New Dealer, Bankhead did oppose the president's plan to reorganize (or pack) the U.S. Supreme Court. Both Bankheads, as well as the senator's son, Walter Will Bankhead, who served in Congress briefly after his uncle died in 1940, were attorneys who had practiced law in Jasper, Alabama.

Congressman Henry Steagall, a lawyer representing Alabama's third district, was another New Dealer, who served as chairman of the Committee on Banking and Currency. He is remembered for the Glass-Steagall Act of 1932, which authorized bank deposit insurance and prohibited commercial banks from owning brokerage firms, generally insuring that the banking system would survive the Depression.

Congressman Lister Hill of Montgomery, another attorney who had entered the House of Representatives in 1923, was instrumental in the creation of the Tennessee Valley Authority in 1933 and, even more importantly, in defending it from private utility, coal, and railroad interests which sought to undermine it later in the decade. Hill entered the Senate in 1938 upon winning Senator Hugo Black's seat which opened up when Roosevelt appointed Black to the U.S. Supreme Court.

Black was another loyal New Deal supporter, particularly in the area of employment and labor, with his chairmanship of the Education and Labor Committee and his leadership in passing the Fair Labor Standards Act of 1938. His role in the passage of that act bought him to President Roosevelt's attention, just when Roosevelt was looking for a liberal southerner to balance out the court. Black would help carry Roosevelt's New Deal liberalism into the post-World War II era with profound impact on the state of Alabama and the nation.

Senator Hugo Black poses for the newsreel cameras following his nomination to the U.S. Supreme Court in August 1937. Although rumors concerning his prior membership in the Ku Klux Klan had started to circulate, he was quickly confirmed.

Bibb Graves is Reelected—1935-1939

After Benjamin Miller's frugal administration, during which powerful financial interests killed proposed tax increases needed to keep schools open during 1933, Alabama voters returned to Bibb Graves for four more years, the first governor to be reelected for a second nonconsecutive, four-year term. He beat attorney Frank Dixon of Birmingham, who was a conservative, in the Democratic primary. This contest well illustrated the two factions which continually vied for political power within Alabama's one party. Graves attracted organized labor, small farmers, and New Dealers, while Dixon represented what Graves dubbed Alabama's "Big Mules" (Alabama's big business interests), Black Belt planters, and small businessmen.

During his second term, Graves created a new state Department of Labor in response to the largest textile strike in American history to that time, appointing labor leaders, including at least two women, to fill important governmental positions. He refused to use troops to quell that and other strikes that occurred during this period, following the lead of his Department of Labor administrators who sought better working conditions as the means to prevent strikes. His policies helped guarantee a strong and politically active labor movement in Alabama for several decades.

Graves was an active supporter of the New Deal, and after passage of the federal Social Security Act, Graves created the Alabama Department of Public Welfare to replace the State Child Welfare Department. Unemployment insurance was developed during his second administration and new government buildings were constructed using New Deal federal public works funds. New roads were built. Much of the funding Alabama received during this period reflected Graves's cooperation with the state's congressional delegation which supported Roosevelt so enthusiastically.

Education again was the focus of reform and efforts to insure funding increases. A sales tax was introduced to fund education, after Graves's proposed gross receipts tax was defeated by the party's conservative element. Thus began the legacy of regressive taxation that continues to burden Alabama's low income population and to fund education from a constantly fluctuating and uncertain financial base.

Graves's career was somewhat parallel to Roosevelt's in that he was extremely popular with ordinary Alabamians and probably could have been reelected. But Alabama's constitution did not allow consecutive terms, and conservative Frank Dixon took over the governorship in 1939. Graves's health failed and he died in 1942, the year that he could have run again. His death left his liberal-labor-New Deal coalition splintered, searching for new leadership and so the conservative arm of the party was able to maintain control for four more years.

Frank Dixon and Chauncey Sparks: Conservative Attorneys and Governors

Frank Murray Dixon was born in California in 1892 but spent most of his youth in the Tidewater region of Virginia. He was the nephew of Reverend Thomas Dixon, who wrote *The Clansman,* upon which the movie *Birth of a Nation* was based. He attended Columbia University and the University of Virginia Law School. He married a Greene County, Alabama, native, came to Birmingham after law school to work in the law firm of Frank S. White, and successfully managed White's campaign for the U.S. Senate. Dixon fought in World War I as a volunteer with the Royal Canadian Air Corps and was shot down and wounded in July 1918 over Soissons, France. He had a leg amputated. The French government honored him by awarding him the Croix de Guerre with palm, making him a chevalier of the French Foreign Legion and promoting him to major. After the war, Dixon helped organize the American Legion in Alabama and served as its state commander and twice as the Birmingham chapter post commander, work that brought him recognition and loyalty among Alabama's war veterans.

Governor Frank M. Dixon's administration is noted primarily for its reorganization and streamlining of the state's government. Politically conservative, he was the leader of opposition to the New Deal in Alabama.

Dixon joined Lloyd Bowers to form the firm Bowers and Dixon, the predecessor firm of today's Porterfield, Harper, Mills & Motlow, P.A., and became a successful corporate lawyer representing the interests of Bibb Graves's "Big Mules." Like others in this faction, he was an open advocate of white supremacy but had opposed the 1920s Ku Klux Klan because it espoused causes adverse to big business interests. He ran for governor for the first time in 1934 and again in 1938, this time beating Chauncey Sparks. Dixon attracted many union leaders, younger voters, and other progressive Alabamians in1938 because he promised to abolish the poll tax, to push for reapportionment of the legislature, and to reorganize state government. He delivered only on his last promise.

Dixon's administration oversaw developments in Alabama during the early years of World War II, when defense projects, especially in Mobile, brought Alabamians a return to prosperity and moved many families into the middle class. He also undertook a reorganization of state government, perhaps the most lasting accomplishment of his administration. He based his efforts on the Virginia model of government and the advice of University of Alabama political scientist Roscoe C. Martin, an expert in the field of administration and civil service reform. (Corporate attorney, James A. Simpson, Birmingham's state senator during this period, became a national leader on the subject of civil service reform and led the efforts both in the state legislature and in the city of Birmingham to create a merit system for public employees.) In his effort to streamline the government, Dixon was able to eliminate 27 government agencies, largely by consolidating related and duplicative functions and creating tighter controls in the office of the governor. He also oversaw the reformation of the tax assessment system.

Dixon was fundamentally antilabor and pro-laissez faire and, some historians say, a white supremacist, even a virulent racist. He led the anti-New Deal forces in the state Democratic Party in their opposition to Roosevelt's third and fourth campaigns, his proposed Fair Employment Practices Commission, and his prolabor programs. He also led a revolt of Southerners from the National Democratic Party in 1948 when Truman sought reelection. Other conservative leaders in

Outgoing governor Frank Dixon, left, congratulates his successor Chauncey Sparks at his inauguration in 1943. Regarded as a conservative, Sparks's administration was unexpectedly progressive, especially in the area of education funding.

Alabama during this period included attorneys Marion Rushton of Montgomery, Gessner McCorvey of Mobile, Sam Hobbs of Selma, and James Simpson of Birmingham. Those attorney political leaders who continued to support the progressive tendencies of the National Democratic Party included Lister Hill, Lieutenant Governor Albert A. Carmichael, Montgomery attorney Richard Rives, and Marc Ray "Foots" Clements of Tuscaloosa.

"Foots" Clements was a politico at the University of Alabama in the 1930s and had a network of friends who were involved in Alabama politics for decades. They included attorneys Hugh D. Merrill, Jr., and Kenneth Roberts of Anniston, Carl Elliott of Jasper, Aubrey Dominick and George LeMaistre (with whom "Foots" practiced law) of Tuscaloosa, and Bob Jones of Scottsboro. Clements used his contacts and his political genius in the service of Senator Lister Hill, who through the 1940s, '50s and '60s led the liberal wing of the Alabama Democratic Party and led many of Clements' friends into the Congress (including Kenneth Roberts, Carl Elliott, and Bob Jones), maintaining Alabama's reputation as the South's most liberal congressional delegation. After the death of Bibb Graves and then President Roosevelt, Hill led the New Deal faction in a struggle against the conservative arm of the party, that would become known as the Dixiecrats.

Attorney Chauncey Sparks, who followed Dixon as governor, was from Barbour County and gave future governor George Wallace, a fellow Barbour County attorney, his first political job as an assistant state attorney general. Sparks was in the Alabama legislature during the 1930s, as part of an "economy bloc" who fought both income and state sales tax proposals. His leadership in this group, which preached against waste and spending, earned him the name "Barbour Bourbon." He ran against Dixon in 1938 in a race that gave him name recognition which then carried him to victory in 1942 against James Folsom, who was little known at that time. Bibb Graves entered the race but died before the primary.

Most Alabamians expected Sparks to continue the conservative positions of Dixon but, to the surprise of many, he became more progressive after taking over state government. The wartime economy gave him additional funds to better the lives of his fellow citizens and he did just that, doubling the state appropriations for education, extending the school term from seven to eight months, emphasizing medical education by moving the University Medical College to Birmingham, and expanding it to a four-year program with double its former appropriations. A School of Forestry opened at Auburn and Tuskegee Institute received increased funding. The state's bonded indebtedness was reduced by twenty-five percent and a constitutional amendment was passed requiring the legislature to meet every two years instead of every four.

Marc Ray "Foots" Clements used his political acumen and wide circle of influential friends to help elect members of the liberal wing of the state Democratic party, including Senator Lister Hill and Congressmen Kenneth Roberts, Carl Elliott, and Bob Jones.

Like others of his Southern contemporaries, Sparks stood against "federal encroachments on the rights of states," particularly in the realm of race relations, and criticized federal handouts that had "strings attached." Toward the end of his administration, the legislature passed the Boswell Amendment that gave county registrars the power to question potential voters on their understanding of constitutional issues and to deny suffrage if their answers were deemed insufficient. Gessner McCorvey, who was chairman of the State Democratic Executive Committee, fashioned this amendment as a means to slow down black and poor white voters. A top-notch attorney, he must have known that the amendment was of questionable constitutionality, but it would take time for the civil rights forces to challenge it. Three years later, the Boswell Amendment was struck down by a three-judge federal district court panel, composed of Alabama natives, as a violation of the Fifteenth Amendment. In the meantime, his conservative forces could take control of the state party and begin to turn the tide away from the New Deal that had controlled state Democratic politics since Roosevelt took office.

Sparks attended the Democratic National Convention in 1948, when the "Dixiecrats" walked out in protest to its racially liberal platform. Sparks and his protégé George Wallace remained at the convention, with Sparks maintaining that the Dixiecrat movement was "ill-starred, ill-conceived, ill-supported and stillborn." He is also quoted as having said, "Orthodoxy is O.K., but it is the unorthodox who bring in fresh breezes, stimulating ideas, and progress. In a world of so many new and newer ideas one is foolish to remain stationary." Sparks proved himself unorthodox for the benefit of the people during his term as governor.

The 1944 United States Senate Race of Lister Hill

Alabama forces who opposed the liberal trend of the National Democratic Party, such as the Farm Bureau Federation and the Associated Industries of Alabama (whose vice chairman was attorney J. Frank Rushton, Jr., of Birmingham, the nephew of attorney Ray Rushton who ran against Hill in 1923 when Hill first ran for Congress) saw Lister Hill's 1944 race as an opportunity to remove one of the New Deal's most loyal supporters. The first challenge for them was how to lure the average Alabama voter away from Roosevelt and Hill.[5]

How had Alabamians been lured away from their own best interests in the past? The false alarm of race had been the successful theme at such possible turning points as the Populist movement in the 1890s, the election to adopt the 1901 constitution, and the successful campaign for Al Smith in the 1920s (as well as the campaign to defeat him). President Roosevelt provided the conservative opposition this alarm in 1944 with his 1941 executive order creating a Fair Employment Practices Committee (FEPC), and with his proposed federal statutes against lynching and poll taxes. Even the efforts of first lady Eleanor Roosevelt on behalf of fair treatment for black Americans could be used to rile the ire of Alabamians to make them forget what most national Democrats deemed the positives of the New Deal, such as rural electrification, TVA, protection for unions, small farm loans, the minimum wage, the shorter work week, and social security.

The second question was who should carry this banner as opposition candidate to Hill? There were two potential challengers, both corporate lawyers from Birmingham, members of Alabama's "gentry," and leading spokesmen for business and industrial interests. One was Frank Dixon, who was described by one correspondent to Hill, as "about to turn into a counterpart of his uncle, Tom Dixon, author of *The Clansman*, etc., and look upon himself as anointed to save Alabama and the South from the Negro." The other was James A. Simpson, a Dixon protégé, who was the popular president pro tem of the Alabama Senate, who had advocated for the state civil service system, old-age pensions, a teacher retirement act, the pardon and parole board, and other progressive legislation, but who also opposed taxes on big corporations, appropriations for education, and rural electrification. Simpson had been voted most valuable legislator in 1939 and 1943 by a group of political reporters who kept up with the legislature. He was considered to be an honest public official, a man of integrity, but one who made "a fetish of financial integrity and frugality in government" at the expense of education, social welfare, highway construction, and other government services. He did not have the statewide name recognition or political network of Lister Hill. A renewed appeal to racism was his only hope of ousting Hill.

Simpson was selected by the conservative power brokers as the one who should take on Lister Hill. He accepted the challenge, even though his chances seemed slim, perhaps to lay a foundation for challenging John Sparkman when he came up for reelection in 1946. He talked about the need to halt the New Deal "wave of socialism and bureaucracy" and the threat of outside interference with the state's handling of race relations. Business leaders, including attorneys such as Sidney Smyer of Birmingham Realty Company and utility executive Thomas Martin, as well as corporate lawyer Forney Johnston, supported Simpson, as did Lister Hill's cousin, attorney T. B. Hill, Jr., and attorney Marion Rushton (Ray Rushton's son), both of Montgomery, and attorney Francis Inge, who was Simpson's campaign manager in Mobile.

As the leader of the liberal faction of Alabama's Democratic Party, when challenged from the right in 1944, Lister Hill had no problem using white supremacist rhetoric to win the election.

This campaign was a battle for the leadership of the Alabama Democratic Party, and Lister Hill took it as such. Still, Hill had the edge because Roosevelt was still alive, and the war was still continuing, and most voters were still appreciative of what the New Deal had done for them during the trying times of the Depression. The timing was wrong for the opposition, but the election did signal the issues which would confront the forces for moderation when the war ended and Roosevelt's demise would create a power vacuum in the national party.

Hill's supporters included the Alabama Education Association, labor leaders, and union members, plus numerous federal employees of TVA, the Rural Electrification Administration, the Farm Security Administration, and numerous military bases in Alabama. Attorney-politicians

Attorney and president pro tem of the state senate James A. Simpson was chosen over former governor Frank Dixon to oppose Lister Hill in the 1944 election for U.S. Senator.

Albert Carmichael and Handy Ellis (both of whom had served as lieutenant governor), Albert Rains, and even Tom Heflin, and most importantly John H. Bankhead, II, (Alabama's other senator) supported him. Foots Clements did much to perfect a sophisticated statewide network of support, whose leadership included Richard Rives (who was a law partner of Hill's uncle, Wiley Hill, and who was a former campaign manager for both Hugo Black and Bibb Graves), and Clarence Allgood (who would later become a bankruptcy judge in Birmingham credited with creating the nation's first effective debtor's court and then a federal district judge.)

In April 1944, the U.S. Supreme Court, with its decision in the case of *Smith v. Allwright*, gave additional ammunition to Simpson when it struck down the all-white Texas Democratic primary by ruling that it was equivalent to race discrimination by the state of Texas forbidden by the Fifteenth Amendment. Hugo Black voted with the majority. Simpson immediately described the case as "the gravest threat to white supremacy since Reconstruction."

Soon, Hill went on the offensive, describing himself as an ardent protector of white supremacy and pointing out that he had voted against funding the FEPC and laws to outlaw lynching and poll taxes and fervently proclaiming his dedication to continued segregation of schools and buses. Thus, while Hill was a New Deal Democrat, he was not in favor of racial equality (and he was aware that his continued political career was contingent on maintaining this stance.) This election foreshadowed the racial demagoguery which would come to play an essential role in Democratic politics in Alabama as Roosevelt's New Deal liberality passed from the political scene.

Hill staved off defeat and his strong political network kept him in the Senate and his allies in the congressional delegation for more than two more decades, but the gauntlet had been thrown and the struggle for control of the state party would be an ongoing struggle during the rest of Hill's political career. It would be a bitter, often ruthless, struggle which would culminate in the rise of a two-party system in Alabama. Alabama lawyers would actively participate on both sides of this divide.

Post-Roosevelt Alabama

Franklin Roosevelt died in 1945 and Harry Truman became president. Things changed for those who had been Roosevelt's favorites as Truman chose his own allies and issues. In Alabama, the governorship passed out of the hands of lawyers in 1946, when James "Big Jim" Folsom beat Lieutenant Governor Handy Ellis, an attorney from Columbiana, and did not return until Attorney General John Patterson became governor in 1959 (after he defeated Judge George Wallace of Barbour County). Still, most of Alabama's congressional delegation continued to be made up of progressive Democratic lawyers such as Senator John Sparkman, who was opposed by James Simpson in 1946 and served as Adlai Stevenson's vice-presidential candidate in the 1952 presidential race when Republican Dwight D. Eisenhower came into office, along with attorney representatives Carl Elliott, Bob Jones, Kenneth Roberts, and Albert Rains. These congressmen owed much to Lister Hill and Foots Clements, whose sponsorship made their elections possible at a time when other Southern state delegations were reflecting strong Republican leanings. Even those Alabama congressmen who were of more conservative philosophy were highly regarded, including attorneys George Andrews, George Grant, and Sam Hobbs.

THE ORIGINS OF ALABAMA POWER AND ITS STRUGGLE WITH THE NEW DEAL, THE TVA, AND DEMAGOGUERY

Alabama Power Company's development and history has probably had more impact on the state than any other single corporation, since it encouraged industrial development, rural electrification, leisure activity facilities, and modernized homes throughout the state. As with many of the state's corporations, and probably more than most, lawyers have been integrally associated with its history. A major Birmingham law firm, now known as Balch & Bingham, LLP, was created primarily to service its legal needs and has furnished it with many corporate leaders.[6]

Thomas W. Martin is the Alabama lawyer most identified with the company since its founding in 1906. At that time, Martin was a young assistant attorney general under Attorney General Massey Wilson, with whom he subsequently practiced law. Martin became familiar with Alabama's laws controlling the generation of electric power at the request of various early investors, including attorneys J. S. Pinckard and Jack Thorington of Montgomery, who needed Alabama law clarified to authorize the building of dams by private, investor-owned companies along Alabama's waterways. At the time, Alabama's laws were not conducive to such development.

Martin and Wilson drafted necessary reform legislation and, with the aid of Thomas Martin's father, William Logan Martin, Sr., who was speaker of the Alabama House at the time, got necessary reform legislation enacted. The result was that different investors began attempts in various parts of the state to organize hydroelectric companies. These included William Patrick Lay and his son, Earl, of Gadsden who, with attorney O. R. Hood, incorporated the Alabama Power Company in 1906, and a group in the Muscle Shoals area who hoped to use the shoals of the Tennessee River to generate power. Often they called upon Wilson and Martin (after they left the attorney general's office and formed the firm of Tyson, Wilson, and Martin) to provide them with legal services.

The main problem these investors had in growing their companies was acquiring sufficient capital.

In the fall of 1911, James Mitchell, a Massachusetts engineer, discussed with Martin his idea of consolidating the groups around the state into one entity structured under a holding company, financed by capital initially from London and later from New York. With this meeting, Martin began his career with what became today's Alabama Power Company, becoming its general counsel and later its president.

Among attorneys whom Martin retained to help in this progressive consolidation and in land transactions needed to build dams were Ray Rushton in Montgomery, George A. Sorrell of Alexander City, James W. Strother of Dadeville, and John L. Burnett, a lawyer who represented the seventh congressional district in the U.S. House of Representatives. Chester A. Bingham of Talladega proved so capable that he soon moved to corporate headquarters, which were located in Montgomery until the fall

tion of Theodore Roosevelt, was also part of national politics. This program included plans for protecting hydroelectric sites for governmental development. An intense debate went back and forth in Congress over what was the best policy for hydroelectric development, private or public. This debate had a strong impact on Alabama's congressional delegation and state politics because Muscle Shoals and the Tennessee River were at its center. This controversy was at its most heated before James Mitchell came to Alabama, at a time when he was away from the United States, so he did not appreciate its potential to reenter the political discussion as he went about purchasing and developing possible dam sites, including the one at Muscle Shoals.

Another aspect of Alabama politics Mitchell could not have been familiar with was its penchant for turning demagogic. This penchant was illustrated in one of the earliest condemnation suits filed by the company (which was called the Alabama Interstate Power Company at the time), involving a small dam at Tallassee Falls owned by the Mount Vernon-Woodberry Cotton Duck Company. After losing at the trial level, Mount Vernon's lawyers, which included the Montgomery firm of Goodwyn and McIntyre, Judge John McElderry Chilton and H. N. Randolph, wrote a brief condemning the power company as a "foreign corporation," an "octopus" (a reference to John D. Rockefeller's monopolistic takeover of the oil industry, which political cartoonists illustrated as an octopus), and "a power trust that wanted to steal the Tallapoosa River, as Ahab, the King of Samaria, in the biblical story stole the garden of Naboth."[7] They distributed their brief to newspapers and politicians as well as to the Alabama Supreme Court. The power company's lawyers and managers, including Martin, were aware in its earliest days that its potential impact and power made the company an easy target for populist politicians at both the state and federal levels, regardless of its good intentions.

During World War I, controversy surrounded the Shoals location because the government needed a plant to produce nitrates for munitions. As an outcome of

OPPOSITE PAGE: *Thomas W. Martin, working with engineer James Mitchell, is the attorney most closely associated with the creation of the Alabama Power Company.* ABOVE: *The Alabama Power Company building in Birmingham was built in 1925.*

of 1912. As historian Leah Rawls Atkins describes him, Martin "proved to be a master at understanding the politics of the local courthouse. For instance, he worked through a cadre of county-seat lawyers, carefully picked for their legal experience and reputation as well as for their knowledge of local politics and canny ability to get things accomplished within the culture of the people."

At the same time that private investors were working to organize hydroelectric companies, a conservation movement, which had started during the administra-

patriotic fervor and frustrated negotiations, Alabama Power gave prime land to the government for a dam and a plant whose construction was not completed before the war ended.

This site became the focal point for President Roosevelt's New Deal program which created the Tennessee Valley Authority (TVA) and its Rural Electrification Program. For entrepreneurs within the hydroelectric community and the many Alabama lawyers involved with Alabama Power Company, Franklin Roosevelt and the liberal Alabama congressmen who supported him were considered adversaries, especially since power company supporters felt that the creation of the TVA effectively robbed the company of its investments in the northern part of the state and all the business that had been developed there. (A major source of anger was the fact that TVA was in direct competition with private companies but was not regulated, had no tax obligations, and could borrow money at low interest.) Lawsuits were filed on several fronts challenging the TVA, including one brought by powerful Birmingham corporate attorney Forney Johnston representing Alabama Power stockholders, but the U.S. Supreme Court was able to avoid ruling on its constitutionality.

President Roosevelt pays a visit to the TVA facility at Muscle Shoals. Seated next to him in the car is Alabama governor Benjamin Miller, while Tennessee governor Hill McAllister turns around to shake Roosevelt's hand. The Muscle Shoals site had been a source of controversy since World War I when Alabama Power was pressured to donate the land to the government.

Company supporters were further provoked when Roosevelt supported legislation to regulate utility holding companies. Alabama Senator Hugo Black investigated the expenditures and activities of some companies trying to defeat the legislation (the Wheeler-Rayburn bill) and found irregularities that raised public animosity toward these companies, helped the bill to pass, and, some maintain, raised Black's profile so that he subsequently was selected by Roosevelt to fill an open seat on the United States Supreme Court. The bill that passed provided the Securities and Exchange Commission some flexibility to allow certain holding companies to operate within the public interest. Out of this came the creation of the Southern Company during the period from 1947 to 1949.

On the state level, in 1915, Governor Charles Henderson signed into law a reorganization of the former Railroad Commission to create the Public Service Commission (PSC), which continues to regulate utility companies in Alabama. In 1920, Governor Thomas Kilby signed the Alabama Public Utility Act which was a far-reaching reform that, among other things, expanded the PSC's authority to regulate utility rates. Having to win approval for rate increases before the PSC made the company vulnerable to political demagoguery within the state. (This vulnerability would be especially intense during the years that George Wallace was governor.) The company faced the same type of vulnerability before the Federal Power Commission, created by the Federal Water Power Act of 1920, which had to approve the building of dams on national waterways.

In that same year, in response to the demand for legal services within the power company, Walter G. Hood was made assistant general counsel of the company. In 1922, Tom Martin's brother, William Logan Martin, Jr. (who had served as attorney general from 1915 to 1918) came to Birmingham, where the company's headquarters had been relocated, to establish a law firm that would eventually absorb the company's legal department and be the predecessor firm to today's Balch & Bingham. He was joined in 1923 by J. Fritz Thompson and Perry Turner, as well as Hobart A. McWhorter. Arthur K. Foster came in 1925, but left three years later to accept an appointment to the Alabama Supreme Court.

During the early 1930s, as part of the continuing national debate concerning the role of private enterprise versus government in the generation of power, the company found itself the focus of investigations by both the Federal Trade Commission and the Alabama legislature. In Alabama, a state legislative panel chaired by attorney representative Finis St.John of Cullman—which included lawyers Richard Bledsoe Kelly, Jr., of Talladega County, Hubert T. Davis of Macon County, Amasa Coleman Lee of Monroe County, Emmett F. Hildreth of Greene County, and Senator Charles S. McDowell of Barbour County—thoroughly reviewed the conduct of Alabama Power in the political realm and its rate structure and tax assessments. After months of investigation, the company was cleared of demagogic charges made against it by Representative Kelly.

Joseph M. Farley, who began his career at Balch & Bingham, was president of Alabama Power Company from 1969 to 1989, one of the more challenging periods in the company's history.

During his years as head of the power company, Tom Martin helped inspire the creation of the Alabama Industrial Development Commission in 1927 and sponsored the creation of the Southern Research Institute in 1941, all to support the industrial development of the state. This development benefited the state and also provided the company with customers for its power "products." Later, the Institute became affiliated with the research programs of the University of Alabama at Birmingham.

Other lawyers have played important roles in the development of Alabama Power and Southern Company history, both within the Balch & Bingham law firm and within company management. These include Hobart McWhorter, labor law expert whom many felt would become president of the company until he died in a car accident in 1950; Walter Bouldin (who served as president); Edwin I. Hatch (primary lobbyist and later president of Georgia Power Company); Eason Balch (expert on federal utility regulation); Jack Bingham; Schuyler A. Baker; Alvin Vogtle (who served as president of Southern Company); Joseph Farley (who led the company during the 1970s when there were multiple rate case crises involving George Wallace and the PSC); Harold Williams; and James C. Blakey, among others. Balch & Bingham continues today as one of the state's largest and most outstanding corporate law firms, whose client base has expanded beyond Alabama Power Company.

CHAPTER TWELVE

DEVELOPMENTS IN THE LEGAL PROFESSION THROUGH 1965

At the time that the Alabama State Bar was given power to police the profession in 1923, there were approximately 1,300 lawyers in practice, if one counted the listings in Martindale-Hubbell's *Law Directory*. By 1960, that number was close to 2,000 with Alabama law licenses. Progressively, as the twentieth century advanced, the profession became predominantly urban, with about thirty per cent of lawyers practicing in Birmingham, and close to twenty per cent combined in Montgomery and Mobile. Still, the lawyers of the smaller towns and cities continued to exert influence since they knew the local judges, the juries, and the prejudices that influenced the outcome of litigation. The local courthouse culture was a factor that urban lawyers representing deep-pocket clients knew had to be taken into account. And since this group of local lawyers was the natural source of political leadership in these communities, the urban lawyers often needed their support in the legislature as well.

Thus, many of Alabama's most influential attorneys were located outside the major cities of Birmingham, Montgomery, and Mobile, and their family names were closely associated with the geographic areas where their practices were located. Many of these names appear in the list of Alabama State Bar presidents during the years of the Klan, the Depression, the New Deal, and the war and postwar eras: C. E. Hamilton of Greenville (1924-1925); John H. Peach of Sheffield (1925-1926); R. H. Powell of Tuskegee (1926-1927); Oscar L. Tompkins of Dothan (1928-1929); J. F. Aldridge of Eutaw (1930-1931); L. F. Gerald of Clanton (1937-1938); C. H. Young of Anniston (1938-1939); Jacob A. Walker of Opelika (whose attorney son invested in the barbell manufacturing business of future two-time governor, Opelika businessman Fob James, to help him get started in

Above: *John H. Peach of Sheffield served as president of the Alabama State Bar from 1925 to 1926. He later served as a legal advisor to Governor Benjamin Miller.* Opposite page: *The headquarters building for the Alabama State Bar on Dexter Avenue was completed in 1963, culminating a process that began in 1950 during the presidency of Francis H. Hare, Sr.*

ASSOCIATION

the business which made him wealthy; 1942-1943); J. Clarence Inzer of Gadsden (1943-1944); John E. Adams of Grove Hill (1945-1946); W. Howell Morrow of Lanett (1947-1948); John A. Lusk, Jr., of Gadsden (1950-1951); John A. Caddell of Decatur (1951-1952); B. E. Jones of Evergreen (1957-1958); Clopper Almon of Sheffield (1960-1961); and Alto V. Lee, III, of Dothan (1974-1975; He was the third Alto V. Lee to practice law and shared his practice with his relative, William L. Lee, another prominent Dothan attorney. They were descendants of Robert E. Lee's family).

Other such lawyers who were important in their communities and active in the bar but who did not serve as president include E.W. Godbey, Tennis Tidwell, John C. Eyster, and Charles H. Eyster of Decatur; Edmund Pettus, II and Archie Reaves of Selma; Thomas F. Seale Sr., and Ira D. Pruitt, Sr., of Livingston; Norborne C. Stone, Sr., of Bay Minette; T. W. Garrett of Grove Hill; Ben H. Lightfoot of Luverne; John D. Rather, Jr., of Tuscumbia; Guy Hardwick and Keener Baxley of Dothan; Robert K. (Buster) Bell and Schuyler Richardson of Huntsville; Abner Powell, Sr. and Jr. of Andalusia; George W. Andrews, Sr. and Jr. and Lawrence K. Andrews of Union Springs; Claud D. Scruggs of Albertville; Nicholas Hare, John Milton Coxwell, and Amasa C. Lee of Monroeville; Ernest Fite and his son Rankin of Jasper; Frank Potts and Doyle Young of Florence; and Robert J. Hooton and his son Paul of Roanoke.

TOP: *Lee C. Bradley, Jr., of the Birmingham firm Bradley, Baldwin, All & White, the largest law firm in the state in 1932. As Bradley Arant Boult Cummings, it is still the largest firm in Alabama.* ABOVE: *Douglas Arant, also a member of Bradley, Baldwin, All & White, served as president of the Alabama State Bar from 1936 to 1937.*

In 1947, Judge Walter B. Jones, who kept a mailing list of practicing lawyers for distributing the bar's official publication, noted that his list showed 1,480 lawyers entitled to practice in the courts of the state, over half of them living above a line dissecting the state at Clanton and half being in Jefferson, Mobile, and Montgomery counties. The largest clusters were in the following counties: Calhoun (25), Dallas (20), Etowah (34), Houston (25), Jefferson (337), Madison (21), Mobile (91), Montgomery (84), and Tuscaloosa (35). He also noted that there were only 178 lawyers in the 14 counties which comprised the Black Belt, with 84 of those being in Montgomery, 20 in Dallas, six in Macon, seven in Perry, three in Greene, seven in Hale, eight in Marengo, seven in Sumter, seven in Pickens, three in Lowndes, four in Bullock, nine in Russell, five in Wilcox, and eight in Barbour. Yet, he pointed out, this section was always powerful in both its political and social influence within the state and had produced 13 of the state's 44 governors and six of its 22 chief justices. The Black Belt's disproportionate power continued until the 1960s when litigation forced a reapportionment of the legislature as required by the 1901 state constitution and the U.S. Constitution.

Solo practice continued throughout this period of the profession's history to be a popular mode of practice, even though multimember firm practices expanded. In the 1932 edition of Martindale-Hubbell, two Birmingham firms were the largest in Alabama: Bradley, Baldwin, All & White (ten partners and five associates) and London, Yancey & Brower (seven partners and three associates). In 1952, the Bradley firm continued to be the largest (nine partners and eight associates) with Martin, Turner, Blakey & Bouldin (six partners and eight associates), and Lange, Simpson, Robinson & Somerville (nine partners and three associates) being second and third, respectively. These corporate firms were specialists at representing certain types of corporations, including insurers and heavy industries. Lange, Simpson even had a branch office in Montgomery. Most Alabama firms, though, had two or three partners and handled the problems of farmers, shopkeepers, and small-scale industrialists.

Forney Johnston, the son of Governor Joseph Forney Johnston, was a vocal opponent of President Roosevelt's New Deal programs.

Up to the 1960s, most attorneys practiced in state courts. Federal court practice was primarily the venue of urban attorneys who specialized, creating a federal court "culture" with which most Alabama attorneys were unfamiliar. Overall, the small size of the bar, its limited venue, and the fact that it was dominated by white males, most of whom were educated at the University of Alabama School of Law, made for a uniformity and provincialism in thinking that kept the bar conservative and even sometimes reactionary when confronted with changes that threatened the culture with which its members were familiar.

Political Philosophy of the Organized Bar

The generally conservative attitudes of bar leaders can be seen in various speeches given and resolutions adopted by bar members at state bar conventions during the thirties and forties. President Roosevelt was excoriated for his proposed court-packing plan, for the expansion of the federal government through commissions, administrative proceedings, and regulatory agencies, and alleged concomitant interference with individual and states' rights, and for proposed expansions of civil rights for minorities.

One of the first such speeches was given in 1935, when Forney Johnston addressed "Certain Constitutional Aspects of Depression Legislation," in which he stated, "Today the chief function of state administrations is to beg and toady the dispensers of federal largesse and rubber stamp laws written by ghost writers for legislative upheavalists, making easy federal waste and aggression." In 1937, then-bar president Douglas Arant (who entered the bar in 1923 and who remained a prominent and generally liberal bar leader until his death after more than 60 years of practice) chose as the subject of the president's annual address "An Independent Judiciary." Although Arant was considered a supporter of Roosevelt and his New Deal, he opposed Roosevelt's court-packing plan and even led a quickly organized national group that worked against the plan. The convention passed a resolution affirming the state bar's "overwhelming... disapproval" of the plan and encouraged all members of Alabama's congressional delegation to work against its passage. The resolution noted with commendation that Senator Bankhead, otherwise a Roosevelt supporter, opposed the bill.

Later in the 1937 program, James Simpson made the following aside in his introduction of another convention speaker, "I was returning from the beautiful city of Washington last week—that beautiful city that used to be the capital of the United States and now has become the capital of the Forty-eight States and is fast becoming the county seat of about four thousand counties." In 1938, president L. F. Gerald, in his address, noted that President Roosevelt's criticisms of the legal profession had lowered the public's esteem for lawyers. He commented, "Our profession is composed of men who are naturally conservative and by their training and life's work value principles above expediency, political or economical." He continued, "These characteristics have placed our profession, as a whole, in opposition to many new and expedient ideas of the day."

In 1944, president Clarence Inzer raised his fears that, due to the requirements of war, the power of the central government was increasing and would not decrease at war's end. The principles of government generally supported by the bar, he noted, included separation of the three functions of government, states' rights and local self government, free enterprise, and the right of every person to develop his or her capacities. He described the threats being made to these principles through the "evils of bureaucracies," many of which contained all three functions of government in one bureau, and the erosion of the right to local self-government through "strained interpretations of the constitutional provisions giving Congress the power to regulate interstate commerce." He further noted that Americans were facing uncertainty regarding federal laws because of the myriad federal regulations that were ever-changing and prone to different constructions. "The net result is that a lawyer cannot with certainty advise his clients." In summary, he made a statement which would be emphasized again and again in subsequent decades as change after change swept through the state, affecting its culture and perception of itself. "It is the duty of lawyers to give attention to all matters that affect the lives of our people. If the rights given to us by our constitution are endangered, if the foundations of our country are being undermined, then the lawyers should speak out. We are the only professional group who takes an oath to support, maintain, and defend the constitution. We are the only class of citizens not on the public payrolls who take that vow. And, too, it is the lawyer who is best qualified for this task."

William Logan Martin, Jr., was Alabama's attorney general from 1915 to 1918, before coming to Birmingham to found the firm that would become Balch & Bingham. He served as president of the Alabama State Bar from 1946 to 1947.

In 1946, Governor Chauncey Sparks addressed the convention on "The Lawyer's Future in Politics." In this talk, he noted the prevalence of communist propaganda and the country's need to act against it to protect democracy, which required the consent of the governed to operate. He urged, "America needs to cleanse itself of traitorous philosophies, Fifth Columnists, and infiltration," and concluded, "Unless the lawyer can help to mold this mass psychology in the protection and preservation of democracy, of a better and more equitable basis of existence, higher economic levels and justice to all, then he ceases to be the leader he should be."

In 1947, president William Logan Martin, Jr., noted, "State self-reliance and resourcefulness as well as states' rights have been reduced and infringed upon as a result of federal aid. But the right of the state to govern is not the most important factor involved. What is most important is that we retain within the people the capacity to govern themselves. That capacity, if not used, will disappear. And there is no opportunity for the use of such capacity, under a centralized, paternalistic, federal government, such as we have had in recent years... We should find opportunity to speak up for those rights which are inalienable from citizenship. We should oppose every effort of the government to change its own status from servant to master of its own people. We should speak in thunderous tones so as to drown out those who are seeking government handouts or special privileges at the expense of the taxpayer—who is none other than you and I...."

In 1948, president W. Howell Morrow of Lanett introduced a new element into the attack on the expansion of the federal government—the issue of race. He argued, "It is the clear and plain duty of the lawyer to explain and make clear to his friends and neighbors the great constitutional issues of the day.... The President of the United States has come out with his so-called Civil Rights program; and both major parties, swept by hysteria, and without reason though as to their actions have joined in an approval of this attack not only on our beloved South but at every citizen of the Republic, north, south, east and west, as well.... With cynicism and hypocrisy they make great questions of states' rights a political football. It cannot be denied that if the national congress has the constitutional right to pass the proposed legislation, in doing so it will take away from each citizen rights even more sacred, the right to select your own associates, the right to freely contract, and even the right to worship as you please....[W]e today shall pitch this contest on a high plane. Not one of race or religious prejudice but on something more real, more important—on the basis of State Sovereignty under the Constitution. (Applause) It is the high privilege of the lawyer to state in clear and impelling words to his neighbors and friends the sacred principles of our free union of states. The base rock of our position is the Constitution—conceived in the minds of men of our profession with the help of other men of liberal education, who were willing to dedicate themselves to the common good....We are unwilling that the Constitution, next to the Holy Book, the most sacred possession of man, that was designed as a bulwark of our strength and freedom, be made a cross of our crucifixion (applause)."

Thereafter, the convention adopted a resolution affirming the bar's support of the concept of state sovereignty whereby "the several States are sovereign in all matters not expressly granted to the United States" and declaring its belief "that among the matters which should be dealt with solely by the States, each for itself, are (a) the qualifications of voters; (b) the segregation of the races, (c) the right of citizens to choose their own associates and employees; and (d) the punishment of crimes not related to the Federal Government."

In his speech accepting the office of president for the period from 1948 to 1949, Gessner McCorvey gave a preview of his political attitude. He stated, "I think one of the outstanding speeches of the whole meeting was that marvelous address by Howell Morrow on states' rights. This is not the time for a political speech, but it is something we are all interested in. When we think about the position taken by the gang up at the Philadelphia convention and the Washington headquarters—I would like to say to you as to that gang that has taken charge of the national Democratic Party, they don't know any more about states' rights than a tom cat knows about a marriage license. I am not going to try to talk to you about what occurred and what we are going to do in the South, or try to do. We are just going to keep on fighting."

Gessner McCorvey of Mobile, president of the Alabama State Bar from 1947 to 1948, in wholeheartedly endorsing the speech given by W. Howell Morrow, signalled the lines of defense that would be taken throughout the segregated South in opposition to the coming civil rights struggle: state sovereignty, and, in Morrow's words, "the right to select your own associates."

Celebrating Legal Education at the University of Alabama and Post-World War II Graduates and Bar Admittees

The 1937 bar convention was held in Tuscaloosa to celebrate the twenty-fifth anniversary of Dean Albert Farrah's coming to the University of Alabama School of Law. Thomas B. Ward, a professor at the law school, was president of the Tuscaloosa Bar and gave the welcoming address. Dr. Richard C. Foster, a lawyer whose ancestors were prominent in the Tuscaloosa Bar, was president of the University of Alabama. He spoke about the law school and those who had served as professors, including H. M. Somerville (remembered as founder of the law department in 1872); John Mason Martin (its second professor); Andrew C. Hargrove; Sterling Wood; A. S. Vandergraff; Ormond Somerville; Judge William S. Thorington (first dean); Charles Bell Verner; William "Buck" Oliver (dean before Farrah); and Albert J. Farrah, who came from the University of Florida, where he had overseen the founding of its law school.

The law school was originally begun in 1845 as a department of the University, under the direction of Benjamin F. Porter, but soon closed due to a lack of students. Another attempt was made in 1860 to establish a school in Montgomery, under the direction of Wade Keyes, to have the status of the law department of the University of Alabama, but only one class was held before the Civil War brought progress to a close. In 1872, the law school was revived as a small department on the campus in Tuscaloosa, but it struggled as a stepchild of the University until the arrival of Albert Farrah in 1913. It grew under his stewardship from 80 students in 1911 to 1912 to a high of 277 students in 1934 to 1935, before European and Asian events disrupted its growth.

Farrah came to the school as the only full-time professor, with W. B. Oliver and Tom Ward as part-time instructors, both also having private practices. By 1937, Farrah had overseen the building of a separate law school facility, Farrah Hall, built in 1927, and the establishment of a law library containing 12,500 volumes, as well as an expansion of the faculty to six full-time professors and one part-time instructor. The school was also granted a class A status by the Association of American Law Schools during his tenure. Farrah taught contracts, constitutional law, and common law pleading. He was also a member, then chair, of the state bar Board of Bar Examiners. Under his deanship, university legal education became the required means to becoming licensed as an attorney in Alabama and University of Alabama law school graduates were given the privilege of becoming members of the bar without the need for a bar exam.

In 1944, Dean Farrah died and William Hepburn, who had taught at the school since 1930, became the new dean. Hepburn's father was a professor at the University of Indiana, where Hepburn had attended undergraduate school. Hepburn attended Yale University School of Law and got his master's degree from Harvard University. Hepburn's father wrote a textbook on torts and his son wrote its second edition. Hepburn spoke at the 1944 convention, noting that the war years had seen a decline of students to an all-time low of 11 students in the summer of 1944.

Dean Albert Farrah came to the University of Alabama in 1913 as the only full-time law professor. The 1937 convention of the Alabama State Bar was held in Tuscaloosa to honor his twenty-five year tenure at the school, which had included the building of Farrah Hall, the University's first law school building, and a three-fold increase in enrollment.

There was optimism that the numbers would increase incrementally as young men returned home at the war's conclusion and this optimism was found to be justified as large numbers of returning veterans soon entered the law school, using the GI Bill to pay their way. This created the law school's largest classes, whose size would not be seen again until the early 1980s.

These postwar graduates (including some who did not graduate from the University of Alabama School of Law) would soon begin making valuable contributions to the profession and to the school. The bar admission classes of 1948 and 1949 produced eight state bar presidents, including Howell T. Heflin of Tuscumbia (1965-1966); Robert E. Steiner, III, of Montgomery (1966-1967); Patrick W. Richardson of Huntsville (1969-1970); Truman M. Hobbs of Montgomery (1970-1971); L. Drew Redden of Birmingham (1972-1973); M. R. Nachman of Montgomery (1973-1974); Thomas G. Greaves, Jr., of Mobile (1975-1976); and Hugh W. Roberts, Jr., of Tuscaloosa (1978-1979). Two 1950 veteran graduates also served as state bar presidents: Bibb Allen (1976-1977) and William B. Hairston, Jr. (1983-1984), both from Birmingham. Future Congressmen Tom Bevill, George Huddleston Jr., and Armistead Selden, Jr., and future U.S. Senator Howell T. Heflin graduated during these postwar years, as did federal judges J. Foy Guin, Elbert Bertram Haltom, Jr., William B. Hand, Truman Hobbs, John C. Godbold, and Robert E. Varner. Judge Alex Travis Howard, Jr., was admitted to the bar in 1950 after war service.

RIGHT: *Yetta G. Samford, Jr., was among the postwar graduates involved in founding the Alabama Law School Alumni Association. A B-17 bomber pilot during the war, he went on to serve in the Alabama State Senate, and as a member of the Executive Council of the Alabama Law Institute.* BELOW: *Tom Bevill was one of three postwar graduates of the University of Alabama School of Law to serve in Congress, representing Alabama's Fourth District for 30 years, from 1967 to 1997.*

Veteran Howell T. Heflin of Tuscumbia led a group of graduates who formed the Alabama Law School Alumni Association in 1949. Other postwar graduates involved in its founding included Yetta Samford of Opelika (1949); Drew Redden of Birmingham (1949), who was the founding editor of the *Alabama Law Review*; Jeff deGraffenreid of Tuscaloosa (1948); Robert M. Smith of Birmingham (1949); J. Jefferson Bennett of Tuscaloosa (1948); Earl Esco, Jr., of Tuscaloosa (1948); John E. Curry of Mobile (1948); William B. Moore, Jr., of Selma (1948); Charles Adair of Dadeville (1948); and Hoyt M. Elliott of Jasper (1949).

Notable Developments within the Alabama State Bar

In 1924, the new Board of Bar Commissioners (BBC) adopted rules governing admission to the bar, rules governing the conduct of attorneys after they were admitted, and rules governing the reinstatement of attorneys who were disbarred. By 1936, the state bar standards for entry into the bar matched those recommended by the American Bar Association, which encouraged at least two years of prelaw college work and a university law school education of at least three years. Reading the law in a law firm was no longer acceptable.

As early as 1935, under state bar president Francis Inge of Mobile, consideration of the establishment of a permanent publication for the bar was underway. In 1940, during the tenure of Richard Rives, Judge Walter B. Jones reported at the bar convention that the first issue of *The Alabama Lawyer* had been published, dated January 1940, with him serving as editor. It was to be a quarterly publication with 1,750 copies to be distributed at the cost of $1,400 per year. He noted that various publications had been issued by the bar during its history: the *Alabama Lawyer's Journal*, 1882-1885; the *Alabama Law Journal*, 1925-1930; and the *Alabama State Bar's Bulletin*, 1939. Shortly after the publication of *The Alabama Lawyer* got underway, the decision was made to no longer distribute printed copies of the proceedings of state bar conventions.

Judge Walter B. Jones, son of Bourbon governor Thomas Goode Jones, was the first editor of The Alabama Lawyer, *which began publication in 1940. Jones continued as editor until 1964. He also helped organize the Bar's first legal institutes, the precursor of its mandatory continuing legal education program.*

In 1937, W. B. Harrison resigned as secretary of the association. His tenure as secretary began in 1923 with the creation of the integrated bar. He was replaced by Harold Cook of Birmingham. Over the next few years, Cook assumed the duties of Henry C. Meader as proctor of the bar to fight the unauthorized practice of law (which was considered by most to be a serious problem for the state's lawyers). James W. Aird was subsequently retained as counsel for the BBC. In 1943, former president Lawrence F. Gerald, Sr., of Clanton became secretary, also assuming the duties of proctor and, in 1944, the duties of attorney for the bar when James Aird resigned. Gerald retired in 1950 and John B. Scott was elected secretary. A city recorder for Montgomery, he had served for 20 years on the Board of Bar Commissioners representing the Fifteenth Judicial Circuit.

Also, in 1937, the Court of Appeals in the case of *State v. Wilson* upheld the validity of a statute which levied a license tax for the privilege of engaging in the practice of law and allocated a portion to the state bar, thereby guaranteeing a greater income for the bar, which had been experiencing financial hard times. The original license fee was $25, of which $10 was credited to the BBC. In 1939, the allocation to the bar was raised to $15, resulting in a steady improvement of the bar's finances. Receipts for the fiscal year 1940 to 1941 were $17,707.56, with disbursements of $15,202.44. A reserve fund of just over $1,000 was retained for emergencies.

CONTINUING LEGAL EDUCATION BECOMES AN OFFIAL FUNCTION OF THE BAR

DURING THE PRESIDENCY OF WALTER P. Gewin (1958-1959), the BBC adopted a proposal to organize a continuing legal education (CLE) function with a paid coordinator. Gewin, John Caddell, and T. B. Hill, Jr., who had been instrumental in organizing ad hoc institutes through the years, served as an advisory committee to Douglas Lansford, who was appointed the first paid coordinator of the Alabama Bar Institute for Continuing Legal Education (ABICLE) in 1960. Other sponsors of ABICLE included the University of Alabama Law School and Cumberland Law School. After being organized with a paid coordinator, the program of continuing education encompassed training not only for private practitioners, but also for circuit judges, intermediate court judges, district attorneys, city attorneys, and various other specialty groups. Camille W. Cook became the director of ABICLE in 1972, followed by Steven Emens.

Judge Walter P. Gewin was state bar president from 1958 to 1959 when the creation of a formal CLE program was proposed.

The Alabama State Bar instituted an award to recognize contributions to continuing legal education in honor of Walter P. Gewin, who had been instrumental in the creation of the ABICLE. In the early 1980s, a committee chaired by William D. Scruggs, Jr., of Ft. Payne (state bar president, 1986-1987) and Lynwood Smith of Huntsville proposed to make continuing legal education mandatory, with a requirement that Alabama lawyers attend at least 12 hours of CLE each year to maintain their licenses. The BBC recommended this proposal to the Alabama Supreme Court, and Alabama became the tenth state to have mandatory CLE, effective January 1, 1982. Bill Scruggs became the first president of the Mandatory Continuing Legal Education (MCLE) Commission. The state bar soon discontinued its function of providing CLE, since its MCLE Commission had the responsibility of accrediting programs offered by outside sources. ABICLE became an independent provider of CLE, and soon, the only CLE offered by the bar would be some credit for attendance at certain annual bar convention programs. Organized sections of the state bar became authorized providers of CLE, as did local bar associations. Later, in 2004, a requirement was adopted to have one hour of the mandatory 12 hours be on the subject of ethics and professionalism.

The bar commission established a Junior Bar Association in 1937 for lawyers under the age of 36, later to be known as the Young Lawyers Section of the state bar. In 1939, a major subject of the convention was the organizing of "legal institutes" as a form of postadmission legal education. In 1940, along with the establishment of *The Alabama Lawyer*, it was announced that the Junior Bar Section, with the aid of Judge Walter B. Jones, had organized seven institutes around the state—in Montgomery, Decatur, Dothan, Selma, Andalusia, Mobile, and Tuscaloosa—with attendance of 655 lawyers, representing 51 of Alabama's 67 counties. They constituted approximately one-half of the lawyers actively practicing in the state. Those who served as instructors included Edward W. Faith of Mobile; Judge

THE WOMEN OF THE CLASS OF 1936

THERE WERE FIVE WOMEN IN THE CLASS OF 1936 at the University of Alabama's School of Law, the largest group of women students in one class up to that time. In 1985, an article in *The Capstone Lawyer* reviewed their accomplishments and where their careers had taken them. Irene Feagin (Scott) was a senior judge on the U.S. Tax Court, having been employed by the Internal Revenue Service in Washington D.C. shortly after graduation. Kathryn McDuff (Rossback) followed Feagin to Washington and worked in the office of the General Counsel for the Treasury Department for 14 years, before taking an extended leave to look after her young son and go overseas with her husband. She returned to the government as an attorney with the National Labor Relations Board in the late 1950s, was transferred to Atlanta with the board in 1960, and retired in 1973. Mae Hammond (Knight) also worked for the Roosevelt administration in Washington, first as an attorney for the Resettlement Administration (a part of the Social Security Board). In 1942, she joined the Reconstruction Finance Corporation and, in 1955, she went to the Small Business Administration, where she rose to the position of assistant general counsel and worked until her retirement in the 1980s.

Elizabeth Johnson (Wilbanks) and Nina Miglionico stayed in Alabama. Johnson married a classmate, Simeon Wilbanks, and they set up a small town practice in Dadeville for some ten years. Then they moved their practice to Alexander City, where they addressed the variety of needs of the clients who came to them. Elizabeth's particular interests lay in the areas of real estate and commercial law. In 1970, they sold their practice and went into the banking business for several years before their retirement.

J. Russell McElroy of Birmingham; Judge E. M. Creel of Birmingham; Professors William M. Hepburn and Bernard Harwood of the University of Alabama Law School; Jack Crenshaw of Montgomery; State Senator James A. Simpson of Birmingham; John S. Tilley of Montgomery; and Fred S. Ball, Jr., of Montgomery. President Richard T. Rives was actively involved in the organization of the institutes.

During this convention, President Rives described other ideas that the bar was working to pursue, including the creation of a legislative reference service to aid the Alabama legislature in the drafting and reviewing of bills presented to them and the establishment of an organized legal aid service to be available to the poor. A policy problem that continued to confront the bar for several years, and soon became a major project of the Junior Bar, was

Professor William M. Hepburn of the University of Alabama School of Law was one of the instructors for the "law institutes" organized by the Young Lawyers Section of the state bar following the 1939 convention. In 1944, Professor Hepburn succeeded Albert Farrah as dean of the law school.

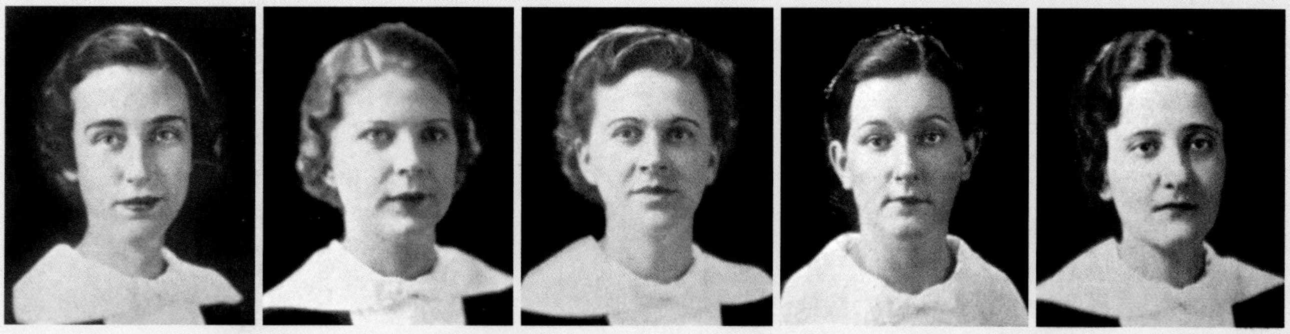

The women of the University of Alabama School of Law class of 1936 as pictured in The Corolla, *from left to right, Irene Feagin (Scott), Kathryn McDuff (Rossback), Sara Mae Hammond (Knight), Elizabeth Johnson (Wilbanks), and Nina Miglionico.*

Nina Miglionico had a private practice throughout her career which emphasized tax law, wills and probate, and domestic relations and family law. In 2009, she was the oldest female lawyer in the state. Her practice remains intact in the firm of Miglionico & Rumore and her partner, Samuel A. Rumore, Jr., served as president of the state bar from 2000 to 2001. Pat Boyd Rumore of that firm is the author of this book.

Miss Nina, as she was called throughout her active career, was elected to the Birmingham City Council in 1963, at the time that the city adopted that form of government, and was its president for one term during her 22-year tenure. She also served a term as president of the Alabama League of Municipalities. She was previously president of both the Alabama Women Lawyers Association and the National Association of Women Lawyers. In 1962, she was appointed by chairman Eleanor Roosevelt to the President's Commission on the Status of Women and served under both presidents John F. Kennedy and Lyndon B. Johnson. In 1996, she won the American Bar Association's Margaret Brent award as one of the five outstanding female attorneys in America that year. She has also been awarded the Maud McLure Kelly service award by the women's section of the state bar and the Sam Pipe's Outstanding Alumnus award by the University of Alabama School of Law. Miss Nina died in 2009 at the age of 95.

what to do about loan sharks and high interest small loan businesses which were injuring low income Alabamians. The Junior Bar would ultimately win a national award for its legislative efforts in confronting this problem. The Junior Bar section began holding its own meeting as part of the annual state bar convention in 1940, during the chairmanship of Bryant A. Whitmire of Birmingham.

The Alabama Women Lawyers Association also met during the 1940 convention and held a luncheon for its members. It was the Alabama chapter of the National Association of Woman Lawyers (NAWL), which two Alabama lawyers have served as president: Nina Miglionico in 1958 and Mahala A. Dickerson, the state's first black female attorney who entered the bar in 1948, from 1983 to 1984. These two also received the Margaret Brent Women Lawyers of Achievement award, presented by the American Bar Association. (Dickerson spent much of her career practicing law in Alaska.) The women lawyers in attendance at the 1940 convention included Jean K. Bynum (admitted to the bar in 1940) of Birmingham; Elizabeth Conerly (1939) of Chatom; Alyxis Gresham (1914) of Birmingham; Nina Miglionico (1936) of Birmingham; Laura Kate Pickett (1936) of Montgomery; Ida D. Rosenthal (1922) of Birmingham; Rossie Rogers (1928) of Birmingham; and Elizabeth Johnson Wilbanks (1936) of Dadeville.

Although women were a small group within the bar, by 1948, 97 women had been bar members, from Luelle Allen, who entered the bar in 1907 but never practiced, and Maud M. Kelly, who joined the bar association in 1909 and was the first woman to actively practice law in Alabama, to Camille W. Cook (who became the University of Alabama Law School's first female tenured professor in 1976) and Ellen G. Irby, who became members of the bar on January 22, 1948. Among these women, two were admitted in the 1900s, eight in the 1910s, over 20 each in the 1920s and 1940s and almost 40 in the 1930s. In an article written in 1951 by Elizabeth J. Wilbanks, it was pointed out that many women left the state to practice (many for government service) and many filled positions that did not require a law license. At the time the article was written, only 16 women were in the general practice of law in Alabama. The article also stated

PIONEER WOMEN OF THE MOBILE BAR

MOBILE HAD FOUR PIONEER FEMALE LAWYERS, including Doris Van Aller (entered the bar 1928), Rosa Gerhardt (entered the bar 1930), Janella Wood (entered the bar 1935), and Alice Meadows (entered the bar 1951, pictured right). Both Van Aller and Gerhardt served the Mobile Bar Association as presidents, "Miss Rosa" in 1948 and Van Aller in 1950. (In 2005, Beth Rouse, whose father and grandfather were also Mobile Bar Association presidents, became the third female president of the Mobile Bar.)

that the percentage of women to men in the profession in Alabama, 1.6 percent to 98.4, was almost exactly the same as existed in the United States as a whole.

In 1941, state bar president Sam Johnston of Mobile reported that the bar, at the request of the American Bar Association, was creating a committee on national defense, to "render legal services without charge to persons in the military or naval service of the United States and their families." At that convention, Lieutenant Colonel Edward C. Betts of Huntsville spoke on the "Constitutional Powers and Limitations Respecting the Military." Colonel Betts was assigned to the JAG Department as professor of law and dean of the law faculty of the West Point Military Academy. He ended his distinguished military career as a brigadier general after having served as legal advisor to General Dwight D. Eisenhower and an organizer of the Nuremburg war crime trials. At the 1944 convention, it was noted that between 500 and 600 bar members were serving in the armed forces, approximately thirty-five percent of the bar.

Other ideas discussed during the forties that took years to bring to fruition included that the bar begin working on the goal of "having a permanent home of its own," and that it work toward the adoption of some form of the federal rules of civil procedure for use in state courts as well as promote judicial reform generally through the creation of a Judicial Council. It was noted that Chief Justice Lucien Gardner of the Alabama Supreme Court was actively involved in American Bar Association studies to formulate standards for judicial self-regulation and improvement of procedures.

At the 1943 convention, President Jacob Walker stressed particularly the need to eliminate the abuses found in the traffic courts, which, he argued, were run merely to collect fees, not administer justice, since the more convictions, the greater the salaries of officials operating the system. He noted the same abuse, to a lesser extent, pervaded the county, inferior, and circuit court systems. He argued that clerks, sheriffs, and peace officers all needed to be placed on salaries unrelated to fees collected. Promoting the adoption of the Federal Rules of Civil Procedures, he stated, "We are living in a museum of procedural antiquities. Perhaps the lawyers are soon to become Egyptian mummies therein.... On two former occasions, I have advocated to you the adoption in our state courts of a system of practice modeled on the Federal Rules of Civil Procedure. As far as the Alabama Bar is concerned, I am still a voice crying in the wilderness. A diet of locusts and wild honey and raiment of camel's hair ill becomes me. Neither by temperament, training, nor environment am I a reformer or an agitator; but I do know that our State rules of practice devised in circuit-riding days can in the light of present knowledge be greatly improved."

A resolution was passed at that convention commemorating Junius M. Riggs, marshal and librarian of the Alabama Supreme Court from 1874 to 1934, who died in 1943. It was noted in 1944 that the Junior Bar Section produced the *Lawyers Handbook* with a view to helping lawyers returning from combat reenter law practice. The American Bar Association presented its award of merit that year in honor of the Junior Bar being named the top junior bar section in the country. The section president, Robert W. Gwin, gave credit to former president Julian Skinner and the officers who served from 1942 to 1943. Julian Skinner was elected secretary of the National Junior Bar Association in 1945 and went on to serve as its president.

In 1945, the state bar created a Judicial Council for the state under a resolution adopted at the 1944 bar convention which required that the council be comprised of "the Chief Justice of the State Supreme Court or some other member of that Court designated by him, two judges of the Circuit Courts of the State appointed by the Chief Justice, the State Attorney General, the Chairman of the Judiciary Committee of the State Senate, the chairman of the Judiciary Committee of the State House of Representatives, and five other members to be selected by the governor, three of whom shall be members of the bar of wide experience." Its duties were "to make a continuous study of the administration of justice of this State, and of the organization, procedure, practice, rules and methods of administration and operation of each and all of the courts of the State," to receive criticisms and suggestions, collect and publish statistical and other information concerning the work of the courts of the state and "to recommend to the Legislature, or the Courts," etc. "such changes in the law or in the rules, organization, operation, or methods of conducting the business of the Courts, or with respect to any other matter pertaining to the administration of justice, as it may deem desirable."

Those named to the Council were Lucien G. Gardner, chief justice; Charles R. Bricken, presiding judge of the Court of Appeals; Walter B. Jones, circuit judge, Montgomery County; J. Russell McElroy, presiding circuit judge of Jefferson County; Charles R. Wiggins, senior judge, Circuit Court of Walker County; William N. McQueen; Charles E. Shaver; Norman W. Harris; Dean William M. Hepburn; John A. Caddell (state bar president, 1951-1952), Crews Johnston; Richard T. Rives (state bar president, 1939-1940); Frank E. Spain; and Edmund Pettus, II. William Logan Martin, Jr., (state president, 1946-1947) was appointed to replace Pettus, who died on July 25, 1945.

Even with such heavy hitters, little headway was made by this group in terms of the enactment of judicial reforms although, in 1955, the legislature embraced federal discovery by statute (in Act No. 375). It has been said that this created the worst of all possible worlds—elaborate pleadings and full-blown federal discovery.[1]

The BBC, on July 7, 1944, repealed its Reciprocity Rule without public explanation, thereby denying lawyers from outside the state the right to practice in Alabama unless they passed the bar's licensing requirements, including the bar exam. (The other side of this coin was that

TOP: *Chief Justice Lucien M. Gardner served on the Alabama Supreme Court for 37 years, from 1914 to 1951.* ABOVE: *The 1943 Alabama State Bar convention honored longtime Supreme Court marshal and librarian Junius M. Riggs.*

Alabama bar members were placed in the same position if they desired to enter another state's bar.) In 1945, the category of "special member," a category that still exists today, was created for lawyers who, because of holding a state or federal office, could not practice law. As "special members," they could still receive the privileges and benefits of full bar membership.

At the 1945 convention, bar president Roderick Beddow invited his brother-in-law, Honorable Bolitha J. Laws, chief judge, District Court of the United States for the District of Columbia, to address the subject "Participation of Judges and Laymen in Improving the Administration of Justice." Judge Laws described "the four stages in the progress of reform: In the first place, when proposed, it is said to be against the laws of God and of man. Then, in the next stage, it becomes un-American; in the third stage, it is unconstitutional; and then, in the fourth stage, when the reform is adopted and found to be effective, the statement is made, 'I was for it all along'."

At the 1947 convention, state bar president William Logan Martin, Jr., noted that a complaint of alleged racial discrimination had been lodged against the University of Alabama law school by "several members of the colored race" who applied to the law school but were not admitted. He reported that he had appointed a committee to study how to respond, since the U.S. Supreme Court had ruled in the case of *Missouri ex rel. Gaines v. Canade, Registrar of the U. of Missouri et al.* (1938) "that the action of a state in providing financial assistance toward the education of a negro in a university outside the state furnishing the funds, resulted in a discrimination repugnant to the 14th amendment, for the reason that the student was entitled to attend the university in the state where he was raised and where he proposed to practice," and this system was exactly that being used in Alabama. He further noted that while the issue was confined to the law school at the moment, "it will probably extend in the future to other departments."

J. Ed Livingston became chief justice of the Alabama Supreme Court in 1951 on the retirement of Lucien Gardner. Before joining the court in 1940, Livingston had practiced in Tuscaloosa, and taught at the University of Alabama School of Law.

A member of the executive committee of the National Junior Bar Conference from Mississippi told the Junior Bar Section that the American Bar Association was considering the policy of changing its bylaws to make membership in the Association easier to attain, the net effect of which would be to expand the number of "colored members" on a wholesale basis. The executive committee member concluded, "I think that the greatest detriment that that foreshadows for the Association is that immediately the Association would become a sounding board for many of the radical ideologies that we down here are constantly fighting against."

Shortly thereafter, the Junior Bar Section held an election for new members of its own executive council and Frank M. Johnson of Jasper nominated his former classmate George C. Wallace of Clio to represent the third congressional district on the council. Wallace was elected.

In 1950, at the behest of President Francis H. Hare, a president's letter first appeared in *The Alabama Lawyer*, so that the president could give an annual report. President Hare recommended in this first President's Report that the bar change its election rules so that a vice president could be elected to succeed the president (which occurred in 1951, when legislation provided for a first vice president who would assume the presidency at the conclusion of the president's term and a second vice president to be appointed by the BBC to serve in the event the president was unable to serve.) He suggested that the office of secretary be made full time.

He also recommended that the bar commissioners begin a search for a permanent home for the state bar, a suggestion that culminated in the building of the state bar headquarters on Dexter Avenue in Montgomery in 1963. (Sam W. Pipes of Mobile led the fundraising effort to raise the $190,000 required to build and furnish the building, which was the first building to be built exclusively for the bar and which at the time was the most expensive public building per square foot ever built in Alabama. Pipes served as state bar president from 1968 to 1969.) Finally, Hare asked the Junior Bar to take the lead in setting up a statewide legal aid society for the poor. By 1954, it had succeeded in establishing legal aid clinics in Birmingham, Mobile, and Montgomery. Herndon Inge Jr., of Mobile cochaired the Legal Aid Committee with Howell T. Heflin of Tuscumbia, and committee members included Frank J. Dishuck, Tuscaloosa; Truman Hobbs, Montgomery; John R. Matthews, Jr., Montgomery; Harry H. Reddick, Mobile (1949); Roderick Beddow, Jr., Birmingham; and Joseph W. Simpson, Birmingham.

In a 1950 article, Walter B. Jones discussed the need and benefits of establishing an Alabama Law Institute (ALI) modeled after the American Law Institute, to continuously study Alabama law and devise ways to strengthen the administration of justice in Alabama. The creation of the ALI did not occur until 1967, but the bar did create a Committee on Jurisprudence and Law Reform, whose purpose was essentially the same. Its first report in 1952 recommended that the promulgation of rules of pleading, practice, and procedure be delegated to the Supreme Court of Alabama in suits at law as they had been for proceedings in equity since 1935. In a 1955 article, Jones reemphasized the need for rule-making authority and for a code of ethics for judges. These reforms again would wait until the late sixties and seventies.

In the spring of 1951, Jefferson County voters approved a constitutional amendment creating the Jefferson County Judicial Commission to aid the governor in filling mid-term court vacancies in the county, of which there had been 97 since 1909. This action followed upon the publication of an article in *The Alabama Lawyer* in 1949 in which William Logan Martin, Jr., (state bar president, 1946-1947) had noted that forty percent of trial judges, and an even greater percentage of appellate judges, were originally appointed by the governor before entering the elective system. In 1951, Justice J. Ed Livingston was appointed chief justice upon the resignation of Lucien Gardner, who had served on the Alabama Supreme Court for 37 years.

Francis Hare, Sr., was considered to be the leading tort lawyer in Alabama. He helped organize both the Association of Trial lawyers of America and the Alabama Trial Lawyers Association, of which he served as the first president.

In 1951, the Alabama Plaintiff Lawyers' Association (APLA) was chartered and reported on its activities in a 1953 article in *The Alabama Lawyer* written by W. E. Brobston. Its membership was comprised of "attorneys who devote themselves to helping injured persons in the field of Workmens' Compensation, railroad, admiralty, and tort law," otherwise known as "damage suit lawyers, trial lawyers, personal injury lawyers, or plaintiffs' lawyers." Its name would later be changed to the Alabama Trial Lawyers Association and ultimately to the Alabama Association for Justice. The attorney considered the premier tort lawyer in Alabama at that time was Francis Hare of Birmingham (state bar president, 1949-1950). The firm of Hare, Wynn, Newell and Newton grew during the 1940s, '50s, and '60s to dominate in this area of the law, especially as the tort field expanded. Later, other lawyers and firms would also create specialties as "plaintiffs' lawyers," including the Montgomery firm founded by Jere Beasley, after his years of service in the Alabama legislature, now known as Beasley, Allen, Crow, Methvin, Portis & Miles, P.C. and the Mobile firm of Cunningham, Bounds, Yance, Crowder & Brown, L.L.C., whose founder, Robert T. Cunningham, was perhaps the first Alabama attorney to obtain a six-figure dollar judgment in such a case.

A Defense Lawyers Association was created in 1964, including founders James Clark of Birmingham (state bar president, 1967-1968); Alto Lee of Dothan (state bar president, 1974-1975); Bibb Allen of Birmingham (state bar president, 1976-1977); Tommy Parker of Montgomery; Paul Brock of Mobile; Ralph Ford of Huntsville;

THE "QUICKIE" DIVORCE SCANDAL

A 1957 ARTICLE IN *THE Alabama Lawyer* written by Judge D. L. Rosenau, Jr., of the Limestone County Court in Athens, Alabama, noted that a divorce granted in his court to a prominent New York City woman lawyer from her husband, a cartoonist for the *New Yorker* magazine, and a divorce he granted to a well-known movie star had drawn national media attention to the laxity of Alabama divorce laws "which stand in danger of permitting Alabama to 'Out-Reno' Reno and gain for the state a rather unsavory reputation." He described a 1945 amendment (which came to be known as the Hooton amendment) to the residence requirements for divorce, which provided that if the court had jurisdiction of both parties, then the one-year bona fide residency requirement for the plaintiff would not apply. As knowledge of the amendment spread outside the state, some courts with equity jurisdiction became swamped with nonresident divorce cases. Judge Rosenau, who had attended Yale University as an undergraduate and Stanford University Law School and had served as a judge for 24 years, discussed the pros and cons of the amendment and the cases its presence in the law generated, stating "it is hard to turn down cases in which your lifelong friends and brother lawyers at your bar are making lucrative fees in cases which they argue are legal under the legislative acts." Still, he concluded that because many were beginning to feel that Alabama was becoming a "hit and run" divorce mecca, he would henceforth impose procedures in his court to assure that only "bona fide" residents of Limestone County would obtain a divorce from his court.

Rankin Fite served as speaker of the Alabama House of Representatives under Governors Jim Folsom and George Wallace. He sponsored legislation used to create a "quickie" divorce mill in Marion County.

Not all judges were as conscientious as Judge Rosenau and some of the lawyers making lucrative fees were attorney-legislators, which probably explains why efforts to repeal the Hooton Amendment failed in 1950, 1954, 1958, and 1960. One legislator, Rankin Fite, who became Governor Folsom's speaker of the house, sponsored legislation in 1953 which created a county court with unlimited ju-

and Clarence Simmons of Gadsden. Its membership was aimed at insurance defense counsel and others who litigated for defendants in business settings. The Alabama Defense Lawyers Association (ADLA) was instrumental in promoting similar organizations in Mississippi, Tennessee, Georgia, and Florida. The Mississippi, Florida, Alabama, and Tennessee organizations met annually at various places within the Southeast for over 20 years, with attorney Don Pierce of Mobile serving as convention chairman the entire time. The organization has had risdiction, particularly as pertained to issues in divorce, in Marion County, where he practiced law. It was described by an article in *The Birmingham News* on March 3, 1953, as offering "all that could be desired to set up a 'quickie' divorce mill." Under it, a party could prove residence by filing a certificate of residence and paying one dollar to the court and have conclusive evidence of residency. (In later years, when court reform was offered to unify the court system, Rankin Fite, then George Wallace's speaker of the house, was a leading opponent because the reform measures would destroy the "superior court" he helped create in Marion County, which was described as "the most powerful of the 78 intermediate courts in Alabama" and which the reform measure would make uniform.)

In response to the quickie divorce scandal, the state bar Grievance Committee in 1960 condemned the practice of attorneys who communicated with individual lawyers in other states about Alabama's divorce laws as unethical solicitation of clients, a violation of Rule 20 of the Rules Governing the Conduct of Attorneys in Alabama. The Grievance Committee included J. H. Perdue, Jr., as chairman, Reid B. Barnes, John O. Harris, Van Waldop, and Douglas Webb.

Subsequently, in 1961, the BBC and the Alabama Supreme Court promulgated Rule 25-A, which prohibited the handling of divorce cases where the attorney knew that neither party was a bona fide resident of Alabama. This rule had been proposed by a special committee appointed by the BBC comprised of Douglas Arant, chairman, C.W. Stringer, and Oliver Brantley. With these two actions and the threat of disbarment they entailed, the number of divorces litigated in the state dropped by one third.

Still, the practice continued in certain courts, such as the court of Judge George Black in Geneva, where more than 2,500 divorces were granted from 1962 to 1963. In 1964, the state bar's Grievance Committee, chaired by Robert E. Steiner, III of Montgomery (who served as state bar president from 1966 to 1967), held hearings in Geneva, as reported in May of that year in *Time* magazine. Local lawyers Edward C. Boswell and Jack Smith were indefinitely suspended from practice and state senator Neil Metcalf was suspended for two years. The judge was suspended as well, when investigators found a locked room containing hidden "quickie" records. The Alabama State Bar won an Award of Merit from the American Bar Association that year for its efforts.

In a final thrust to end the scandal, U.S. Attorney Wayman Sherer and his assistant R. Macey Taylor prosecuted to conviction three disbarred attorneys, K. C. Edwards, John I. Griffiths, and Robert Huie, who continued to hold themselves out to out-of-state attorneys as licensed to practice and who counseled clients to file *pro se* documents they furnished through the mails. They also prosecuted Bob Moore, a circuit judge in the Winston County Circuit Court in Double Springs, who allegedly aided them, for conspiracy to defraud by use of the U.S. mails. This case continued through appeal to the Fifth Circuit until 1971. (One finding that came out of the disbarment proceedings was that the Rules of Conduct for Attorneys did not apply to judges. This finding created momentum for a code of ethics for judges.) This divorce ring had been investigated by the Unauthorized Practice of Law Committee of the Birmingham Bar, chaired by Frank Bainbridge, Jr., who worked with postal inspectors and state bar investigators and federal prosecutors to shut down the ring.

In 1965, Roy Smith of Phoenix City, an attorney who supported the "quickie divorce" system, attempted to change the prosecutorial attitude of the bar by running for bar president. His position was that the bar should not have the right to disbar an attorney. He maintained that the attorney should have a right to trial by jury. He was beaten by Robert E. Steiner, III, who chaired the Grievance Committee which prosecuted several attorneys charged with violating Rule 25-A. A loss by Steiner might have taken away from the bar its role as the regulatory arm of the state to police the ethics of attorneys.

As a result of the federal prosecution and continued pressure from the bar, the legislature finally repealed the Hooton amendment in 1971, after 26 years and untold thousands of "quickie divorces."

a close affiliation with the Defense Research Institute since its beginnings as well.

The formation of these two organizations marked the continuation of a sometimes adversarial split in the integrated bar between lawyers who represented plaintiffs and lawyers who represented defendants in personal injury, products liability, medical malpractice, and other tort related lawsuits. These organizations had no formal affiliation with the Alabama State Bar and were evidence of the early beginnings of a trend for lawyers to gravitate to specialty bars,

CUMBERLAND SCHOOL OF LAW MOVES TO BIRMINGHAM'S SAMFORD UNIVERSITY

Cumberland Law School was founded in 1847 in Lebanon, Tennessee. Many early members of Alabama's legal community were Cumberland graduates and it was well thought of generally in the Alabama legal community. By the late 1950s, it and its sponsoring institution, Cumberland University, had fallen on hard times. At this crucial time in its history, attorney Memory L. "Toby" Robinson, a member of the prominent Lange, Simpson, Robinson & Somerville firm, was chairman of the Executive Committee of the Howard College (now Samford University) Board of Trustees. Under Robinson's guidance, the college acquired the historic law school and undertook to build a building to house it. That building, the Memory Leake Robinson Law Building, was dedicated in 1964.

The legal community was well represented on the board of trustees of Howard College when this affiliation was made, including Harwell G. Davis, a former attorney general and former president of the college; Edgar Bowron, then presiding judge of the Tenth Judicial Circuit; Lee C. Bradley, partner at Bradley Arant Rose & White; Frank E. Spain of Spain, Gillon, Grooms, and Young; H. Hobart Grooms, U.S. district judge; and William H. Brantley, a Lange, Simpson partner and benefactor to the college, who left it one of the best private history collections in the state. Cumberland would soon attract students from all over the United States to attend law school in Birmingham. Alva Caine, who entered the bar in 1970, was the first Cumberland graduate to serve as president of the Alabama State Bar (1989-1990).

including, later, the Alabama Criminal Defense Lawyers Association, the Alabama Lawyers Association (comprised of African-American lawyers), and the Alabama chapter of the Association of Corporate Counsel, among others. The Alabama State Bar would respond to this trend by establishing practice sections and identity groups within the state bar itself, currently having 22 practice sections, many of which sponsor annual meetings focusing on specialized continuing legal education programs.

During this same period, with the founding of the American College of Trial Lawyers in 1950, there began a trend to create national and international organizations with selective membership limited to a small percentage of the population of lawyers in a state to designate the best within particular specialties. The American College of Trial Lawyers, whose statement of purpose describes it as "composed of the best of the trial bar from the United States and Canada," with membership being by invitation only, includes members from both civil plaintiff and defense trial bars as well as criminal prosecution and defense bars. Thereafter, such groups as the American College of Labor and Employment Lawyers, the American College of Bond Counsel, the American College of Trust and Estate Counsel, the American Academy of Matrimonial Lawyers, the American College of Bankruptcy, the American Academy of Appellate Lawyers, the American College of Construction Lawyers, and the American College of Hospital Attorneys were created as each of these areas of the law became significant areas of specialization. Alabama attorneys are represented in each of these organizations, and the designation of Fellow in any of these organizations indicates selection as a prominent specialist by one's peers.

By a special supplement to *The Alabama Lawyer* dated April 1958, the state bar's Committee on Jurisprudence and Law Reform published a proposed Business Corporation Act which had been worked on continuously by its Sub-committee for Revision of Business Corpora-

The Board of Trustees of Howard College view a rendering of the proposed new building, later named Memory Leake Robinson Hall, planned to house Cumberland Law School. From left to right are John B. Scott, Executive Secretary of Alabama State Bar; Harwell G. Davis, past president of Howard College; Judge Edgar Bowron; Richard J. Stockham of Stockham Valves and Fittings; Memory L. Robinson of Lange, Simpson, Robinson and Somerville; Lee C. Bradley of Bradley Arant Rose & White; Frank P. Samford, Jr.; Frank P. Samford, Sr., of Liberty National Life Insurance Company and Chairman of Trustees of Howard College, for whom the university was later renamed; Leslie S. Wright (standing), President, Howard College; Frank E. Spain of Spain, Gillon, Grooms, and Young; Judge H. Hobart Grooms; and William H. Brantley, early partner in Lange, Simpson.

tion Law since1953. The subcommittee was chaired by Sam Earle Hobbs and its membership included Dean M. Leigh Harrison of the University of Alabama Law School, Jack Crenshaw of Montgomery, William F. McDonnell of Sheffield, and Roy M. Woolf of Anniston. Also noted for their contributions were Walter Gewin of Tuscaloosa and Reid Barnes of Birmingham. This effort was the state bar's first significant exercise in major law reform. It was a prelude to the creation of the Alabama Law Institute, which would in the future coordinate many such efforts within the state. The Business Corporation Act was adopted by the legislature in 1959. In 1960, the committee also reported its conclusion from an in-depth study that Alabama's state courts needed statewide court administration to ensure that those circuits with crowded dockets and backlogs could be assisted by judges from circuits without these problems.

A paper presented by Truman Hobbs entitled, "Products Liability—Legal Battleground of the 1960s" foreshadowed the trend toward expansion in the field of tort law which would play an increasingly important role for Alabama lawyers in coming years as Alabama juries awarded huge punitive damage awards and Alabama plaintiff lawyers perfected the tort of "bad faith."

In January 1964, Richard W. Neal replaced Walter B. Jones as editor of *The Alabama Lawyer.* At that time, Neal was not only serving as editor of *The Alabama Lawyer*, but was also marshall and librarian, as well as acting clerk, of the Alabama Supreme Court. Upon Neal's death in 1967, J. O. Sentell was appointed clerk of the Supreme Court and assumed the task of editing *The Alabama Lawyer.*

In 1964, Lawrence K. "Snag" Andrews was selected by the BBC as the first general counsel of the state bar. He died in 1966 and was replaced by William H. Morrow, Jr. The year 1964 saw the elimination of the "diploma privilege" for University of Alabama Law School graduates and thereafter all applicants for admission to the bar were required to take the bar examination.

CHAPTER THIRTEEN

DIXIECRATS AND DEMOCRATS

As Harry S. Truman gained confidence in himself as president, he increasingly committed to press for greater rights for African Americans, promising to back an antilynching bill as well as establishing a President's Committee on Civil Rights and charging its members to study and report on all aspect of that explosive issue. Lister Hill, who had previously been progressing into the circles of party leadership on the national level, began to back away, seeing an upcoming clash between Truman and the Southern segregationist wing of the Democratic Party. Since he was the leader of the state's loyalist forces in Alabama, he did not want to become embroiled in this clash over racial issues as a floor leader for Truman if he could help it.

In February 1948, Truman made his move, asking Congress to abolish the poll tax, make lynching a federal crime, prohibit segregation on interstate trains and buses, curtail job discrimination, establish a permanent Federal Employment Practice Commission, and set up a civil rights division within the Justice Department. In response, 21 Southern senators, including Hill and Sparkman, vowed to fight Truman.

Back in Alabama, Frank Dixon, Gessner McCorvey, and Horace Wilkinson, as leaders of a State Democratic

This tumultuous scene at the 1948 Democratic National Convention in Philadelphia shows the moment when 14 of the 26 Alabama delegates walked out in protest of the civil rights plank in the party's platform. Beneath the Alabama placard, Senator Lister Hill, in a white shirt, can be seen taking the microphone from the departing Handy Ellis.

Executive Committee (SDEC) controlled by Big Mules and Black Belt interests, began preparing to foment a rebellion within the national party at the 1948 Democratic convention. In addition to the issue of civil rights, they added the issues of outside federal intervention in state matters and centralization of government powers over the economy and labor. Other attorneys who supported the rebellious State Democratic Executive Committee included John D. McQueen of Tuscaloosa (who had served as state bar president from 1932 to 1933 and was a previous chairman of the party's executive committee); Talladega judge D. H. Riddle; Robert B. Albritton of Andalusia (who served on the SDEC for 20 years and also served as state bar president from 1971 to 1972); and Birmingham's Hugh Locke. The struggle in Alabama encompassed who would control the state delegation to the Democratic convention in Philadelphia and who would comprise the slate of electors that would appear under the official party emblem in the November presidential election.

On May 4, 1948, Alabama Democrats chose 14 convention delegates pledged to walk out if a civil rights plank was adopted and 12 who opposed a walkout under any circumstances. In the race for presidential electors, the Dixon-McCorvey-Wilkinson wing of the party had fielded a slate of presidential elector candidates who claimed the right to vote for someone else if Truman or anyone who favored civil rights became the Democratic nominee. This slate won, making Alabama the only state in the union in November 1948 on whose ballot the

national Democratic nominees for president and vice-president were not represented.

When the delegates at the Democratic convention adopted a civil rights plank even stronger than that proposed by Truman, Alabama's 14 anti-Truman delegates left the convention, while the remaining delegates reorganized and remained. Within days, the anti-Truman forces, soon to be dubbed "Dixiecrats," joined segregationists and states' righters from across the South in Birmingham at a convention to form a new party, the States' Rights Democrat, or "Dixiecrat," Party. Frank Dixon served as temporary chair and keynote speaker, while Horace Wilkinson gave the nomination speech for Strom Thurmond of South Carolina and Fielding Wright of Mississippi as presidential and vice-presidential nominees of the new party. Although few states' rights electors won, it had been a goal of that party, if they had won sufficient electors, to persuade all the various presidential electors from throughout the country that they were constitutionally free and independent to cast their votes in the Electoral College for whomever they chose. They hoped to achieve a national political realignment with significant Southern influence, denial of the presidency to either Truman or Dewey, and election in the Electoral College of a coalition choice for president who would be acceptable to the South, possibly Dwight D. Eisenhower.

The States' Rights Democrat Party convention was held at the Municipal Auditorium in Birmingham. Former Klan attorney Horace Wilkinson gave the speech nominating Strom Thurmond.

A TALE OF TWO PRESIDENTS

ROBERT BYNUM ALBRITTON was the grandson of Edgar Albritton, who had founded the Andalusia, Alabama, firm of Albritton, Givhan & Clifton back in 1887, the oldest firm which has had a family member practicing since its inception. Edgar's son Harold had 11 children and three of them joined the firm, including Robert, William, and Marvin. Robert was a leader in the Alabama states' rights movement and ran for the Democratic nomination for state senator from Covington, Conecuh, and Butler counties in 1954 (being defeated by a Jim Folsom loyalist). His brother William at the same time was affiliated with the Republican Party, and served Covington County as the party's county chairman. William was an Alabama delegate to the 1952 Republican National Convention which nominated Dwight Eisenhower for the presidency, where he supported Ohio senator Robert Taft.

During this period, Marvin Albritton was a war veteran who was attending law school and who joined the firm upon passing the bar in 1950, too late to be a part of the national states' rights party movement. He served for many years as an important member of the state bar Board of Bar Commissioners during his legal career.

All three brothers were charter members of the Alabama Defense Lawyers Association (created in 1964), as was their firm partner Albert Rankin, who was also elected a Fellow in the International Society of Barristers.

Robert served as president of the Alabama State Bar from 1971 to 1972. Robert's son, William Harold Albritton, III, named for his grandfather Harold and his uncle Bill and known as Harold, joined the firm in 1962. He followed his uncle's lead into the Republican Party and his father's lead into bar leadership, serving as president of the Alabama State Bar from 1990 to 1991. After this service, he was appointed a federal district judge in Alabama's Middle District by Republican president George H.W. Bush in 1991.

Robert Bynum Albritton, above left, and his son, District Judge W. Harold Albritton, left.

THE STRUGGLE FOR CONTROL OF THE STATE DEMOCRATIC EXECUTIVE COMMITTEE

During his first term as governor from 1947 to 1951, Jim Folsom was thwarted at every turn by the legislature. His first major challenge had been the struggle to be able to name the speaker of the House, which previous governors had been able to do as a legislative courtesy. Perhaps because he had no elective political experience in Montgomery before he was elected governor, Folsom did not immediately let his wishes be known once he became the Democratic nominee. Three legislators put their names forward as candidates for speaker, two of whom were members of the conservative wing of the party and one of whom was not an announced Folsom man but did represent DeKalb County in the northeastern corner of Alabama and had many of the same political views as Folsom. This legislator, William M. Beck, was a young attorney from Fort Payne. Governor Folsom used substantial political capital fighting for Beck's election. Beck won, but this struggle publicly

ANNIE LOLA PRICE

THE STATE'S FIRST FEMALE APPELLATE JURIST WAS from Cullman and first entered the law through her work as a stenographer in the offices of Judge A. A. Griffith and attorney Joel B. Brown. While working for them, she also studied law and gained admission to the bar in 1928. She worked in private practice and also worked as a court reporter in Judge Griffith's court for a number of years.

When Jim Folsom became governor in 1947, Price went to Montgomery as an assistant legal advisor to the governor and then Folsom made her his legal advisor in 1950. In 1951, just before leaving office, he appointed her to fill a vacancy on the Court of Appeals caused by the death of Judge Charles R. Bricken. Price was elected to a full term, then reelected three times. In 1969, she was sworn in as presiding judge of the newly created Court of Criminal Appeals, where she served until her death in 1972.

Price was inducted into both the Alabama Women's Hall of Fame and the Alabama Lawyers Hall of Fame.

demonstrated the weakness of Folsom's influence on the legislature and the long odds that he would pass his agenda of rewriting the state constitution, repealing the poll tax, reapportioning the state legislature, overhauling the state's corporate tax structure, and expanding the social welfare role of state government.

The lieutenant governor, presiding over the Senate, which as a body was thoroughly controlled by conservative forces, was J. Clarence Inzer, a Gadsden attorney, who appointed legislators of a decidedly anti-Folsom cast to key positions in the Senate. (Clarence Inzer served as president of the state bar from 1943 to 1944.) Wielding their power through the legislature's committee structure, the conservative legislature effectively stymied Folsom during his first term in office. One significant accomplishment of his first administration was his appointment of attorney Annie Lola Price to a seat on the Alabama Court of Appeals at a time when women were barred by law from serving on the state's juries.

During the election year that followed Folsom's first administration, the struggle for control of the state Democratic party played out in the selection of its executive committee. Folsom had the opportunity upon his election in 1947 to propose a new committee chairman to replace Gessner McCorvey, who had served since 1939 when he won the post with the support of then-Governor Frank Dixon. Folsom passed up this opportunity, not realizing the power that could be wielded from the chairman's position. It proved a costly error in the dynamics of the continuing struggle between liberals and conservatives in the party. It was the right wing of the committee, under McCorvey's leadership, which led the Dixiecrat revolt in 1948.

In 1950, there was a renewed struggle for control, and there was a possibility that the conservative wing would win, but both public opinion and geography worked against the states' righters. The fact that the incumbent president of the country was not on the 1948 ballot left many voters upset, regardless of whether they supported him or not and they directed their ire at the states' righters. Further, the SDEC was elected by congressional districts and the conservative candidates for positions outside the Black Belt and industrial Jefferson and Mobile counties were not well known. Thus, the Loyalists were able, under the leadership of Lister Hill (who asserted that the states' righters were really Republicans in everything but name), to elect a lopsided majority of the executive committee and maintain the loyalty of the state Democratic party to the national party. One journalist asserted that "the Dixiecrat movement is washed up, unless something else comes along in the next few years to revive it." In 1954, something else would come along: *Brown v. Board of Education* which would usher in "a decade of demagoguery."

Governor James E. "Big Jim" Folsom, below, was relatively liberal on issues of civil rights and social welfare, but found his efforts to move the state forward blocked by the conservative legislature, led by Lieutenant Governor J. Clarence Inzer.

Where did the Alabama State Bar Stand on the Issues of Race, States' Rights, and Economics?

A review of the proceedings of the 1949 state bar convention, held in Mobile, clearly shows where the bar stood on the split in the state democratic party. The president of the bar that year, who presided at the convention, was Gessner McCorvey. The chairman of the Resolutions Committee, appointed by McCorvey, was former governor Frank Dixon and the keynote speaker was the Dixiecrat candidate for president, Strom Thurmond of South Carolina.

Hugh Morrow (admitted to the bar in 1894), who was a founder of the state's first large corporate firm, known in its early days as Tillman, Grubb, Bradley and Morrow, and now known as Bradley Arant Boult Cummings LLP, gave an address entitled "Trend of the Times." A brief quote captures its tenor, "For many years there have been eager and busy beavers in Washington gnawing away at the rights of the states until now, the heavy hand of Truman's 'F.E.P.C.' (Hell Bent for Election) Bill is angrily reaching for the very windpipe of the Nation. And this brings me to a subject that is today of vital interest not only to the people of the South, but also to the people of the entire country. I refer to what some call 'local self-government,' some, 'home rule,' and what down South is called by the quaint old name, 'states rights,' all meaning the same thing—'the liberty of being governed at home on things belonging to home.'" "States' rights" was the order of the day.

A deliberation of the convention, involving three proposed resolutions, also demonstrates where the leadership of the state bar stood politically in 1949. Frank Dixon, chairman of the Resolutions Committee, introduced two of the resolutions, which opposed the ratification by the United States of "the Convention on the Prevention and Punishment of the Crime of Genocide" and "the International Covenant on Human Rights" based on the Universal Declaration of Human Rights approved by the United Nations Assembly on December 10, 1948. He stated, "Gentlemen of the Bar, the next two resolutions deal with matters as to which there is a considerable lack of information; and on that account, the Resolutions Committee, after a reading of the two resolutions, because they deal with similar subjects, will ask Mr. Logan Martin, who has been working with the American Bar Association on these matters, to explain the resolutions and the meaning behind them to you."

Martin, who was the founder of the predecessor firm of today's Balch & Bingham and was the state bar's delegate to the American Bar Association House of Delegates, as well as president of the state bar from 1946 to 1947, then described the reasoning behind the American Bar's opposition to the conventions, the thrust of which was that they would impose international obligations that might interfere with U.S. constitutional rights and responsibilities and the operation of both federal and state governments. After Martin concluded, attorney Ben Turner of Mobile, who was McCorvey's law partner in the law firm McCorvey, Turner, Rogers, Johnstone & Adams (currently known as Johnstone, Adams, Bailey, Gordon & Harris, L.L.C.) moved the adoption of the resolutions, whereupon Montgomery attorney Richard Rives, who had been president of the bar from 1939 to 1940, moved that the resolutions be tabled until they could be further studied. Borden Burr, at this time a very senior member of the bar, having been admitted in 1898, and having served as state bar president from 1931 to 1932, made a statement which concluded, "I would hate to see a body of lawyers hesitate for one moment and not vigorously and enthusiastically take a position that we don't want by treaty to surrender the domestic affairs of this country to international courts or commissions."

South Carolina governor Strom Thurmond, the "Dixiecrat" nominee for president, was the keynote speaker at the 1949 convention of the Alabama State Bar. He went on to serve in the United States Senate until the age of 100 in 2002.

Devane K. Jones, a Tuscaloosa attorney who served as state bar president from 1941 to 1942, argued, in part, that "it is sufficient for us...to vote favorably on both resolutions and to adopt the resolutions unhesitatingly for us to know and to understand one thing about the resolutions and what is attempted in the proposed treaties, namely, as has already been said, the proposal to put into effect international and local laws down to the county courthouses and city halls merely by treaty." Jones pointed out that the Covenant on Human Rights would give people the right to marry anyone of their choosing. Horace Wilkinson asked, "Does it abolish the miscegenation laws by treaty?" and Jones responded in the affirmative. "Does it outlaw segregation," asked Ernest Jones, and Devane Jones responded, "Yes." He then argued that it would be difficult for any of the convention attendees to write senators Hill and Sparkman as individuals if they failed to pass the resolutions while at the convention, where they were "a study group, selected group, this group of men who left home and their business and their offices to come down here to undertake to look after these matters."

Most of this discussion took place after it had been pointed out that the meeting schedule called for the members to proceed to a fish fry. Even so, Richard Rives spoke up again, stating, "I...don't know whether I will stand alone on this matter or not; but as a conscientious lawyer I couldn't sit out there and say that I was a member of any study group which had information on the Treaty on Genocide and the Treaty on Human Rights, and whose advice would be worth anything to the Senate of the United States or to the President...

There are many things, Mr. Chairman and fellow members of the Bar, about which we honestly disagree. We are here in a Bar Association, an integrated bar association, different from the American Bar Association where anyone can join or abstain from joining. We are in a Bar Association every man is a member of. In controversial matters, they have a right to study those controversial matters; they have got a right to express themselves on those controversial matters. We ought not to adopt a resolution of this kind upon the mere reading by any man, Judge Martin or anyone else. I have been railroaded enough into this kind of thing; and I am not going to be railroaded into adopting a thing I don't know anything about any more."

Rives also asserted, "I consider it as much a function of government to protect human welfare as property rights." To this Borden Burr asked, "What government, the Federal government?" Rives responded, "No, our government. I have listened to states' rights preached..." to which another member asserted, "It is a good doctrine." Rives continued, "It may be a good doctrine. I didn't vote for Governor Thurmond last fall. For the first time I was deprived of the right to vote. I came down here to attend a Bar Association convention and not a Dixiecrat convention; and I don't propose to have Logan Martin, Borden Burr, or anybody else dictate to me."

"I haven't studied the subject. I didn't read it; I didn't study it; but I say that it has got no part in our deliberations when we know nothing about it." Here "applause" was indicated. As the proceedings continued, a vote was called on Rives's motion to table the resolutions. At this point, chairman Frank Dixon took over. After noting that a motion to table is not debatable, he stated, "On this resolution, and in spite of the motion to table, which is not debatable, I am going to impose on you to say this: that under the genocide convention, they can reach into Alabama and pick up your Governor and carry him to be tried before a foreign tribunal if he attempts to enforce the miscegenation law or statute." Then the vote was taken. The resolution to table failed and the resolutions were passed.

Richard T. Rives, state bar president from 1939 to 1940, was a lone voice against the resolutions opposing congressional ratification of two international treaties at the 1949 bar convention. He later served on the U.S. Court of Appeals for the Fifth Circuit.

Then the third resolution was put forward. This resolution was one that called upon the state senate "to adopt and submit to the people the proposal now pending in the Senate known as the Voter Qualification Amendment." Again Richard Rives spoke against the resolution, stating, "[T]hat is something I have studied and I have studied the Boswell Amendment which was declared unconstitutional. This amendment—it is a proposed substitute for the Boswell Amendment—in my opinion is just as unconstitutional as the Boswell Amendment. And in the opinion of one of the Justices of the [Alabama] Supreme Court it is unconstitutional. [Justice Lawson]. And I may safely say in the opinion of the Dean of the Law Department of the University."

Rives continued, "I came here not to be railroaded into this kind of resolution. It has got nothing to do with our Bar Association. And I submit to you that the opinion of the Federal Court of Appeals, on which certiorari was denied by the Supreme Court, says we must have reasonable and definite rules for determining the right to vote...that will make this a government of laws and not of men.

"The proposed amendment to the constitution..." Here Ben Turner inserted a question. "Didn't you appear before the Committee charged with the enactment of the resolution?" Rives responded, "I appear before everybody I know." "Did you tell them your thought?" "Yes, sir," Rives answered. "Did they adopt your thought?" "No, sir," Rives replied. Turner then stated, "It ought to be closed."

Rives continued his argument, "I appear before everybody I know to oppose an amendment in my opinion unconstitutional, when I have sworn to support the Constitution.

"This proposed amendment imposes two additional tests for the right to vote, any one of which could be interpreted by registrars in different ways. Those tests are to be submitted to the sixty-seven Boards of Registrars throughout the State, with liability on the part of those Boards, if they refuse a man the right to vote, to be dragged into court and sued."

Horace Wilkinson moved the previous questions, which Frank Dixon acknowledged and then stated, "I make this preliminary statement: the House has passed the voters qualification amendment, and it has gone to the Senate and is on the Senate special order calendar, about fourth place. Those who prepared the resolution are convinced it is urgent that it be adopted," whereupon the vote was taken and Dixon continued, "It is the opinion of the Chair that the motion has been carried."

LISTER HILL, RICHARD T. RIVES, AND DEMOCRATIC APPOINTMENTS TO THE FEDERAL JUDICIARY

IT IS NOT SURPRISING THAT RICHARD RIVES, A former president of the bar, was not able to influence the states' righters who controlled the 1949 bar convention. The primary adversary of the conservative faction of Alabama's Democratic Party which ran that convention was Senator Lister Hill, and as Hill's biographer Virginia Van der Veer Hamilton has pointed out, Dick Rives was "practically a Hill." He had been trained in the law by Lister Hill's uncle, Wiley Hill, and had been Will and Wiley Hill's law partner for many years. The Rives and Hill families owned adjoining plantations before the Civil War, so the two families had been longtime friends and acquaintances. Rives had a well-known history of support for progressive politicians, including Bibb Graves, Hugo Black, and especially Lister Hill and was esteemed in liberal circles as a political tactician. Originally Rives was a gradualist on civil rights, but he was influenced to a more activist stance by his only son, educated at Harvard, who was killed in a car accident in 1949.

In 1951, Leon McCord, who had been appointed to the Fifth Circuit in 1938 by President Roosevelt, was ready to retire, having entered the practice of law in 1900. He handpicked Richard Rives to succeed him. With the backing of Lister Hill and John Sparkman, and a quiet endorsement from Hugo Black, President Harry Truman made the appointment.

President Roosevelt had appointed Birmingham attorneys Thomas Alexander Murphree and Clarence Mullins to district judgeships in 1938 and 1943 respectively, and both of them were politically savvy allies of Lister Hill. In 1951, Lister Hill engineered another appointment, this time for a federal district court judgeship in the Southern District of Alabama, for Democratic Party loyalist Daniel H. Thomas of Mobile, a law partner of his uncle, Joseph H. Lyons, in the firm Lyons, Pipes & Cook. Sam W. Pipes of this firm was state bar president from 1968 to 1969.

Other appointments to the federal bench were made from the firm that Richard Rives left. John C. Godbold

U.S. District Court Judge Virgil Pittman served on the federal bench before retiring at the age of 90. One of his most notable cases, Bolden v. City of Mobile, *changed the process of city government elections, allowing for the representation of minorities.*

ABOVE: *Robert S. Vance was active in state and national Democratic Party politics before being appointed to the Fifth Circuit Court of Appeals in 1977. A progressive on civil rights cases, he was killed by a letter bomb in 1989.* RIGHT: *Lister Hill's influence was felt again in 1962 when Clarence Allgood was named a federal district judge by President John F. Kennedy.*

was selected to succeed Rives on the circuit bench in 1966 by President Johnson and Truman Hobbs, who had been Hugo Black's law clerk in 1949 and state bar president from 1970 to 1971, and was named a federal district judge by President Carter in 1980. The firm is now known as Copeland, Franco, Screws & Gill, P.A. Robert D. Segall of that firm served as state bar president from 2005 to 2006.

President Johnson also appointed Mobile attorney Thomas Virgil Pittman to the U.S. District Court for the Southern District in 1966. President Carter named Birmingham attorney Robert S. Vance, who had served for 11 years as chairman of the State Democratic Executive Committee, to the Fifth Circuit Court of Appeals in 1977. (In December 1989, Vance was tragically killed by a letter bomb sent to his home.) Carter also named Elbert Bertram Haltom, Jr., of Florence and Robert B. Propst of Anniston to the U.S. District Court for the Northern District in 1980.

In an act of providence that would become evident soon after his appointment, Senator Lister Hill chose to approve the appointment of Republican Frank M. Johnson, Jr., to the federal district court in Montgomery in 1955 rather than supporting his own cousin, Thomas Bowen Hill, Jr., who had been president of the state bar from 1952 to 1953 and who was partner in another prominent Montgomery firm with a corporate clientele (Hill, Hill, Stovall and Carter, now known as Hill, Hill, Carter, Franco, Cole & Black P.C.). Relations between Senator Hill and his cousin had soured over the years as T. B. Hill supported the Dixiecrat movement and thereafter drifted toward Republicanism. By 1952, he called himself an "Eisenhower Democrat." In 1955, Senator Hill considered him a turncoat. There is little doubt that history would be very different if T. B. Hill had been appointed federal judge rather than Frank M. Johnson, Jr., who teamed up with Rives and, later, Godbold to create a judicial revolution in Southern mores. T. B. Hill's firm represented the state of Alabama and other defendants in several of the important civil rights cases brought by black plaintiffs in the next several years. (T. B. Hill's firm produced state bar president James R. Seale, 1993-1994.)

When John Kennedy became president in 1960, Senator Hill had two more opportunities to influence the judiciary: Clarence Allgood was named a federal district judge in Birmingham in 1962 and Walter P. Gewin, Foots Clement's law partner, was appointed judge of the Fifth Circuit Court of Appeals in 1961. (Gewin served as state bar president from 1958 to 1959.) That appointment had been promised to Clements himself, but he learned that he had a terminal illness and asked that his partner be named instead.

CHAPTER FOURTEEN

THE STRUGGLE FOR CIVIL RIGHTS

Many white Alabama attorneys played significant roles in the struggle of African Americans for civil rights and in the expansion of civil liberties for all Americans in the decades of the fifties, sixties, and seventies. There were five whose roles were critical: Supreme Court Justice Hugo Black, Fifth Circuit Judge Richard T. Rives, District Court Judge Frank M. Johnson, Jr., Governor John Patterson, and Governor George Wallace. The background against which they played their roles developed during the period that Justice Hugo Black was on the Supreme Court, culminating with the issuance of the opinion in the case of *Brown v. Board of Education of Topeka* by the United States Supreme Court in 1954, which held that state-sanctioned segregation deprived African Americans of "equal protection of the laws."

The *Brown* opinion specifically dealt with the issue of education, but its use in subsequent litigation gradually changed Alabama's "Southern way of life" to eliminate the legal doctrine of "separate but equal" in all areas of life. The court's opinion was unanimous, and Justice Hugo Black was one of the justices who took a leadership role in arriving at that unanimity.

For most white Alabamians of that time, Justice Black's participation in this decision and other decisions of the court which were expanding the application of the Bill of Rights made him a traitor, a "Judas Iscariot," the "Benedict Arnold" of Alabama, and a scalawag. He became a pariah in his home state; the state senate passed a resolution which stated that it was the sense of that body that when Black died, his remains should not be mingled with the soil of Alabama. The state house of representatives passed a resolution proclaiming *Brown* "null, void and of no effect" in Alabama.

The outrage among conservatives grew throughout Black's time of service on the court because Black ruled in favor of a progressively broader construction of the Constitution's protection of such rights as the right to vote, the right to free speech and association, freedom of religion, freedom from unlawful search and seizure, procedural rights in criminal prosecutions, and rights to privacy. Hugo Black's Supreme Court gave new meaning to the entire Bill of Rights, but most especially to their application to African Americans through the post-Civil War constitutional amendments—the Thirteenth, Fourteenth, and Fifteenth amendments—which were passed to protect the civil liberties of the freed slaves. The purpose of these amendments had been frustrated by the court's decision in the case of *Plessy v. Ferguson* in 1896 and by the continual failure of the federal government to enforce them, even within the framework of *Plessy*.

Richard Rives joined the Circuit Court in 1951 and served as chief judge of the circuit from 1959 to 1966. He positioned himself with other liberal judges of the Fifth Circuit to produce a court which developed the principles set out in *Brown v. Board of Education* into a broad mandate for racial justice and equality under law in the South and, by extension, throughout the country. With Judge Frank M. Johnson, Jr., who was appointed federal district judge for the middle district of Alabama in 1955, he formed a unit that gave backbone and structure to the developing civil rights movement in the state.

Johnson's location in Montgomery, the seat of government in Alabama, made his courtroom the focus of

litigation challenging state-sponsored violations of civil rights in Alabama. Many of his detractors, and especially governors Patterson and Wallace, described him, and the circuit judges with whom he often sat, as judicial activists, giving rights where none had been before. Scholars who have studied their decisions more closely have described

Supreme Court Justice Hugo Lafayette Black was a key member of the court that issued the decision in the pivotal Brown v. Board of Education *case that ignited the civil rights movement and its opposition throughout the South. As a native of Alabama, Black was branded as a traitor to his race by the white conservative establishment of his home state.*

Johnson and other like-minded Southern federal judges as being willing to accept the constitutional philosophy set out by the Supreme Court in *Brown* and other cases involving constitutional rights and liberties and to reinforce it, upward and outward, stretching and expanding the law to protect rights and liberties granted by the Constitution which had been denied in error in the past.[1]

The roles played by Patterson and Wallace were adversarial and often demagogic, demonstrating a political failure to accept the Supreme Court's expression that the time had come to recognize the equal positions of black and white Americans before the law and under the Constitution and to uphold the federal rights and privileges of individual Americans as being paramount to the sovereignty of individual states. By being rigid and obvious in their denial of equal protection and due process to more than a third of the population of the state, they invited both litigation and mass action to challenge the very legal system they described themselves as protecting. What otherwise might have come about progressively and quietly instead came about in a way that, for a time, brought infamy and shame to the reputation of white citizens of the state of Alabama and unnecessary injury to many of its black citizens. Both men later expressed regret for their earlier positions as the change that ultimately came was obviously for the good of all.[2] And the progress that has been made with time has ameliorated the shame of the past.

Renowned Birmingham defense attorney Rodderick Beddow was in charge of the defense in the Sumter County peonage case. He was famous for his participation in high-profile cases, including, briefly, the Scottsboro boys case, and the 1954 murder of attorney general candidate Albert Patterson in Phenix City.

U.S. Attorney Frank Johnson Prosecutes a Peonage Case

When Frank Johnson served as U.S. attorney of the Northern District of Alabama, prior to his appointment to the bench, his one experience involving civil rights was his prosecution of several family members of a prominent Sumter County farming family under an indictment charging slavery, involuntary servitude, peonage, the use of interstate travel for such offenses, and conspiracy. The family had a practice of going to neighboring Mississippi jails and prison camps, paying the fines of African Americans imprisoned for relatively minor offenses, and then forcing them to work in the fields on one of their plantations. Those who tried to escape or otherwise displeased their masters were beaten. One victim died during a beating.[3]

The black owners of the funeral home where his body was brought, seeing that local authorities were not taking any action, informed Johnson of the circumstances and he asked the FBI to investigate. Soon various family members were brought before District Judge Seybourn Lynne for trial. The defendants retained attorney Thomas F. Seale, Jr., of Livingston to represent them. He in turn hired Roderick Beddow, the state's preeminent criminal defense attorney at the time, to direct the defense. Beddow was well known throughout the state, having represented clients from Ku Klux Klan members to policemen to poor blacks, including one black youth whose trial for murdering a prominent white woman required National Guard protection.

Johnson produced witnesses to the conduct of all the men who were being prosecuted that painted a grim picture of the defendants and the operation of their plantations, where brutal treatment of African-American workers was the norm. It became evident that only two of the family members were responsible for most of the conduct charged in the indictment and Johnson, on the second day of the trial, asked that certain counts of the indictment be dismissed for lack of evidence (after getting testimony allowed that might not have gotten in if the dismissal had happened earlier or the indictments had not been issued). Johnson also got one character witness to admit that beating black workers in Sumter County would not be held against a white man's character.

Beddow and his associate, Robert Gwin, gave a vigorous defense without interjecting racial commentary that others might have used to prejudice the jury. As federal prosecutor, Johnson emphasized the duty of the jury to make their decision based solely on the evidence and to understand their role in the government's action as protectors of the rights of citizens who had no other protection. When the all-white, male jury returned its verdicts, after 15 hours of deliberation, the two defendants were found guilty.

Phenix City attorney Albert Patterson ran in the Democratic primary for attorney general on a platform of cleaning up the notoriously corrupt town.

John Patterson and the Clean-Up of Phenix City

From the earliest days of white settlement, the area that became today's Phenix City, Alabama, had a reputation for turning a blind eye to criminal activity. Being right across the river from a settled area of Georgia, people on the run from the law had merely to cross the water into Indian lands to avoid capture and prosecution. As time went on, a settlement grew where the criminals congregated. It was called Girard.[4]

Girard was known as a den of gambling and a haven for bootleggers. In May 1916, Attorney General William Logan Martin, Jr., sent a special train to Girard carrying 40 hand-picked deputies who seized and destroyed close to $1 million worth of illegal liquor under Alabama's prohibition laws. A young Hugo Black was appointed special prosecutor for the state of Alabama and Judge A. H. Alston of Clayton was appointed to impanel a blue ribbon grand jury to clean up the town. After the criminal element was prosecuted, Girard merged with the nearby town of Phenix City with the hope that expansion and new leadership would keep the town clean into the future.

Soon after the cleanup, though, the United States entered World War I. In 1918, the War Department established Fort Benning as a military training center in nearby Columbus, Georgia. With the influx of hundreds of young military personnel, gambling, bootlegging, and prostitution returned and gradually increased so that Phenix City itself became notorious. Its notoriety derived not only from criminal activity but also from the corruption of its local and county government and law enforcement personnel.

In 1933, attorney Albert Patterson came to Phenix City and set up a law practice. He was joined in his practice in the early 1950s by his son, John, who earned his law degree from the University of Alabama in 1949. Albert Patterson ran for attorney general in the 1954 Democratic primary against attorneys Lee "Red" Porter and MacDonald Gallion, with the platform of cleaning up Phenix City again. Patterson ended up in a runoff with Porter. The incumbent attorney general was Silas "Si" Garrett, III. He supported Lee Porter and was later accused of conspiring with attorney Lamar Reid, who was chairman of the Jefferson County Democratic Executive Committee, and Arch Ferrell, the Russell County circuit solicitor, to alter the primary runoff vote tally in Jefferson County in order to steal the election from Patterson. (In spite of the alleged fraud, the official state canvass conducted on Thursday, June 10, revealed that Patterson won the election by 854 votes out of approxi-

JUDGE ALTA KING EXPANDS THE GRAND JURY PROBE

UPON HEARING A RUMOR THAT the death of Albert Patterson might be tied to the alleged voter fraud that the grand jury was investigating, Judge King gave special instructions to the Birmingham grand jury.

"Albert Patterson was to have appeared before this inquisitorial body today to bring information he had about the vote fraud tally in Jefferson County. On Friday night, he was ambushed and assassinated in one of the most heinous and cowardly crimes in the annals of Alabama history.

"Those responsible for the murder of Albert Patterson have flouted the will of the people of Alabama, first, by endeavoring to steal the election from him and when this failed, they ruthlessly took his life...showing to what extent such lawless elements will go.

"The gravity of this crime strikes at the very vitals of our form of government and is a direct threat to our free elections and to our very way of life, for should we ever lose our freedom of election and the expression of the will of the people at the ballot box, all our other freedoms would soon be lost.

"We should and must do all in our power to pinpoint and bring to justice those who have violated our elections laws and to discover, as nearly as possible, the facts of any connection between what happened in Phenix City and the vote stealing in Jefferson County."[5]

A blackboard displays the results of the 1954 Jefferson County attorney general primary, showing Albert Patterson as the winner.

(Alta King's son, attorney Tom King, ran for mayor of Birmingham in 1961 against Art Hanes. His grandson Tom King, Jr., currently serves Jefferson County as a circuit judge and his grandson Alan King serves the county as probate judge.)

mately 400,000 votes cast in the runoff). On Monday, June 21, 1954, Albert Patterson was to go to Birmingham to testify before a grand jury impaneled by Circuit Judge Alta King to investigate the alleged vote fraud, but, the Friday night before, Patterson was shot and killed outside his office in Phenix City.

In response to the killing, Governor Gordon Persons placed Russell County under martial law and sent in National Guard troops to protect citizens from the criminal element that dominated the city and to drive that element away. Chief Justice Ed Livingston appointed Judge Walter B. Jones to take over the duties of the local circuit judge, Julius Hicks, and ordered a special grand jury impaneled to again conduct a cleanup of the criminal activities in Phenix City. (Judge Jones was well known in the state bar for having founded Jones Law School in 1927, for

A crowd mills around the scene of the murder of Albert Patterson, whose car, with its door still open, can be seen parked in the alley. Standing in the doorway of the Elite Cafe is deputy sheriff Albert Fuller who was ultimately convicted of the murder, a classic example of the criminal returning to the scene of the crime.

being the founding editor of *The Alabama Lawyer*, the state bar magazine which began in 1940, and for being the incoming president of the bar, 1954-1955.) George Johnson, circuit solicitor of the Eighth Judicial Circuit, was appointed special prosecutor, with Conrad "Bulley" Fowler, circuit solicitor of the Eighteenth Judicial Circuit, being appointed to assist him. Fowler had already made headlines for bringing down gambling kingpins in Shelby County.

After testifying before the Birmingham grand jury, Si Garrett, who had a history of mental illness, left the state at the behest of his family, including his brother, Broox Garrett, who served as state bar president from 1981 to 1982, for treatment in a clinic in Galveston, Texas, remaining unavailable during much of the ensuing turmoil resulting from the murder of Patterson. During his absence, several assistant attorneys general conducted the investigation into Patterson's murder, with Bernard Sykes serving as coordinator of the investigation, which became the biggest murder investigation Alabama had ever seen.

In the meantime, the State Democratic Executive Committee considered what to do to fill the position of attorney general, since their elected candidate had been killed. Because of the charges of corruption which surrounded Patterson's death, the committee determined that its only recourse was to call a special election. Albert Patterson's son John, who had previously avoided politics as a career, decided to carry on his father's legacy and declared himself a candidate for the special election. Lee Porter, who allegedly had received contributions from several Phenix City criminal kingpins during the primary runoff election, decided not to run. MacDonald Gallion also did not run, upon Patterson's promise to name

him first assistant attorney general. (He subsequently served two terms as Alabama's attorney general.) The Republicans did not submit a candidate for the general election, and Patterson assumed the office his father had initially won.

John Patterson took over the investigation of his father's death upon his inauguration and added assistant attorneys general Joe Robertson, Albert Rosenthal, MacDonald Gallion, Lee Barton, and Maury Smith to the team of investigators and prosecutors, with Bernard Sykes retained because of his overall knowledge of the investigation.

After the corruption prosecutions involving both crime figures and local officeholders were concluded, Judge Jones withdrew and returned to Montgomery. Soon after, indictments were returned against Arch Ferrell, Silas Garrett, and corrupt local sheriff's deputy Albert Fuller for the murder of Albert Patterson. Chief Justice Livingston appointed Circuit Judge J. Russell McElroy, presiding judge of the Tenth Judicial Circuit, to hear the

Attorney General Silas Garrett holds an informal press conference following the murder of Albert Patterson. Behind him, leaning against the window, is Albert Fuller. Garrett and Fuller would eventually be two of the three men indicted for the murder. Seated in the corner is Phenix City mayor Elmer Reese.

trials in Birmingham, with Cecil Deason, an assistant circuit solicitor for Jefferson County, being named special prosecutor. Judge McElroy, at the age of 53, had already been on the bench for 28 years. He is still regarded as one of the most outstanding trial judges in the state's history, and was the state authority on the rules of evidence, having written a treatise on evidence and having served as a part-time professor at various times at Birmingham School of Law, the University of Alabama School of Law, and Cumberland School of Law, as well as at the Medical College of Alabama.

Si Garrett employed criminal defense attorney Roderick Beddow to represent him for all actions that came out of both the vote fraud case and the death of Patterson. Because of his treatment by psychiatrists in Texas, Garrett also faced a "lunacy" action brought by Jefferson County's circuit solicitor Emmett Perry, who was the prosecutor of the vote fraud case. Beddow was also retained by defendant Albert Fuller. (Beddow was familiar with crime and criminals in Phenix City, having served as a special prosecutor in 1946 in a case where crime boss Hoyt Shepherd was tried for the murder of competitor Fayette Leebern. Shepherd was defended by a team which included, ironically, Albert Patterson and Arch Ferrell. Beddow, with his associate Robert Gwin, also represented several of the criminal kingpins prosecuted before Judge Jones, even challenging the constitutional validity of the declaration of martial law and the appointment of Judge Jones to sit in place of Judge Hicks.)

Russell County circuit solicitor Arch Ferrell, above center, was indicted in the original voter fraud case and was the third man indicted for the Patterson murder. He was respresented by George Rogers, left, and his young associate L. Drew Redden, right.

Arch Ferrell chose to have separate counsel, turning to George Rogers and his associate L. Drew Redden, who had been practicing together since 1952. George Rogers, at the age of 49, already was considered second only to Beddow in his reputation as a criminal defense attorney. At the age of 32, Redden was in line to fill both their shoes as his career progressed. He served as president of the state bar from 1972 to 1973. (William N. Clark, a partner in the firm that Redden founded with Rogers, served as president of the state bar from 2003 to 2004.)

When all litigation, including one of the longest murder trials in the state's history to that time, was concluded, Albert Fuller was found guilty of the murder of Albert Patterson. Arch Ferrell was found not guilty in both the vote fraud case and the murder trial. Silas Garrett, as coconspirator, was not tried in either case after his alleged coconspirator was found not guilty.

The death of Albert Patterson launched the final cleanup of Phenix City and it also, and perhaps more importantly for the history of the state, launched the political career of attorney John Patterson, who followed his four years as attorney general with four years as governor, during the years when the modern civil rights movement began in Montgomery.

The Ambition of George Wallace

George Wallace was born in 1919 in Clio, Alabama. Clio is in Barbour County, where many prominent Alabama political figures were born, including Eli and John Gill Shorter and their relative, Reuben Kolb, as well as U.S. Senator James Pugh, and governors Braxton Bragg Comer and Chauncey Sparks. Perhaps that legacy of statewide political success was the inspiration for Wallace's political ambitions, which blossomed quite early in his life and which almost immediately included visions of being Alabama's governor. Later Wallace's ambition would ultimately include the U.S. presidency.[6]

Wallace became a senate page in 1935, at the age of 16, being sponsored by attorney Archie M. McDowell, the senator from his district whose brother, Charles S. McDowell, Jr., with whom Archie practiced law in Eufaula, had served as president of the state bar from 1915 to 1916 and as lieutenant governor from 1923 to 1927. (Charles McDowell ran for governor in 1926, but was beaten by Bibb Graves. Archie McDowell served as legal advisor to Governor Chauncey Sparks in the early days of his administration.) Wallace not only wrote to each of the 35 state senators asking for their votes, but also went to the capitol and walked the halls shaking hands and introducing himself. He won a page position easily. While working as a page, he became close to Barbour County's representative, Chauncey Sparks, whom Alabama historian Harvey Jackson has described as being "like an uncle" to Wallace, mentoring him over the years in the workings of traditional Southern politics and giving him his first political job.

Another Clio-born attorney, Elton B. Stephens, who at the time was a magazine distributor in Montgomery (and who became well known later when he established his hugely successful distribution company, EBSCO, in Birmingham) gave Wallace a summer job as a magazine salesman, while he was in high school. Stephens was so impressed with Wallace's enthusiasm and sales talent that he made Wallace crew leader for the following summer. Such jobs were a necessity for young Wallace whose family was poor. His economic position became even more precarious when his father died in 1937, just as George was heading off to college.

After successfully taking on the political elite at the University of Alabama, the young George Wallace served as an assistant attorney general and as a progressively minded state legislator before running for circuit judge in Barbour County, winning easily.

Wallace attended the University of Alabama, a training ground for would-be politicians. Politics at the University were dominated by the fraternity machine, normally leaving independents out in the cold, but Wallace almost immediately mobilized a coalition of independents and unpledged freshmen and won election as class president.

Later, during his undergraduate career, he again took on the fraternity machine when he ran for president of the Cotillion Club, whose officers arranged almost all social activities on campus and worked closely with the fraternities to control most honorary and elected student positions. Although he was defeated twice for this position, his ambition seemed only to become more intense. His approach was that of the outsider, the populist, the independent—in the tradition of fellow Barbour County politician Reuben Kolb.

Wallace attended law school and became friends with a fellow student whose path would become entwined with his later in their legal careers, Frank M. Johnson, Jr. They both entered the bar in 1943. In 1955, when Frank Johnson was named a federal district judge, Wallace had already served as an assistant attorney general under Attorney General William N. McQueen (a Tuscaloosa attorney whose father, John D. McQueen, was president of the state bar from 1932 to 1933) and as a state legislator representing Barbour County. He gained a reputation for proposing legislation for the "furtherance of education, welfare and health," and as an exemplary member of the board of trustees of Tuskegee Institute (seeming to have a genuine, paternalistic interest in black education). He ran for and won a circuit judgeship in Barbour County, beating Preston Clayton, a state senator, wealthy breeder of Arabian horses, distinguished lawyer, and legislative floor leader for Governor Persons. Wallace won the 1950 judicial election with 75 percent of the vote.

His dedication to cultivating his political reputation among the voters of his circuit, even while he had served in the military during World War II, paid off as he began laying the foundation for a run for the governorship after Jim Folsom's second term. He mimicked the Folsom style of person-to-person campaigning, which bypassed the traditional conservative interest groups that dominated state politics, and became known for his prodigious ability to remember voters' names. He also earned a reputation for being a racial moderate in the image of his ally, Governor "Big Jim" Folsom.

How could he have planned for the abrupt entry on the political stage of John Patterson or the upheaval which would come with the *Brown v. Board of Education* decision and the efforts to implement it? His response led him to demagoguery.

Attorney Fred D. Gray Versus the State of Alabama

There are several African-American attorneys in Alabama's history who are acknowledged champions of civil rights, but only one was Rosa Parks's lawyer who guided most of the early litigation arising out of the Montgomery bus boycott and the leadership of Reverend Martin Luther King, Jr. That lawyer was Fred Gray, who was only 25 years old when Rosa Parks refused to give up her seat on a Montgomery bus to a white person, an action which precipitated the bus boycott that is considered by most historians as the trigger for the modern-day movement that many call the Second Reconstruction.[6]

Gray was born in Montgomery in 1930, the youngest of five children, whose father, a carpenter, died when Fred was two years old. He and his siblings were raised by their mother, who had only a sixth grade education and who worked as a domestic in several white homes. His neighborhood, a typical black community of the time, had no paved streets, no running water, and no inside sanitary facilities. There were no hospitals for black children to be born; he was delivered by a midwife.

Gray's parents were devout members of the Church of Christ and his mother's ambition was for him to become a minister, so he attended high school at the all-black Nashville Christian Institute (NCI), a boarding school operated by members of the Church of Christ. While attending NCI, whose 300 students came from about 25 states, Gray made friendships which lasted his whole life and who served as resources during the years when he worked to break down segregation in the state of Alabama. Gray fulfilled his mother's desire that he become a minister and he served various churches throughout his legal career, regularly preaching on weekends in communities he visited for business reasons during the week.

Gray attended Alabama State College (ASC), where he was a member of the Omega Psi Phi fraternity, which continued to provide social and business contacts after his graduation. He also worked as distribution manager for the *Alabama Journal* over 13 routes that included the ASC campus and most of Montgomery's black neighborhoods. He did not have a car so he traveled on the bus as many as six times a day, seven days a week.

Montgomery attorney Fred Gray was forced the leave the state in order to receive a legal education, but he was determined to return and take up the fight against segregation. His chance came quickly, when, at the age of 25, he represented Rosa Parks following her arrest on a Montgomery bus.

All the bus drivers were white, even though ninety percent of the riders were black. There was strict segregation on the buses, with blacks relegated to the back, even on routes through mostly black neighborhoods. A constant aggravation to black riders, and the black community generally, was the invariably discourteous treatment they received from the drivers, especially the black women who used the buses to go to their domestic jobs in white homes, and the fact that the drivers often made blacks give up their seats to whites even when they were sitting in the area of the bus designated for blacks. Refusal to give up a seat could result in arrest.

Suffering this denigrating treatment and seeing others suffer as well inspired Gray to consider a career in the law, a path his political science teacher encouraged and which he decided to pursue during his junior year. His goal was to attain a law degree and return to Montgomery "to destroy everything segregated he could find."

Gray had to leave the state to get a legal education, because no law school in Alabama admitted African-American students. The state developed a plan to comply with Supreme Court mandates for equal opportunity in professional education by providing African-American law students round-trip transportation once a year to their chosen school, as well as reimbursing the difference between tuition fees at the University of Alabama School of Law and the particular university chosen by the student (which in Gray's case was Case Western Reserve in Cleveland, Ohio), and the difference between room and board costs. These sums were available only on a reimbursement basis, which was a burden for students like Gray, who came from poor families. The program was administered by the state superintendent of education, who at the time was Austen Meadows, a man who became a defendant in many subsequent lawsuits that Gray filed upon his return to Alabama with his law degree.

Arthur Shores was the first black attorney in Birmingham, beginning his practice in 1937. He frequently represented the NAACP during the civil rights era, and acted as a mentor to the younger generation of black attorneys, including Fred Gray.

From the beginning of his law school career, Gray studied with the Alabama bar exam in mind, learning those areas where Alabama law differed from that of other states. He ordered a copy of Title 7 of the Alabama Code, which encompassed "pleadings and practice," where Alabama law was uniquely its own, and studied it as part of his overall legal studies. Whenever he had a research paper to do, he would do his paper on some aspect of Alabama law.

Upon completing law school, he studied for the Ohio and Alabama bar exams, taking a bar review course in Cleveland for the Ohio bar exam (which he determined to take in case examiners in Alabama failed him because of his race.) He wrote to Judge Walter B. Jones, who was incoming president of the state bar and who offered a bar review course for law graduates in Alabama, but Jones replied that he did not know when he would offer another course. Jones suggested that Gray study Title 7 and read various articles in *The Alabama Lawyer.*

Judge Jones was known as a staunch segregationist and used his ties with the bar and the community to voice his views, including writing a weekly article for the *Montgomery Advertiser.* An article he wrote on March 4, 1957, entitled "I Speak for the White Race," illuminates the mindset of the political elite during the Montgomery bus boycott. His first sentence was, "I speak for the White Race, my race, because today it is being unjustly assailed all over the world. It is being subjected to assaults here by radical newspapers and magazines, Communists and the Federal Judiciary. Columnists and photographers have been sent to the South to take back to the people of the North untrue and slanted tales about the South."

This quote illustrates why many historians consider the civil rights era a second Reconstruction. The notions of outside interference (carpetbaggers) and homegrown radicals (scalawags) as well as the power of the federal government (now through both Congress and the judiciary) forcing unwanted change in race relations on a beleaguered white race reflected the same mindset prevalent during the post-Civil War Reconstruction era. Thrown into the modern mix was the threat of communism. It was a mindset that did not take into account the legitimate rights of local African Americans, who made up forty percent of Montgomery's population, and their willingness to struggle to enforce their rights. Judge Jones was a highly regarded jurist and member of the Alabama State Bar, from a family with a long history of service to the state. The fact that he published his views, even though he was a judge before whom matters he was making reference to could possibly and, in some cases, did come, illustrates the posture of many in Alabama's white legal community as far as the pressure to change racial relations was concerned. It was a posture of defiance.

Fortunately for Fred Gray, he entered the bar before this posture of defiance developed. He was able to come up with five white members of the bar who supplied affidavits vouching for his character, a prerequisite for taking the bar exam. They included Clifford Durr, a white attorney known for his progressive politics (and for being Justice Hugo Black's brother-in-law) who would serve as a behind-the-scenes mentor for Gray until Durr's death, as well as Nesbitt Elmore, Woodley C. Campbell, Henry Heller, and Kenneth McGee. Charles Henley, a black attorney who was Grand Master of the Masons and did not practice, and Arthur Shores, a black attorney from Birmingham who was considered the dean of black attorneys in the state because he had been practicing since 1937, also signed affidavits for him.

One of Fred Gray's law professors had encouraged his students to "always seek assistance and never be afraid to share a fee with an older lawyer who has more experience." Gray took this lesson to heart throughout his career, but particularly in the early days. Clifford Durr was available, with a law library, when Gray needed help, probably serving as his most important mentor in his development as a lawyer. There were other black lawyers, including Charles Langford in Montgomery, who would later become Fred's partner. In Birmingham, there were black attorneys Oscar Adams, Orzell Billingsley, Jr., Peter Hall, and David Hood, all of whom were young lawyers like Gray, as well as Arthur Shores, who served as an inspiration and mentor for all the state's black attorneys until his death in 1997. As time passed and Gray became actively involved in civil rights litigation, he often sought out these attorneys, because of their experience and interest and to share the complex work, both mental and physical, these cases entailed. Another source of aid for Gray was the NAACP Legal Defense and Education Fund and the lawyers who guided its use, such as Thurgood Marshall and Constance Motley, who litigated civil rights cases throughout the United States and who executed the legal strategy which resulted in the *Brown v. Board of Education* decision. Robert Carter was NAACP general counsel and was available as needed. These three lawyers were not from Alabama, but their involvement in litigation in the state has had a significant effect on its modern culture and its laws.

Orzell Billingsley, Jr., a law graduate of Howard University, was one of the group of young black attorneys in Birmingham who came of age during the civil rights era. Billingsley and Peter A. Hall were the first black attorneys to appear in court in Selma.

The civil rights movement is thought of by most nonlawyers as a series of events: the Montgomery bus boycott; the freedom riders in Anniston, Birmingham, and Montgomery; the demonstrations, fire hoses, and police dogs in Birmingham; the deaths of four young black girls in Birmingham when their church was bombed; George Wallace's stand in the schoolhouse door; the Selma to Montgomery march; and the death of Viola Liuzzo. All of these events were undertaken, though, to assert or defend legal rights or to retaliate against the assertions of these rights, and most of them precipitated or resulted in litigation or changes in the law in one way or another. Many would argue that the litigation and changes in the law, both state and federal, are the cause of lasting changes in American society, and particularly in Southern society, that came about as a result of the massive actions undertaken by private citizens. Lawyers and judges, most of whom were well known in the bar, were intimately involved, both as agents of change and as agents of reaction.

For the legal profession, it is the litigation, the precedent-setting cases, and the expansion of constitutional rights that resulted which make the civil rights era both interesting and inspiring. More than a dozen cases arising from events in Alabama became constitutional benchmarks filling the textbooks used by law schools for decades thereafter.

CHAPTER FIFTEEN

THE MOVEMENT BEGINS

Rosa Parks's prosecution in 1955 for refusing to give up her seat on a bus was for disorderly conduct, not for violating Montgomery's segregation laws. Still, the case precipitated the bus boycott, which in turn precipitated the civil rights movement and the call for Martin Luther King, Jr., to be its leader. Parks was tried in Montgomery Recorders Court before Judge John B. Scott, with D. Eugene Loe prosecuting and Fred Gray defending. She was found guilty and fined $10.[1]

At the time, Judge Scott was also the secretary to the Alabama State Bar; he had checked in law school graduate Fred Gray when he took the bar examination. Scott later served as the reporter of decisions for the Alabama Supreme Court. He was a nephew of attorney William A. Gunter, who served as mayor of Montgomery and who, together with his brother Gaston, ran a political machine which controlled the city's politics for many years after defeating the machine of the powerful Hill family of lawyers. One of Scott's forebears, General John B. Scott, was a pioneer settler of Montgomery.

Rosa Parks's case did not present the proper venue for challenging segregation but the African-American community was ready for this challenge, as proved by the strength of their boycott. First, though, Gray and other representatives of the Montgomery Improvement Association (MIA), of which Martin Luther King, Jr., was president, approached the city and the bus company with a proposal for moderate changes (short of a legal challenge to the segregation ordinances). These changes, which would have made segregation more tolerable to the black community, included that all drivers display more courtesy toward the "colored" riders, that seating be arranged on a first-come, first-serve basis, and that the company hire "colored" bus drivers on buses running into areas heavily populated by "colored" people. City officials categorically refused to discuss reforms or suggest alternate plans or to compromise on any point. In effect, they forced the MIA to continue their boycott, which resulted in the bus company losing hundreds of dollars a day in fares.

Left: *Rosa Parks was tried before Judge John B. Scott, longtime secretary of the Alabama State Bar, who fined her $10 for disorderly conduct.* Opposite page: *Rosa Parks's arrest and the boycott of city buses that followed are frequently cited as the first major salvo in the war for civil rights for African Americans. This photograph is the mugshot taken when she was arrested for her participation in the boycott.*

7053

Attorney Walter Knabe, named partner of Capell, Howard, Knabe and Cobb (today's Capell & Howard, P.C.), represented the city of Montgomery, while Jack Crenshaw represented the bus company. Crenshaw, a Harvard law graduate and the "proctor" of the state bar, was regarded as an excellent lawyer. His father, Hervey Files Crenshaw, Sr., was president of the state bar from 1935 to 1936 and Jack and his brother, Files Crenshaw, Jr., practiced law with him after their entry into the bar in 1926. Jack Crenshaw was a political ally of Jim Folsom, a racial moderate, but it was Crenshaw who was most intransigent in his position, refusing the request to make the seating first come, first serve, arguing that the change could not be made because of state and local segregation laws.

At least one historian, J. Mills Thornton,[2] has pointed out that Crenshaw's intransigence, and Knabe's compliance with his position, drove the MIA to challenge in federal court the laws the lawyers quoted to justify their stands. Thornton stated, "Despite [his] background, [Crenshaw] proved incapable of understanding the strategic advantage of accepting a modest compromise in order to forestall a full-scale assault on segregation. He dismissed Gray's arguments out of hand and informed his client...that the law left the bus company absolutely no room for compromise." He took this position even though the city of Mobile and several other Southern cities served by Crenshaw's client were using the very approach to seating being put forth by the African-American delegation.

In his biography, Fred Gray stated that he believed that Crenshaw let his personal feelings interfere with the best interests of his client. Crenshaw dismissed out of hand legal arguments made by Gray, even though Gray had written an exhaustive brief setting out the legal principles which could have been the foundation for a reasonable compromise. It appears that there was a breakdown in communication concerning what the pertinent law said and how it was to be applied. Crenshaw was unwilling to hear what Gray had to say.

Frank M. Johnson, Jr., spent 24 years as a judge for the U.S. District Court for the Middle District of Alabama, participating in many of the momentous civil rights cases of that tumultuous era. One of the first was Browder v. Gayle, *which found Montgomery and Alabama segregation laws to be unconstitutional.*

The result was the case of *Browder v. Gayle,* filed February 1, 1956, brought before a three-judge panel comprised of district judges Frank M. Johnson, Jr., and Seybourn Lynne and Fifth Circuit judge Richard T. Rives. It sought a ruling that the Montgomery segregation ordinance and the state segregation statute were unconstitutional. An injunction enjoining their enforcement, and the ruling, based in part on an extension of *Brown v. Board of Education*, was forthcoming when the decision was rendered on June 19, 1956, and later affirmed by the U.S. Supreme Court. The various defendants, which included the city's commissioners individually and as members of the city commission, the chief of police, the bus company, and a few of its drivers, as well as the members of the Alabama Public Service Commission, were represented by Walter Knabe, Drayton N. Hamilton, Herman H. Hamilton, Jr., and Jack Crenshaw. Joining Fred Gray in representing the plaintiffs were Charles Langford, Arthur Shores, Peter Hall, Orzell Billingsley, Jr., Robert Carter, and Thurgood Marshall.

Martin Luther King, Jr., pastor of the Dexter Avenue Baptist Church, just a block from the state capitol, and president of the Montgomery Improvement Association, was arrested for his participation in the bus boycott.

The filing of the case had been preceded in January by a letter to the editor printed in the *Montgomery Advertiser* from attorney Fred S. Ball, Jr., (son of the founder of today's Ball, Ball, Matthews & Novak, P.A.) arguing that all the black leaders of the bus boycott should be indicted under an Alabama statute making a boycott illegal. Given Ball's stature in both legal and social circles, Circuit Solicitor William F. Thetford and Circuit Judge Eugene W. Carter instructed a grand jury to determine whether the antiboycott law had been violated. On February 21, the grand jury returned indictments against 89 African Americans for the misdemeanor of conspiring to boycott. Martin Luther King, Jr., was brought to trial under these indictments, but, although convicted, he served no jail time. Given previous interpretations of the boycott statute by the Alabama Supreme Court, it was debatable that it even applied in the Montgomery situation, and subsequently no other prosecutions took place. Defendant King's attorneys cited the case of *Thornhill v. Alabama*, where the U.S. Supreme Court in 1940 had declared a similar antipicketing statute unconstitutional. Rationally, the whole effort to gain these indictments was a waste of time and resources, but rationality did not rule the day.

In his study of the history of the city of Montgomery's civil rights struggles, J. Mills Thornton reviewed the conduct of each of the white groups, including politicians, civic leaders, and business leaders, participating in the events surrounding the boycott. He pointed out that "from the outset the most inflexible of the whites were lawyers" which he found most perplexing. He argued that, from the perspective of history, it would seem that Crenshaw, Knabe, and Ball, all highly educated and well regarded in the legal community, should have had an interest in compromise, since that approach would have guaranteed the continuation of segregation in that particular circumstance. Thornton concluded that their position as lawyers, advocating for their clients, made them, and all lawyers, poorly prepared to participate in the give and take of negotiations and this explained why they acted as they did. Most members of the legal profession would probably disagree with this assessment, since negotiation and compromise are highly prized tools in the lawyer's work of constructing the resolution of client, as well as societal, problems. Obviously, Fred Gray was working for compromise before he brought the lawsuit.

Another conclusion drawn by Thornton, perhaps more directly, points to why it was most often well-educated, well-placed lawyers who defended the status quo so vigorously, even when it might have been in the best interests of their clients to compromise. Thornton notes that segregation in the South was an inflexible system built into the law. "Compromise with segregation was impossible because segregation so forged and underlay social relationships that even the most modest reform of its requirements threatened the entire social fabric. In such a situation reform was impossible; only 'revolution' would do;"[3] and the revolution had to be in the system of law, since it was the legal system that entrenched the social system of segregation. An all-out battle had to be waged, but it had to be a battle to change the law. That was the lesson of the Montgomery bus boycott. Perhaps the lawyers Thornton highlighted did not act consciously from recognition of this truth, but

ALABAMA STATE BAR CONVENTION, JULY 1958

FOLLOWING ARE EXCERPTS FROM THE ADDRESS OF state bar president Burnie E. Jones of Evergreen, Alabama, at the Alabama State Bar convention of July 1958:

"I do not claim to be a great Constitution lawyer, and what I shall say has been better said by others. It is my hope, however, that because of my position some few members of the Bar may be caused to stop and consider as to where we are headed.

"During the period of time that I have practiced law, and especially in the past 20 years the interpretation of the Constitution has so changed that an old timer can hardly recognize our government, though not a comma has been changed in the Constitution. We are fast approaching a Socialistic state, where all rights are regulated by committees and authorities in the Soviet way, and it disturbs me....

"Our courts were reasonably steadfast until Mr. Roosevelt became President. He was almost power mad. Congress passed a great number of New Deal laws, taking authority from the states and giving it to the central government. Several were declared unconstitutional. The President became enraged at the court. He first attempted to pack it by adding additional members. This failed, but as vacancies occurred, he placed on the court political hacks whom he could control. No one was appointed who did not believe the Constitution was outmoded and many of its principles should be abandoned. The first appointment was Senator Black, who became a justice of the court in August, 1937.

"Each subsequent appointment has been of like kind. Constitutional lawyers of integrity no longer can aspire to the Federal Bench. An appointee to the highest court since 1937 need know no law but he knows he cannot reach this court unless he agrees by accepting appointment to carry out the wishes of the appointing power. No longer do we have checks and balances in government but supreme power. The members who have gone on the court since 1937 have shown by their acts that they did not in good faith take the oath to support the Constitution.

"If you think these are strong statements, let's examine a small part of the record since the Court became purely political and see the continual attempts being made to destroy constitutional government."

At this point, Jones described Supreme Court cases in the realms of schools (especially the *Brown* case); restrictions on the use of real estate (*Shelley v. Kraemer*, making unenforceable restrictive covenants involving race, national origin, etc.); advocating the overthrow of the government (*Yates v. The United States*, asserting the primacy of the rights to free speech and association); state primaries (*Smith v. Allwright*, prohibiting white-only primaries); saluting the flag (*West Virginia State Board of*

that knowledge was probably operating at some level of consciousness. Their conduct joined the battle; no quarter was to be given.

The Alabama State Bar and the Civil Rights Movement

All the Alabama lawyers who participated in the litigation and political decision-making during the civil rights era were members of the Alabama State Bar. Because the bar was headquartered in Montgomery, attorneys who were members of that bar were positioned to have a significant impact on its culture, and its culture had the potential to influence the conduct of all of its members. Statewide, lawyers had the choice of being part of the "fraternity" of the law or being considered aberrant. What philosophy controlled the legal fraternity at this time? And who were the members who set the tone?

Education, et al., v. Barnette, et al., preventing a school from forcing a student to salute the flag, as a violation of free speech); admission to the Bar (*Konigsberg v. The State Bar of California,* prohibiting the state from denying a license to practice law because the applicant failed to respond to questions concerning past membership in the Communist Party, as a violation of speech and association); and various other cases where the Warren Court (after Chief Justice Earl Warren) had overturned established precedent by liberalizing interpretations of the rights guaranteed by various constitutional provisions and amendments.

Then Jones continued, "These cases are only samples of the sorry record of our highest Court in the last twenty years. There are many more just as astonishing. While the Court was consistently destroying the authority of the states, the federal government was dishing out our tax monies to the states so as to keep them quiet. Governors of the states would have protested loudly at loss of the rights of local government, but for the fact they could go to Washington and 'shake the apple tree.' The state governments have simply sold their birthrights for a mess of pottage and at the same time have paid for the pottage.

"Since state authorities have been bought with their own money, and have ceased to fight for their Constitutional rights, the trend continues. The only possibility of preserving our government in some semblance of that established by the patriots of old is to get the lawyers aroused. They, better than anyone else, can realize what is taking place. There is much evidence that our brothers in other parts of the country are beginning to realize that the rights of the people of the South cannot be destroyed without danger to them. Lawyers in all parts of the country are becoming uneasy at the actions of an unbridled Court and are attempting to devise means to save some shadow of Constitutional government. Southern lawyers are more awake to the problems than others have been, but we must keep working and help arouse all sections of the country to the immediate danger.

"Right after the War between the States, when animosities were strong and feelings high, and just at the beginning of 'The Tragic Era,' the Supreme Court declared, 'The Constitution, in all its provisions, looks to an indestructible union, composed of indestructible states.'

"Now, nearly ninety years later, the Federal Government, with the enthusiastic support of the Court, is rapidly destroying the 'indestructible states.'

"The Supreme Court is continually and apparently with great relish destroying the Constitutional landmarks set up by the founding fathers. The doing of this is condemned by both sacred and profane law. Back under the law of the Hebrews the right to remove ancient landmarks was repeatedly denied. In Proverbs 22:28, it is written: 'Remove not the ancient landmark, which thy fathers have set.' The penalty is provided in Deuteronomy 27:17, where Moses, the lawgiver, said: 'Cursed be he that removeth his neighbor's landmark.'

"If this old law were still in effect, the present members of the Supreme Court would face a dismal future in the hereafter.

"I have at some length tried to point to the dangers which confront us. We older members of the Bar have fallen down on the job. My hope is that some of the younger lawyers may be aroused to the situation. They have grown up under changed conditions and do not remember a time when Constitutional law was more or less fixed and a person could determine what were his rights. If just a few of the younger lawyers of Alabama will inform themselves as to the danger and make a resolve "They shall not pass," then my labors will have been worth while."

(These comments may be found in *The Alabama Lawyer*, Vol. 19, p. 341, 1958.)

The philosophy that dominated the bar can best be illustrated by a resolution promulgated at the state bar convention on July 20, 1957, by a resolutions committee chaired by Birmingham attorney Kirkman Jackson (state bar president, 1959-1960), which read:

"Be It Resolved by the Alabama State Bar in convention assembled in Tuscaloosa, Alabama, on July 20, 1957, that this association renews its condemnation expressed one year ago at its meeting in Birmingham, two years ago at its meeting in Mobile and three years ago at its meeting in Montgomery, of the decisions of the Supreme Court of the United States in the school segregation cases, and that we reaffirm our determination to resist by every proper, legal, and honorable means at our disposal the enforcement of these decisions." When the vote on the resolution was taken by the meeting chairman, bar president John D. Higgins of Birmingham, there was only one "no" vote.

The first time the resolution was adopted was at the July 1954 convention, held shortly after the issuance of the *Brown* decision in May. At that meeting, Walter B. Jones assumed the presidency of the bar. He had a unique and powerful influence on the state bar because he was the son of one of its most famous founders, Thomas G. Jones. In 1927, Walter Jones had founded Jones Law School in Montgomery to honor his father. He was also the founder and only chief editor of the official mouthpiece of the bar, *The Alabama Lawyer*, which he often used to honor the almost mythlike legacy of his father and those who led the bar with him during the Bourbon period of Redemption that followed the original Reconstruction.

S. Palmer Gaillard, Sr., born in 1856, was thought to be the oldest lawyer in the American Bar Association when he celebrated his 103rd birthday in 1959.

Jones did not attend the 1957 convention, but sent a telegram to convey his regrets. He said, "Please extend to Bar of Alabama, ever *loyal defenders of our constitutional rights and way of life,* my warm and kindest regards. In all periods of our state's history lawyers have faithfully done their part to build in Alabama a government of laws based in principles of justice, honor, and freedom. Alabama owes a debt of gratitude to her lawyers." (Italics added.) When Judge Ben Turner, who entered the bar in 1908, rose to nominate the next president of the bar, he said, "I am distressed our good friend Judge Jones is not here. He has been a stabilizing influence in every Bar meeting in my recollection." Jones entered the bar in 1909.

Drayton Hamilton, one of the defense attorneys in the *Browder* case, was on the editorial board of *The Alabama Lawyer,* edited by Judge Jones during the years of the civil rights era, and was a recent past president of the Montgomery Bar Association. Some of the articles that were published in the journal while he was on the editorial board during the late fifties included "The White South is a Minority Group: The Supreme Court Cannot Bestow White Man's Inheritance on Another Race," "The Federal Invasion of Arkansas in the Light of the Constitution," and "We Must Save the Constitution" (authored by Walter B. Jones). There was a "timely" reprint of a tribute written by Governor Thomas Hill Watts in 1889 on the occasion of the death of Jefferson Davis entitled, "The Relation of the Separate States to the Union," defending the doctrine of states' rights, and another "timely" reprint of a lecture given by Dean William Sewell Thorington on the subject "The Federal Constitution and the Sovereign States."[4] In this article, Thorington disputed the assertion in the constitutional law text book entitled *Handbook of American Constitutional Law* published in 1897 that "the organic act, the Constitution, was formed by delegates representing the several States in Convention, but it was submitted to the consideration and acceptance of the people; the States did not act upon it. It was ratified and adopted by the people of the United States." Thorington's article was a defense of states' rights.

Two articles written by S. Palmer Gaillard, Sr., of Mobile were published during this period. Gaillard was described as "probably the oldest active practicing lawyer in the United States," being over 100 years old (born in Mobile in 1856; entered the bar in 1881). One article was the reprint of a letter he wrote to historian Arnold Toynbee in 1954 disputing his comments in *A Study of History* concerning the degradations of slavery. Gaillard, among other things, recalled his childhood and fond memories of the slaves who had served his family. The second article was entitled "Origin of the Races and Their Development for Peace (Separate but Equal)" which discussed the Bible story of the Tower of Babel and the separation of the races and which contained such comments as "Touch the white race when or where you can throughout their past ages and you find it a race of progress and stamping itself upon the civilization of the ages. Touch the black race when or where you can, throughout the unnumbered ages, (until they came in contact with the white race in modern times), and you find a race so far below the race that could conceive great things and build cities and towers that reached toward the skies, and we wonder what spirit of sloth could have so benumbed mind and body of a race possessed of the same living soul of the advanced races of the earth." The article continued as a defense of segregation and states' rights. (Refer to the sidebar on pages 216-217 for a sample of the stories that the official state bar was telling itself from the presidential address of President Burnie E. Jones of Evergreen, Alabama (1957-1958, admitted in 1914.)

Attorney General John Patterson, standing left, listens attentively as Judge Walter B. Jones reads his decision fining the NAACP $100,000 for contempt of court for refusing to name its members.

The Younger Lawyers

The classes of lawyers graduating in the years following World War II were comprised, for the most part, of large numbers of young men who had had to postpone their career plans in order to fight. This group of men was large not only because they had delayed law school entry, but also because many who might not otherwise have gone to law school were able to pay their way using the GI Bill. These post-World War II graduates have had a tremendous impact on the bar, but most were still in the Junior Bar organization during the early period of the civil rights era. They were not yet positioned to set the tone or philosophy from which the institutional bar operated. Instead, the bar was being run by men whose gaze was turned to the past and whose power was based on the action and thinking of their elders.

John Patterson and His Politics

One young lawyer, a veteran who had graduated in 1949, did command a position of influence. He was the chief legal officer of the state, beginning in 1955, having replaced his murdered father as the Democrat who won the race for attorney general. That lawyer was John Patterson, who quickly made a name for himself as an opponent of corruption in government. How did he respond to civil rights activities?

On June 1, 1956, Patterson, positioning himself for a run for governor in 1958, sued the NAACP for operating in Alabama without having qualified to do business there. The suit was filed before Judge Walter B. Jones, who immediately issued a temporary restraining order enjoining the NAACP from doing business in the state. More importantly, he granted Patterson's motion to compel the NAACP to produce the names, addresses, and phone numbers of all its members. The NAACP refused to produce the list, based on the threat of harassment posed to its members if the list were to be made public. Judge Jones cited the NAACP for contempt of court and fined the organization $100,000. He also enjoined it from qualifying to do business until such time as it purged itself by producing the list of its members and by paying the $100,000 fine. Fred Gray and Arthur Shores were local counsel who worked with NAACP

General Counsel Robert L. Carter to defend the organization. It took eight years and four trips to the U.S. Supreme Court, twice through the state court system, and twice through the federal court system, before the NAACP again was permitted to do business in Alabama. The 1958 Supreme Court case of *NAACP v. Alabama* is considered a principal case in the development of the first amendment right to freedom of association.

Fortunately, Fred Gray incorporated the Montgomery Improvement Association (MIA) as the organization which sponsored the Montgomery bus boycott. In making this recommendation, he recognized that the NAACP was perceived by many whites as threatening, because it was the nation's oldest and most effective civil rights organization, and the very name often provoked hatred and overreaction. In Birmingham, the response of the leadership of its NAACP chapter was to organize the Alabama Christian Movement for Human Rights (ACMHR) headed by Reverend Fred Shuttlesworth. This group led the civil rights efforts in Birmingham with Shuttlesworth being the named plaintiff 11 times in civil rights-related cases (thereby becoming the most litigious individual in U.S. Supreme Court history.)

On August 15, 1957, Patterson attacked another black civil rights organization, the Tuskegee Civic Association (TCA), which dated back to 1941 and was known for sponsoring an action in federal court to have the Boswell Amendment, which required that applicants for voter registration be able to read, write, and interpret the Constitution, declared unconstitutional. Patterson's 1957 action sought to enjoin the TCA and its members from refusing to trade with white merchants and businesses[5] in downtown Tuskegee after the town was gerrymandered by the legislature to remove black neighborhoods from the city limits so as to prevent most blacks from voting in city elections. This action also was a prelude to a run for the governorship in 1958 and it gained Patterson notoriety even though nothing actually came of it when the decision was finally announced after the 1958 election was concluded.

The actions he had taken against civil rights organizations as attorney general gave John Patterson the political recognition to run for governor in 1958. Here he is seen greeting supporters during a campaign stop in Jefferson County.

These actions as attorney general gave the 38-year-old Patterson credibility in the governor's race, which had three viable candidates including Barbour County Circuit Judge George Wallace, Bay Minette publisher and Folsom ally Jimmy Faulkner, and Patterson. Historian Wayne Flynt described the campaign in *Alabama: History of a Deep South State*:

John Patterson faced George Wallace in the runoff for the Democratic nomination for governor. Here they are seen visiting the Alabama Military Academy at Fort McClellan in Anniston. Patterson defeated Wallace by well over 100,000 votes in part by portraying Wallace as soft on race issues.

"Wallace...conducted the most issue-oriented of all his campaigns. Leaning heavily on his populist instincts, he promised to modernize the state's economy, recruit new industry, build trade schools, raise teacher salaries, improve medical care, and provide higher pensions for the elderly. But Patterson made race the central issue of the campaign. He reminded voters that as a probate judge [sic] Wallace had halted a purge of black voters and had sentenced a white man to death for murdering a black. Patterson portrayed himself as the premier segregationist in the race who had fought the Tuskegee boycott and dismantled the state's NAACP. Folsom backers, blacks, and labor split between Faulkner and Wallace, allowing Patterson to lead the primary with 32 percent of the vote.

"In the runoff, Wallace tried to depict Patterson as an extremist on race and as a tool of the Big Mules who would threaten the Tennessee Valley Authority. In a time of racial polarization, he tried to emphasize traditional economic issues and lost the initiative on race even though he proclaimed himself a segregationist. The Klan, which endorsed Patterson, denounced Wallace as 'NAACP-loving George Wallace.' Despite the support of labor, blacks, Jewish organizations, Democratic loyalists, well-educated people, and eight of the eleven large daily newspapers, Wallace lost to Patterson by a vote of 250,000 to 365,000. Wallace attributed his loss to being 'outsegged' and vowed that it would never happen again. Nor did it."

John Patterson's inaugural address, published in *The Alabama Lawyer* in April 1959, reads in places like it could have been written by Burnie Jones or Walter B. Jones:

".... [W]e are being undermined from within by the usurpation of the rights of the states through the unconstitutional encroachment of the Federal Government. The Federal Courts have decreed that we must send our children to integrated schools contrary to our customs and traditions. They have told us how we must sit on city buses in Montgomery. We have seen paratroopers with bayonets try to ram integration of the races down our throats. We should bear in mind that the Federal Government is a government of delegated powers only—that it has only those powers that were granted to it by the states—and that any encroachment by the Federal Government on these rights of the states is tyranny.

"I think we should pause a moment and pay tribute to a great American whose birthday is today—Robert E. Lee. Lee, a Southerner, was a champion of States' Rights and saw in them, as did Jefferson and the other drafters of our Constitution, a means by which the people would be protected against the tyranny of an all-powerful centralized government. He so believed in this that he gave up a bright career in the United States Army and gave his life and fortune to defend these principles. I think we should also pay tribute to a great Alabamian, a former Governor of our State, who served on General Lee's staff, Honorable Thomas Goode Jones. We are honored by the presence of his son...here today, Honorable Walter B. Jones....

"I want to pledge to you that as your governor, I will be unyielding in my opposition to this wrongful usurpation of power by the Federal Government and I will use every power at my command to prevent any further usurpation by the Federal Government of the sovereign powers of Alabama. My administration will be dedicated to the preservation of our Constitutional form of Government.

"I will work in every way possible with the other States, particularly the Southern States, here to form a common front, so that we can better protect ourselves from the unlawful actions of the Federal Government....

"There can be no compromise in this fight. There is no such thing as a 'little integration.'

"The determined and ruthless purpose of the race agitators and such organizations as the NAACP is to bring about as fast as possible an amalgamation of our society. They seek to destroy our culture, our heritage, and our traditions. If we compromise or surrender our rights in this fight, they will be gone forever, never to be regained or restored....

"...We must put our life and meaning into the motto of our State—"WE DARE DEFEND OUR RIGHTS."

Fred Gray and Gomillion v. Lightfoot

Fred Gray was another young lawyer. He was not part of the power structure of the bar or the state's political system, but he was having an impact putting life and meaning into his own motto "to destroy everything segregated he could find."

In the fall of 1960, he found himself arguing the case of *Gomillion v. Lightfoot* before the United States Supreme Court (with the help of Robert Carter, NAACP General Counsel, who still was able to share responsibility for the case with Gray, regardless of the legal status of the NAACP in Alabama). The case attacked the racially motivated gerrymandering of Tuskegee, Alabama. The defendants, who included most of the city and county officials who were empowered to enforce the gerrymandering, were represented before the court by James J. Carter of the law firm of Hill, Hill, Stovall & Carter, the firm founded by T. B. Hill, Jr. (again raising the question of how differently the civil rights era might have unfolded if T. B. Hill, Jr., had been appointed U.S. federal district judge instead of Frank M. Johnson, Jr.). James J. Carter was president of the state bar from 1962 to 1963.

The Supreme Court ruled in favor of the plaintiffs, finding that the statute which had established new boundaries for Tuskegee was unconstitutional under the Fifteenth Amendment because it was so blatantly racially motivated. This decision established precedent which would allow all gerrymandering to be evaluated by federal courts.

The Young Men's Business Club Lawyers, Reynolds v. Sims, *and Birmingham's Change of Government*

The Young Men's Business Club (YMBC) in Birmingham was a civic club comprised of young men who were seeking to broaden the political outlook of both Birmingham and the state of Alabama. They wanted to change both the narrow political and economic leadership that had a stranglehold on the city and state. Among its members were five activist post-World War II attorneys: David Vann and J. Vernon Patrick (both of whom had been law clerks of Justice Hugo Black), George Peach Taylor, Charles "Chuck" Morgan, Jr., and C. H. Erskine Smith.

This group of young attorneys challenged the state legislature's failure to reapportion legislative districts, as required by the 1901 constitution. Their action was in part precipitated by the 1960 census, which showed that Alabama had lost population and would lose a congressional seat. In response, the legislature was considering a "chop-up" plan which would divide Birmingham among the remaining congressional districts so that the city's urban voters would not be proportionally represented

David Vann, above, and the other lawyers of the Young Men's Business Club, joined with older lawyers like Sydney Smyer, right, to change the form of Birmingham's city government from a commission to a city council and end the reign of notorious police commissioner Eugene "Bull" Connor, opposite page, seen here campaigning against the change. David Vann later served on the city council and as mayor of Birmingham.

in Alabama's congressional delegation. This proposal created such controversy that even the "Big Mules" of Birmingham's business community, and their powerful spokesman, attorney and state senator Larry Dumas, were up in arms against the Black Belt-controlled legislature. Only a historic filibuster, by young attorney legislators Ryan deGraffenreid of Tuscaloosa, E. B. Haltom, Jr., of Lauderdale County (appointed a federal district judge in 1980 by President Jimmy Carter), and Larry Dumas of Jefferson County kept Jefferson County as a unified district.[6]

The historic failure to reapportion had allowed the Black Belt counties of south Alabama to have power in the legislature disproportionate to the number of voters represented, especially when compared to Birmingham's large urban population. The YMBC lawyers were able to use the precedent established, in part, by *Gomillion v. Lightfoot*, that federal courts had jurisdiction to protect voters whose right of suffrage was being unconstitutionally violated. *Reynolds v. Sims,* the case they litigated, became a precedent-setting case which established the principle of "one man, one vote," serving as a guideline for legislative reapportionment thereafter.

District Judge Frank M. Johnson, Jr., had ordered, as temporary relief, that a special election be held to give Jefferson County more representation in the state legislature. The YMBC lawyers, with the aid of older attorneys Abe Berkowitz (a member of a Birmingham Bar Association committee which had recommended that Birmingham change its form of government from a commission to a council form of government)[7] and Sidney Smyer (who was both the president of the Birmingham Realty Company and the Birmingham Chamber of Commerce at the time) were able to use this election as an opportunity to garner signatures on petitions to change the form of government in Birmingham. With this effort, they were eventually able to replace Police Commissioner Eugene "Bull" Connor and attorney Mayor Art Hanes who were seen as responsible for the racial crisis in Birmingham which had smeared

Birmingham's reputation worldwide during the civil rights demonstrations led by Reverend Martin Luther King, Jr.

David Vann, along with attorney Arthur Shores, helped mediate the crisis between the black and white communities in Birmingham and set up a structure of government-sponsored groups which allowed these communities to stay in communication in order to forestall future racial crises. Thereafter, both Vann and Shores were elected to the city council, as well as attorney Nina Miglionico, the first woman to be a part of Birmingham's governing body and a future president of the council. Vann would later become mayor of Birmingham during a critical period of desegregation.

Young Lawyers and the City of Mobile

Mobile, as Alabama's second largest city, was able to avoid the national, and even international, spotlight that shone on other Alabama cities and towns during the fifties and sixties because it was fortunate enough to have an enlightened leader during this period, attorney Joe Langan. Langan entered the bar in 1936, but had only gotten his feet wet in both law and politics before leaving Mobile to serve in World War II, where his experience of black soldiers fighting and dying for their country challenged his earlier acceptance of racial segregation. He is quoted as having said, "We are all creatures of God. . . . I could not consider any person to be less entitled to anything in life than I was."[8]

Upon his return to civilian life, he was elected to the state senate in 1946 and was there to oppose fellow Mobilian Gessner McCorvey in his effort to pass the Boswell amendment as a way to slow down the progress of African Americans in registering to vote. When the amendment passed, Langan was instrumental in the successful litigation which challenged its constitutionality[9] and in a filibuster which prevented the passage of a comparable follow-up amendment, known as Boswell, Jr. The consequence of this success, though, was defeat in his 1951 reelection campaign.

Subsequently, he became involved in city politics and in 1953 was elected to Mobile's city commission with the help of African-American voters, whose block vote

TOP: *Pioneering female attorney Nina Miglionico was the first woman to serve on the Birmingham City Council, eventually becoming its president.* ABOVE: *Mobile attorney Joe Langan, as a state senator, opposed the Boswell amendment in the legislature and later challenged it in court. He lost his seat as a result.*

resulted in filling all three commission seats that year with progressive political leaders. The Non-Partisan Voters League was the premier civil rights organization in Mobile after the NAACP was outlawed in Alabama and it secured black votes for Langan throughout his political career. Because of this support, African Americans were able to win many concessions in Mobile without the need for the demonstrations and boycotts that brought negative attention to Montgomery and Birmingham.

When political participation did not achieve results, the Non-Partisan Voters League used the courts, bringing lawsuits that opened up job opportunities for blacks throughout city and county government, with major private employers, and even the Alabama National Guard. The legal resources of the national NAACP Legal Defense Fund were available to black attorney Vernon Crawford, Mobile's first civil rights attorney, who entered the bar in 1956 at the age of thirty-six. Crawford, who was a merchant marine in World War II, was a 1951 graduate of Alabama State University and a friend of Fred Gray, who he had defeated in a contest for the presidency of the senior class. Back in Mobile, Crawford worked as a waiter at the Mobile Country Club, even continuing this employment during the summers while he attended the Brooklyn Law School in New York because he was able to make a considerable income to use to cover his expenses.

TOP: *Vernon Crawford, left, seen here with client Willie Nicholson, was Mobile's first civil rights lawyer. As a student at Alabama State, he became friends with Fred Gray.* ABOVE: *Vernon Crawford mentored many of Mobile's young attorneys, including Frankie Fields Smith, the city's first black female attorney.*

Over the years, Crawford practiced law with black attorneys A. J. Cooper (who became the mayor of Prichard, Alabama); Michael Figures (who was elected to the Alabama Senate and served as its first African-American president pro tempore); Cain Kennedy (who became a Mobile County circuit judge); Frankie F. Smith, the first black female attorney in Mobile; David Coar (who became a United States district judge for the Northern District of Illinois); and Mercuria Ludgood (who served as executive director of the Legal Services Corporation of Alabama and as a Mobile County commissioner.) After 1971, white attorneys James Blacksher, Larry Menefee, and Greg Stein carried on Crawford's civil right legacy after his attention turned to other areas of the law. Blacksher, Menefee, and Stein were all born in the Mobile area

ABOVE: *The participants in the* Birdie Mae Davis *case leaving court are, from left to right, plaintiff Rosetta Gamble, attorneys Derrick Bell and Wiley Bolden (of* Bolden v. City of Mobile*), plaintiffs Birdie Mae and Ann Davis, attorney John Leflore, and plaintiff Alyea Bolton.* LEFT: *Michael Figures was the first black legislator to serve as president pro tem of the state senate.*

with roots in the community and were graduates of the University of Alabama School of Law. They left Crawford in the late 1970s, forming their own firm, and continued in the civil rights arena until these cases became unproductive in the federal judicial climate dominated by conservative Republican appointees.

Some of the important civil rights cases litigated in Mobile included *State of Alabama v. Willie Seale*, whose conviction for rape by an all-white jury was challenged on the grounds that African Americans had been systematically excluded from the grand jury that indicted him and the jury that convicted him; the *Birdie Mae Davis* case which continued for decades battling segregation in the Mobile County public school system; and the *Brown v. Moore* and the *Bolden v. City of Mobile* cases, which challenged at-large elections for county and city offices on the grounds that they unconstitutionally diluted black voting strength. The *Bolden* case, decided by U.S. District Judge Virgil Pittman, resulted in the 1985 election of three black Mobile city council members, the first such occurrence since Reconstruction.

WHITE CIVIL RIGHTS LAWYERS

BESIDES JIM BLACKSHER, LARRY Menefee, and Greg Stein, the University of Alabama School of Law has produced other white attorneys who became civil rights lawyers during the years that the federal courts made their efforts worthwhile. Jack Drake, Ralph Knowles, and Ed Still practiced together in the 1970s in Tuscaloosa. A substantial portion of their practice during those years involved representing the American Civil Liberties Union in its funding of litigation that included not only African-American rights, but the rights of patients in Alabama mental health facilities and prisoners in Alabama's prison system.

Morris Dees, a Montgomery native who graduated from law school in 1960, joined Joseph J. Levin, Jr., and Julian Bond in founding the Southern Poverty Law Center (SPLC) in Montgomery in 1971. Its most important work has been in litigation against hate groups such as the Ku Klux Klan (KKK). A wrongful death action brought by the center on behalf of a 1981 KKK lynching victim's mother in Mobile resulted in a $7 million verdict, which bankrupted the United Klans of America in the 1980s. This case served as a model for other litigation against racist groups throughout America. (Morris Dees had previously practiced law and partnered with fellow University of Alabama Law School graduate Millard Fuller in a publishing business that they sold to Times Warner which made them both millionaires. Dees used his fortune to found the SPLC, while Fuller and his wife used their resources to establish Habitat for Humanity, now an international organization building low-cost housing across the globe. Both men have received innumerable honors and awards for their respective work.)

The ultra-modern Southern Poverty Law Center building in Montgomery houses the civil rights organization founded in 1971 to combat the power of hate groups in the United States.

CHAPTER SIXTEEN

EXPANDING THE APPLICATION OF THE BILL OF RIGHTS AND THE CIVIL RIGHTS AMENDMENTS

As time progressed, the U.S. Supreme Court, under the leadership of Chief Justice Earl Warren, continued to expand the application of the Constitution's Bill of Rights in other realms that did not specifically deal with segregation. Some important cases came out of litigation that began in Alabama.

Times v. Sullivan and the Right to Free Speech

In early1960, a Montgomery County grand jury indicted Martin Luther King, Jr., on two counts of perjury in connection with the filing of his 1956 and 1958 Alabama income tax returns. It appeared that Governor Patterson, or someone in his administration, took the opportunity of a tax audit to trump up charges in an effort to reduce King's effectiveness as the premier civil rights leader in the country. This maneuver was in keeping with the kinds of legal actions Patterson took in response to civil rights activities. He had brought an action against the NAACP for failing to qualify to do business even though very few nonprofit agencies qualify to do business in any state other than the state of their incorporation and the NAACP had been operating in the state for decades. He had sued the Tuskegee Civic Association, raided its headquarters, and confiscated its records on the basis of a law he probably knew was not enforceable. And he had ordered the president of Alabama State College to expel and suspend students who had participated in a sit-in at the lunch counter at the Montgomery County Courthouse, in violation of their rights to free speech and to a public education. He knew how to use the legal system to harass civil rights activists.

Friends of King in New York formed The Committee to Defend Martin Luther King and the Struggle for Freedom in the South and took out an ad in *The New York Times* to raise funds for King's defense in the tax case and to fund other civil rights activities throughout the South. Funds were raised and King was subsequently exonerated

defense team were Solomon Seay, Jr., and Vernon Crawford from Mobile. The commissioners were represented by the law firm of Steiner, Crum & Baker, with Roland "Rod" Nachman, Jr., as the lead counsel. The Birmingham firm of Beddow, Embry, and Beddow represented *The New York Times*, with Eric Embry (later to become a justice on the Alabama Supreme Court) as lead counsel. The Beddow firm was known for its representation of unpopular clients, so it was natural that it would be brought into the case when the *Times's* local counsel felt compelled to withdraw because of pressure brought to bear by its other media clients.

Fred Gray, in writing about this case, pointed out that the ministers' names were attached to the ad without their knowledge. There were factual inaccuracies in the text of the ad which were not discovered because those who wrote the ad were in New York and did not submit their text to Gray or others on the scene to have it read for accuracy. If the ad had been submitted for his review prior to its publication, Gray wrote, there probably would not have been a lawsuit. But, Gray noted, "Then we might not have had a major advance in the nation's libel law, and L. B. Sullivan, Rod Nachman, and Eric Embry might not have become famous. God and the law work in mysterious ways."

Thomas Eric Embry, who represented The New York Times *in* Times v. Sullivan, *was a member of the firm of Beddow, Embry, and Beddow, which had never shied away from representing unpopular clients. Embry was elected to the Alabama Supreme Court in 1974, serving for 10 years before returning to private practice in 1985.*

of the perjury charges by an all-white jury based on the defense provided by an all-black defense team.

Referencing some of the statements in the ad, Montgomery's three commissioners sued four ministers who were named as endorsers of the ad as well as *The New York Times* for alleged libel. Fred Gray represented the four ministers, who included Ralph Abernathy, Solomon Seay, Sr., (whose son practiced law with Gray), Joseph Lowery, and Fred Shuttlesworth. Joining Gray as part of the

Katzenbach v. McClung and Public Accommodations

Another advance in civil rights law arising from a lawsuit brought in Alabama came with the Supreme Court's decision in the Ollie's Barbecue case, *Katzenbach v. McClung,* in 1964. In part because of the well-publicized demon-

H. H. Grooms, above center, was appointed a federal district judge in 1953. Along with Seybourn Lynne, left, he participated in many important civil rights cases, including Katzenbach v. McClung, *and the integration of the University of Alabama.*

strations against segregation in Birmingham's businesses, Congress enacted the 1964 Civil Rights Act. Title II, which prohibited discrimination in public accommodations, was challenged by Birmingham restaurateur Ollie McClung as an unconstitutional extension of federal powers under the commerce clause. A three-judge panel composed of federal district judges Seybourn Lynne and H. H. Grooms, and Fifth Circuit judge Walter P. Gewin heard the case. These judges demonstrated the conservative approach of most of the Northern District's federal judges toward cases involving the potential extension of federal power into new areas of the law, when they ruled that Title II of the act was an unconstitutional usurpation of an area of law previously controlled by the states. The U.S. Supreme Court reversed the decision, extending recent precedents that had greatly expanded congressional authority to regulate both intrastate and interstate commerce. The court held that a prohibition against racial discrimination could be incorporated into the commerce clause and applied to commerce within a state.

Selma and Voting Rights

Historian J. Mills Thornton, III, in his book *Dividing Lines: Municipal Politics and the Struggle for Civil Rights in Montgomery, Birmingham, and Selma* described Selma in the 1950s and 1960s, by stating, "In any ranking of Alabama cities…Selma would very likely have emerged as its single most inflexibly and fervently segregationist." Various white Selma lawyers stood out in its segregationist history. Thornton points to a criminal prosecution in the mid-1950s as the beginning point of black assertion of rights and strongly negative white reaction.[1]

The case involved a black man with a previous criminal record who was arrested for the criminal invasion of several homes over the course of three months in 1953. In one home, he raped a woman and in another he attempted a second rape. He was tried first for the rape. In that case, he was vigorously defended by white attorneys Sam Earle Hobbs (the son of former Congressman Hobbs) and Hugh S. D. Mallory (the grandson of a former mayor and former state bar president of the same name), who had been appointed to represent him. The prosecutor was Circuit Solicitor James A. Hare. Although the defendant was found guilty, the fact that he was given a sentence of 99 years instead of death was considered a triumph for the defense and stunned the community. Solicitor Hare decided to try him on the attempted rape charge hoping to garner the death penalty in that case, because the victim was the daughter of the town's sitting mayor.

In the second trial, the NAACP entered the case, furnishing defense attorneys Peter A. Hall and Orzell Billingsley, Jr., of Birmingham. They asserted multiple violations of the defendant's constitutional rights including the intentional exclusion of blacks from the grand jury and jury venires and the involuntariness of the defendant's confession. Hall and Billingsley were the first black attorneys to appear in Selma's court and they were aggressive in their questioning of white county officials who maintained the jury rolls. They demonstrated the county's failure to follow applicable law in the creation of the grand jury venire and the judge, Walton E. Callen, was forced to quash the indictment.

The error was corrected, the indictment reissued, and the case was retried, this time with a guilty verdict and the death penalty as the outcome. Appeal proceeded to the United States Supreme Court which reversed the decision on a 6-3 vote, finding that the trial court had improperly admitted a confession that was not voluntarily given. Since the confession was the main evidence for the state, the case was thereafter dropped. (The defendant did go to prison on the basis of the first trial, since it was not appealed, but black Selma attorney J. L. Chestnut, Jr., was able to get him freed in 1975, arguing that the confession was the convicting evidence in the original trial and should not have been used there either.)

Mills Thornton argues that this case demonstrated that blacks were willing and capable of asserting their rights and gave hope to the local black population that efforts to act on their own behalf would be rewarded. It also created outrage among white citizens of Selma toward both the U.S. Supreme Court and the NAACP and the mayor developed an intense personal animosity against both these organizations and against any show of black militancy in asserting civil rights.

One result of the anger stirred up by the case, and a subsequent effort to petition the local school board to integrate the Selma school system, was the founding of the first White Citizens' Council in Alabama. Its first president and moving force was attorney M. Alston Keith, who was also chairman of the Dallas County Democratic Party and president of the Dallas County Bar Association. He told the *Selma Times Journal*, "The white population of this country controls the money and this is an advantage that the Council will use in a fight to legally maintain segregation of the races. We intend to make it difficult, if not impossible, for any Negro who advocates de-segregation to find and hold a job, get credit or renew a mortgage." The council became so strong that by 1961 it was chosen as the top individual council in the United States by its national organization.

Membership throughout the state grew to as many as 80,000 at the peek of the White Citizens' Council movement. The councils were seen by many as an "upscale ver-

The White Citizens Council movement began in Mississippi in response to early desegregation efforts and soon spread to Alabama. Here, George Wallace is seen addressing a White Citizen Council audience while running for governor of Alabama.

sion of the Klan" since they did not espouse violence, and the State Association of Citizens' Councils, headquartered in Montgomery, counted among its sympathizers some of the brightest legal minds in the state, including judge Walter B. Jones, who, historian Wayne Flynt maintains, "made the [*Alabama Lawyer*] a forum for segregationists."

The mayor's political machine in Selma allied itself to the council so intimately that it was often hard to tell the two organizations apart and it was this connection between these two groups which was the foundation of the unusually forceful and uniform defiance of civil rights efforts for almost a full decade in Dallas County. Part of the apparent unanimity among whites against integration actually arose from the council's intimidation of any white who showed any kind of sympathy toward black aspirations.

The main frustration for Selma's black community was the obvious impediments put up by the Board of Registrars to prevent blacks from registering to vote. Even when blacks were gaining voting rights in areas within the jurisdiction of the Middle District of Alabama, under the auspices of the Justice Department's Civil Rights Division and the judicial authority of U.S. District Judge Frank M.

Following the events of "Bloody Sunday," and a ruling by Judge Frank Johnson upholding the marchers' First Amendment rights, the Selma to Montgomery march was finally accomplished, starting on March 21, 1965, and taking five days to reach its goal.

Johnson, Jr., blacks in the Southern District of the state under the jurisdiction of District Judge Daniel H. Thomas made little headway. He had become a judge in 1951, appointed by President Harry Truman. His approach in cases involving racial matters was to delay, with the hope that matters would be resolved through voluntary action. The Justice Department worked for several years to promote voting rights in Dallas County, but Judge Thomas was an impediment to progress rather than a help.

Thornton noted, "[I]n Selma, Judge Thomas' desire to avoid judicial compulsion in order to allow the community to find its own path to accommodation, ironically had the effect of forcing the city toward just the sort of direct-action movement that Thomas most wanted to avoid." African Americans had no faith in his court at all.

Former solicitor James Hare subsequently was elected circuit judge and he was replaced as solicitor by Blanchard McLeod, both men soon becoming recognized for their extreme racial views and near paranoia about civil rights groups and even about supposed communist influence in the administrations of Presidents Kennedy and Johnson.

These men, as well as segregationist city attorney McLean Pitts, reacted to locally organized voting rights demonstrations which began in September 1963 by not cooperating in the issuance of permits, harshly prosecuting demonstrators, and ultimately enjoining further demonstrations. Their conduct set the stage for local black leaders to invite the Student Nonviolent Coordinating Committee (SNCC) to organize a voter registration drive and the Southern Christian Leadership Conference (SCLC), led by Dr. Martin Luther King, Jr., to lead a march from Selma to Montgomery.

The extreme reaction of law enforcement personnel in beating and clubbing the first group to attempt a march over the Edmund Pettus Bridge leading out of Selma toward Montgomery inspired the filing of a lawsuit by attorneys Fred Gray, Solomon Seay, Jr., Peter Hall, and several lawyers of the Legal Defense Fund to require Governor George Wallace and state law enforcement officials to protect the marchers. The state officials were represented by assistant attorneys general Maury Smith and John Goodwin. The suit was heard by Judge Johnson, who designated the United States of America as a party (a step he regularly took in civil rights cases). Justice Department attorney John Doar represented the United States. Judge Johnson granted the relief sought, on the basis that the march for the purpose of petitioning the state government for redress of grievances, particularly the right to vote, was a reasonable exercise of the constitutional right of assembly and freedom of movement and outweighed the state's interest in denying the march due to its alleged concerns for public safety. Upon an immediate appeal to the Fifth Circuit, that court upheld the district court ruling and the march was held.

The attention drawn to the issue of voting rights by the conduct of local, county, and state officials in Alabama (many of whom were attorneys) helped inspire the passage of the 1965 Voting Rights Act which completely revamped the conduct of voting officials in Alabama and the rest of the United States and gave the vote to millions of black people. It was a major milestone on the journey of black Alabamians to political power and it was the final death knell for the intentional legal interference with black voting rights which dated back to the Bourbon governments of the post-Civil War era.

Ending Legal Segregation of Education in Alabama

In the second opinion of the U.S. Supreme Court in the case of *Brown v. Board of Education*, the court wrote that relief should be implemented "with all deliberate speed." No specific instructions were given as to how that was to be accomplished. The specifics were to be worked out as cases developed in the lower courts.[2]

In Alabama, Birmingham attorney Arthur Shores was involved with NAACP Legal Defense Fund attorney Thurgood Marshall, even before the decision in the *Brown* case, in the efforts of Autherine Lucy to integrate the University of Alabama as early as 1953. Although the University was ordered to admit her in 1956, she was subsequently expelled for statements she and her lawyers allegedly made about certain state and school officials.

The first attempt to integrate the University of Alabama was made by Autherine Lucy in 1953. Here, she is emerging from the courthouse with her attorneys, Thurgood Marshall, center, and pioneering Birmingham civil rights attorney Arthur Shores, right.

In 1953, segregationist attorneys in the Alabama legislature were aware of the cases which had been consolidated and argued before the U.S. Supreme Court in 1952 and could see the writing on the wall which became the *Brown* opinion. The state senator from Jefferson County, attorney Albert Boutwell who would be elected lieutenant governor in 1959, then mayor of Birmingham when its form of government changed in 1963, proposed the appointment of a legislative committee to consider how the state should respond to the predicted decision. This Joint Interim Legislative Committee, which included Boutwell as well as attorneys J. Miller Bonner (Camden) and Ira D. Pruitt (Livingston), endorsed the right of white parents to send their children to all-white schools. They sought aid from the Alabama State Bar to formulate possible responses to the predicted ruling from the Supreme Court.

TOP: *State Senator Albert Boutwell, anticipating the* Brown *decision, proposed the creation of a legislative committee to plan a response.* ABOVE: *J. Paul Meeks suggested a school enrollment plan that led to the passage of the Alabama School Placement Law.*

Birmingham attorney Joseph F. Johnston, who was well versed in constitutional law, led a group of four, which included J. Kirkman Jackson of Birmingham (state president, 1959-1960, and later a member of the State Sovereignty Commission created by George Wallace); Gessner T. McCorvey of Mobile; and Norman Harris of Decatur, in studying ways that integration of schools might be avoided. They pointed out to the committee that section 256 of the 1901 constitution required a racially segregated, publicly funded statewide school system. They recommended that this section be eliminated to remove the "smoking gun" statement of governmental intent to maintain segregated schools. They recommended that a passage in section 256 which gave children a right to a public school education be eliminated as well. In this way, they believed, the state could divert public funds to private schools and even discontinue public education altogether. They also wanted the sections eliminated so that it could be argued that each school system was an individual entity not under the control of the state. When their plan, which also permitted parents the freedom to choose the racial composition of the particular school their children attended, was passed into law, only one legislator voted against the bill, attorney Charles Nice, Jr., of Birmingham. The required constitutional amendment was overwhelmingly approved and Nice was defeated in his subsequent bid for reelection.

In a letter to Governor Persons, Birmingham attorney J. Paul Meeks proposed that the state rely on its police powers "for the protection of life and health" to develop a pupil assignment law which did not name race as a consideration but which could then be used to maintain segregation by its application. Part of the strategy was to develop a legal structure which would require desegregation cases to be brought on an individual basis. The hope was that the energy and will of plaintiffs and their sponsors (such as the NAACP), as well as their financial resources, would diminish in the face of legal roadblocks before full integration could be accomplished. This approach was ultimately followed by the legislature with the adoption of the Alabama School Placement Law in 1955 which

allowed superintendents to assign students based on academic preparation, kinds of academic programs, availability of transportation, and other similar considerations.

When the placement law was challenged by some black parents in Birmingham at the end of 1957, a three-judge federal panel comprised of judges Richard Rives, Seybourn Lynne, and H. Hobart Grooms found that, on its face, it was not unconstitutional. They did note in their opinion, "All that has been said in this present opinion must be limited to the constitutionality of the law *upon its face*. The School Placement Law furnishes the legal machinery for an orderly administration of the public schools in a constitutional manner by the admission of qualified pupils upon a basis of individual merit without regard to their race or color. We must presume that it will be so administered. If not, in some future proceeding it is possible that it may be declared unconstitutional in its application. The responsibility rests primarily upon the local school boards, but ultimately all of the people of the State." In that case, the firms of Lange, Simpson, Robinson & Somerville (Reid B. Barnes and Ormond Somerville) and Cabaniss & Johnston (Joseph F. Johnston and Thad Holt, Jr.) represented the defendant, the Birmingham Board of Education.

Governor George Wallace's "stand in the schoolhouse door" (actually the entrance to Foster Auditorium) has become one of the iconic moments in the civil rights struggle.

In 1963, Vivian Malone and James Hood sought admission to the University of Alabama. They brought suit to ensure their admission after their applications were rejected. Fred Gray, Arthur Shores, Constance Motley, and Leroy D. Clark were their attorneys. The university was defended by the law firm of Moore, Thomas, Taliaferro, Forman and Burr of Birmingham, today's Burr & Forman, LLP. Judge H. H. Grooms heard the case and ordered their admission. (Hood later withdrew for personal reasons.)

George Wallace had been elected governor in 1962, beating attorney Ryan deGraffenreid of Tuscaloosa in the Democratic primary runoff on a straight segregation platform. He had vowed in his inaugural address, "Segregation now, segregation tomorrow, and segregation forever." Soon after his election, he proposed, and the legislature passed, numerous resolutions of nullification and interposition defying the U.S. Supreme Court and its various orders commanding an end to segregation.

FRED SHUTTLESWORTH AND THE BIRMINGHAM STALEMATE

ERNEST D. JACKSON, SR., OF JACKSONVILLE, Florida was counsel for the plaintiffs in the School Placement case, which included Fred Shuttlesworth, a Baptist minister who was not originally from Birmingham. Shuttlesworth was at odds with most of the established black leadership of Birmingham, being a younger, more aggressive activist than the older generation of leaders, and could not find a black Birmingham attorney willing to represent him. There were only seven black lawyers at the time and they had many ties to community leaders who wanted to take a more conservative approach than Shuttlesworth did in confronting segregation. They were not prepared to accept the leadership of a relative newcomer to Birmingham.[3]

Later, when Shuttlesworth planned to bring a lawsuit challenging segregation of Birmingham's parks, Judge Seybourn Lynne brought to his attention a local rule which required that an out-of-state lawyer retain a local lawyer as cocounsel. (This rule had not been applied when Jackson brought the Pupil Placement law challenge.) At this point, Shuttlesworth was stalemated. First, he retained attorney Demetrius Newton, who was practicing in Fairfield, but Newton withdrew after being put under pressure by both the judge and the other black attorneys. Later, Shuttlesworth hired Willie L. Williams, who began his practice in Birmingham in 1959. Williams was the eighth black lawyer to practice in Birmingham and was young enough and "hungry" enough to disregard the pressures which had blocked Newton, thereby breaking the "cartel."

In subsequent litigation, Judge Grooms ordered the parks integrated. In response, the city commission ordered them closed, including 67 parks, 38 playgrounds, eight swimming pools, and four golf courses, together with the zoo, art museum, state fair, municipal auditorium, and Legion Field stadium. This action by the commission in 1961 helped inspire the movement to change Birmingham's form of government to a city council form, in order to remove the intransigent mayor, attorney Art Hanes, and public safety commissioner, Eugene "Bull" Connor.

After their decision not to cooperate with Fred Shuttlesworth, who criticized them openly during an anniversary dinner for his Christian Movement, the other seven black lawyers took the opportunity to "explain" their reasons. Young Selma attorney J. L. Chestnut, Jr., who had been admitted to the bar only six weeks earlier (and who would later become the premier civil rights lawyer in Selma) presented the case. He was introduced by Orzell Billingsley, Jr., at a convention of the black Alabama Independent Beauticians Association held in Birmingham on June 14, 1959. As Mills Thornton described his speech, "Chestnut assured his audience with extraordinary condescension that 'when these learned lawyers refuse to go along with some 'Johnnie Come Lately' who overnight has decided, for reasons best known

Wallace was the ex-officio chairman of the Board of Trustees of the University of Alabama and, in that capacity, proposed to defy Judge Grooms's order by "standing in the school house door" to block Vivian Malone and James Hood from registering for classes. After much orchestration, and an injunction issued by Judge Lynne, Wallace stood in the door of Foster Auditorium but backed down at the request of federal officials, including U.S. Attorney Macon Weaver and federal marshal Peyton Norville, both graduates of the university's law school, and Malone and Hood entered the university. The publicity generated by Wallace's defiance propelled him before a national audience, soon leading him into presidential politics. His conduct as a state official who would deny constitutional rights to a substantial portion of his state's citizenry helped motivate President John Kennedy to announce plans to propose national civil rights legislation which would open public facilities and institutions

Baptist minister Fred Shuttlesworth, left, marches with Ralph Abernathy, center, and Martin Luther King, Jr., right.

to him, that his unlearned and unlettered plan is the only means of deliverance for the Negro people then these lawyers, trained in the law and the constitution, in their refusal have unquestionably adopted the best policy, the best approach, to preserve the dignity [and] security of every Negro in the Jefferson County area.' Chestnut then launched into a truly slanderous attack on Shuttlesworth, implying that Shuttlesworth's only real goals were to feed his ego and to line his own pocket."

The rhetoric that went back and forth almost resulted in tearing the black community apart at the beginning of the civil rights movement in Birmingham and also ultimately resulted in Shuttlesworth's decision to turn to mass action to speed up the integration process. Even though the federal judges in Birmingham were not vigorous (especially as compared to Frank Johnson in Montgomery) in asserting new constitutional principles, Shuttlesworth never completely gave up on his original intent of using the courts and laws to challenge segregation and, by 1971, was a plaintiff in 11 civil-rights related cases that came before the U.S. Supreme Court.

and job opportunities to all American citizens regardless of race, creed, sex, or national origin. Wallace's defiance helped bring about the very thing he ostensibly fought, intervention of the federal government into what had previously been seen as areas of "states' rights." It also promoted what he actually fought: desegregation.

In 1963, various federal courts in the state ordered the desegregation of schools in Birmingham, Huntsville, Tuscaloosa, and Mobile and in Macon County. The school boards in each of these locations planned to acquiesce. George Wallace, though, planned to prevent the integration of these school systems by closing them down with the excuse that integration would be attended by the threat of violence and possible injury of students.

The Macon County system was the first to be closed when state troopers appeared on the first day of school and blocked the entrance to the high school as students arrived for class. Governor Wallace asserted his authority to close the school based on his powers as governor and as ex-officio chairman of the state board of education.

After closing the school, Wallace announced the formation of a private academy in Tuskegee, publicly soliciting funds from state employees and from the white citizens of the state to pay for its opening. He also encouraged white parents to boycott public schools and to form private schools instead, inspiring a private school movement which spread across the state and across the South as a means for whites to avoid integrated schools. He then introduced legislation which provided for tuition grants from state funds to fund private school education.

Prior to the governor's assertion of power to close a school, the state had maintained that each county and city board of education was an independent entity which had complete control over the operation and supervision of its school. On this basis, civil rights attorneys had brought actions against individual boards to seek desegregation, a daunting enterprise since there were over 100 different boards within the state. When Wallace asserted his right as governor to close a school to prevent its desegregation, attorney Fred Gray responded by immediately preparing a motion for a temporary restraining order and a motion to show cause as well as an amendment to the complaint in *Lee v. Macon County Board of Education,* the lawsuit under which the Macon County Board of Education had been ordered to integrate.

The motion to show cause sought to join Wallace as a party defendant and then to restrain him from interfering with the court's previous order requiring racial integration of the schools in Macon County. The amendment sought to add Wallace, as president of the Alabama State Board of Education, and other state board officials and to enjoin them from operating a dual school system based upon race throughout Alabama and to order them to desegregate public schools statewide. It also sought to enjoin as unconstitutional the tuition grant law which Wallace had introduced to allow diversion of tax money to segregated private schools.

Attorney General Richmond Flowers represented the Macon County Board of Education in the pivotal case that finally broke the back of segregation in Alabama's public educational institutions.

When the complaint was amended, a three-judge federal panel, comprised of Circuit Judge Rives and district judges Grooms and Johnson, was convened to hear the amended case. The law firm of Goodwyn and Smith represented the governor and the state board of education, with T. W. Thagard as chief attorney. Attorney General Richmond Flowers, with assistant attorneys general Robert Bradley and Gordon Madison, represented the Macon County Board of Education. Gray was joined by his partner, Solomon Seay, Jr., and by NAACP Legal Defense Fund attorneys Jack Greenburg, Charles H. Jones, and Constance Motley as well as Justice Department attorney John Doar and the local U.S. attorney, in litigating the case.

This case ultimately resulted in a statewide desegregation order covering 98 school systems not already under court order, all trade schools, junior colleges, vocational schools, and other educational institutions under the control of the state board of education. This 1967 order, which also declared the private tuition program unconstitutional, was appealed to the U.S. Supreme Court and affirmed, thereby integrating all of Alabama's remaining segregated schools, including colleges and trade schools, through this one lawsuit, saving hundreds of thousands of dollars in legal costs and saving many individuals from harassment as named plaintiffs in individual lawsuits. It also integrated the state high school athletic association, thereby allowing many black high school athletes to gain recognition for their achievements, attracting the attention of coaches from larger colleges and universities. The case also provided an ongoing forum for desegregation issues in education to be placed before the court. Again, it was the demagogic conduct of George Wallace that provided the basis for massive legal action which resulted in the very thing he sought to avoid: desegregation. History provides many ironies.

The Birmingham school system was already under the jurisdiction of the federal court in the Northern district, and so did not fall under the *Lee v. Macon County* decision. Judge Grooms had traditionally handled these cases, but he went on senior status in 1969 and newly appointed judge Sam C. Pointer, Jr., took over. When it was shown that the virtually all-white Pleasant Grove school system had been created by local authorities to avoid compliance with a busing order governing Jefferson County schools, Judge Pointer ruled that since Pleasant Grove had previously been part of the county system, it would be "deemed to have elected to transfer responsibilities for general administration and supervision of public education within the Pleasant Grove zone to the Jefferson County Board of Education." This was a creative remedy which continued the desegregation of Alabama's school system and showed that the judges of the Northern District were ready to forcefully compel compliance with what had become well established precedent.

Although *de facto* segregation of many schools continues in Alabama, due primarily to the private school movement and white flight, the legally mandated segregation of public school children has ended. Funding of all schools continues to be a major issue in Alabama due to its regressive and unpredictable tax structure. Efforts to equalize funding through litigation has proven futile because the removal of section 256 of Alabama's 1901 constitution, which had granted Alabamians a right to public education, also removed the basis for an equal protection argument concerning disparate property tax rates and other sources of funding which vary from school district to school district. Thus, the legislative plan to thwart *Brown v. Board of Education* failed to have that desired effect but instead "survives to weaken Alabama's attempts to create a superior system of public education."[4]

Another legal battle arose over higher education and the vestiges of segregation in the case of *United States of America v. State of Alabama*, a lawsuit brought by the Justice Department in 1983. The theory of the case was that the state had never provided blacks in Alabama proper educational opportunities in higher education, even though promises had been made during Reconstruction that it would provide and fund universities for blacks comparable to the University of Alabama and Auburn University. Alabama State University in Montgomery and Alabama A&M in Huntsville were the colleges mandated for this purpose, but they had never been granted the funding or attention paid to the white-only universities. And, when it would have seemed appropriate to integrate them as part of a fully integrated higher education system after *Brown,* instead an extension of Auburn was founded in Montgomery and an extension of the University of Alabama was established in Huntsville, thereby duplicating services and encouraging the maintenance of a dual system.

Sam C. Pointer was only 35 years old when President Richard Nixon appointed him to be a U.S. District Judge in 1970, the youngest in the country at that time. Judge Pointer participated in a number of important civil rights decisions in the 1970s.

Over 50 lawyers[5] participated in the trial of this case, which was held before Judge Harold L. Murphy of the Northern District of Georgia, who was assigned the case because the judges of the Northern District of Alabama had recused themselves due to their relationships with various parties in the lawsuit. The trial was held between October 1990 and April 1991. The judge ordered that state officials attend a settlement conference, based on his belief that it was their responsibility to settle the issues in the case rather than spending millions of state dollars in litigation. But the case was not settled and Judge Murphy issued a wide-ranging, 850-page decision, finding that there were vestiges of discrimination, as alleged by the plaintiffs, and provided remedial relief. This case concluded in 1995, but the court retained jurisdiction to review compliance with the relief ordered.

CHAPTER SEVENTEEN

THE REIGN OF GEORGE WALLACE, THE RISE OF THE REPUBLICAN PARTY, AND BLACK POLITICAL POWER

GEORGE WALLACE WON THE 1962 GUBERnatorial election by using racial hyperbole, calling Judge Frank Johnson "a low-down, carpetbaggin', scallawaggin', race-mixin' liar" and promising to stand in the schoolhouse door. His appeal to the raw emotions of his followers is illustrated by the most famous lines from his inaugural address on January 14, 1963: "I draw the line in the dust and toss the gauntlet before the feet of tyranny. And I say, Segregation now! Segregation tomorrow! Segregation forever!"[1]

With this self-serving challenge to federal authority, he began a reign in Alabama politics where he "wasted state resources fighting the inevitable and sullying the image of Alabama." When he was questioned by a longtime supporter about his pandering to racist emotion, he was quoted as saying, "I started off by talking about schools and highways and prisons and taxes—and I couldn't make them listen. Then I began talking about niggers—and they stomped the floor." Wallace's biographer, Dan T. Carter, concluded that "he had stepped past an invisible line of hyperbole and fallen down a dark hole of the bleakest demagoguery."[2]

He quickly learned that his appeal went beyond the borders of Alabama and he entered America's presidential politics in the1964 Democratic primary. Although he had limited impact, the run whetted his appetite for national politics. To keep his momentum going, he had to continue to hold office, even though Alabama law limited him to nonconsecutive, four-year terms. He attempted to change the constitution to provide him a second consecutive term, but was filibustered in the Alabama Senate by adversaries such as young attorneys Ernest C. "Sonny" Hornsby (state bar president, 1977-1978), Larry Dumas, and John Tyson (none of whom were reelected after taking this stand, although Sonny Hornsby would ultimately serve as chief justice of the Alabama Supreme Court).[3]

When the proposed constitutional change did not occur, Wallace ran his wife Lurleen B. Wallace in the Democratic primary as his stand-in and she easily won.

George Wallace's first try for the presidency was as a candidate for the Democratic Party nomination in 1964. Here, he shakes hands with a supporter outside the Alabama State Capitol during his 1968 campaign, when he ran as an independent. Like Ross Perot after him, his campaign started well, and then he made a disastrous choice of a running mate.

Thereafter, he entered the 1968 presidential race as an independent candidate. His campaign began strong, but took a nosedive when his candidate for vice president, Curtis LeMay, suggested using atomic weapons to end the Vietnam War.

Albert P. Brewer, who had served as Wallace's speaker of the house, was elected lieutenant governor and became governor when Lurleen Wallace died of breast cancer on May 7, 1968. He served for 33 months, and during that period the state made the largest appropriations for education in its history as well as establishing the Alabama Commission for Higher Education. Brewer created the Alabama Development Office and helped modernize and economize state government operations. During his tenure, the Alabama Court of Appeals was divided into the Court of Civil Appeals and the Court of Criminal Appeals, the state Supreme Court was expanded by two judges, and the state Ethics Commission was created. Albert Brewer, who taught at Cumberland Law School for two decades, continues to be honored for his service to the state and has been described as representing the best of the progressive strain of Alabama politics.

Although George Wallace pledged not to run against him in 1970, when the time came for Brewer to run for a full term, Wallace reneged on that promise, having realized that his access to campaign funds would be limited without the governorship to back up his stature as a presidential primary candidate. Wallace ultimately ran as a Democrat for president, rather than as an independent, in 1972, after allegedly striking a deal with Richard Nixon's Justice Department, which threatened to prosecute Wallace's attorney brother, Gerald, on charges that he had rigged state bid procedures, received illegal campaign

George Wallace is greeted by supporters in Tyler, Texas, during his 1972 campaign for president, this time as a member of the Democratic Party. On May 15, 1972, at a campaign stop in Laurel, Maryland, he was shot four times by Arthur Bremer and remained paralyzed for the rest of his life.

contributions, and accepted kickbacks and payoffs on which he neglected to pay taxes. (A Wallace advisor, attorney, and finance director, Seymour Trammell, had been convicted on similar charges and served a term in jail.) Brewer was the top vote getter in the primary election, where Wallace came in second. (Years later, during Brewer's 1978 campaign for governor, it came out that Brewer's campaign had received $400,000 from Nixon's Committee to Reelect the President (CREEP). This disclosure derailed the later campaign.) Wallace again used racially bigoted rhetoric to defeat his opponent, beating Brewer in the primary runoff. Author Kerwin C. Swint in his book *Mudslingers*[4] credits this runoff battle as the most negative election of all times in American politics, and one of the last openly racist campaigns. He quotes Albert Brewer as saying, "This was the dirtiest campaign I've ever observed. If it takes that to be governor, then I'll pass it up."

Ever the campaigner, George Wallace was generally inattentive to administering state affairs, leaving the day-to-day operations in the hands of his cronies, who often used their positions for personal gain. Historian Glenn Eskew noted that under Wallace, "Graft abounded as friends won lucrative state contracts and bought state surplus at discount while making large political donations to Wallace's numerous campaigns." Although he gained positive acclaim for creating a system of technical schools and junior colleges throughout the state, these institutions "became political plums placed in counties as payoffs or incentives for votes rather than according to student demand or need." (The two-year college system continues to attract attention as the seed-bed of political corruption even in 2009.) Wallace spent huge amounts of federal dollars to pave highways and interstates throughout the state, awarding contracts to his supporters, but refused to build them in or around Birmingham, the state's most populous city, because a majority of its voters did not support him.

The governor had a populist agenda which helped the average citizens who were his constituency. He promoted industrial development, attracting nearly $350 million in expanded and new industries, which added 19,000 new jobs in 1963 alone. He gave pay raises to teachers and fringe benefits to state employees and expanded the state's free textbooks to include the state's high schools. He used bond issues to benefit colleges and universities and rarely meddled in the administration of schools, but he never identified a stable formula or source to support public education. Instead, he increased the state's regressive sales tax, raised the state's bonded indebtedness, and depended on increased revenues from expansion of the state's industrial base.

After African Americans became a substantial voting block, Wallace saw that state largesse flowed to their communities, where local roads suddenly were paved by the state. His 1975 inaugural featured a black choir, and he spoke to black congregations, apologizing for his former racial rhetoric, arguing that his conduct was "federally provoked."

As described by historian Glenn Eskew,[5] "a number of federal court orders affected Wallace's second and third terms. On March 12, 1971, federal district judge Frank M. Johnson, Jr., ordered the state to provide adequate and effective treatment to all patients being held in Alabama's mental health facilities," ultimately resulting in significant increases in funding. In January 1976, Judge Johnson declared that the Alabama prison system was operating in a manner that violated the "cruel and unusual punishment" section of the Bill of Rights. Remedial measures required huge outlays of money.

Another federal lawsuit found Alabama's property tax system to be discriminatory, required equalization of those taxes, and demanded a rational basis for any differences that were left in Alabama's property tax rates. The response of the legislature and lobbyists for large landowners was the creation of a system whereby the tax on large landowners actually declined, being based on "current use" rather than market value, while state and local taxes levied on all Alabamians without regard to their ability to pay increased.

After issuing so many orders forcing state government to meet its constitutional obligations, some political observers maintained that federal district judge Frank M. Johnson, Jr., was "the real governor" of Alabama. Wallace maintained that "thugs and federal judges" had taken over the state.

George Wallace liked to reward his supporters and curry the favor of voters by building new roads and highways. When blacks started to vote in larger numbers during the 1970s, Wallace made sure that new roads would be built to serve their communities.

Wallace's fourth term has been described as perhaps "his most productive," in spite of the fact that his health was in decline due to complications that resulted from the 1972 assassination attempt which left him in a wheelchair and in constant pain. One important contribution of Wallace during his fourth term was the establishment by constitutional amendment of the Alabama Trust Fund that protected the corpus while paying the interest derived from offshore leases on Alabama oil and natural gas into the general operating fund of the state. During this administration he appointed more than 100 blacks to advisory panels.

Historian Glenn Eskew sums up the career of George Wallace in these words, "There is an irony about Wal-

RACIALLY MODERATE LAWYER CANDIDATES DEFEATED BY GEORGE WALLACE AND THE CAREER OF DON SIEGELMAN

THROUGHOUT THE PERIOD HE HELD THE GOVERNORSHIP, Wallace defeated several attorney candidates running racially moderate campaigns. In 1962, he beat attorney and state senator Ryan deGraffenreid of Tuscaloosa in the primary runoff. deGraffenreid, considered a possible front-runner, was killed early in the 1966 race when the aircraft in which he was flying to a campaign stop crashed.

In 1966, moderate attorney Carl Elliott (former U.S. congressman from Jasper) was defeated by Lurleen Wallace, when Martin Luther King, Jr., endorsed liberal attorney general Richmond Flowers (who had taken a pro-civil rights stance throughout his tenure in opposition to Wallace, but who also was being investigated for political corruption by the Johnson administration) and newly

George Wallace looks on as Albert Brewer is sworn in as governor following the death of Lurleen Wallace. Wallace broke his promise not to run in 1970, and defeated Brewer in the Democratic primary runoff. Brewer ran again in 1978, losing to Fob James.

registered black voters voted as a block in Flowers's favor.[6] (In 1964, Elliott, with an almost New Deal-like political record during his 16 years in Congress, had come in last in an at-large race to fill eight congressional seats from the nine incumbent candidates, when Wallace forces printed a sample ballot endorsing all the candidates but Elliott. In 1966, he was the candidate considered most likely to attract both white moderates and newly enfranchised blacks, before the King endorsement of Richmond Flowers. Thereafter, whites voted as a block for Lurleen Wallace and Elliott gleaned only eight percent of the vote.)

Wallace defeated Albert Brewer in 1970 and had no significant opposition in 1974, when he won his third term as governor in his own right (the law having been changed in 1968 to allow two terms in succession). In 1982, he defeated moderate lieutenant governor George McMillan in the Democratic primary runoff, but only by one percentage point. Ironically, he won this unprecedented fourth term by receiving over thirty percent of the black vote. (In 1978, when he was constitutionally barred from running for the governorship, the Democratic nomination was sought by the "three Bs": former governor Albert Brewer, lieutenant governor Jere Beasley (who had been governor for almost a month in 1972 when George Wallace was shot by a would-be assassin while out of state), and attorney general Bill Baxley (who had successfully prosecuted the Klan bomber responsible for the explosion at the 16th Street Baptist Church in 1963, which killed four young black girls), who served as lieutenant governor during the period from 1983 to 1987. These three attorneys were beaten in the Democratic primary by little known, but wealthy Opelika businessman Forrest "Fob" James, whose extensive media advertising paid off. James's decision not to seek a second term at the time opened the way for Wallace to seek his fourth term in 1982. James served a second term from 1995 through 1999.)

In 1999, attorney Don Siegelman, a Mobile native, became governor. Siegelman is the only Alabamian to have held all of the state's major constitutional offices, including secretary of state, attorney general, lieutenant governor, and governor. In 1973, he worked for the Alabama Democratic Party under party chairman Robert Vance, and then took Vance's place as executive director of the party until 1978, when he entered politics as a candidate for secretary of state, an office he held for two terms. He thereafter successfully ran for attorney general, then ran in the Democratic primary for governor in 1990 and lost to Paul Hubbert, leader of the Alabama Education Association, who then lost to incumbent Republican governor Guy Hunt.

Don Siegelman, seen here at the time of his first campaign for secretary of state in 1978, has since served as attorney general, lieutenant governor, and governor.

In 1994, he won the office of lieutenant governor, where he exerted enormous power during a period when the business community was seeking tort reform. Although he was blamed by that community for the defeat of their tort reform package, he later came back to support tort reform and to receive the support of the business community when he defeated incumbent Republican governor Fob James who sought his third term as governor in 1998.

Siegelman was the first governor born and reared in Mobile and the first Catholic governor in the state. His wife was the first Jewish woman to serve as first lady in Alabama. Siegelman's successful campaign theme was the funding of education through implementation of a state lottery. His election race drew more voters than any previous gubernatorial candidate in Alabama's history and he won with fifty-seven percent of the vote. Yet, when the legislature passed the necessary constitutional amendments to implement his campaign promise, it was defeated by Alabama voters by a fifty-six percent to forty-four percent margin. He came up with no new way to fund education and was defeated by Republican Bob Riley when he sought reelection.

As he prepared to contest Riley's 2005 bid for reelection, he was charged and tried for misconduct while in office. After 11 days of jury deliberation, he was found guilty of bribery, conspiracy, mail fraud, and obstruction of justice and immediately imprisoned. After serving nine months of a seven-year sentence, he was released on bond in March 2008 and is still free while his case is being considered on appeal.

lace as governor. It is possible, indeed likely, that because of his constant forays into presidential politics Wallace may have spent less time at actually running the state than anyone else previously in the position. Nonetheless, he is unquestionably the most significant of the state's governors. He entered office during a period of social transition, and, instead of endorsing the fundamental changes taking place, he chose to defend a dying system. After encouraging a violent atmosphere, he became the victim of violence. Wallace recanted and repented, seeking forgiveness from those he had wronged. Yet his conservative influence was widespread; his antigovernment rhetoric and demonization of the federal government had affected the language and policies of both national political parties. Certainly, in Alabama, the indelible images of the racist Wallace, like the phantom pains he felt in his body after being shot, continue to haunt the state."[7]

The Rise of the Republican Party in Alabama

As the national Democratic Party promoted the expansion of civil rights and began attracting newly enfranchised black voters, the Republican Party developed a southern strategy, which some historians argue had racial undertones, that began to appeal to those whites disillusioned with the Democratic Party. This strategy bore fruit in much of the South, but George Wallace's presence in national politics during the sixties and early seventies wreaked havoc with both parties' agendas by driving them to the extremes of their traditional constituencies.

Republican presidential candidate Barry Goldwater was the first Republican to have "coattails" in Alabama in the post-World War II era, although President Eisenhower had drawn many Republican (and "Eisenhower Democrat") votes in 1952 and had made being a Republican fashionable in the wealthy suburbs of Montgomery, Birmingham, and Mobile. Goldwater's brand of conservatism appealed to Southerners, and young Birmingham attorney John Grenier, whose "Young Turk" supporters had taken control of the Alabama party in 1962, led the efforts to find committed Republicans throughout the South to support him and searched for candidates in Alabama to win local contests.

Grenier's success in promoting the party's "Operation Dixie" encouraged Republican attorney James D. Martin of Gadsden (a former Democrat) to challenge Lister Hill for his Senate seat in 1962 and to give him a close race, so close that Hill retired from politics rather than run again in 1968. Martin went on to win a congressional seat in the Goldwater sweep in 1964. (Hill was replaced in 1968 by a supporter of George C. Wallace, conservative Democratic Lieutenant Governor James B. Allen, a Gadsden attorney, who beat Democrat Armistead Selden and Republican Perry Hooper, both attorneys, and remained in the Senate until his death in 1978.) Grenier himself challenged Senator John Spark-

Top: *Birmingham attorney John Grenier was one of the first Alabama Republicans to make a serious search for viable candidates to run in local elections.* Above: *U.S. Senator Richard Shelby, elected as a Democrat in 1986, announced in 1994 that he was switching to the Republican Party.*

man when he ran for reelection in 1966, but lost, as Sparkman polled sixty percent of the vote in the general election. Grenier's candidacy for the Senate seat left Martin, who wanted to parlay his congressional win into higher office, to run against Lurleen Wallace; he carried only thirty-one percent of the vote in the general election and he lost the tacit help of Wallace, who had quietly cooperated with the Republicans in earlier fights.

Attorneys William Dickinson and Jack Edwards were also elected to Congress on Goldwater's coattails in 1964 and remained in Congress until their retirements in 1992 and 1984 respectively. Martin, after his failed attempt to parlay his win into the governorship in 1966, challenged John Sparkman for his Senate seat in 1972 and ran for Jim Allen's Senate seat in 1978, upon Allen's death (a race that was won by Anniston attorney Donald W. Stewart, a Democrat). Although he never won office after 1964, Martin did make a serious, creditable candidate, leading the way for others to fill Republican slots on the ballot thereafter. Attorney Spencer Bachus won a congressional seat in 1993 running as a Republican and was joined in 1997 by attorney Robert Aderholt and in 2003 by Mike Rogers, a 1991 graduate of the Birmingham School of Law, both Republicans.

ABOVE: *Attorney Bert Nettles of Mobile, above center, was the first Republican to be elected to the state legislature in the modern era.* RIGHT: *Jeff Sessions, also from Mobile, was elected to the United States Senate as a Republican in 1997, assuming the seat left vacant by the retirement of Howell Heflin, a Democrat.*

Another coming trend began in 1966 when attorney Don Collins, who had won a state legislative seat as a Democrat, even though he had actively supported Richard Nixon's 1960 campaign for president, stood up in the legislature and declared himself to be a Republican convert, stating, "I campaigned as a conservative or Southern Democrat...and my thinking has not changed; I have not changed. While I have not changed, and while the people of Alabama have not changed, the political philosophy of the national Democratic party has changed and has left me an orphan...At a recent point in time, the Republican party philosophy became that of the Southern Democrat."[8] Collins ended his speech with an announcement that he would run as a Republican for the office of attorney general. He was beaten by McDonald Gallion, the Democratic incumbent, and subsequently lost a bid for lieutenant governor as well. He, Martin, and Grenier were trailblazers. They did not win, but they led the way.

Mobile attorney Bert Nettles was the first Republican to win a seat in the Alabama legislature during this

REPUBLICAN PATRONAGE FILLS THE FEDERAL JUDICIARY

In the post-World War II era, Republican patronage in the form of federal appointments brought Alabama Republicans into the federal judiciary before the party was able to elect candidates to state office and the pace picked up during periods that Republicans controlled the White House as the judiciary expanded. President Eisenhower appointed Harlan Hobart Grooms to the Northern District in 1953 and Frank Johnson, Jr., whose father had served as the only Republican in the Alabama House of Representatives in 1942, to the Middle District in 1955.

President Nixon appointed Frank H. McFadden to the Northern District in 1969, Sam C. Pointer, Jr., to the Northern District in 1970, Robert E. Varner to the Middle District and William Brevard Hand to the Southern District in 1971, and J. Foy Guin, Jr. (who had run for the U.S. Senate as early as 1954) and James H. Hancock to the Northern District in 1973. President Reagan appointed William Acker, Jr., to the Northern District in 1982, Emmett R. Cox to the Southern District as district judge in 1981 and to the Eleventh Circuit in 1988, and Alex Travis Howard, Jr., to the Southern District and Joel F. Dubina to the Middle District in 1986.

W. Brevard Hand of Mobile was appointed to the Southern District of Alabama by President Nixon in 1971. In all, Nixon appointed six federal district judges in Alabama. Presidents Reagan and Bush added ten more.

President Bush appointed Joel F. Dubina to the Eleventh Circuit, Edwin L. Nelson to the Northern District, and Richard Wade Vollmer, Jr., to the Southern District in 1990; William Harold Albritton to the

period. His victory came about in a special election to fill a position in the state house of representatives held in Mobile on April 1, 1969. Many Democrats referred to his victory as an April Fools' Day surprise. He was reelected for one full term in 1970. By 2009, Republicans were well represented in the legislature, including four attorney-legislators, senators Ben Brooks, Bradley Byrne, and Arthur Orr and Representatives Paul DeMarco and Cam Ward.

In 1994, U.S. Senator Richard Shelby, a Tuscaloosa attorney whose political career had led him to be elected a state legislator, a congressman, and ultimately a United States senator, all within the Democratic Party, announced that he had decided to become a Republican. He is the highest ranking of many Alabama officeholders who switched parties during the decades since Don Collins announced his conversion. His fellow senator, former attorney general Jeff Sessions, ran and won his Senate seat as a Republican in 1997, upon the retirement of Senator Howell Heflin, a Democrat who entered the Senate in 1979. Thereafter, the attorney general's office continued to be controlled by the Republican Party when attorney Bill Pryor took over in 1997, remaining in office until 2004 when he was appointed to the Eleventh Circuit Court of Appeals by President George W. Bush and was replaced by Republican Troy King. Steve Windom of Mobile was elected as a Republican to be lieutenant governor in 1998, having previously served as a member of the state senate for over a decade.

Middle District and Sharon Lovelace Blackburn to the Northern District in 1991; and Edward E. Carnes, an assistant Alabama attorney general from 1975 to 1992, to the U.S. Eleventh Circuit Court of Appeals and Ira DeMent to the Middle District in 1992.

This group photograph of judges of the Northern District of Alabama includes five of seven Republican appointees: H. H. Grooms, seated right, and standing, left to right, Sam C. Pointer, Jr., Frank McFadden, J. Foy Guin, and James H. Hancock. Also pictured are Clarence Allgood, seated left, and Seybourn Lynne.

The Democratic Party and Black Political Aspirations

Soon after the passage of the 1965 Voting Rights Act, blacks began to offer themselves for political office. Attorney Fred Gray became the first black attorney to serve in the Alabama legislature following the "Second Reconstruction" when he was elected to represent Macon, Bullock, and Barbour counties in the Alabama House of Representatives in 1970. Birmingham attorneys U.W. Clemon and J. Richmond Pearson were elected in

Civil rights attorney and state senator U.W. Clemon was the first black appointed to a federal district judgeship in Alabama.

THE DEMOCRATIC RACE FOR GOVERNOR THAT ELECTED A REPUBLICAN

GEORGE WALLACE RETIRED from Alabama politics in 1986, whereupon Lieutenant Governor Bill Baxley, a Birmingham attorney, and Attorney General Charles Graddick, a Mobile attorney, faced each other in the Democratic primary runoff. Baxley represented the progressive, populist faction of the state's politics, the heir of Hugo Black, Lister Hill, John Sparkman and "Big Jim" Folsom, while Graddick represented the conservative, states' rights Democrats.[9]

Perennial gubernatorial candidate Guy Hunt took advantage of public reaction to the imbroglio over the Democratic nomination to become the first Republican governor of Alabama since Reconstruction.

In the runoff, Graddick invited voters who had voted in the Republican primary to cross over and vote in the Democratic runoff. He even had an assistant attorney general issue an opinion that it was perfectly legal for Republican voters to vote in the Democratic runoff, even though it was forbidden by Democratic Party rules. A letter was mailed from the Attorney General's office to election officials stating that they would face possible prosecution if they interfered with crossover voters. Thousands of Republicans who had voted for Guy Hunt, a part-time Primitive Baptist preacher and Amway salesman, in their own primary, helped Charles Graddick win the Democratic runoff by a vote of 470,051 to Baxley's 461,295.

Almost immediately a Pike County couple, represented by attorney Jack Drake, filed suit to challenge the validity of the runoff election under the 1965 Voting Rights Act. A three-judge federal panel found Graddick guilty of violating the act and ordered a new runoff unless Baxley could prove he would have won the election but for the crossover votes. The Alabama State Democratic Executive Committee held a hearing, the first of its kind in Alabama history, to judge the outcome of its primary election. David Cromwell Johnson, along with Jack Drake and Ed Still, all Birmingham attorneys, were able to convince the committee that Bill Baxley should be the Democratic Party's gubernatorial candidate.

Graddick appealed the decision, and the federal district judge who heard the case, Foy Guin, Jr., a former corporate attorney who had held several Republican offices before being appointed to the federal bench by President Nixon in 1973, found that a new runoff election should be held. Upon appeal of this decision to the Eleventh Circuit, a three-judge panel comprised of the Eleventh Circuit's Alabama judges, including former Democratic Party chairman Robert Vance, held that the State Democratic Executive Committee had acted entirely within the law in giving the nomination to Baxley.

The runoff victory was a Pyrrhic victory for Baxley, because the entire spectacle so angered Alabama's voters that they elected Republican Guy Hunt governor in the general election, ending the long tradition of the Democratic primary winner being automatically elected to office. After this election, both Baxley and Graddick ended their aspirations to be Alabama's governor.

ABOVE: *Carole Smitherman has served as a municipal court and circuit judge, as well as president of the Birmingham City Council* RIGHT: *After first having been appointed by Governor Fob James, Oscar W. Adams became the first black justice elected to the Alabama Supreme Court in his own right.*

1974 to become the first blacks to serve in the Alabama Senate since Reconstruction. Clemon received an appointment to a federal district judgeship in 1980 from President Jimmy Carter, while Pearson later became a state circuit court judge.

President Carter also appointed black attorney Myron Thompson of Tuskegee to a federal district judgeship in the Middle District of Alabama in 1980, following a thwarted effort to appoint Fred Gray. Attorney Hank Sanders, a Harvard Law School graduate who practices in Selma, is currently serving his seventh term as a state senator. Attorney Demetrius Newton of Birmingham was elected to the state house of representatives in 1986 and was the first black to serve as its Speaker Pro-Tempore. Birmingham attorney Rodger Smitherman was elected to the state senate in 1994. His wife, Carole Smitherman, with whom he practices law, has served as a Birmingham municipal court judge and as a circuit court judge and in 2009 was the president of the Birmingham City Council. Myron Penn of Union Springs was elected to the state senate in 2002. Yusuf Abdus-Salaam of Selma was elected to the state house of representatives in 2002. Attorney Christopher England of Tuscaloosa is a young black state representative in 2009.

In 1982, Birmingham attorney Oscar W. Adams became the first black Alabamian to win a statewide election for a constitutional office in the state when he was elected to the Alabama Supreme Court, after having first been appointed to the court by Governor Fob James. Bessemer attorney Ralph D. Cook, a Bessemer circuit judge, was appointed to the court in 1993 by Governor Jim Folsom and elected for a full term in 1994. John H. England, Jr., was appointed to the court in 1999 by Governor Siegelman but he and Cook lost their election bids in 2000 as Republicans beat them in the general election. Subsequently, John England was appointed to serve on the University of Alabama Board of Trustees.

In 1992, Birmingham attorney Earl Hilliard was elected to Congress from Alabama's Seventh District, after having served in both the Alabama House of Representatives and Senate. He became the focus of controversy when he was seen as presenting a pro-Arab foreign policy position and, in 2002, was beaten by black attorney Artur Davis, who was born in Montgomery, educated at Harvard University and its law school, clerked for Judge Myron Thompson, and served as a U.S. attorney in the Middle District of Alabama. Davis ran unopposed in 2008 and in 2009 announced his candidacy for governor of Alabama.

CHAPTER EIGHTEEN

THE BAR AFTER 1964: NEW LEADERSHIP AND REFORM

THE YEAR 1965 WAS A WATERSHED YEAR FOR the legal profession in Alabama. In a 1965 study for *The Alabama Lawyer* (published in 1966), Professor John Payne did a statistical analysis of the bar, noting that of the 2,716 licensed lawyers (of whom 50 were women) listed in Martindale-Hubbell's *Legal Directory*, there were approximately 1,900 Alabama lawyers in active private practice, predominantly in small partnerships or solo practices. Over 1,700 of these attorneys practiced in the five counties where Alabama's five largest cities were located: Jefferson (851), Mobile (319), Montgomery (311), Madison (128), and Tuscaloosa (118), denoting a continued urbanization of the bar. All counties had at least one lawyer, and there continued to be an unexpectedly large number of lawyers still practicing in smaller communities. He also noted that sixty percent were under the age of 50 and that fifty-eight percent had fewer than 20 years' experience in the bar (this relative inexperience being accounted for by the disruption caused by World War II and, to some extent, the impact of the Depression). Roughly sixty-seven percent of the bar had graduated from the University of Alabama's Law School (1,822), approximately 9.5 percent were graduates of the Birmingham School of Law, Jones Law School, and Cumberland Law School, with the remaining 23.5 percent having matriculated out of state.

Why was 1965 a watershed year? For one thing, Walter B. Jones was no longer editor of *The Alabama Lawyer*, a position he held for 24 years, which had given his views inordinate influence in the bar for someone who was born in 1888 and had entered the bar in 1909. Although his service to the bar had been tremendously positive in many areas, his attitudes in his later years had been regressive during the period of civil rights turmoil in Montgomery, reflecting poorly upon the organized bar. His death in 1963 opened the way for both new leadership and reform.

Also in 1965, the state legislature, under court order, redistricted itself, making one-voter, one-vote a legal reality. Thus, the concentration of power in the Black Belt was broken, and the power of the "Big Mules" in Birmingham dissipated. With the passage of the 1964 Civil Rights Act and the 1965 Voting Rights Act, the legal rights of Alabama's African-American citizens were basically in place, even though there would be continuing litigation and political effort to secure the reality of those rights. Still, the era of demonstrations and marches in Alabama was coming to an end so that attention and energy could turn to other matters.

The Alabama State Bar was in new headquarters (groundbreaking for which had taken place during the

As president of the Alabama State Bar from the watershed year of 1965 to 1966, Howell T. Heflin, a "country lawyer from Tuscumbia," set in motion the reorganization and reform of both the state bar and Alabama's judiciary system. He went on to serve for six years as chief justice of the Alabama Supreme Court, and for 18 years as an influential U.S. senator.

1963 to 1964 presidency of J. Edward Thornton of Mobile). The position of bar secretary became a full-time job for John B. Scott, who had served as secretary since 1950, and the position of part-time proctor was converted to a full-time general counsel, filled by Lawrence "Snag" Andrews, with an office in the new bar building. Finally, the many attorneys who had entered the bar as returning veterans of World War II were now seasoned and ready to bring a new forward-looking, reformist energy to bar leadership and, beyond that, to the state's legal system. The 1964 bar convention presented them with this opportunity, when they elected Howell T. Heflin to be president, beginning in July 1965, the first post-1945 bar admittee to be president. His presidency, as much as anything else, made 1965 a watershed year.

Howell Heflin, center, as a U.S. marine on Guadacanal with Conrad Fowler, left, and Bill Pfeifle. Fowler was Heflin's company commander and, following the war, his classmate at the University of Alabama School of Law.

Howell T. Heflin Brings Reform to the Bench and Bar

At the time, bar presidents were chosen at the convention by the vote of convention attendees, first to serve as first vice president and then to move into the presidency. The 1964 convention was held in Mobile and Winston McCall, a 1934 bar admittee, was slated to be the nominee. (No one had yet served as president who entered the bar during the decade of the forties, much less anyone who had entered the bar after World War II.) At the convention, there was a rumor, later proven untrue, that McCall was being investigated by the Internal Revenue Service for not paying taxes on cribbage winnings at his country club and therefore it was thought that his election might end up embarrassing the bar. With this excuse, a number of convention attendees approached Howell Heflin of Tuscumbia, who was present at the convention, about challenging McCall for the presidency.[1]

Heflin agreed to run after much persuading and the word went out to various groups throughout the state that they needed to get to the convention before the business meeting at which the election would be held. And come they did. Since it was not the norm for the slated candidate to be challenged at the convention, it might be stated that the election of Howell Heflin was a coup by the postwar contingent of the bar to take control. Those concerned, especially Heflin himself, have described the "coup" as spontaneous, but the result was the coming on the scene of a president who was able to corral and direct the energy of a new generation of attorneys to bring about profound change in the bar, the profession, and the state.

Why Howell Heflin?

At the time of his election, Howell Heflin was not a member of the power structure of the state bar, never having served as a bar commissioner. He was, though, a well-known and highly regarded attorney who regularly attended bar conventions and who had shown support in the past for various judicial reforms. He was from a family who had been active in Alabama politics and the legal profession for decades. He was a decorated war veteran who acknowledged that his wartime experience had greatly broadened his views, especially his understanding of the value of pluralism and diversity.

Heflin had been recruited into the Marines by Conrad Fowler, who also ended up being Heflin's company commander during most of Heflin's service as a platoon leader. Fowler would become a prominent member of the law school class of 1948 with Heflin and an important leader of the reform movements that Heflin helped instigate. Another prominent class member and close personal friend was George Huddleston, Jr., who was Heflin's apartment mate during law school and would soon become a congressman. Roy Greene, who lived upstairs from Heflin with another classmate, Peyton Finch, returned to Phenix City and became a wealthy and prominent businessman. Bert Haltom, a classmate who practiced in Florence, near Tuscumbia where Heflin established his practice, remained a close friend and peer in service to the law school and the bar, finishing his career as a federal district judge. Charlie Carmichael, who also entered practice in Tuscumbia, was a first cousin of Heflin's future wife, Elizabeth Carmichael, whose family also had a history of public service (her grandfather was Archie H. Carmichael, who had served both as a state and federal legislator).

Heflin's dean at the law school was M. Leigh Harrison, who encouraged Heflin to form an alumni association and who later served as reporter to the Alabama Constitutional Commission.

With so many outstanding members of the profession entering during the postwar era, 1947 to 1950, why was Heflin the one to be recruited as this group's first president? There were many reasons. Heflin was known in law school as a great raconteur and was quite popular among both students and faculty, having a penchant for making friends. He was also politically astute and racially moderate, choosing to support the National Democrats against the Dixiecrats in 1949 and thereafter, as did many of his peers. He became friends with Tuscaloosa attorney-politico Marc Ray "Foots" Clements while a student, even then contemplating following his various relatives who had entered state politics.

Almost immediately out of law school and at Dean M. Leigh Harrison's request, Heflin helped organize and was the first president of the Alabama Law School Alumni Association, giving his time to travel the state recruiting members. Thus, he had the opportunity to continue and deepen friendships with classmates and peers as they spread throughout the state, while also getting to know those already well established in the profession. Later he helped organize and led the Alabama Law School Foundation, serving as president from 1964 to 1966, again having the opportunity to continue law school friendships and acquaintances while also reaching out to other members of the bar raising funds to support their alma mater. In these roles he made long-lasting friendships.

Heflin was a "country lawyer" in northwest Alabama, with a general practice. He had such success with criminal cases that he earned the nickname "Perry Mason" of North Alabama and also became well known for his trial work in the personal injury arena, both on the plaintiff and the defense side. He handled divorces, estate matters, collections, and any other matters that might be brought to him, and he handled them well. He gained a reputation for competence, professionalism, and reliability, and was serving as president of the Alabama Trial Lawyers Association in 1964 when he was chosen as first vice president of the Alabama State Bar. He had already shown a flair for organization, becoming active in the American Legion (which he served as state vice commander), in Methodist

HOWELL HEFLIN AND OTHER MEMBERS OF THE POST-WORLD WAR II BAR

NELLE HARPER LEE, WHOSE SISTER, ALICE Finch Lee, had entered the bar in 1943, studied law with Howell Heflin and his classmates at the University of Alabama Law School, but did not seek admission to the bar. She wrote *To Kill a Mockingbird* in 1960 and contributed the character of attorney Atticus Finch (drawn, in part, from her father Amasa Lee, a Monroeville attorney) to the Alabama legal profession and to the world. In honor of her achievement in authoring one of the twentieth century's most famous and well-loved novels, the Alabama Supreme Court presented her with an honorary membership in the bar in 2008.

There were many others in law school with Howell Heflin during the postwar period who gained prominence in the profession, aside from the bar presidents and other officeholders mentioned earlier in this book, including Charles Adair; Hugh Nash; James M. (Marvin) Albritton; Frank Dominick; Walter Fletcher; Clifford Emond; Neal C. Newell; Roscoe B. Hogan; Doug Corretti; Herndon Inge; William S. Pritchard, Jr.; Max Hudson; William J. Sullivan, Jr.; John W. Williams, Jr.; Ralph Bland; Robert Straub; L.A. Farmer, Jr.; Richard Poellnitz; Ralph Gaines; Gordon Rosen; Olin Zeanah; Sam Earle Hobbs; Jane Kimbrough Dishuck; Camille Wright Cook; John M. Puryear; Stancil Starnes, Sr.; Ryan deGraffenreid, Sr., (who ran for governor); Schuyler Baker; Charles A. Beavers; William L. Chenault, Jr.; Thomas W. Christopher (who later became dean of the law school); James Jefferson Bennett (who became the president of the University of the South in Sewanee, Tennessee); Robert Guilott (who later became president of the University of North Alabama in Florence); Charles H. Eyster, Jr.; Richmond M. Flowers (who served one term as attorney general); Ralph A. Franco; Karl B. Friedman; Dwight McInish; William B. Fernambucq; James C. Barton; Jack Livingston; Huel

church activities, and serving as chairman of the Tuscumbia Board of Education for ten years. During his period of school board service, he received an appointment to the Alabama Educational Study Commission, created by the legislature to study the state's education system, and worked with the legislature for passage of a $100 million bond issue for school buildings. He later served as president of the Alabama Teachers Tenure Commission and the Alabama Committee for Better Schools. Thus, Howell Heflin had a reputation for being able to get things done. He also was on the other end of the political spectrum from George Wallace. He was the perfect choice for those who wanted to bring new energy to the bar and to the state.

ABOVE: *These pages from the 1947* Corolla *show Howell Heflin, second row, third from the right, during his junior year at the University of Alabama law school. In the fifth row, third from the right is Harper Lee.* OPPOSITE PAGE: *In 1997, the Alabama State Bar placed this monument to "Atticus Finch, Lawyer-Hero" on the grounds of the Monroe County Courthouse. Harper Lee was honored by the Alabama Supreme Court in 2008 with honorary membership in the bar.*

M. Love Sr.; Byron D. Boyett; McCoy Davidson; Lynn W. Jink; Louis Salmon; Glenn F. Manning; Robert D. Norman; Joe C. Cassady; Edward L. Colebeck; Maurice Bell; Joseph Kellett; William W. Watson; John C. Wear; James W. Kelley; Nelson Vinson; Joe L. Payne; Roscoe O. Roberts, Jr.; Hoyt Elliott; Caine O'Rear, Jr.; Robert T. Wilson, Sr.; James E. Wilson; John W. Johnson, Jr.; James H. Caldwell; Marshall DeMouy; Fred G. Collins; Thomas M. Calloway; Paul W. Brock; Robert B. Wilkins; Edward J. Azar; Clarence Simmons, Jr.; Jack W. Torbert; Alfred W. Goldthwaite; William B. Hand; Richard L. Jones, Jr.; Eric Embry; James Faulkner; James N. Bloodworth; Vivian G. Johnston, Jr.; James C. Inzer Jr.; Ralph D. Porch; Bruce Sherrill; James W. Woodroof; Frank H. Hawthorne; Jack W. Wallace; John R. Matthews, Jr.; Woodley C. Campbell; William B. Moore, Jr.; Roy H. Phillips; A. Jackson Noble, Jr.; Sam M. Johnston, Jr.; and John Patterson (who served as attorney general, governor, and a judge of the Court of Criminal Appeals). Among others admitted to practice during this period who studied out of state were Oscar W. Adams, Jr.; Samuel E. Balch; John Bingham; Ira Burleson; Sam Burr; Walter Cook; Robert T. Cunningham; Percy W. Johnston, Jr.; Willis C. Darby, Jr.; Peter Hall; Frank Hill; David Hood, Jr.; J. Reese Murray, Jr.; William K. Murray; Harry Reddick; Clarence Rhea; Jacob A. Walker, Jr.; Meade Whitaker, Sr.; and Cecil H. Young, Jr.

HEFLIN BEGINS THE PROCESS OF CHANGE

There were many issues which had confronted the bar for years, with resulting study and discussion, and even lots of proposals, but little successful action. Most of these issues arose from the antiquated rules of pleading and procedure, as well as the outdated structure and judicial philosophy of Alabama's court system, as established in the 1901 Constitution and later amendments to it. Other subjects of concern included effective policing of the profession by the bar (illustrated by the "quickie divorce" scandal) as well as improving the admissions process and the overall professionalism of lawyers. Many lawyers and judges understood the issues that confronted the state's legal system and the Alabama State Bar itself, but no spark plug had yet ignited the movement for change. Howell Heflin served as that spark plug.

Upon becoming president of the bar, after a year of review and consideration as first vice president, president Heflin appointed over 25 study committees[2] and instructed all those he appointed as chairmen that he expected all committees to meet, research the subjects presented to them, and produce reports that would inspire action. More than 250 lawyers were appointed to these committees, representing every geographical area of the state and every type of practice and bringing into leadership many new faces from the postwar classes of bar admittees. Heflin established a series of uniform dates and sites for all committees to meet, holding the "organizational conference of committees" in Birmingham in October 1965, with two more "conferences" held in February and April of 1966. In this way, he could be assured that work would get done and preliminary reports be made before his term as president ended. The act of meeting at the same time and at the same location promoted a sense of joint enterprise that generated momentum to "stay the course" when legislative action was required. As his term in office drew to a close, a resolution was adopted to continue holding mid-winter meetings so that effective committee activity could continue to be encouraged.

TOP: *Former student Daniel J. Meador became dean of the University of Alabama School of Law in 1966, serving until 1970.* ABOVE: *In 1967, J. O. Sentell assumed the editorship of* The Alabama Lawyer, *and became clerk to the Alabama Supreme Court, succeeding Richard W. Neal in both jobs.*

A quote from state bar secretary John Scott in a letter to Dean Daniel J. Meador, who was newly selected to lead the University of Alabama Law School, captures some of the enthusiasm and diligence with which the committee work was being done: "You will come to Alabama at a time when its Bar Association has a breadth of interest surpassing anything that it has experienced before. I will not attempt to go into any details as to the good work being done by our numerous committees and sections, but will only say that if the interest that now exists in the better administration of justice does not cool or waste itself, it should produce significant and happy results."

The list of committee reports in the General Index of the 1966 volume of *The Alabama Lawyer* shows the broadness of the issues considered by the committees. This list provides an opportunity to trace some of the results that accrued and changes that continued well into the future.[3]

Advisory Committee on The Alabama Lawyer

Its assignment was to make the *Lawyer* a "bread and butter" publication for Alabama lawyers. The committee's name was changed to the Board of Editors and it became a permanent fixture of the editorial process. The Advisory Committee appointed by Heflin was chaired by Sam Earle Hobbs of Selma. J. O. Sentell, who replaced Richard W. Neal upon his death in 1967, continued as editor until 1983, when Robert Huffaker, the current editor, took over. At that time, under the chairmanship of J. Mark White (state bar president, 2008-2009), the format was changed to a magazine instead of a journal, and it was published six times a year. The new format included a president's page, a secretary's report, an article by the president of the Young Lawyers Section (beginning with Tom King, Jr., of Birmingham), and a legislative wrap-up by the director of the Alabama Law Institute. Later, information about lawyer discipline was included as were articles by the general counsel on ethical issues and the Code of Professional Conduct. Always, there were "nuts and bolts" articles about applying the law. In 1987, attorney Samuel A. Rumore, Jr., began a series on the courthouses of Alabama which continued until 2001, at the end of his year of service as state bar president.

Alabama Law Books

This committee's work started the movement for the recodification of the Alabama Code, published in 1975, and also inspired the publication of the *Alabama Bar Reports*, which made judicial decisions promptly available to subscribers, and the creation of a series of "How To Do It" books and forms by the Alabama Bar Foundation, the Alabama Law School Foundation, and the bar's Committee on Professional Economics in 1973. The committee was chaired by Walter R. Byars, Montgomery, state bar president from 1984 to 1985. Clement C. "Bo" Torbert, Jr., chaired the Committee on the Revision of the Alabama Code which accomplished its recodification in 1975. The bar supported this revision effort by funding the clerical help necessary to complete the project in the amount of $10,000.

TOP: C. C. *"Bo" Torbert chaired the Committee on the Revision of the Alabama Code and later served as chief justice of the Alabama Supreme Court.* ABOVE: *Sam W. Pipes, III, served as state bar president from 1969 to 1970, and was a special justice for the case of* Johnston v. Public Service Commission *in 1971.*

Bail & Recognizance Report

This committee's work resulted in reform of Alabama's bail bond laws to allow release on personal recognizance for those charged with misdemeanors. It was originally chaired by William H. Cole of Birmingham. The bail bond reform effort was led by the Young Lawyers Section of the bar, much of the work being done while Ernest Potter was president from 1972 to 1973.

Client Security Fund

This committee's work resulted in the creation, in 1971, of a state bar fund to protect clients from attorney malfeasance, with an initial funding of $15,000. The committee was chaired by Edward J. Colebeck of Florence. A 1997 article in the *Lawyer* noted that, in 1987, contributions to the Client Security Fund became mandatory and that between 1989 and 1997, the fund had paid more than $214,000 in claims.

Congestion in Appellate Courts

This committee's work led to the expansion of the Alabama Supreme Court from seven to nine judges and the creation of a separate Court of Criminal Appeals and a reconstituted Court of Civil Appeals in 1969. It was originally chaired by Sam W. Pipes, III, of Mobile, president of the state bar from 1968 to 1969. Francis Hare, Sr., of Birmingham was chair in 1969, while Robert Vance, also of Birmingham, made important contributions to the committee, which also recommended that appellate salaries be set at $25,000 per year.

Pattern Jury Charge

In recognition that many appeals had as their underlying issue a challenge to the jury charges given by the trial judge, a Pattern Jury Charge Committee was established in 1967 and soon was designated an ongoing commission. The commission's original chairman was James N. Bloodworth, who became a justice of the Alabama Supreme Court in 1968, and was replaced by Judge Ingram Beasley. Beasley had presented a paper at a circuit judges seminar sponsored by Continuing Legal Education in 1966 which served as a foundation for the commission's work. Judge William Sullivan chaired the commission for 25 years after Judge Beasley stepped down. The commission's reporter was Professor Janie Shores of Cumberland Law School, who would soon become the first female justice on the Alabama Supreme Court. In 1973, the Alabama Supreme Court authorized the publication of *Alabama Pattern Jury Instructions.* The commission incorporated as a nonprofit organization in 1973 and thereafter the royalties collected from the sales of its book were retained and used to fund scholarships at the University of Alabama Law School and at Cumberland Law School

TOP: *James N. Bloodworth served as chairman of the Jury Pattern Charge Committee until joining the Alabama Supreme Court in 1968.* ABOVE: *Mobile attorney Thomas Greaves chaired the Congestion in Circuit Courts Committee. He was president of the Alabama State Bar from 1975 to 1976.*

Congestion in Circuit Courts

This committee promoted the centralization of court administration under the Supreme Court so that judges from one circuit could be assigned to another circuit to reduce congestion. The first court administrator, Charles Y. Cameron, was named in 1971, after authorizing legislation was passed that year and Howell T. Heflin became chief justice. This committee was chaired by Thomas Greaves of Mobile, state bar president from 1975 to 1976.

Discovery in Criminal Cases

This committee promoted the granting of rule-making authority to the Supreme Court and its work eventually led to the adoption of the Rules of Criminal Procedure. It was originally chaired by Jeff D. Smith of Huntsville.

Educational Cruise Program

This committee studied the tax implications of conducting continuing education programs on cruises outside the country and was chaired by William B. Moore, Jr., of Montgomery. Out of this effort developed a travel program sponsored by the bar, directed at its senior members, which continued for years, although for most of its history, it promoted collegiality rather than continuing education.

Judicial Commission

The goal of this committee, chaired by M. Roland Nachman of Montgomery (state bar president, 1973-1974), was to study the need for a state entity other than the legislature, to address retirement, discipline, and removal of judges. Its work resulted in the creation of Alabama's Judicial Inquiry Commission and the Court of the Judiciary by constitutional amendment in 1973. Stewart O'Bannon of Florence was an important member of the bar committee and would later be the primary sponsor in the Alabama Senate of much of the legislation which would reform the judicial system. In 1975, the Alabama Supreme Court adopted Alabama's first Canons of Judicial Ethics.

Judicial Salaries

The work of this committee, chaired by Jack Crenshaw of Montgomery, resulted in legislative attention to the competitiveness of salaries being paid to all judges in the state. At the time, circuit judges were paid $12,000 per year, the lowest salary for judges in the nation. Over the years, judicial salaries have increased enough to attract ever more qualified candidates to these positions.

Law and Poverty Recommendations

This committee, chaired by Paul Johnston of Birmingham, considered indigent defense and access to justice issues in light of federal funds being made available through the Office of Economic Opportunity (OEO). Its work resulted in the creation of the position of public defender in some circuits.

The OEO proposed to establish legal aid clinics for the poor without the participation of the state bar association. In July 1968, the bar requested by resolution that the governor not approve any applications for establishing such clinics unless and until they had first been presented to the bar for comments and recommendations. It took some years before OEO and the federally funded Legal Services Corporation were able to work congenially with the state bar.

Bernard Sykes of the Attorney General's office did much during the 1960s to see that the legislature provided funds to be used for the defense of indigents. Stova McFadden also worked to increase the fair trial tax in 1969. William N. Clark, state bar president from 2003 to 2004, chaired the Committee on Indigent Defense during much of the 1970s and worked to increase the hourly rate paid to appointed counsel to provide more equitable pay.

TOP: *Birmingham attorney Paul Johnston served as chairman of the Law and Poverty Recommendations Committee, which considered the issue of indigent defense.* ABOVE: *Professor Dallas Sands represented the University of Alabama School of Law on the Legal Internships Committee.*

Law Clerks for Circuit Judges

This committee was chaired by Patrick W. Richardson of Huntsville, state bar president from 1969 to 1970.

Lawyers and Title Insurance Companies

Chaired by Roy L. Smith from Phenix City, this committee considered whether the title work done by title insurance companies constituted the unauthorized practice of law.

Legal Internships

The work of this committee resulted in the development of clinical programs manned by law students at the various law schools and the adoption of a limited third-year law student practice rule in 1974. It was chaired by Thomas F. Parker of Montgomery, with Professor Dallas Sands representing the University of Alabama School of Law and Professor Walter Sowa representing Cumberland School of Law.

New Judicial Building

This committee studied the feasibility of a new judicial building for the state which was accomplished when Alabama's Heflin-Torbert Judicial Building was occupied in 1993. The committee was originally chaired by Albert P. Brewer of Decatur. Ernest C. "Sonny" Hornsby of Tallassee (state bar president, 1977-1978) was instrumental in seeing this project through to completion when he served as chief justice during the period of its funding and construction. At that time, Maury Smith of Montgomery was chairman of the state bar committee.

Committee on Public Relations

Chaired by Jack Porterfield, this committee began to study more effective ways for the profession and the state bar to relate to the general public positively. At its recommendation, the bar retained the services of a professional public relations consultant in 1971, when Frank Bainbridge of Birmingham was committee chairman, and later established its own communications function.

Montgomery attorney Maury Smith, above left, as chairman of the state bar committee for the new judicial building, and Ernest C. "Sonny" Hornsby, right, as chief justice of the Alabama Supreme Court, were two of the people who helped oversee the funding and completion of the new Heflin-Torbert Judicial Building, above right, located opposite the state bar headquarters.

Revision of Canon of Ethics

This committee studied the question of whether the Code of Ethics needed to be updated especially in the area of indigent defense. It was chaired by Truman M. Hobbs of Montgomery, state bar president from 1970 to 1971. An important member was Professor Harry Cohen of the University of Alabama Law School who undertook a thorough explication of the state of the rules in 1965 and whose work laid the foundation for the later recommendations of the committee. The work of this committee soon led to the adoption of an updated model Code of Professional Responsibility in 1974 (under the leadership of Julian Harris and Marshall Neilson) and then, effective January 1, 1991, to the Rules of Professional Conduct, which replaced the Code. The Alabama Supreme Court would later create an advisory committee on rules for defending indigents, chaired by William N. Clark of Birmingham (state bar president, 2003-2004), with Wade Baxley of Dothan (state bar president, 1999-2000), as vice chairman. A major issue in the realm of ethics throughout the last part of the twentieth century was whether lawyers should be allowed to advertise and what the parameters of ethical advertisement should be. The Alabama state bar was "unalterably opposed" to lawyer advertising until the U.S. Supreme Court ruled that the first amendment protected it; thereafter the bar considered appropriate limitations to advertising.

Harry Cohen, a professor at the University of Alabama School of Law played an important role on the Revision of Canon of Ethics Committee. His work was the basis for the later recommendations made by the committee.

Revision of Procedures in Connection with Grievances

This committee's work resulted in the adoption by the Alabama Supreme Court of the state bar's Rules of Disciplinary Enforcement, effective in 1977. The committee was chaired by James J. Carter of Montgomery, who was state bar president from 1962 to 1963. The Rules created a three-member disciplinary commission to replace the earlier Grievance Committee, plus the appointment of three disciplinary panels composed of bar commissioners. The first members of the Disciplinary Commission were William Hairston, Jr. (state bar president, 1983-1984), chairman; Norborne Stone (state bar president, 1982-1983), and Hugh A. Nash.

The grievance function is one of the most important functions of the bar, being part of its regulatory role as a state entity and has continued to receive constant attention throughout the years. Those who chair the Grievance Committee often receive the Award of Merit for service to the bar: for example, Drayton T. Scott in 1969, Max Pope in 1973, George P. Howard in 1975, Broox Holmes (state bar president, 1994-1995) in 1978, and Norborne Stone in 1980.

TOP: *Champ Lyons, Jr., receives congratulations following his investiture as a justice of the Alabama Supreme Court.* ABOVE: *University of Alabama law professor Harry Haden was one of three members added to the Board of Bar Examiners in 1964.*

Revision of Rules Pertaining to Board of Bar Examiners

This committee's work resulted in the use of the multistate bar exam as part of the Alabama bar examination, beginning in July 1973. It was originally chaired by Henry H. Mize of Tuscaloosa. The role of the Board of Bar Examiners (BBE) is critical to the policing function of the bar and is always subject to review. (The bar confronted litigation in the 1970s concerning the fairness of the exam to minorities and won. Truman Hobbs, state bar president, 1970-1971, served as lead trial counsel with Champ Lyons, Jr., assisting as counsel for the state bar.) Some of the outstanding chairmen of the BBE over the years include E.T. Brown, Jr.; T. Bowen Hill, III; L. Tennent Lee, III; Robert Potts; David R. Boyd; Michael D. Waters; Delores R. Boyd; Edward Gentle; Ann Stone Sumblin; and David G. Hymer.

Until 1963, there were only three members of the BBE: Marion Rushton of Montgomery, Dean M. Leigh Harrison of the University of Alabama Law School, and Lawrence K. Andrews (who later served as the first general counsel of the state bar). When the diploma privilege formerly granted to graduates of the University of Alabama School of Law was removed, the board was expanded to six members, with two from the University of Alabama Law School faculty, two from Cumberland Law School, and two from the general bar membership. In January 1964, Dean Arthur A. Weeks and Professor C. E. Bankester of Cumberland Law School and Professor Harry Haden from the University of Alabama Law School were added at the recommendation of the three incumbents. By 1969, two additional examiners were added. At that time, the BBE included Frank Donaldson and Claude E. Bankester, from Cumberland

Law School; M. Leigh Harrison and M. Clinton McGee, from the University of Alabama Law School; E.T. Brown, Jr., from Birmingham; James J. Carter and Roland Nachman from Montgomery; and Vivian G. Johnston, Jr., from Mobile. By 1973, the number of examiners had increased to 14 at the time when E. T. Brown Jr., was chairman of the board and the board recommended use of the multistate bar exam.

In 1975, some changes were made to the BBE: 1. Rotation of bar examiners began with the February 1977 bar exam, with no examiner serving more than one four-year term thereafter; 2. The chairman was to serve as administrator of the board only; and, 3. The creation of an advisory committee composed of members of the Board of Bar Commissioners (BBC) to serve as a nominating committee to recommend persons as examiners when vacancies occur. In 1985, major changes in the rules used to score the bar exam were adopted, based on recommendations made by a committee chaired by David R. Boyd, who received a 1985 Award of Merit for his work on bar examination issues, including representing the bar in a lawsuit brought by disgruntled examinees.

In 1997, President Dag Rowe appointed a new task force, headed by Robert Potts of Florence, which concluded that changes were needed to ensure continued quality, fairness, and impartiality of bar examiners. The task force proposed adding a multistate essay exam (MEE), a multistate performance test (MPT), and to continue the multistate bar exam. The format of testing on Alabama law was changed from twelve 45-minute essays on six subjects to six 30-minute essays dealing with one subject—civil litigation. The state bar commissioners approved the changes in October 1999 and the Alabama Supreme Court in May 2001, and they became effective in July 2003.[4]

By 1969, the number of examiners on the BBE had been increased to eight. Two of the members at that time were Professor M. Clinton McGee of the University of Alabama Law School, top, and Mobile attorney Vivian G. Johnston, Jr., above.

Rules of Civil Procedure

This committee promoted the granting of rule-making authority to the state supreme court and advocated the task of revising Alabama's antiquated procedural rules, resulting in the adoption of the Alabama Rules of Civil Procedure, effective July 3, 1973. It was chaired by E. B. Haltom, Jr., of Florence. A subcommittee comprised of Charles E. Poellnitz of Florence, chairman; Charles E. Shaver of Huntsville; Broox Garrett of Brewton; James E. Clark of Birmingham; and Jacob Walker, Jr., of Opelika worked with the Alabama Supreme Court to coordinate the legislative effort to grant the court rule-making powers. Oakley Melton, president of the state bar from 1979 to 1980, served as the chairman of the court's Advisory Committee on Civil Practice and Procedure and the Standing Committee on Alabama Rules of Civil Procedure at the time the rules were adopted.[5]

Champ Lyons, Jr., who subsequently became a justice of the Alabama Supreme Court, served as reporter for the advisory committee and he, along with Melton and other committee members, became the acknowledged experts on the subject of procedure at continuing education programs which were held during the period between passage of the rules and their implementation. Lyons wrote extensive annotations to the rules that explained how Alabama's previously antiquated and complicated system of procedure had been simplified. (After the adoption of the rules, he also wrote a practice book to help practitioners become familiar with the new rules.)

Legal educators Professor Jerome Hoffman of the University of Alabama School of Law and Professor Frank Donaldson of Cumberland served on the rules committees, as well as prominent circuit judges James O. Haley of Birmingham and Joseph M. Hocklander of Mobile. Sam W. Pipes, III, who had previously served as state bar president from 1968 to 1969, was also on these committees. (He was named Outstanding Alumnus of the University of Alabama in 1973. The Farrah Law Society named its own Outstanding Law School Alumnus award after Mr. Pipes in later years.) Other members of this important committee included Timothy M. Conway, Jr., Birmingham; J. Foy Guin, Jr., Russellville; Francis H. Hare, Sr., Birmingham; James L. Klinefelter, Anniston; Jack Livingston, Scottsboro; Mayer W. Perloff, Mobile; Ira D. Pruitt, Livingston; and Thomas E. Skinner, Birmingham.[6] Their work profoundly changed and modernized the procedural system of civil justice in the state which had been earlier described by then-president Jacob Walker, Sr. (1943) as "a museum of procedural antiquities."

Circuit judges James O. Haley of Birmingham, top, and Joseph M. Hocklander, above (on the right, with Dr. Coles of Cumberland School of Law), both served on the rules committee. Judge Hocklander, in 1973, achieved the almost impossible task of clearing his docket of all pending cases.

Traffic Courts

The work of this committee resulted in the elimination of this level of court in the Judicial Article, which promoted uniformity of courts statewide, and its responsibilities were transferred to municipal or district courts, depending on the size of the city or its choice under the Judicial Article. The committee was chaired by James R. Knight, Cullman.

Uniform Commercial Code (UCC)

This committee was formed to help Douglas Lanford, the state bar's director of Continuing Legal Education, develop an educational program in connection with the UCC, which was to go into effect on January 1, 1967. It was chaired by Joseph F. Johnston of Birmingham. George Maynard, also of Birmingham, was especially involved in this educational project, producing an important bibliography of articles on the UCC, published in *The Alabama Lawyer*. Both men, as well as J. Vernon Patrick, Jr., of Birmingham (who had been a law clerk to Justice Hugo Black), were instrumental in its passage into law in 1965.

THE ALABAMA LAW INSTITUTE

In March 1966, president Heflin appointed a Special Committee, headed by G. M. Harrison, on the Feasibility of a State Law Institute, to be "an official advisory law revision, law reform, and legal research agency of the State of Alabama." The Special Committee quickly recommended that an Alabama Law Institute (ALI) be created and the BBC, in turn, made the same recommendation to the legislature. Hugh D. Merrill, Jr., who was a member of the BBC and the Special Committee, as well as a legislator, provided the leadership, energy, and enthusiasm to guide a bill through the legislature which was signed into law by Governor Lurleen Wallace on August 24, 1967. No funding was initially provided, but the bar commissioners still proceeded to appoint a Council of the Institute, comprised of two members from each congressional district. The Council was comprised of: District 1: Sam W. Pipes and Tom Johnston, Mobile; District 2. Oakley W. Melton, Jr., Montgomery and Broox G. Garrett, Brewton; District 3. G. M. Harrison, Dothan and Pelham Ferrell, Phenix City; District 4. Hugh D. Merrill, Jr., Anniston and Ralph Gaines, Talladega; District 5. Perry Hubbard, Tuscaloosa and Ira D. Pruitt, Livingston; District 6. L. Drew Redden and E.T. Brown, Jr., Birmingham; District 7. John D. Petree, Jr., Jasper and J. Foy Guin, Jr., Russellville; and District 8. Howell T. Heflin, Tuscumbia and Eugene McLain, Huntsville. The University of Alabama Law School provided office space and staff support for the initial organizational activities.[7]

Hugh D. Merrill, Jr., served as the Institute's first president from 1967 to 1978, Howell Heflin was vice president and chairman of the Projects and Program Committee; and Vastine Stabler, a professor at the University of Alabama Law School, served as first acting director. Oakley W. Melton, Jr., (state bar president, 1979-1980) served as chairman of the Nominating Committee, which was charged with screening the practicing bar to recommend to the council the names of not more than 150 practicing lawyers to be elected to membership in the Institute. By 1969, with the help of Governor Brewer and his legal advisor Hugh Maddox, the institute had received state funding for its administration. After 40 years of existence, the ALI has had five presidents, with Senator Finis St. John following Hugh Merrill, from 1978 to 1984; Oakley Melton, from 1984 to 1991; Speaker Pro Tem James M. Campbell, from 1991 to 2001; and Speaker Pro Tem Demetrius Newton, from 2001 to the present.

Professor Jerry Gibbons and Professor Thomas L. Jones served as acting directors before Robert L. McCurley, Jr., took over as director in 1975. McCurley continues to direct the institute in 2009. In 1975, its first three major projects were before the legislature, including a revision of the Criminal Code, reported by University of Alabama law professor Clinton McGee; a revision of the Business Corporation Act, reported by Birmingham attorney George Maynard and University of Alabama law professor J. William Futrell; and Land Title Reform, reported by University of Alabama law professor John Payne. University of Alabama law professor Timothy Hoff served as reporter on a revision of Alabama's Rules of the Road, which was also before the legislature in 1975. These pieces of legislation began the ALI's career of service to the state in its continual

TOP: *Attorney and legislator Hugh D. Merrill, Jr., was instrumental in the passage of the law that created the Alabama Law Institute.* ABOVE: *University of Alabama law professor John Payne, known as "Black Jack" by his students, served as reporter to the ALI committee on land title reform.*

consideration of needed improvements in Alabama law and in providing legal research and advice to legislative committees. Its annual report for 2007-2008 listed 75 pieces of enacted legislation, 24 publications and associated training projects, and close to 25 active projects underway. This list represents millions of dollars of donated legal talent contributed to the state by its legal profession during the 40 years of the ALI's existence.

In 2002, the ALI recognized the following attorneys for 25 years of service to the Institute by making them life members: Charles Adair, Jr.; Lee E. Bains; E.T. Brown, Jr.; Walter Byars; John Caddell; T. J Carnes; Joe C. Cassady; A. J. Coleman; Camille W. Cook; Jerome A. Cooper; Homer W. Cornett; Robert T. Cunningham; Frank Dominick; George P. Ford; Conrad M. Fowler, Jr; James M. Fullan, Jr.; Ralph Gaines; John W. Johnson, Jr.; Joseph H. Johnson; Jack Livingston; Louis B. Lusk; William H. McDermott; Richard S. Manley; John R. Mathews; Jr.; Oakley N. Melton, Jr.; Roland M. Nachman, Jr.; E. B. Peebles, III; Ernest L. Potter; James D. Pruitt; Ira D. Pruitt, Jr.; L. Drew Redden; Morgan Reynolds; William M. Russell, Jr.; Yetta G. Samford, Jr.; Maury D. Smith; Robert McD. Smith; Harold Speake; C. Stephen Trimmier; and Jacob Walker, Jr.

Also in 2002, Representative Demetrius Newton was president of the ALI and Senator Roger Bedford was vice president, with an executive committee comprised of David Boyd; James M. Campbell; William N. Clark; Representative Mark Gaines; Representative Ken Guin; Richard S. Manley; Oakley W. Melton, Jr.; and Senator Rodger Smitherman. Legislator Marcel Black has been active in the ALI for many years as well.

Associate Justice Pelham Merrill represented the Alabama Supreme Court on the Committee on Feasibility of a Citizens' Judicial Conference. A former state legislator representing Cleburne County, he was twice elected speaker pro tem of the house. He was elected to the Alabama Supreme Court in 1952.

The Citizens' Conference on Alabama State Courts, the Alabama Constitutional Revision Commission, and the Adoption of a New Judicial Article to the 1901 Constitution

One of the original Heflin committees was particularly productive, the Committee on Feasibility of a Citizens' Judicial Conference, chaired by Robert T. Cunningham of Mobile. Justice Pelham Merrill was an important member of this committee, as representative of the justices of the Alabama Supreme Court. (He served as the keynote speaker at the conference the committee organized.) At its first meeting, the committee voted to recommend to the BBC that the Alabama state bar sponsor a conference, whose purpose was to bring together a group of Alabama civic leaders from all walks of life to study the state judicial system and consider changes that needed to be made. The BBC accepted the recommendation and allocated funds to underwrite the conference. The American Judicature Society, which had participated in similar conferences in approximately 20 other states, also pledged its help and financial support.

The conference, called the "Citizens' Conference on Alabama State Courts," was scheduled for December 3, 4, and 5, 1966, in the Jefferson Davis Hotel in Montgomery. Douglas Arant of Birmingham, state bar president from 1936 to 1937, although not a committee member, was asked to chair a subcommittee to select those citizens to be invited, a step all believed to be of critical importance. Others of the Heflin-appointed committees dealing with judicial issues coordinated their efforts with the Citizens' Judicial Conference committee

Howell Heflin poses in the voting booth prior to casting his vote for the new judicial article to the Alabama constitution, overwhelmingly approved by voters in 1973. In many ways, the vote was the culmination of the reform efforts Heflin had set in motion as president of the Alabama State Bar in the 1960s.

because all knew that its success was crucial to the goal of bringing about judicial reform.

At the conference, during which expert speakers had addressed the latest thinking about judicial reform, reporters were assigned to each of four groups of conferees to draft a consensus statement which was adopted at the end of the conference proceeding. The reporters were Julian D. Butler of Huntsville, Lister Hill, Jr., of Montgomery, Bert S. Nettles of Mobile, and Clarence M. Small, Jr., of Birmingham (state bar president, 1992-1993). A Liaison Committee from the bar was appointed by 1966-1967 bar president Robert E. Steiner, III, to work with a steering committee appointed by the conferees to do follow-up work to get their suggestions adopted by the legislature. That Liaison Committee included Douglas Arant; Roland Nachman; Robert McD. Smith; Howell T. Heflin; C. C. "Bo" Torbert, Jr.; Robert T. Cunningham; and Jack Giles.

A meeting of these two groups in February 1967, resulted in the incorporation of the Citizens' Conference on Alabama State Courts, with the conference attendees being charter members and a group being selected by the steering committee to serve as an executive committee, in order to have an entity which could carry on citizen efforts to bring about judicial reform. Roland Nachman was given the duty of doing the legal work involved in its incorporation and tax qualification. The members of the Liaison Committee, with the addition of James J. Carter, Jacob A. Walker, Jr., and Bert Nettles, were assigned the task of drafting legislation and constitutional amendments necessary to effect the recommendations of the conference. Their work was approved by the BBC by resolution adopted on July 22, 1967. By September 1969, in response to the activities of the bar and the Citizens' Conference, the state legislature, at Governor Brewer's urging, created a joint house-senate constitution revision commission called the Alabama Constitutional Commission, with Howell Heflin's former Marine commander,

Conrad Fowler, as its chairman. The commission had 21 members, including the senate president, the speaker of the house, three designees of the speaker, two designees of the senate president, and 14 members appointed by the governor. These commission members, with Dean M. Leigh Harrison serving as reporter, worked diligently to draft a new constitution for the state, including a new judicial article.

In 1972, state bar secretary Reginald Hamner submitted an account of the state bar's accomplishments from 1971 to 1972, under the presidencies of Truman Hobbs and Robert B. Albritton, as an entry in the 1972 American Bar Association Award of Merit competition, which was awarded to the Alabama State Bar that year. In his report, he called 1971 "the year of the legislature." President Robert B. Albritton in his farewell remarks summarized the legislative accomplishments toward the goal of "comprehensive judicial reform" of that year, which included: 1. Vesting rule-making power in the Supreme Court of Alabama as to civil procedure in the trial courts as well as procedure in the appellate courts; 2. Creating a department of court management; 3. Allowing the retirement of judges at age 70 without losing the benefit of their services in a supernumerary capacity; 4. Expanding membership on the Court of Criminal Appeals together with a case transfer measure to control an ever-increasing appeals docket and a measure to expedite the submission of appellate cases; and 5. Two acts enabling a public vote on constitutional amendments to abolish the office of Justice of the Peace and create a Judicial Commission.

Howell Heflin was elected chief justice of the Alabama Supreme Court in 1971, the first chief justice elected by the popular vote without having first been appointed to the court. He served one term on the court before being elected to the U.S. Senate in 1978. As one of the most influential members of the Senate Judiciary Committee, he voted against the controversial nominations of Robert Bork, Clarence Thomas, and Jeff Sessions.

Both amendments were adopted by an overwhelming vote of the electorate.

In 1971, Howell T. Heflin was elected chief justice of the Alabama Supreme Court (after having served as chairman of the newly created Alabama Ethics Commission). He continued efforts to bring about judicial reform, primarily aimed at educating the public about the great need to improve the court system. He also used the piecemeal powers that had already been granted by the legislature and the people to make improvements where he could. His efforts were rewarded, through the work of the bar, the Citizens' Conference (which held a Second Citizens' Judicial Conference in April 1973), and the Constitutional Commission, with the passage by a vote of the people of a new Judicial Article to the 1901 Constitution in December 1973. One of the outstanding features of the new Judicial Article was the creation of a unified court system, through the establishment of a new lower court called the "district court" which replaced all of the special courts that had previously lacked any uniformity of jurisdiction or procedure. The Alabama Supreme Court was given rule-making authority governing the administration, the practice, and the procedures in all courts within the state, thereby extending rule-making to the criminal arena. A Judicial Inquiry Commission and Court of the Judiciary replaced the judicial commission previously created, to separate the investigative and trial functions when a judge was being tried for ethical violations or judicial misconduct.[8]

THE "TEN COMMANDMENTS" JUDGE AND THE COURT OF THE JUDICIARY

Roy Moore was a circuit judge in Etowah County who made a wooden plaque of the Ten Commandments and displayed it in his courtroom in 1997. Both the governor, Fob James, and the attorney general, Bill Pryor, supported him when his conduct was challenged by the Alabama Civil Liberties Union on the issue of separation of church and state. Subsequently, Moore parlayed this controversy into a victory in a race for the position of chief justice in 2001, calling himself the "Ten Commandments" judge. Upon his election, he had a two-and-one-half-ton stone monument engraved with the Ten Commandments and took it upon himself to have the monument placed in the rotunda of the Supreme Court Building.

Former chief justice of the Alabama Supreme Court Roy Moore made use of his notoriety to make an unsuccessful run for the Republican nomination for governor in 2006.

He and the state were subsequently sued to have the monument removed, as a violation of the separation of church and state. Not unexpectedly, federal district judge Myron Thompson ordered the monument removed. Moore refused, calling for demonstrations of support and generating national media coverage.

When Judge Thompson ordered the state to pay a penalty of $5,000 each day that the monument remained, the eight other justices, acting under the leadership of senior justice Gorman Houston who served as interim chief justice during the period of Moore's suspension and removal from office, voted to have the monument removed, on the basis that they had a duty to comply with a federal court order. Their decision was supported by Attorney General Pryor and Governor Bob Riley, both citing the supremacy of federal constitutional requirements over personal principle, and the monument was removed.

Moore was suspended by the Judicial Inquiry Commission pending a trial on charges that he violated six ethical standards of the Code of Judicial Ethics. The trial resulted in the order for his removal from office. He appealed this decision, whereupon all members of the Supreme Court recused themselves and the governor appointed seven special judges to hear the appeal, including judges Harry J. Wilters, Jr.; Braxton Kittrell; Janie L. Shores; J. Richmond Pearson; John M. Patterson; Edward Dwight Fay, Jr.; and Kenneth Ingram. These judges upheld the order of the Court of the Judiciary in 2005. Governor Bob Riley then named Drayton Nabers, who had been serving as state finance director (after many years of service as an executive of Protective Life Insurance Company) to complete Moore's term as chief justice. The institutional structure of the Judicial Inquiry Commission and the Court of the Judiciary, with its appointed membership and its appeals procedure, was able to depoliticize the removal of the chief justice in highly political circumstances.

CHAPTER NINETEEN

EXPANSION OF THE ROLE OF THE ALABAMA STATE BAR IN SERVICE TO ITS MEMBERS AND THE PUBLIC

When William B. Hairston, Jr., of Birmingham became president of the state bar in July 1983, he had already proven himself a committed bar leader through many years of active service as a bar commissioner, having assumed representation of the Tenth Judicial Circuit in 1973 from Walter L. Mims. At the February 1983 meeting of the Board of Bar Commissioners (BBC), the commission acted on several proposals made by Hairston to go into effect prior to his assuming office. Hairston had reviewed the committee structure of the bar and asked the commission to actively reaffirm those to which he intended to appoint members, to create new standing committees, and to authorize the task forces for the year of his presidency. As part of this request, he requested authorization to appoint committee membership prior to the bar's annual convention and to have the committees meet at a special breakfast held in connection with the convention, with committee chairmen to be recognized by "appropriate identification on the convention badges" and to authorize a mid-winter meeting in Montgomery as well.

In taking these steps, Hairston took a cue from the presidency of Howell Heflin and effectively set the agenda of the bar for the next 25 years. The BBC reaffirmed 24 standing committees (many of which continued the reforms begun during the Heflin presidency), established 11 new standing committees, and authorized 12 presidential task forces. Selected task forces and committees show some of the important issues which confronted the state bar in the last years of the twentieth century:

(1) Task force on judicial evaluation, election and selection (Hugh Nash of Oneonta, chairman); (2) Task force to evaluate the lawyer explosion in Alabama and its effect on the practice of law (Ernest Potter of Huntsville, chairman); (3) Task force to evaluate the place of lawyer advertising and solicitation in Alabama (Wade Baxley of Dothan, chairman); (4) Task force on legal services to the poor (Hollis Geer Swift of Birmingham, chairman); (5) Task Force on lawyer alcohol and drug abuse (Judge Val McGee of

When William B. Hairston, Jr., seen here at a University of Alabama School of Law function, assumed the presidency of the Alabama State Bar in 1983, he had already gained authorization for 11 new committees and 12 presidential task forces.

Ozark, chairman); (6) Task force on a client security fund for the state bar (James Ward of Birmingham, chairman); (7) Task force on the disciplinary function of the state bar (William B. Matthews, chairman); and (8) Indigent Defense Committee (Dennis Balske, chairman).

While he was president, Hairston also announced that the Birmingham Bar intended to seek reapportionment of the BBC. In response, president-elect Walter Byars requested approval to establish a committee to review the whole question of bar governance. Gary Huckaby of Huntsville (state bar president, 1988-1989) chaired this committee, which considered not only the composition of the BBC, but also the election of officers and its governance structure vis-a-vis judicial authority over the operations of the state bar.

From this committee's recommendations, the BBC approved a plan that each judicial circuit would have at least one commissioner, while those circuits with more than 300 members would have one commissioner for each increment of 300 members, up to a maximum of ten. Further, the Bessemer "cutoff" in Jefferson County would have its own commissioner. No commissioner would serve more than three consecutive terms. The election of the president-elect would be by mail ballot, with a candidate nominating petition with 25 names on it to be filed by March 15. A picture and biographical sketch would appear in *The Alabama Lawyer* prior to the ballot being sent out. The board also approved seeking passage of legislation to put supervision of the state bar wholly under the Alabama Supreme Court, removing supervision by the legislature. This plan went into effect in 1987, with expanded representation for urban areas such as Birmingham, Mobile, Montgomery, Tuscaloosa, Huntsville, and Gadsden and with sole supervision by the Alabama Supreme Court.

HIGHLIGHTING SUPERIOR BAR LEADERS

THERE HAVE BEEN SEVERAL important leaders of the Board of Bar Commissioners (BBC) who never served as president, but whose presence as commissioners had an important impact. One such leader is Richard S. Manley of Demopolis, who served as Bill Hairston's vice president and ran unsuccessfully for president-elect in 1984. Although he never served as president of the bar, he served as vice president and on the bar executive committee many times, on a variety of important committees, and was a commissioner for more than 20 years. He received an Award of Merit in 1988 for his many years of service to the bar and to the legislature, the award being given specifically for outstanding legislative services to the profession and the judiciary.

Attorney and legislator Richard S. Manley served on the BBC and as vice president of the Alabama State Bar. He received an Award of Merit in 1988.

Oliver W. "Pi" Brantley of Troy was another commissioner with long, distinguished service on the board, having served for 27 years when he was replaced in 1979 by Joe C. Cassady, who received an Award of Merit in 1991 for his length of service and membership on the Disciplinary Commission. Brantley and Charles A. Poellnitz of Florence, another influential commissioner, were the first commissioners to serve on the Judicial Inquiry Commission when it was created in 1974. Jacob Walker, Jr., of Opelika, whose father served the state bar as president from 1942 to 1943, was another servant of the bar with an outstanding record who many considered worthy of the presidency. Walter Crownover of Tuscaloosa was on the BBC for many years in various capacities, including the executive committee, while Hugh A. Nash chaired an important committee during the 1970s to evaluate the disciplinary function of the bar and was on the first three-member Disciplinary Commission in 1978.

Patrick H. Graves of Huntsville proposed several worthy ideas during his tenure on the commission during the 1990s and was awarded the Walter P. Gewin CLE Award in 1986. Sam Franklin of Birmingham was elected to the BBC in 1991 and provided substantial leadership during the 1990s, as did John Earle Chason of Bay Minette. These are a few examples of the many well-known and highly regarded members of the BBC throughout the years.

Merit Selection of Judges

The Alabama State Bar continues to support improvement of the process of selecting judges and has consistently promoted the nonpolitical merit selection of judges with elections to affect retention only. It even sponsored a Third Citizens Conference on Alabama State Courts to study the selection of judges and judicial campaign financing during the presidency of Broox G. Holmes (1994-1995).

The idea of merit selection did not catch the imagination of the legislature or the general populace sufficiently to bring about change as part of the judicial reform movement, even though it was proposed. At the time that the

Judicial Article was being considered, Alabama was becoming a two-party state and judicial offices began to be contested and won by Republicans, who rejected the idea of merit selection as a possible ploy to defeat their success at the polls.

Over the course of time, judicial races became the arena of great Republican success. With this success, though, Alabama judicial races have also included some that were negative, controversial, and expensive. The changing political climate resulted, in 2009, in eight of the nine Supreme Court justices and all of the other appellate judges being Republican. Only the chief justice, Sue Bell Cobb, is a Democrat. In spite of the negativity, controversy, and expense (and the fact that contributions are often described by the general populace as attempts by special interests to purchase influence), party-based elections are still the preferred method of judicial selection. Bar leaders continue to promote removing the selection process from the political arena. This subject received particular emphasis during the presidencies of William N. Clark, Douglas McElvy, Robert Segall, and Fournier J. Gale. A special task force headed by retired Justice Gorman Houston has worked to keep the issue before the public and its leaders.

The first full-time secretary of the Alabama State Bar, Judge John B. Scott, left, retired in 1969 from the post he had held for almost 20 years. He was succeeded by Reginald T. Hamner, right, who would hold the job for 25 years.

Expansion and Diversification of the Bar

In 1969, bar secretary John B. Scott retired to become Reporter of Decisions for the Alabama Appellate Courts. His successor was Reginald T. "Reggie" Hamner, admitted to the bar in 1965, who had served as law clerk to Justice Pelham Merrill in 1965 and would serve as secretary of the state bar until 1994. At the time Reggie Hamner was selected, William H. Morrow, Jr., was general counsel and advisor to the Grievance Committee. Hamner and Morrow proved to be excellent choices, as evidenced by resolutions passed in February 1970 commending them both for their excellent performance and diligence in carrying out their duties.[1]

John Scott, after leaving his bar post, could look down from his office in the Supreme Court building and observe the state bar headquarters next door. His observations became reflections and his reflections became poetry. One of his poems, titled "A Glum Look Into the Future,"[2] captures the beginnings of a seventies trend and the profession's reaction to it:

Lawyers now multiply like mice
Their numbers are so increasing
Soon every layman can have two
To advise him without ceasing.

CHANGING PERSONNEL ON THE ALABAMA APPELLATE COURTS

In 1963, the Supreme Court's seven justices included Chief Justice J. Ed Livingston, who had served on the court since 1940 (and who left the court upon the investiture of Howell Heflin in 1971); Justice James S. Coleman (1957-1975); Justice John Goodwyn, who came to the court in 1951 and served until his death in 1968 (when James N. Bloodworth was appointed to serve out his term); Thomas S. Lawson (1942-1973); Pelham J. Merrill (1953-1976); Robert T. Simpson, (1944-1973); and Robert B. Harwood (1962-1975). Justices Hugh Maddox and Daniel T. McCall, Jr., were appointed to the court by Governor Albert P. Brewer in 1969, when it was expanded to nine members.[3]

A decorated veteran of World War II, James F. Faulkner received his law degree from the University of Alabama in 1949. He became an associate justice of the Alabama Supreme Court in 1972, remaining on the bench until 1986.

In 1963, the Alabama Court of Appeals was comprised of Presiding Judge Annie Lola Price, Judge Aubrey Cates, and Judge George C. Johnson. This court was converted to the Court of Criminal Appeals in 1970 and later expanded to five members. A newly constituted Court of Civil Appeals began service in 1970, with T. Werth Thagard named presiding judge, and L. Charles Wright and Robert P. Bradley named as judges. This court was also later expanded to five members.

By 1975, the Alabama Supreme Court acquired five new members, as the older justices began to retire, including Justices James H. Faulkner, Janie L. Shores, Richard L. Jones, Reneau P. Almon, and T. Eric Embry, while retaining Justices Heflin, Maddox, Merrill, and Bloodworth. Justice Merrill retired on May 31, 1976, and was replaced by Justice Samuel A. Beatty, previously a professor at the University of Alabama Law School and Dean of the Walter F. George School of Law at Mercer University. This court was the first to have a perceptible plaintiff orientation at a time when the law of torts and concepts such as bad faith and punitive damages as well as expansion of class action lawsuits under the new Rules of Civil Procedures were trends in the law. For a period, Alabama became known for large jury verdicts (including punitive damages) in personal injury lawsuits and for forum shopping to maximize these verdicts.

Howell Heflin left the court in 1977 and C. C. "Bo" Torbert was elected chief justice. As a member of the state senate, Torbert led the 1975 effort to pass the legislative package prepared by a 55-member Judicial Article Implementation Commission appointed by Heflin and chaired by attorney Joseph F. Johnston of Birmingham. The commission had studied every preexisting statute on the subject of the court system in the Alabama Code to ensure conformance with the new Judicial Article or to recommend changes to guarantee conformance. Torbert carried on the court's leadership in implementing all changes required by the Judicial Article when Heflin left the court and was elected to the United States Senate in 1978. Torbert served two terms, until 1989, and was followed by Ernest C. "Sonny" Hornsby (who served as state bar president in 1977, when Torbert first became chief justice).

Hornsby was active in the Alabama Trial Lawyers Association during a period when tort reform had become a major issue and the court was seen as unduly proplaintiff. When he ran for reelection, the Alabama Business Council hired Republican political consultant Karl Rove to help them get probusiness Republicans elected to the appellate courts. Republican Perry Hooper and Democrat Hornsby clashed in a hard-fought election that ended up in the courts and was resolved in Hooper's favor by the U.S. Supreme Court more than a year after the election. Harold See likewise used Rove's help in his win against incumbent Democrat Kenneth Ingram in 1996. Thereafter, Republicans began to dominate the Alabama appellate courts, with a probusiness stance.

Justice Bloodworth died in 1980 and Oscar Adams, Jr., the court's first black justice, was appointed by Governor Fob James, then elected for a full term in 1982, serving until 1993. He was replaced by African-American Ralph

ABOVE: *John H. England, Jr., was appointed to the Alabama Supreme Court by Governor Don Siegleman in 1999.* BELOW LEFT: *Perry O. Hooper, Sr., a Republican, was elected chief justice of the court in 1995.*

D. Cook, appointed by Governor Jim Folsom, who served until 2000, when he and John England, another black lawyer who was appointed to the court in 1999 by Governor Don Siegelman, were swept out of office as Republicans extended their success at the polls. One Democrat who won in 2006 was Sue Bell Cobb, elected the first female chief justice, after serving on the Court of Criminal Appeals from 1995 to 2007. She joined two other female justices on the court, Lyn Stewart (2001 to present) and Patricia Smith (2005 to present). Jean W. Brown had also served on the court from 1999 to 2005, after having served on the five-member Court of Criminal Appeals from 1997 to 1998. Pamela W. Baschab (1997 to present) and Alisa Kelly Wise (2001 to present) also serve on the criminal appeals court. On the five-member Court of Civil Appeals, Judge Sharon Yates served from 1993 to 2005, when she sought election to the Alabama Supreme Court and lost. Terri W. Thomas was elected in 2007. Their presence on the appellate courts could be deemed the successful arrival of the expanding corps of female attorneys to the heights of the profession.

A TREND TO CLUSTER INTO SPECIALTY GROUPS

With so many areas in which one could develop one's practice, and with the membership of the bar rapidly expanding, a trend began to develop of lawyers identifying with independent specialty bar groups and disassociating themselves from the Alabama State Bar except as required for regulatory purposes. The result was a problematic segmentation of the bar and a loss of collegiality and professional respect. In some instances, particularly where groups represented different client interests, adversarial posturing became prevalent. Still, this group identification also symbolized vibrancy within the bar, and much of the group identification now is with the 22 practice sections of the state bar itself, which members look to for relevant continuing legal education and networking with peers having similar practices. The establishment of sections had been proposed by Douglas Lansford, director of CLE, in late 1961 as a means to promote pertinent educational programming. He was authorized to "develop ways and means of creating sections." The first section to be created was the Section on Taxation, in May 1962. In 1963, a resolution was approved which authorized the bar president to instigate the creation of sections, which not only promoted specialized educational opportunities, but also provided a resource for promoting legislative change. During his presidency, President Hairston established committees to work on sections for Family Law, Bankruptcy Law, Military Law, Energy Law, and a task force on the establishment of a litigation section.

Under presidents Broox Holmes (1994-1995); John Owens (1995-1996); Warren Lightfoot (1996-1997); and Dag Rowe (1997-1998), the state bar began a concerted effort to exert itself in the role of being the official umbrella organization of the profession, serving all lawyers where common interests could be emphasized. These presidents, as well as presidents Vic Lott, Wade Baxley, and various other presidents, held summit meetings of the various independent groups to promote collegiality, beginning with the first Bench and Bar conference sponsored by the bar in 1995 as a "summit on the profession." President Sam Rumore's administration (2000-2001) developed a Pledge of Professionalism, drafted by Pat Graves of Huntsville, which promoted collegiality and civility among all lawyers, emphasizing professionalism over self-interest.

Strange new cases we soon will see
Finding their way to the docket
We'll sue the barber for falling hair
To put something in our pocket.

Lawyers will no more ask the hours
When seeking their employment
Or mention any extra benefits
To add to their enjoyment.

Near four hundred lawyers every year
Do come to this state's profession
This fact alone should tend to prove
The bar is headed for depression.

So fawn on your judge with respect
Yea, do treat him like a caliph
If fortune smiles you have hope
He'll appoint you as his bailiff.

In the January 1980 edition of *The Alabama Lawyer*, a report on the first demographic survey of lawyers undertaken since 1965 was published by William M. Kimmelman, Ph.D., a UAB professor and member of the Survey Research Center. It was funded by the state bar under the auspices of its Committee on the Future of the Profession. The survey was conducted in 1978, being sent to each of the 4,588 lawyers licensed to practice law at that time (up from 2,700 in 1965, an increase of approximately

A prime example of the state bar's role of impartiality, made essential by the fact that it is an integrated bar which requires all lawyers to be members, was demonstrated during the late 1980s when tort reform was a controversial political issue in which members of the plaintiff and defense trial bars had competing interests. The state bar was able to play the role of mediator, working out a compromise between the plaintiff and defense bar groups and the interests of their various clients. President William D. Scruggs, Jr., was instrumental in this effort, giving his time to analyze each bill of the proposed civil justice reform measures and determine the impact it would have on existing statutes and case law.

Upon presenting this study to the Board of Bar Commissioners, he was authorized to speak to the state senate committee considering the legislation on behalf of the bar, and his thoughtful and impartial testimony to the committee is remembered as the turning point of the legislative debate, which up to that time might have been described as irrational. Scruggs, from Fort Payne, Alabama, was a small town general practitioner with years of service to the bar. He was also recognized as one of the state's finest trial lawyers, having been elected to the selective American College of Trial Lawyers in recognition of his courtroom talents. His years of consistent service to the bar had made him well known and well liked. As a consequence of his presentation and because of the esteem in which he was held by both the plaintiff and defense bars, he, together with the drafting assistance of Champ Lyons, Jr., and legislative assistance from commissioner/legislator Richard Manley, was able to rewrite a significant portion of the original legislation to address impartially the interests of all parties involved. The state bar as an institution was able to speak to the issues of the parties from the perspective of what was best for the state and what proposals most reasonably worked within the framework of the state's legal system, thereby promoting acceptable compromise. Bar secretary Reggie Hamner, in a tribute to Scruggs shortly after his death at the age of 58 in 2001, described this episode as one of the Alabama State Bar's greatest successes, primarily because it demonstrated that the bar as an institution was not a "special interest" group.[4]

During his term as president of the state bar from 1986 to 1987, William D. Scruggs, Jr., played an important role in mediating between the opposing sides on the issue of tort reform.

sixty percent.) The report noted that from 1960 to 1978 there had been a seventy-eight percent increase in bar membership. Judge Scott's poem reflected reality.

The report showed that lawyers continued to cluster in the urban centers of Jefferson (1,495), Montgomery (581), Mobile (538), Madison (223), and Tuscaloosa (202), making up approximately sixty-six per cent of the bar. Seventy percent of Alabama's lawyers were in private practice and forty-one percent of those had less than five years' experience (reflecting the bar's rapid growth.) Most practiced solo (23.3 percent) or in firms of six or less (51.8 percent), although a fairly large number of lawyers in Jefferson and Mobile counties practiced in firms with more than 30 lawyers (in Birmingham) or 20 lawyers (in Mobile).

Insurance, negligence, and compensation law, plaintiff (19.8 percent) or defendant (13.1 percent), were dominant fields of concentration in 1978 with real property law (19.3 percent) and corporation, banking, and business law (13.1 percent) also competing for first in producing "highest source of income." Domestic law, estate planning, and probate law were other areas which lawyers listed as first, second, or third highest sources of income. Nineteen possible areas of practice were listed in the survey, including administrative, bankruptcy, criminal, labor, municipal, taxation, and mineral, water and natural resources law along with such specialties as antitrust, government contracts, patent, trademark and copyright, public utility, securities, and environmental law.

In the 1978 survey, there was no discussion of diversity, since women and African Americans remained a small percentage of the bar's population. It is worthy to note that 1975 marked the first entering class for a law school established in Birmingham at predominantly black Miles College, which joined Cumberland Law School (which began its Birmingham operations in 1961); Birmingham School of Law (which dated back to 1915); and Jones Law School in Montgomery (which dated back to 1927) as in-state private law schools. The University of Alabama School of Law was still the school of choice for the majority of Alabama's would-be lawyers. (Only Alabama and Cumberland law schools were accredited at the time.) It celebrated the opening of a new building in 1978 and also saw a growing trend in the number of women applicants matriculating and graduating from the school, as did the other schools.

Expansion of the number of black students would be slower, although Cumberland quietly admitted its first black student, Audrey Gaston, in 1966. In 1970, she became the first black student to graduate from an Alabama law school. African Americans Michael Figures and Booker Forte graduated from the University of Alabama Law School in 1972, Donald Watkins in 1973, and John England in 1974 as the first group of black male graduates. Sarah "Sue" Thompson became its first black female graduate in 1974.

In July 1983, Fred Gray became the first African-American member of the BBC, soon followed by J. Mason Davis, who had served as the first black president of the Birmingham Bar Association in 1985. African Americans Ernestine Sapp of Tuskegee and Anthony Joseph of Birmingham also served on the board before its membership was expanded to promote more diversity. A year after Gray, Lynn Robertson Jackson became the first woman elected to the board. Those who followed her before the membership expansion included Wanda Devereaux of Montgomery; Cathy Wright of Birmingham; Cecelia Collins of Mobile; Donna Pate of Huntsville; Carol H. Stewart of Birmingham; Alyce M. Spruell of Tuscaloosa; and Maibeth Porter of Birmingham.

In 2002, Gray was the first African American to be elected president of the Alabama State Bar. Several women, including Lynn Robertson Jackson, Carol Ann Smith, and Carol H. Stewart, sought this honor over the years. During his 2007 to 2008 term, president Sam Cosby selected Alicia Bennett as the first black female to serve as vice president of the state bar. In 2009, as this book was preparing for publication, Alyce Manley Spruell of Tuscaloosa became the first female president-elect when she qualified for the position without opposition. She is now in line to become the first woman to be president of the Alabama State Bar.

At the same time Fred Gray was president of the state bar in 2002, Judge Charles Price was serving as the first African American to head the Alabama Circuit Judges Association and Tyrone C. Means completed his term as the first African-American president

TOP: *Donald Watkins, in 1973, was among the first black students to graduate from the University of Alabama School of Law.* ABOVE: *J. Mason Davis was the first black president of the Birmingham Bar Association. He also served on the BBC.*

JANIE LEDLOW SHORES

Janie Shores was born on a farm outside a small town in Butler County, Alabama, in 1932, where she worked in the strawberry fields at age five. Her family moved to Loxley in Baldwin County when her father found employment in Mobile after the beginning of World War II. She worked in the potato fields there to earn money to buy school clothes. At Robertsdale High School, she developed excellent shorthand and typing skills and, after high school, got a secretarial job with an outstanding Mobile attorney, Vince Kilborn, Sr., who soon became her mentor, recommending that she go to college and law school and earn her law degree. Shores often gave credit to Kilborn for changing her life by his encouragement and help.

Shores went to the University of Alabama Law School, one of five female students at the time. As well as being an excellent student, she also served as editor of the *Alabama Law Review* and won the Phi Alpha Delta Moot Court Competition Award. Because of her shorthand and transcribing skills, her lecture notes and case summaries created such a demand by other students that they were soon put in marketable form and sold at a bookstore, where they became the store's bestseller in the legal realm for a number of years.

Janie L. Shores was elected to the Alabama Supreme Court in 1974, the first woman to serve on the state's highest court.

After graduation in 1959, she served as law clerk for Justice Robert T. Simpson (who also had previously employed 1953 graduate Marge Sparks (Fullan) as his clerk), practiced for a short time in Selma, worked in the law department of Liberty National Life Insurance Company in Birmingham, then became a member of the faculty of Cumberland Law School, the first female law school teacher in the state. She was an excellent law professor and legal scholar and was honored when the moot court competition began to bear her name. She was active in the work and the campaign to adopt a new judicial article, and, with substantial encouragement by a large number of lawyers, she offered herself as a candidate for the Alabama Supreme Court in 1974, winning overwhelmingly. She served on the court for 24 years, as its first female justice and as the third in the nation of a state's highest court. There are 1,362 opinions that bear her name. Because of her willingness to work hard, she also wrote opinions for other justices when necessary to help the court stay current as its terms ended. She proved such an excellent jurist that she was put on the short list of jurists considered to fill the position on the Supreme Court of the United States to which Ruth Bader Ginsburg was ultimately nominated by President Clinton in 1993.

of the Alabama Trial Lawyers Association. Throughout this period, black lawyers in Alabama actively supported the Alabama chapter of the National Bar Association as well.

By 1986, a survey similar to the one in 1978 reported that approximately eleven percent of the bar was female, while one percent was African American. In 1986, the median age of attorneys was 38 and the median income was $55,000. Seventy-two percent of the members were in private practice and the average hourly rate was $75.

In 1998, *The Alabama Lawyer* reported on a new survey that showed that close to twenty percent of the bar was female and three percent African American. Fifty-seven percent of Alabama lawyers were 41 years or older. Median income was between $70,000 and $90,000. Seventy-five percent had access to the Internet and seventy-seven percent used computerized legal research. The average hourly rate was $129. Bar membership had reached approximately 12,000. By 2006, the makeup of the bar was twenty-eight percent female and 5.6 percent African American and its total membership was nearing 15,000.

In 1999, the BBC approved the creation of a Women's Law Section. In 2002, the section created the Maud McLure Kelly Award to honor outstanding women lawyers in the state. The first recipient of the award, named after the first woman to practice law in Alabama, was former Justice Janie Shores. The award is given annually at a luncheon during the state bar convention. Other recipients include Alice Finch Lee; Nina Miglionico; Judge Phyllis Nesbit; Mahala Ashley Dickerson; Camille Wright Cook; Louise Turner; Jane Dishuck; and Frankie Fields Smith. In 2006, the Women's Section and the Alabama Law Foundation established the Justice Janie L. Shores Scholarship for one or more female residents of Alabama attending an Alabama law school.

TOP: *Tuscaloosa attorney Alyce Manley Spruell is set to became the first female president of the state bar in 2010.* ABOVE: *Camille W. Cook, the first female tenured professor at the University of Alabama School of Law, was the 2007 recipient of the Maud McLure Kelly Award.*

THE ALABAMA STATE BAR'S EXPANDING ROLE OF SERVICE TO ITS MEMBERS

Since its founding, the bar association has given its members opportunities for networking and continuing education. In 1923, it became the second bar in the country to be integrated into state government as the regulatory agency of the state to license and discipline the profession, under the supervision of the state supreme court and the legislature. Membership in the state bar became mandatory for attorneys practicing before the courts in the state and the bar became responsible for establishing and policing the qualifications of its members as well as disciplining them for violations of ethics and professional misconduct.

Over the years, the state bar also began providing benefits and services to its members. With the founding of its professional publication and law institutes in 1940, it provided a reliable source of continuing professional training and information for and about its membership. In 1949, under president Francis Hare of

Birmingham, its first group insurance plan was made available to bar members. In 1967, it entered a relationship with Insurance Specialists, Inc., of Atlanta, Georgia, to serve as its agent in the group insurance arena, a relationship which continues to exist. In 1959, under president Walter P. Gewin, its Alabama Bar Institute for Continuing Legal Education became a formal program of the bar.

In 1962, Alabama joined 13 other states when the state legislature passed the Professional Association statute at the bar's urging. This type of organization gave lawyers the same tax advantages enjoyed by business corporations without offending ethical prohibitions against incorporation, which was seen as a possible means of avoiding liability for professional misconduct. In 1973, president L. Drew Redden of Birmingham saw that a WATS line was installed at state bar headquarters to make statewide communication with members more convenient.

Norborne Stone, as president of the Alabama State Bar, provided the first cover subject for The Alabama Lawyer *when it changed its format from a journal to a glossy magazine in 1983.*

George Azar. Another topic which began to be discussed during this period was a program under which a lawyer could certify a specialty.

During the presidency of Norborne Stone (1982-1983) of Bay Minette, the BBC changed the format of *The Alabama Lawyer* from a journal to a magazine and authorized its publication six times a year, upon the recommendation of the Publication Committee chaired by J. Mark White of Birmingham (state bar president, 2006-2007). Stone began a tradition by being pictured on the cover of the *Lawyer* when his presidency began. William B. Hairston included his wife in his picture and soon new presidents appeared with their families. In 1984, the first bar directory edition of *The Alabama Lawyer* was published (an idea first put forward by Ernest C. Hornsby while he was president from 1977 to 1978). The last printed edition was the 2004-2005 directory.

In 1978, during the presidency of Ernest C. "Sonny" Hornsby, the bar established its Lawyer Referral Service, an effort led by a committee chaired by Ralph D. Gaines of Talladega. (In 2002, the referral service was added to the bar's website, so that online referrals could be made.) Also in 1978, lawyer Joe Carpenter of Montgomery served as the bar's first legislative analyst to represent member interests to the legislature and to report on legislation of interest to lawyers. His first assignment was to aid the Practice and Procedure Section in undertaking the passage of reforms to Alabama's jury selection laws. His efforts were successful when reform legislation was passed which eliminated any systematic exclusion of particular groups from jury rolls. A Legislative Steering Committee was appointed to assist him, whose membership included Joe C. Espy; Reginald T. Hamner; W. Mike House; Floyd Minor; Randolph P. Reaves; Perry Roquemore; and

Thereafter, the directory of state bar members was maintained on the bar's official internet website, which was created in 1996. Use of the website has grown exponentially from year to year since its founding. The most commonly accessed pages are the list of members online, the CLE calendar, bar exam results, Office of General Counsel opinions, admissions, the extensive materials of the Practice Management Assistance Program, the Alabama Center for Dispute Resolution, a divorce brochure published on the site, and the Lawyer Referral service.

In 1985, E.T. Brown, Jr. (state bar president, 1980-1981) and Roy Crawford, both of Birmingham, undertook the legal work to create the IOLTA (Interest On Lawyer Trust Accounts) program, an idea proposed by Norborne Stone during his presidency. Under this program, interest could be earned on lawyer trust accounts for the benefit of a bar-sponsored foundation, the Alabama Law Foundation,

and used for charitable purposes, since attorneys could not ethically earn interest on client funds. Rowena Crocker of Birmingham received an Award of Merit in 1987 for her work chairing the committee which recommended the IOLTA plan. In 1987, it was adopted by the Alabama Supreme Court. As originally adopted, it was a voluntary program but later participation became mandatory and the bar worked actively with various banks to maximize the interest paid on lawyer trust account funds. The Alabama Law Foundation, with its director Tracy Daniels, became an important charitable arm of the bar, with a fellows program and a society, known as the Atticus Finch Society, for fundraising, to compensate for the loss of funding when interest rates were low. By 2008, the Law Foundation had awarded millions of dollars in charitable grants.

In 1985, during the presidency of James L. North of Birmingham, the state bar followed the recommendations of a committee chaired by Harold L. Speake of Moulton and hired an office automation consultant, then purchased its first computers and began computerizing all its records in 1986. The Professional Economics Committee, headed by David Arendall of Birmingham, proposed that the bar find a consultant it could recommend to its membership to help them with the economic aspects of practice, particularly with automation, word processing equipment, and filing systems. A consultant was found, but the ultimate goal was to have a program run by the state bar itself. In 1997, the bar hired attorney Laura Calloway to direct a new program entitled the Practice Management Assistance Program. Its purpose was to help attorneys, especially in small and solo practices, to operate their offices in a businesslike and efficient way, assisting with computerization, case management, timekeeping, scheduling, billing, accounting, docketing, time management, filing systems, and other management issues.

The addition to the Alabama State Bar headquarters building, begun in 1990, was completed in stages as the need for space increased, until the entire building was completed in 2008.

Under President William D. Scruggs, Jr., of Fort Payne, the bar began studying the feasibility of starting a captive professional liability company, in the face of the fact that the state suffered from the lack of a reliable professional liability insurance market. This study was guided by Henry Henzel of Birmingham and resulted in the creation of Attorneys' Insurance Mutual of Alabama in 1988. Scruggs served as chairman of the board of the new company, while Henry Henzel served as president and vice chairman of the board. Other officers included Cathy S. Wright, vice president; Charles H. Moses, III, secretary; and Reginald Hamner, treasurer. Efforts to capitalize it began in July 1988. By late spring of 1989, it reached its goal of $2 million in capital and began writing policies, writing more than $1 million in premiums in less than a year.

Mail ballots for electing the president-elect began in 1989. The new method expanded participation in the election process and immediately resulted in a shift to a younger generation of leaders, lawyers who graduated during the 1960s and 1970s (although the first such president, James L. North, admitted in 1965, was in office when the change came about.)[5] The legislation authorizing the change also expanded the number of bar commissioners, to give greater representation to the urban areas where large numbers of lawyers practiced. Much of the work on this effort took place during the presidency of Walter Byars of Montgomery (1984-1985). Alex Newton, Richard Ogle, and John Proctor (in addition to Gary Huckaby) were also instrumental in the formulation of the legislation authorizing it. Legislator-lawyers Lieutenant Governor Bill Baxley, Senator Roger Bedford, Jr., and Representatives Jimmy Clark, Jim Campbell, and Bill Fuller guided the act through the legislature. The first contested race for the presidency under the new mail ballot system involved Dagnal Rowe and Lynn R. Jackson (the first female lawyer to run for the presidency). Rowe won and served as president from 1997 to 1998. Later, in 2005, the commission was expanded to include nine at-large members for the purpose of promoting more diverse representation, including race, gender, age, and geographic region as factors in the selection of the at-large members by the remaining bar commissioners.

Law professor, and later Alabama Supreme Court justice, Harold See was vice chairman of the committee that evaluated the Uniform Arbitration Act.

In the 1980s, Governors George Wallace and Guy Hunt transferred lands adjacent to the bar building to the Alabama State Bar Foundation so that the bar could enlarge its headquarters. In 1990, ground was broken on a new $3.5 million addition to the state bar headquarters, including a third floor which was left unfinished for future expansion. The addition allowed room for the meetings of a larger bar commission and also included committee meeting rooms. The addition also gave the bar room for new staff as additional programs providing service to the membership were being contemplated. In 1999, when the bar reached a membership of 13,600, half of the third floor constructed in 1990 was built out to accommodate further growth of staff. The remaining part of the floor was finished in 2008 to further accommodate staff and program growth.

Effective January 1, 1994, the state bar implemented its Rules of Specialization under which a lawyer could declare a specialty and advertise himself or herself as such. That same year, the Alabama Supreme Court created a Commission on Dispute Resolution to promote alternative methods of dispute resolution, such as mediation, to reduce the volume of litigation in the courts. Nick Gaede chaired the bar's Alternative Dispute Resolution Committee, which in 1985 proposed the introduction of the Uniform Arbitration Act in Alabama, which had formerly not recognized the right to arbitration in the state. The BBC sought input from the Alabama Law Institute to study the act and determine how it would impact existing statutes and cases, before proposing passage of an arbitration statute by the legislature. The committee, whose vice chairman was then-professor, later-Justice Harold See, also proposed that the bar promote the use of mediation and support local mediation centers, with appropriate rules to guide mediation, as a preferred means of dispute resolution.

In 1998, the Alabama Lawyers Assistance Program, headed by Jeanne Marie Leslie, became operational, joining 38 other states with similar programs whose members worked with lawyers whose substance abuse and/or mental health problems were affecting their practices and, thereby, the public. Subsequently, the Alabama Lawyer's Assistance Foundation was created to raise funds to make loans to those lawyers unable to pay for treatment for drug and alcohol addiction. This program arose from a task force originally created by President William Hairston in 1983. The task force created a Lawyers Helping Lawyers Foundation in 1986, through which a system of referrals for lawyers and their families needing assistance or drug or alcohol dependency intervention was established to provide confidential help.

During the term of president Douglas McElvy (2004-2005), Chief Justice Drayton Nabers of the Alabama Supreme Court established the Chief Justice's Commission on Professionalism. This commission was continued by Chief Justice Sue Bell Cobb who, in conjunction with the Alabama State Bar and Cumberland Law School, held a Professionalism Consortium in February 2008 to consider problems of professionalism facing both the bench and the bar. Chief Justice Cobb created the Chief Justice's Professionalism Award to recognize attorneys whose careers were models of professionalism. The first recipient, who received the award at the consortium, was Charles Gamble, former dean and professor of the University of Alabama Law School, who also taught at Cumberland Law School and who has been known throughout his career for his publications on legal evidence. Judge Harold Crow was named as the first director of the commission.

Under President Bobby Segall (2006-2007), a Mentoring Task Force was established, led by Professor Pam Bucy of the University of Alabama Law School and Ted Hosp of Birmingham, whose focus was to work with new lawyers in the areas of networking within the profession and to provide models of professionalism.

TOP: *Chief Justice Drayton Nabors, Jr., of the Alabama Supreme Court formed the Chief Justice's Commission on Professionalism.* ABOVE: *Charles Gamble, former dean of the University of Alabama School of Law, was the first recipient of the Chief Justice's Professionalism Award.*

"Lawyers Render Service"

When Fred Gray became president of the state bar in 2002, he was described as "probably the most influential African-American trailblazer in Alabama's law profession." He was also one of the country's most respected lawyers, regardless of his race. His decision to become a lawyer and "destroy everything segregated he could find" is perhaps the premier example of the ability of a lawyer to dedicate his career to service. In discussing the agenda for his presidency, he noted that he wanted to do something to improve the image of lawyers to the public, who often do not realize the service lawyers provide to their community, state, and country, in both their professional and private lives. Upon assuming the office of president, he announced his theme: "Lawyers Render Service: Service to the Client, Service to the Public, and Service to the Profession."

In keeping with that theme, he pointed out that the participation of lawyers in important public events and in day-to-day life often goes unrecognized and, therefore, unappreciated. Gray appointed a task force to explore the possibility of establishing an Alabama Lawyers Hall of Fame,[6] chaired by past president Sam Rumore (2000-2001), to recognize those lawyers in Alabama who have made a positive difference. Out of this task force came the establishment of the Alabama Lawyers Hall of

Sam Rumore, left, served as president of the Alabama State Bar from 2000 to 2001 and chaired the task force that led to the establishment of the Alabama Lawyers Hall of Fame. His wife and law partner Pat Boyd Rumore, right, is the author of this book.

A project promoted by president Douglas McElvy, (2004-2005), under the auspices of the History and Archives Committee, which ultimately became a joint project with the Bench and Bar Historical Society, was the writing and publication of a history of the legal profession in Alabama. Ben Spratling chaired the History and Archives Committee during this period. Pat Boyd Rumore, a Birmingham attorney who had written a similar book for the Birmingham Bar Association about the legal profession in that city, was asked to write the book, with the goal of providing a record of the impact of lawyers and the profession on the developing history of the state of Alabama.

When 2003-2004 president William N. Clark took over as president, he recommended to the bar commission that the phrase "Lawyers Render Service" be made the permanent motto of the Alabama State Bar. This outward expression of the profession was in keeping with the state bar's own goal of rendering service to its members.

In reviewing the many initiatives of the legal profession through the Alabama State Bar, it becomes obvious that this formal motto is merely an expression of what has been true for several decades. Some examples of lawyers as a profession rendering service already discussed in this book include:

Fame, housed in the Heflin-Torbert Judicial Building, which continues to be chaired by Sam Rumore. A list of the inductees is found on the bar's website. The first induction was made in 2004.

The bar already had in place a "legal milestones" marker program which Sam Rumore oversaw during his chairmanship of the History and Archives Committee. It recognized important cases, events, or personalities in Alabama's legal history. In 1999, a marker was placed in front of the bar's headquarters highlighting events in the establishment of the bar. It was the third such marker, one already having been placed in Monroeville, commemorating Harper Lee's book *To Kill a Mockingbird* and its main character Atticus Finch, and one in Huntsville, honoring the state's first constitution and statehood. The marker program was first proposed by Pat Graves of Huntsville.

The bar's constant efforts to improve its members' professionalism and ethical conduct and to protect the public from unethical and impaired lawyers through its policing of the profession (with the addition of lay people in the disciplinary process in the 1980s) and through its Client Security Fund and Lawyers Assistance Program; The many improvements to the state's legal system which derived from the bar-driven effort to adopt a new Judicial Article to the 1901 Constitution and to reform court rules and procedures; The thousands of hours of service donated by lawyers to the improvement of Alabama's legal system through the efforts of the Alabama Law Institute; The millions of dollars in charitable grants made by the Alabama Law Foundation since its founding in 1987, including, in 2007 for example, $190,000 in grants to programs providing legal services to the poor, another $164,000 aimed at administering programs for the defense of indigents in capital cases and other prison-related programs, and $10,000 to the Center for Law and Civic Education to help pay for their "Play by the Rules" pro-

A historical marker, the third in a series commemorating legal milestones, was placed in front of the Alabama State Bar headquarters building in 1999. The marker gives a brief summary of the founding of the Alabama State Bar and of the significant developments in its history.

gram that educates high school students about the law, as well as other calls to the profession by the state bar for contributions to various funds, which included a request in 2007 to contribute to a fund to grant scholarships to new judges to attend the National Judicial College at a time when no state funds were available which raised over $100,000; and the bar's ongoing efforts to promote the rewriting and replacement of Alabama's antiquated 1901 constitution and the restructuring of Alabama's regressive tax system.

Two other programs operated under the auspices of the state bar are worthy of note when discussing the phrase "Lawyers Render Service"—The Volunteer Lawyers Program and the Alabama Center for Dispute Resolution.

In 1990, with the encouragement of president W. Harold Albritton, III, the Committee on Access to Legal Services, chaired by Kenneth Battles, worked closely with the Indigent Defense Committee, chaired by Dennis Balske, to propose the funding of a program to coordinate and encourage the provision of pro bono services by individual lawyers and by law firms. A grant was made by the Alabama Law Foundation to fund the employment of the coordinator, Melinda Waters, whose initial task was to organize the program on a statewide basis, working with existing local pro bono organizations, and to develop a structure for delivery of needed services where no local organizations currently existed. Waters became a member of the state bar staff and worked with existing local bar programs in Mobile, Montgomery, Huntsville, Birmingham, and Tuscaloosa, as well as the Legal Services program funded by federal funds. She was later replaced by Kim Oliver. Currently Linda Lund runs the program and the combined efforts of these staff members have produced a substantial increase in the legal resources available to the poor in Alabama.

Part of the success of the program has been due to the recognition given to pro bono volunteers in *The Alabama Lawyer* and at the state bar annual convention. In the January 2007 edition of the *Lawyer*, a substantial portion of the magazine was given to celebrating the sixteenth anniversary of the program. Highlighted was a Pro Bono Honor Roll listing hundreds of members of the Volunteer Lawyers Program from around the state, including those in almost every county, who have given thousands of hours of free legal services to those who could not otherwise afford representation by an attorney. Public service given by law students under the auspices of the University of Alabama Law School's Public Interest Institute and the Cumberland Law School's Public Interest Project and Community Service Organization was also highlighted, as was the sponsoring of a pro bono divorce clinic by members of major corporate law firm Maynard, Cooper, & Gale, P.C. Also recognized were 18 public interest groups whose focus involved, in part or whole, providing access to legal services to low income

THE RETIREMENT OF REGGIE HAMNER AND THE EMPLOYMENT OF KEITH NORMAN, ED PATTERSON, AND OTHER IMPORTANT STAFF

AFTER 25 YEARS AS EXECUTIVE DIRECTOR OF THE state bar, Reginald T. Hamner retired in 1994. His replacement, whose appointment became effective on October 1, 1994, was Keith B. Norman. When Hamner took over as state bar secretary in 1969, there were approximately 3,000 members of the bar. During the course of his service, the membership expanded to over 10,200. Hamner's staff had five members, but, by 1994, there was a staff of twenty-nine. From these figures, it can be seen that Reggie Hamner presided over a tremendous amount of change in the bar and was involved in the consideration and resolution of many important issues facing the bar and the state. (After his retirement, he presided over a totally different undertaking, becoming project coordinator when the Middle District federal judiciary determined to build a new United States courthouse. In affectionate recognition of his excellent work, the court named the eagle statuary adorning the building's front entrance "Reggie.")

Hamner was instrumental in the selection of Keith Norman, a young Montgomery attorney who had been an active and successful volunteer in bar activities, to be his potential replacement. Norman was recruited to Reggie's staff as program director in 1989, soon after Hamner made his plans to retire known to the BBC. Thus, Norman had five years to gain the experience to make him a success when the bar commission officially chose him as Hamner's successor.

Keith B. Norman became executive director of the Alabama State Bar in 1994.

Soon after Norman became executive director, Ed Patterson was hired to fill the position of program director. Patterson had worked for the bar from 1976 to 1980 as its first assistant general counsel under then-General Counsel William Morrow (who retired in 1987). Even though Patterson had been in private practice for a number of years, his return to the bar staff brought additional continuity to a period of change. He was made assistant executive director in 2008. Robert W. Norris, who had joined the staff in 1988 after retiring as the judge advocate general of the Air Force, retired as the bar's general counsel in 1995 and was replaced by then-Assistant General Counsel Tony McLain, whose staff in 2008 included three assistant general counsels: Robert E. Lusk, Jr., Samuel S. Partridge, and Jeremy W. McIntire. The general counsel and his staff are housed in the "Center for Professional Responsibility," which oversees ethics advice and opinions, client security fund claims, and attorney discipline. The year 1995 saw the creation of a full-time position of director of communications and public information, which was filled by Susan Andres and is currently held by Brad Carr. Staff member Margaret Murphy has served as director of publications since 1984.

MAYNARD, COOPER & GALE SETS A NEW STANDARD FOR PROFESSIONAL LEADERSHIP

THE BIRMINGHAM FIRM of Maynard, Cooper & Gale is active in leadership within the profession, as evidenced by one of its members, N. Lee Cooper, who served as president of the American Bar Association from 1996 to 1997. At that time, he was only the second Alabamian (Henry Upson Sims having served from 1929 to 1930) to be elected president of this national professional organization which currently has approximately 413,000 members. In 2007, another firm member, H. Thomas Wells, Jr., served as the third president of the American Bar Association from Alabama during the period 2008 to 2009, (an extraordinary accomplishment, producing two national presidents within the same firm and so close in time). During 2007, firm member Fournier J. "Boots" Gale was serving as president of the Alabama State Bar, while Anthony A. Joseph was serving as president of the Birmingham Bar Association. Firm member Daniel H. Markstein, III, also served as president of the American College of Trust and Estate Counsel that year. Firm member Maibeth Porter, who was president of the Birmingham Bar Association in 2003, served with Anthony Joseph on the state bar Board of Bar Commissioners in 2008.

H. Thomas Wells of Maynard, Cooper & Gale, was only the third Alabamian to serve as president of the American Bar Association.

Alabamians, including six clinics run by the University of Alabama Law School: the Civil Law Clinic; the Elder Law Clinic; the Criminal Law Clinic; the Capital Defense Law Clinic; the Community Development Law Clinic; and the Domestic Violence Law Clinic.

Another effort to enhance legal access to the poor came about in 2004, when Alabama's three legal services corporations united to form a single, comprehensive, statewide program, Legal Services Alabama, under one executive director. This merger was recommended by the Alabama Task Force on Reconfiguration and assisted by the Alabama Law Foundation. One major reason for the merger was to be able to focus fundraising activities and to share resources, with the hope of better providing equal access to justice throughout the state.

In 2007, the Alabama Law Foundation joined Alabama Chief Justice Sue Bell Cobb in creating the Access to Justice Commission, an organization whose mission is to provide funding and civil legal services for low-income residents of the state. One focus of the commission is to bring together organizations that serve the poor to maximize the use of current limited resources available for providing civil legal services. At the time of the commission's creation, Alabama ranked last in the nation in governmental spending for legal aid to the poor. The commission's goal is to close the gap of providing equal access to civil justice for all Alabamians.

A subcommittee of the bar committee which oversees the Volunteer Lawyers Program and Access to Legal Services issues was formed to study how to aid *pro se* (parties without lawyers) before the courts. Chairman Al Vreeland and his committee assembled a collection of *pro se* forms to be disseminated through Legal Services and Volunteer Lawyers Program offices for those persons who choose, for whatever reason, to represent themselves.

Another longstanding activity of the state bar which provides service to the public is its Center for Dispute Resolution,[7] housed in the offices and sponsored by the bar's Committee on Alternative Dispute Resolution. The movement to provide alternative approaches to resolving disputes other than through litigation in the court system parallels issues addressed by the Access to Justice Committee. The center opened in August 1994, under the direction of Judith M. Keegan, as an alternative dispute resolution management, coordination, research, and development office. It was set up under the supervision of the Alabama Supreme Court's Commission on Dispute Resolution, which was newly created under a proposal of the Alternative Dispute Resolution (ADR) Committee of the state bar.

The mission of the commission was to develop guidelines for alternative dispute resolution, to implement and supervise the Center for Dispute Resolution, to develop standards for "neutrals" (such as mediators), to implement community-based ADR programs and to provide ADR technical assistance, education, and training. The commission was initially chaired by Marshall Timberlake of Birmingham and included 19 members appointed to represent various entities such as the Alabama Supreme Court, the Court of Civil Appeals, the Alabama State Bar, the Alabama Trial lawyers Association, and the Alabama Defense Lawyers Association, as well as three at-large members chosen by the other commissioners. A subcommittee worked on implementing a mediation program in domestic relations, and another subcommittee, by means of advertisements, public service announcements, and bar newsletters, worked to get ADR information out to all areas of the state. The National Conference of Bar Presidents selected the Alabama Center for Dispute Resolution as one of its "Best Bar Projects of 1994."

As a service to both clients and attorneys, a program of fee dispute resolution has also been sponsored by the state bar to help resolve this type of dispute, which generates numerous grievance complaints but which is not a grievance under the Rules of Professional Conduct. Another aspect of the ADR Commission is the creation of an ADR program in the appellate court system, as well as at the trial court level. The state bar has a standing committee on Alternative Methods of Dispute Resolution whose mandate is to promote increased use of mediation in the state as a process for facilitating voluntary settlement of disputes.

One of the programs that state bar leadership and staff hope will enhance the profession's rendering of service to the profession and the public is its Leadership Forum program, adopted in 2004, during the presidency of William Clark of Birmingham. Its mission is "to produce committed and involved lawyers willing and able to fill significant leadership roles in the local and state bar associations, in communities and in state organizations, and to serve as role models in matters of ethics and professionalism."

Its goals are to raise the level of awareness of lawyers as to the purpose, operation, and benefits of the Alabama State Bar; to build a core of practicing lawyers to become leaders with respect to ethics and professionalism, resulting in raising the overall ethical and professional standards of lawyers in the community; and to form a pool of lawyers from which the state bar, state and local governmental entities, local bar associations, and community organizations can draw upon for leadership and service. Many future leaders of the state bar and of state and local governments will come from this group. The emphasis of the training is leadership through service and ethical conduct, based on professionalism.

In Conclusion

The organized bar, through the vehicle of the Alabama State Bar, has arrived at a place where service to clients, the profession, and the community outweighs power. This fact has been institutionalized in both the bar's motto of "Lawyers Render Service" and its mission statement, which reads: "The Alabama State Bar is dedicated to promoting the professional responsibility and competence of its members, improving the administration of justice, and increasing the public understanding of and respect for the law."

No longer does the defensive posture of the state's motto dominate the bar's attitude. Instead, it has assumed a proactive orientation of servant leadership. Hopefully, its commitment to addressing longstanding problems faced by the state will result in continued improvement in the lives of Alabama's citizens and its promotion of professional responsibility and competence among its members will benefit not only the profession but their communities and, most importantly, their clients.

FROM POWER TO SERVICE

PRESIDENTS OF THE ALABAMA STATE BAR

1879
Walter L. Bragg
Montgomery County

1879-1880
Edmund W. Pettus
Dallas County

1880-1881
John Little Smith
Mobile County

1881-1882
Edward A. O'Neal
Lauderdale County

1882-1883
M. L. Stansel
Pickens County

1883-Aug. 7, 1884
Henry C. Semple
Montgomery County

Aug. 7 to Dec. 3, 1884
N. H. R. Dawson
Dallas County

1884-1885
W. H. Barnes
Lee County

1885-1886
William M. Brooks
Dallas County

1886-1887
H. C. Tompkins
Montgomery County

1887-1888
W. F. Foster
Macon County

1888-1889
Milton Humes
Madison County

1889-1890
Thomas H. Watts
Mobile County

1890-1891
Hannis Taylor
Mobile County

1891-1892
A. B. McEachin
Tuscaloosa County

1892-1893
A. C. Hargrove
Tuscaloosa County

1893-1894
J. R. Dowdell
Chambers County

1894-1895
James E. Webb
Hale County

1895-1896
Daniel S. Troy
Montgomery County

1896-1897
Richard H. Clarke
Mobile County

1897-1898
John P. Tillman
Jefferson County

1898-1899
John D. Roquemore
Montgomery County

1899-1900
Joseph J. Willett
Calhoun County

1900-1901
Thomas G. Jones
Montgomery County

1901-1902
Edward L. Russell
Mobile County

1902-1903
Lawrence Cooper
Madison County

1903-1904
Edward deGraffenreid
Hale County

1904-1905
Thomas R. Roulhac
Colbert County

1905-1906
George P. Harrison
Lee County

1906-1907
Fred G. Bromberg
Mobile County

1907-1908
H. S. D. Mallory
Dallas County

1908-1909
William S. Thorington
Montgomery County

1909-1910
Emmet O'Neal
Lauderdale County

1910-1911
John London
Jefferson County

1911-1912
John Pelham
Calhoun County

1912-1913
Frank S. White
Jefferson County

1913-1914
Thomas M. Stevens
Mobile County

1914-15
Ray Rushton
Montgomery County

1915-1916
Charles S. McDowell, Jr.
Barbour County

1916-1917
Joseph H. Nathan
Colbert County

1917-1918
Henry Upson Sims
Jefferson County

1918-1919
J. Manly Foster
Tuscaloosa County

1919-1920
J. T. Stokely
Jefferson County

1920-1921
J. Kelly Dixon
Talladega County

1921-1922
W. O. Mulkey
Geneva County

1922-1923
B. P. Crum
Montgomery County

1923-1924
R. B. Evins
Birmingham

1924-1925
C. E. Hamilton
Greenville

1925-1926
John H. Peach
Sheffield

1926-1927
R. H. Powell
Tuskegee

1927-1928
Norville R. Leigh, Jr.
Mobile

1928-1929
Oscar L. Tompkins
Dothan

1929-1930
Bernard Harwood
Tuscaloosa

1930-1931
J. F. Aldridge
Eutaw

1931-1932
Borden H. Burr
Birmingham

1932-1933
John D. McQueen
Tuscaloosa

1933-1934
A. Leo Oberdorfer
Birmingham

1934-1935
Francis J. Inge
Mobile

1935-1936
H. F. Crenshaw, Sr.
Montgomery

1936-1937
Douglas Arant
Birmingham

1937-1938
L. F. Gerald
Clanton

1938-1939
C. H. Young
Anniston

1939-1940
Richard T. Rives
Montgomery

1940-1941
Sam M. Johnston
Mobile

1941-1942
DeVane K. Jones
Tuscaloosa

1942-1943
Jacob A. Walker
Opelika

1943-1944
J. Clarence Inzer
Gadsden

1944-1945
Roderick Beddow, Sr.
Birmingham

1945-1946
John E. Adams
Grove Hill

1946-1947
William Logan Martin, Jr.
Birmingham

1947-1948
W. Howell Morrow
Lanett

1948-1949
Gessner T. McCorvey
Mobile

1949-1950
Francis Hare, Sr.
Birmingham

1950-1951
John A. Lusk, Jr.
Gadsden

1951-1952
John A. Caddell
Decatur

1952-1953
T. B. Hill, Jr.
Montgomery

1953-1954
W. H. Mitchell
Florence

1954-1955
Walter B. Jones
Montgomery

1955-1956
Francis H. Inge
Mobile

1956-1957
John D. Higgins
Birmingham

1957-1958
B. E. Jones
Evergreen

1958-1959
Walter P. Gewin
Tuscaloosa

1959-1960
J. Kirkman Jackson
Birmingham

1960-1961
Clopper Almon
Sheffield

1961-1962
John W. Vardaman
Anniston

1962-1963
James J. Carter
Montgomery

1963-1964
J. Edward Thornton
Mobile

1964-1965
Frank J. Tipler
Andalusia

1965-1966
Howell T. Heflin
Tuscumbia

1966-1967
Robert E. Steiner, III
Montgomery

1967-1968
James E. Clark
Birmingham

1968-1969
Sam W. Pipes, III
Mobile

1969-1970
Patrick W. Richardson
Huntsville

1970-1971
Truman M. Hobbs
Montgomery

1971-1972
Robert B. Albritton
Andalusia

1972-1973
L. Drew Redden
Birmingham

1973-1974
M. R. Nachman
Montgomery

1974-1975
Alto V. Lee, III
Dothan

1975-1976
Thomas G. Greaves, Jr.
Mobile

1976-1977
Bibb Allen
Birmingham

1977-1978
Ernest C. Hornsby
Tallassee

1978-1979
Hugh W. Roberts, Jr.
Tuscaloosa

1979-1980
Oakley W. Melton
Montgomery

1980-1981
E.T Brown, Jr.
Birmingham

1981 (To Nov. 20)
Harold V. Hughston
Tuscumbia

Nov. 20, 1981-Jul. 17, 1982
Broox G. Garrett
Brewton

1982-1983
Norborne C. Stone, Jr.
Bay Minette

1983-1984
William B. Hairston, Jr.
Birmingham

1984-1985
Walter R. Byars
Montgomery

1985-1986
James L. North
Birmingham

1986-1987
William D. Scruggs, Jr.
Fort Payne

1987-1988
Ben H. Harris, Jr.
Mobile

1988-1989
Gary C. Huckaby
Huntsville

1989-1990
Alva C. Caine
Birmingham

1990-1991
W. Harold Albritton, III
Andalusia

1991-1992
Phillip E. Adams, Jr.
Opelika

1992-1993
Clarence M. Small, Jr.
Birmingham

1993-1994
James R. Seale
Montgomery

1994-1995
Broox G. Holmes
Mobile

1995-1996
John A: Owens
Tuscaloosa

1996-1997
Warren B. Lightfoot
Birmingham

1997-1998
S. Dagnal Rowe
Huntsville

1998-1999
Victor H. Lott, Jr.
Mobile

1999-2000
Wade H. Baxley
Dothan

2000-2001
Samuel A. Rumore
Birmingham

2001-2002
Larry W. Morris
Alexander City

2002-2003
Fred D. Gray, Sr.
Tuskegee

2003-2004
William N. Clark
Birmingham

2004-2005
J. Douglas McElvy
Montgomery

2005-2006
Robert Segall
Montgomery

2006-2007
Fournier J. Gale, III
Birmingham

2007-2008
Samuel N. Crosby
Daphne

2008-2009
J. Mark White
Birmingham

2009-2010
Thomas J. Methvin
Montgomery

2010-2011
Alyce M. Spruell
Tuscaloosa

FOOTNOTES

INTRODUCTION

1 For instance, see "Alabama: A Prospect" in *Alabama: The History of a Deep South State* by William Warren Rogers, Robert David Ward, Leah Rawls Atkins, and Wayne Flynt, The University of Alabama Press, Tuscaloosa, AL, p. xv, 1994.

CHAPTER 1

1 William Warren Rogers, Robert David Ward, Leah Rawls Atkins, and Wayne Flynt, *Alabama, The History of a Deep South State,* The University of Alabama Press, Tuscaloosa, AL, p. 65, 1994.
2 Ibid., p. 64.

CHAPTER 2

1 Thomas Perkins Abernathy, *The Formative Period in Alabama, 1815-1828,* The University of Alabama Press, Tuscaloosa, AL, p. 119, 1965.
2 Ibid.
3 Willis Brewer, *Alabama: Her History, Resources, War Record, and Public Men: From 1540 to 1872,* 1872, reprint, Tuscaloosa, 1964, p. 349, Willo Publishing Company, quoted in Harriet E. Amos Doss, "The Rise and Fall of an Alabama Founding Father, Gabriel Moore" *The Alabama Review*, Auburn, AL, Vol. 53, No.3, pp. 163-176, 2000 (quotation found on p. 166).
4 J. Mills Thornton, III, *Politics and Power in a Slave Society: Alabama 1800-1860,* Louisiana State University Press, Baton Rouge, LA, p. 20, 1978
5 William H. Brantley, Jr., "Law and Courts in Pioneer Alabama," *The Alabama Lawyer,* Montgomery, AL, Vol. 6, pp. 390-400, 1945.
6 *Politics and Power in a Slave Society,* see footnote 4, p. 25.
7 Samuel Webb and Margaret E. Armbrester, eds., *Alabama Governors: A Political History of the State,* The University of Alabama Press, Tuscaloosa, AL, pp. 31-33, 2001; John Craig Stewart, *The Governors of Alabama,* Pelican Publishing Company, Gretna, LA, pp. 66-70, 1975.

CHAPTER 3

1 The author would like to acknowledge her extensive use of an unpublished manuscript authored by Paul M. Pruitt, Jr., and to thank Mr. Pruitt for making this manuscript, entitled *The Legal Profession in Antebellum Alabama, 1819-1860,* available.
2 This story comes from Val L. McGee, "Escape from Slavery: The Milly Walker Trials," *The Alabama Review,* Auburn, AL, Vol. 49, No. 4, pp. 243-252, 1966.
3 Tony Freyer and Timothy Dixon, *Democracy and Judicial Independence: A History of the Federal Courts of Alabama, 1820-1994,* Carlson Publishing Inc., Brooklyn, NY, pp. 7-17, 1995.

CHAPTER 4

1 Sources for this section include Ralph B. Draughon, Jr., "The Young Manhood of William L. Yancey, *The Alabama Review,* Auburn, AL, Vol. 19, 1966; Malcolm C. McMillan, "William L. Yancey and the Historians: One Hundred Years," *The Alabama Review,* Auburn, AL, Vol. 20, No. 3, 1967; Henry Mayer, "'A Leaven of Disunion': The Growth of the Secessionist Faction in Alabama, 1847-1851," *The Alabama Review,* Auburn, AL, Vol. 22, No. 2, 1969; Austin L. Venable, "The Public Career of William Lowndes Yancey," *The Alabama Review,* Auburn, AL, Vol. 16, No. 3, pp. 200-212, 1963.

2 This quote was taken from *Politics and Pen Pictures*, New York, p. 258, 1892, and reported in Malcolm C. McMillan's "William L. Yancey and the Historians: One Hundred Years," *The Alabama Review*, Auburn, AL, Vol. 20, No. 3, p. 177, 1967.

3 Another old Whig lawyer-politician who fought to maintain the Union until Alabama seceded was Julius Caesar Alford—lawyer, Indian fighter, politician, U.S. congressman and orator, known as "The Old War Horse." Alabama was Julius C. Alford's second home. He was admitted to the bar and in 1828 set up practice in the Alabama-Georgia border town of Columbus, Georgia and shortly thereafter in nearby LaGrange, Georgia (which was "named for Lafayette's home, the Chateau de LaGrange, on motion of Julius C. Alford"). He was one of the more "notable men who figured on the pages of Georgia history between the Revolutionary and Civil War periods." According to the Biographical Directory of the United States Congress, Alford "commanded a company in the Creek War of 1836; (was) elected (in Georgia) as an Anti-Jacksonian candidate to the Twenty-fourth Congress to fill (a) vacancy... and served from January 2 to March 3, 1837...; (was) elected (in Georgia) as a Whig to the Twenty-sixth and Twenty-seventh Congresses and served from March 4, 1839, to October 1, 1841, when he resigned; moved to Tuskegee, Ala., and subsequently settled near Montgomery, Ala.; (was a) delegate to the Union convention at Montgomery in 1852; resumed the practice of law; (was an) unsuccessful candidate (in Alabama) for election in 1855 to the Thirty-fourth Congress...; died on his plantation near Montgomery, Ala., January 1, 1863." (Julius C. Alford's fourth great-grandson, Benjamin B. Spratling, III, currently serves as chair of the History and Archives Committee of the Alabama State Bar.)

4 Wallace T. Hettle, "Curing the 'Sir Walter Disease': The Politics and Fiction of Jeremiah Clemens," *The Alabama Review*, Auburn, AL, Vol. 52, No. 3, p. 163, 1999.

Chapter 5

1 This story is taken from Peter Branum, "General Joe Wheeler and the Dandrige Galey Murder Trial, 1871-1873," *The Alabama Review*, Auburn, AL, Vol. 50, No. 3, pp. 163-173, 1997.

2 Ibid., p. 163.

3 See Malcolm McMillan, *The Disintegration of a Confederate State: Three Governors and Alabama's Wartime Home Front, 1861-1865*, Mercer University Press, Macon, GA, 1986; Samuel Webb and Margaret E. Armbrester, eds., *Alabama Governors: A Political History of the State*, The University of Alabama Press, Tuscaloosa, AL, 2001.

4 Resources used include Michael W. Fitzgerald, "Wager Swayne, the Freedmen's Bureau, and the Politics of Reconstruction in Alabama," *The Alabama Review*, Auburn, AL, Vol. 48, No. 3, pp. 189-218, 1995; and Kenneth B. White, "Wager Swayne: Racist or Realist?" *The Alabama Review*, Auburn, AL, Vol. 31, No. 2, pp. 92-109, 1978.

Chapter 6

1 The attorneys who called for the bar's formation included Daniel S. Troy, Thomas H. Watts, Sr., Walter L. Bragg, John A. Minnis, Joseph Wheeler, LeRoy Pope Walker, Francis Bernard Clark, Jr., Gaylord B. Clark, Neil McCarron, George F. Moore, James J. Robinson, E. J. Fitzpatrick, John W. A. Sanford, H. C. Thompkins, John Enochs, Leroy F. Box, A.H. McClung, William G. Cochrane, H. A. Woolf, Alexander Troy, Thomas Mann Arrington, E. P. Morrissett, C. J. Watson, Thomas G. Jones, Milton Humes, W. G. Little, Jr., Jefferson M. Falkner, Lester C. Smith, J. S. Winter, Martin L. Stansel, William S. Thorington, John Little Smith, William P. Chilton, David Clopton, George P. Harrison, Jr., J.L. Cunningham, A. C. Hargrove, L. A. Dobbs, John D. Roquemore, John A. Padgett, J. R. Satterfield, W. E. Clarke, J.W. Bush, John T. Heflin, C. F. Hamill, John A. Foster, Malachi Riley, A. L. Brooks, Thomas W. Williams, F.W. Bowden, G. D. Campbell, H.A. Sharpe, W. P. Jack, James T. Holtzclaw, Wade Keyes, W. A. Gunter, and H. C. Semple. *Proceedings of the Alabama State Bar Association*, Vol. 46, p. 274, 1923.

2 See p. 715 in the book.

3 Sheldon Hackney, *Populism to Progressivism in Alabama*, Princeton University Press, Princeton, NJ, p. 36, 1969.

4 This section draws on attorney David A. Bagwell's "The 'Magical Process': The Sayre Election," *The Alabama Review*, Auburn, AL, Vol. 25, No. 2, pp. 83-104, 1972; and Sheldon Hackney, *Populism to Progressivism in Alabama*, see footnote 3. Sayre would later serve as an Alabama Supreme Court justice. He was the father of Zelda Sayre, who is remembered as the wife of novelist F. Scott Fitzgerald.

5 See Bagwell, "The Magical Process," footnote 4, p 95.

6 Quoted in the Montgomery *Advertiser*, April 18, 1899,

and taken from Malcolm Cook McMillan, *Constitutional Development in Alabama, 1798-1901: A Study in Politics, the Negro, and Sectionalism*, The Reprint Company, Spartanburg, SC, p. 258, 1978.

Chapter 7

1 The author notes that much of the information in this section comes from an unpublished manuscript written by Paul M. Pruitt, Jr., of the University of Alabama, entitled *The Legal Profession in New South Alabama, 1861-1915*.
2 Ibid., pp. 20-23.
3 Refer to Wayne Cline, *Alabama Railroads*, The University of Alabama Press, Tuscaloosa, AL, 1997.
4 See Kenneth R. Johnson, "The Peabody Fund: Its Role and Influence in Alabama," *The Alabama Review*, Auburn, AL, Vol. 27, No. 2, pp. 101-126, 1974.
5 See Kit C. Carter and Jerry C. Oldshue, "N.H.R. Dawson: Soldier, Statesman, and U.S. Commissioner of Education," *The Alabama Review*, Auburn, AL, Vol. 34, No. 3, pp. 202-213, 1981.
6 See Tennent S. McWilliams, "'No Sterile Monster': Hannis Taylor, the New South, and American Expansion," *The Alabama Review*, Auburn, AL, Vol. 30, No. 1, pp. 34-50, 1977.
7 See Hugh C. Davis, "Hilary A. Herbert: Bourbon Apologist," *The Alabama Review*, Auburn, AL, Vol. 20, No. 3, pp. 216-222, 1967.
8 See Thomas Adams Upchurch, "Senator John Tyler Morgan and the Genesis of Jim Crow Ideology, 1889-1891," *The Alabama Review*, Auburn, AL, Vol. 57, No. 2, pp. 110-131, 2004.
9 Ibid., p. 111.
10 Ibid., p. 113.

Chapter 8

1 Sheldon Hackney, *Populism to Progressivism in Alabama*, Princeton University Press, Princeton, NJ, p. 141, 1969.
2 Malcolm Cook McMillan, *Constitutional Development in Alabama 1798-1901: A Study in Politics, the Negro, and Sectionalism*, The Reprint Company, Spartanburg, SC, p. 261, 1978.
3 Moore, Albert B., *History of Alabama and Her People*, The American Historical Society, Inc., Chicago, IL, and New York, NY, p. 265, 1927.
4 Ibid., pp. 338-339.
5 Ibid., p. 339.

Chapter 9

1 Quote taken from James F. Doster, "Comer, Smith, and Jones: Alabama's Railroad War of 1907-1914," *The Alabama Review*, Auburn, AL, Vol. 10, No. 2, 1957.

Chapter 10

1 See Glenn Feldman, *Politics, Society, and the Klan in Alabama, 1915-1949*, The University of Alabama Press, Tuscaloosa, AL, 1999, which the author used as a reference for much of the information in this chapter.
2 See J. Mills Thornton, III, "Alabama Politics, J. Thomas Heflin, and the Expulsion Movement of 1929," *The Alabama Review*, Auburn, AL, Vol. 21, No. 2, pp. 83-112, 1968; Glenn Feldman, *Politics, Society and the Klan in Alabama, 1915-1949*, The University of Alabama Press, Tuscaloosa, AL, pp. 160-193, 1999.

Chapter 11

1 See Dan T. Carter, *Scottsboro—A Tragedy of the American South*, Louisiana State University Press, Baton Rouge, LA, 1969, 1979, from which the information in this sidebar was taken.
2 *Powell v. Alabama*, 287 U.S. 56 (1932). This case is considered by many as a landmark constitutional law case, providing the foundation for the development of the constitutional principle that criminal defendants have the right to adequate counsel.
3 See footnote 1.
4 *Patterson v. Alabama*, 294 U.S. 599 (1933).
5 See, generally, Virginia Van der Veer Hamilton, *Lister Hill: Statesman from the South*, University of North Carolina Press, Chapel Hill, NC, 1987.
6 See Leah Rawls Atkins, *Developed for the Service of Alabama: The Centennial History of the Alabama Power Company, 1906-2006*, Alabama Power Company, Birmingham AL, 2006, used by the author in writing this segment.
7 Ibid., p. 53.

Chapter 12

1 See Justice Champ Lyons, Jr., "Reminiscences on Adoption of the Rules of Civil Procedure" *The Alabama*

Lawyer, Montgomery, AL, Vol. 65, No. 2, 2004, where he also points out that, in 1957, a Commission for Judicial Reform was formed, which promoted judicial reform but saw little of substance accomplished.

Chapter 14

1 See Jack Bass, *Unlikely Heroes*, The University of Alabama Press, Tuscaloosa, AL, 1981, for a discussion of the role of the Fifth Circuit in developing the case law that derived from *Brown v. Board of Education*.

2 See Warren Trest, *Nobody But the People: The Life and Times of Alabama's Youngest Governor*, New South Books, Montgomery, AL, 2008; and Gene L. Howard, *Patterson for Alabama: The Life and Career of John Patterson*, The University of Alabama Press, Tuscaloosa, AL, 2008, for information about Patterson's later career. Also, see Jeff Frederick, *Stand Up for Alabama: Governor George Wallace,* The University of Alabama Press, Tuscaloosa, AL, 2007, for more about George Wallace.

3 See Frank Sikora, *The Judge: The Life & Opinions of Alabama's Frank M. Johnson, Jr.,* Black Belt Press, Montgomery, AL, 1992; and Tinsley E. Yarbrough, *Judge Frank Johnson and Human Rights in Alabama*, The University of Alabama Press, Tuscaloosa, AL, 1981, from which much of the information about Judge Johnson and his cases was taken for this book.

4 See Margaret Anne Barnes, *The Tragedy and the Triumph of Phenix City, Alabama,* Mercer University Press, Macon, Georgia, 1998; and Alan Grady, *When Good Men Do Nothing: The Assassination of Albert Patterson,* The University of Alabama Press, Tuscaloosa, AL, 2003.

5 Quote taken from Margaret Anne Barnes, *The Tragedy and the Triumph of Phenix City, Alabama,* Mercer University Press, Macon, GA, p. 208, 1998.

6 See Dan T. Carter, *The Politics of Rage: George Wallace, The Origins of the New Conservatism, and the Transformation of American Politics*, second edition, Louisiana State University Press, Baton Rouge, LA, 2000.

7 See Fred D. Gray, *Bus Ride to Justice*, Black Belt Press, Montgomery, AL, 1995.

Chapter 15

1 See Burt M. Rieff, "*Browder v. Gayle:* The Legal Vehicle of the Montgomery Bus Boycott," *The Alabama Review*, Auburn, AL, Vol. 41, No. 3, pp. 193-208, 1988.

2 J. Mills Thornton, III, "Challenge and Response in the Montgomery Bus Boycott of 1955-1956," *The Alabama Review*, Auburn, AL, Vol. 33, No. 3, pp. 163-235, 1980 (quotation found on p. 192). See also, Thornton's book, *Dividing Lines: Municipal Politics and the Struggle for Civil Rights in Montgomery, Birmingham, and Selma*, The University of Alabama Press, Tuscaloosa, AL, 2002.

3 See footnote 2, Thornton, "Challenge and Response in the Montgomery Bus Boycott of 1955-1956," p. 233.

4 The editor's comments concerning this article and its author provide insight into his attitude, which held sway in the Alabama State Bar at this time. They read: "The author of this lecture...was one of Alabama's ablest lawyers. He was admitted to the Bar in 1867, and at various times was associated in the practice of his profession with such eminent lawyers as...John T. Morgan [primary defender of Jim Crow laws], and Walter L. Bragg [the architect of "the Redemption"]. He was Judge of the City Court of Montgomery and in February, 1892, was appointed an Associate Justice of the Supreme Court of Alabama by Governor Thomas Goode Jones....In August, 1909, Judge Thorington was appointed by lifetime friend, Judge Thomas G. Jones, as special master for the Middle District of Alabama in the noted railroad rate cases. Judge Thorington was Dean of the Law School at the University for eighteen years, 1897-1915. The Editor of the *Alabama Lawyer* studied law under Judge Thorington for two years, 1907-1909. Judge Thorington was an able lawyer, a great jurist and a gifted teacher and withal, a Christian gentleman of the Old School...This valuable paper was the first lecture on Constitutional Law delivered by Judge Thorington while dean of the Law School at the University of Alabama, to the Junior Law Class in May 1908."

5 One white Tuskegee attorney, Henry Neill Segrest, was never boycotted. Segrest, born in 1898 to an old and politically prominent Macon County family, was active in the American Legion after World War I and had been instrumental in establishing its statewide Tenth District, composed of black veterans who had previously not been allowed to join. He was elected to the legislature in 1938 and worked to get state money for Tuskegee Institute, on whose board he served for 11 years. He also represented blacks and worked to insure their rights throughout his career, resulting in his ultimately being "boycotted" by white voters and clients, so that he lost his elected position and barely

made enough money from his law practice to feed his family. He died in 1974.

6 See Anne Permaloff and Carl Grafton, "The Chop-Up Bill and the Big Mule Alliance," *The Alabama Review*, Auburn, AL, Vol. 43, No. 4, p. 243, 1990; and Albert P. Brewer, "Famous Filibusters: High Drama in the Alabama Legislature," *The Alabama Review*, Auburn, AL, Vol. 43, No. 2, p. 83, 1990.

7 This committee was formed by then-Birmingham Bar Association president Walter Mims at the request of the Chamber of Commerce. Its membership was described by J. Mills Thornton: "The bar association appointed no black attorneys to the committee, but its membership otherwise was carefully and fully representative; spokesmen for the full spectrum of attitudes within the white bar were included, from the rigid segregationist J. Kirkman Jackson, who had been a member of the state bar's committee to advise legislators on ways to circumvent the Supreme Court's school desegregation decision, and was later appointed to the Alabama State Sovereignty Commission by Governor George Wallace, to William E. Mitch, son of the socialist former state CIO president who had led the United Mine Workers' Birmingham organizing campaign in the 1930s, and law partner of a son of U.S. Supreme Court Justice Hugo Black. Other members included District Judge Hobart Grooms; Tarrant City municipal judge and former and future state legislator Paschal P. Vacca; M. Camper O'Neal, a son of the powerful longtime state president of the Farm Bureau Federation and a law partner of Jefferson County's state senator Lawrence Dumas; former circuit judge Leigh M. Clark, the committee's chairman, who was a law partner of Joseph F. Johnston, the arch-segregationist who headed the bar's anti-integration advisory committee on which Kirkman Jackson had served; Waldrop Windham, a leading trial lawyer who was a brother of Circuit Judge Whitten M. Windham, the president of the segregationist Methodist Laymen's Union; Erle Pettus, Jr., a Princeton graduate and former assistant U.S. attorney who was a son of a leading delegate to the disfranchising Constitutional Convention of 1901; Douglas Arant, the prominent corporate attorney who had chaired the Interracial Committee's subcommittee on black police; Abraham Berkowitz, a labor lawyer, Jewish community leader, and vigorous spokesman for Birmingham's liberals; and George Peach Taylor, the young liberal and future Peace Corps official who was the immediate past president of the Young Men's Business Club." J. Mills Thornton, III, *Dividing Lines: Municipal Politics and the Struggle for Civil Rights in Montgomery, Birmingham, and Selma,* The University of Alabama Press, Tuscaloosa, AL, p. 239, 2002.

8 See Michael V. R. Thomason, ed., *Mobile: The New History of Alabama's First* City, The University of Alabama Press, Tuscaloosa, AL, p. 251, 2001.

9 *Davis v. Schnell*, 81 F. Supp. 872 (S.D. Ala. 1949), aff'd per curiam, 336 U.S. 933 (1949).

Chapter 16

1 See J. Mills Thornton, *Dividing Lines*, Chapter 15, footnote 2. Also, William Warren Rogers, et al., *Alabama: The History of a Deep South State,* see Chapter 1, footnote 1.

2 See Edward R. Crowther, "Alabama's Fight to Maintain Segregated Schools," *The Alabama Review*, Auburn, AL, Vol. 43, No. 3, p. 206, 1990; William Warren Rogers, et al., *Alabama: The History of a Deep South State*, pp. 545-565, see footnote 1; J. Mills Thornton, *Dividing Lines*, see footnote 1; Fred Gray, *Bus Ride to Justice*, see Chapter 14, footnote 7.

3 *Dividing Lines,* pp. 223-225, see footnote 1.

4 Edward R. Crowther, "Alabama's Fight to Maintain Segregated Schools, pp. 206, 225, see footnote 2.

5 These lawyers included Joe R. Whatley, Robert D. Hunter, Solomon S. Seay, Jr., Fred Gray, John C. Falkenberry, Demetrius Newton, C. Glenn Powell, Thomas W. Thagard, Armand Derfner, Jeffrey A. Foshee, Craig M. Crenshaw, Donald Watkins, David Boyd, Stanley J. Murphy, James Blacksher, and Leslie Proll, among others.

Chapter 17

1 See Samuel L. Webb and Margaret E. Armbrester, eds., *Alabama Governors: A Political History of the State*, see Chapter 2, footnote 6, essays by Glenn T. Eskew, pp. 216-234.

2 See Dan T. Carter, *The Politics of Rage: George Wallace, The Origins of the New Conservatism, and the Transformation of American Politics*, second edition, Louisiana State University Press, Baton Rouge, LA, p. 109, 2000.

3 Albert P. Brewer, "Famous Filibusters: High Drama in the Alabama Legislature," *The Alabama Review*, Auburn, AL, Vol. 43, No. 2, p. 83, 1990.

4 Kerwin C. Swint, *Mudslingers: The Top 25 Negative Political Campaigns of all Time,* Praeger Publishers, Westport, CT, 2006.

5 Samuel L. Webb and Margaret E. Armbrester, Eds., *Alabama Governors: A Political History of the State*, See Chapter 2, footnote 6, essays by Glenn T. Eskew, p. 227.

6 See Jason J. Battles, "Racial Politics and the 1966 Alabama Gubernatorial Election," *The Alabama Review*, Auburn, AL, Vol. 49, No. 2, pp. 108-122, 1996.

7 Webb and Armbrester, footnote 1 above, pp. 229-230.

8 Wayne Greenhaw, *Elephants in the Cottonfields: Ronald Reagan and the New Republican South*, MacMillan Publishing Co., New York, NY, p. 92, 1982.

9 See Pat Boyd Rumore, *Lawyers in a New South City: A History of the Legal Profession in Birmingham,* second edition, Association Publishing Company, Birmingham, AL, pp. 163-164, 2006.

Chapter 18

1 See John Hayman with Clara Ruth Hayman, *A Judge in the Senate: Howell Heflin's Career of Politics and Principle*, New South Books, Montgomery, AL, 2001, which was used as a reference on the life of Howell T. Heflin.

2 See *The Alabama Lawyer*, Montgomery, AL, Vol. 26, p. 351, 1965, and *The Alabama Lawyer,* Vol. 27, p.108, 1966, for lists of the committees and their memberships. The point of highlighting this seminal year in the life of the Alabama State Bar is that the work of the committees represent a moment in time when the legal profession in Alabama studied itself and its self governance, its judicial system, its substantive laws, and procedural structure and then took the momentum of the collegiality that developed from the process to bring about profound change. Shortly after Heflin's tenure ended, but in recognition of what was accomplished, the American Bar Association awarded Alabama its coveted Award of Progress as having the most progressive bar for that year in the nation.

3 Ibid.

4 The task force went through a methodical effort, under the guidance of the Auburn University Center of Business and Economic Development, to develop the essay portion of the Alabama test. They determined that the principal subject critical to new lawyers, that was not covered by the multistate tests, was pleading and practice. Out of this endeavor, an Alabama Civil Litigation Outline was developed and approved by the Board of Bar Examiners to be provided to those preparing to take the bar exam to guide their preparation. Ed Gentle, who was presented an Alabama State Bar Award of Merit in 2003, was the Board of Bar Examiners chairman who implemented these changes.

5 See article by Justice Champ Lyons Jr., entitled "Reminiscences on Adoption of the Rules of Civil Procedure," published in the March 2004 issue of *The Alabama Lawyer* for a full review of the history of the development and passage of the Alabama Rules of Civil Procedure. He pointed out the important roles of state senators Richard Dominick, Richard Shelby, Tom King, Sr., Pat Vacca, Lionel "Red" Noonan, and Stewart O'Bannon, all attorneys, in the passage of the legislation authorizing the court to make its own rules.

6 Skinner had previously chaired a 1957 "blue ribbon committee" known as the Commission for Judicial Reform which had offered proposed rules patterned on the Federal Rules to the legislature which failed to pass them. The work of that commission served as a foundation for the rules which were eventually passed. That committee included E.T. Brown, Jr., of Birmingham; John Caddell of Decatur; James J. Carter of Montgomery; John D. Higgins of Birmingham; Truman Hobbs of Montgomery; Francis Inge of Mobile; Judge Walter B. Jones of Montgomery; and Jacob A. Walker of Opelika, all of whom served as presidents of the Alabama State Bar, as well as Judge Hobart H. Grooms of Birmingham; Dean M. Leigh Harrison of Tuscaloosa; Judge Robert M. Hill of Florence; Chief Justice J. Ed Livingston of Montgomery; Attorney General John Patterson; Williams S. Pritchard of Birmingham; Marion Rushton of Montgomery; Judge John B. Scott of Montgomery; Justice Davis F. Stakely of the Alabama Supreme Court; and Judge Reuben H. Wright of Tuscaloosa.

7 See L. Vastine Stabler, Jr., "The Alabama Law Institute—A Legal Adviser to the Legislature," *The Alabama Lawyer*, Montgomery, AL, Vol. 30, pp. 134-146, 1969, for a thorough explanation of the founding of the Alabama Law Institute, which has been described as perhaps the seminal event in terms of modernization of the law and improvement in the output of the legislature in Alabama. Other lawyer-legislators who cosponsored the bill included Richard Manley, Ira D. Pruitt, and Henry B. Stegall. Other bar leaders involved in the original committee work included

Walter P. Gewin, Francis H. Hare, Jr., Hugh Maddox, Pelham Merrill, Roland Nachman, Professor Dallas Sands, J. Ed Thornton, Dean Arthur A. Weeks, James E. ("Red") Clark, Sam Pipes, Patrick W. Richardson, C. C. "Bo" Torbert, Jr., and Bryant Whitmire.

8 Awards of Merit were given by the Board of Bar Commissioners for work on the Judicial Article to the following: Howell T. Heflin, A. Stewart O'Bannon, Jr., Robert M. Hill, Jr., Joseph F. Johnston, Conrad Fowler, M. Leigh Harrison, Carl Bear (chairman of the Alabama Citizen's Conference on State Courts Inc.), Ronnie G. Flippo, M. Roland Nachman, Jr., and William Michael House.

Chapter 19

1 Throughout his tenure as state bar secretary, Reginald T. Hamner proved his excellence. In July 1972, the Board of Bar Commissioners passed a resolution commending not only his operation of the bar but also the importance of his contribution in the passage of the programs of judicial and legal reform that were presented to the legislature during this period, noting that he had "rendered exceptional and outstanding service to the Alabama State Bar, often under trying circumstances." In 1975, he successfully passed a nationwide examination to attain the CAE designation of the American Society of Association Executives. In 1977, a resolution recognized his election as president-elect of the National Association of Bar Executives.

2 This and other poems by John B. Scott were published in *The Alabama Lawyer*, Montgomery, AL, Vol. 39, p. 168, 1978, as part of a tribute memorializing him upon his death on February 23, 1978.

3 See the April 1970 edition of *The Alabama Lawyer* for a Commemoration, celebrating the one hundred fiftieth anniversary of the Supreme Court of Alabama, which contains a biographical sketch and portrait of several chief justices, as well as highlights of the court's early decisions, and which includes a listing of all judges on Alabama's appellate courts from 1820 to 1970, with "a glimpse" written by J. O. Sentell, the Reporter of Decisions and editor of the *Lawyer*.

4 Because of this and his other important service to the bar, the Board of Bar Commissioners, in 2002, inaugurated the William D. "Bill" Scruggs, Jr., Service to the Bar Award, to recognize outstanding, long-term service by living members of the bar to the Alabama State Bar as an organization. The award's creation stands as a tribute and memorial to Bill Scruggs, who is considered as a model for those the award would honor.

5 This new generation included presidents William D. Scruggs, Jr., admitted 1968, Fort Payne (1986-1987); Ben H. Harris, Jr., 1962, Mobile (1987-1988); Gary C. Huckaby, 1962, Huntsville (1988-1989); Alva C. Caine, 1970, Birmingham (1989-1990); W. Harold Albritton, III, 1960, Andalusia (1990-1991); Phillip E. Adams, Jr., 1968, Opelika (1991-1992); Clarence M. Small, Jr., 1961, Birmingham (1992-1993); James R. Seale, 1969, Montgomery (1993-1994); Broox G. Holmes, 1960, Mobile (1994-1995); John A. Owens, 1967, Tuscaloosa (1995-1996); Warren B. Lightfoot, 1964, Birmingham (1996-1997); S. Dagnal Rowe, 1972, Huntsville (1997-1998); Victor H. Lott, Jr., 1975, Mobile (1998-1999); Wade H. Baxley, 1968, Dothan (1999-2000); Samuel A. Rumore, Jr., 1974, Birmingham (2000-2001); Larry W. Morris, 1968, Alexander City (2001-2002); William N. Clark, 1971, Birmingham (2003-2004); J. Douglas McElvy, 1971, Montgomery (2004-2005); Robert D. "Bobby" Segall, 1971, Mongomery (2005-2006); Fournier "Boots" Gale, 1969, Birmingham (2006-2007); Sam Crosby, 1978, Daphne (2007-2008); John Mark White, 1974, Birmingham (2008-2009). Only five presidents were admitted during the 1950s: Bibb Allen, 1950, Birmingham (1976-1977); Oakley W. Melton, 1951, Montgomery (1979-1980); William B. Hairston, Jr., 1950, Birmingham (1983-1984); Walter R. Byars, 1952, Montgomery, (1984-1985), and Fred D. Gray, Sr., 1954, Tuskegee, whose election as the first African-American president of the bar from 2002 to 2003 was a vindication and commendation by the predominantly white Alabama bar of the value to the state of his work to "eliminate everything segregated" he found. The president-elect for 2009 to 2010 is Thomas Methvin of Montgomery, who was admitted to the bar in 1988, perhaps signaling a new shift to a younger generation of leadership. The election of Alyce Spruell (1983) in 2009 is further evidence of such a shift.

6 As president of the National Bar Association in the mid-1980s, Gray initiated the National Bar Association Hall of Fame, into which he was inducted in 1995.

7 For articles on the successes of this program and its history see *The Alabama Lawyer,* Vol. 65, whose theme is *Advancing ADR in Alabama: 1994-2004*, Issue No. 3, p. 154.

BIBLIOGRAPHY

I was asked by the Alabama State Bar to write about lawyers. Being a lawyer gave me an idea what other lawyers might be interested in knowing about those who came before them. I have used the work of many of the professional historians who write about Alabama, digging out the references to lawyers and hoping that I correctly interpreted the context and the facts. I have also used the work of some nonprofessional historians, such as myself, whose writings have appeared in *The Alabama Review*, *The Alabama Lawyer*, and the *Alabama Law Review*. Since I have covered the profession and its historical surroundings from Mississippi territorial days to the present, I felt it was important to show what sources I used, because many of the sources were, by necessity, secondary.

I was particularly fortunate that the man who established and first directed Alabama's Department of History and Archives and produced over 100 years of biographical sketches, Thomas McAdory Owens, was himself a lawyer. This fact guaranteed that I was able to find information about most of the early lawyers of historical consequence, including the almost 100 lawyer delegates to the 1901 constitutional convention.

I had access to the Alabama State Bar's library of printed proceedings of many of the early state bar conventions, even for some years where the proceedings were only in the form of a court reporter's typed manuscript. These proceedings were my most valuable primary source of information, because they were taken verbatim and often captured the personalities of speakers through their comments. I have spiced the manuscript where I could with comments that I thought personalized the lawyers I was writing about.

I read 35 years of Board of Bar Commission minutes, from 1960 to 1994, trying to capture the inside sources of the many changes that occurred during that important era. I relied heavily on a summary of the first 60 years of articles in *The Alabama Lawyer* undertaken by the Alabama State Bar executive director Keith Norman in 2000-2001 to guide me to specific articles that I used to explore those changes and to glean facts about bar operations and personnel.

I interviewed several older members of the bar and watched video interviews of others to capture information about the years that preceded my entry into the bar in 1975. And, of course, I used the collective knowledge and memories of members of the History and Archives Committee of the Bar who read the manuscript era by era as I completed chapters. I could have written many more pages about lawyers and the practice of law as it has evolved in the past 50 years, but hopefully I have written enough.

Bibliography

Abernathy, Thomas Perkins, *The Formative Period in Alabama, 1815-1828*, The University of Alabama Press, Tuscaloosa, AL, 1965.

Andrews, Carol Rice, Paul D. Pruitt, Jr., and David I. Durham, *Gilded Age Legal Ethics: Essays on Thomas Goode Jones' 1887 Code and the Regulation of the Profession,* Occasional Publications of the Bounds Law Library, The University of Alabama School of Law, Tuscaloosa, AL, No. 4, 2003.

Atkins, Leah Rawls, "*Developed for the Service of Alabama": The Centennial History of the Alabama Power Company, 1906-2006,* Alabama Power Company, Birmingham, AL, 2006.

Bagwell, David A, "The 'Magical Process': The Sayre Election Law of 1893," *The Alabama Review*, Auburn, AL, Vol. 25, No. 2, pp. 83-104, 1972.

Barnard, William D., *Dixiecrats and Democrats: Alabama Politics, 1942-1950,* The University of Alabama Press, Tuscaloosa, AL, 1974.

Barnes, Margaret Anne, *The Tragedy and the Triumph of Phenix City, Alabama*, Mercer University Press, Macon, GA, 1998.

Bass, Jack, *Unlikely Heroes,* The University of Alabama Press, Tuscaloosa, AL, 1981.

Battles, Jason J., "Racial Politics and the 1966 Alabama Gubernatorial Election," *The Alabama Review*, Auburn, AL, Vol. 49, No. 2, pp. 108-122, 1966.

Brantley, William J., Jr., "Law and Courts in Pioneer Alabama," *The Alabama Lawyer*, Montgomery, AL, Vol. 6, p. 390, 1945.

Branum, Peter, "General Joe Wheeler and the Dandrige Galey Murder Trial, 1871-1873," *The Alabama Review*, Auburn, AL, Vol. 50, No. 3, pp. 163-173, 1977.

Brewer, Willis, *Alabama: Her History Resources, War Record, and Public Men, from 1540 to 1872,* reprint, Willo Publishing Co., Tuscaloosa, AL, 1964.

Carter, Dan T., *From George Wallace to Newt Gingrich: Race in the Conservative Counterrevolution, 1963-1994,* Louisiana State University Press, Baton Rouge, LA, 1996.

Carter, Dan T., *Scottsboro: A Tragedy of the American South,* Louisiana State University Press, Baton Rouge, LA, 1969.

Carter, Dan T., *The Politics of Rage: George Wallace, the Origins of the New Conservatism, and the Transformation of American Politics,* Louisiana State Press, Baton Rouge, AL, second edition, 2000.

Cline, Wayne, *Alabama Railroads,* The University of Alabama Press, Tuscaloosa, AL, 1997.

Doss, Harriet E. Amos, "The Rise and Fall of an Alabama Founding Father, Gabriel Moore," *The Alabama Review*, Auburn, AL, Vol. 53, No. 3, pp. 163-176, 2000.

Draughon, Ralph B., Jr., "The Young Manhood of William L. Yancey," *The Alabama Review*, Auburn, AL, Vol. 19, 1966.

DuBose, John Witherspoon, *Alabama's Tragic Decade 1865-1874,* Reprint: Webb Book Company, Birmingham, AL, 1940.

Feldman, Glen, *Politics, Society, and the Klan in Alabama, 1915-1949,* The University of Alabama Press, Tuscaloosa, AL, 1999.

Fitzgerald, Michael W., "Wager Swayne, the Freedmen's Bureau, and the Politics of Reconstruction in Alabama," *The Alabama Review,* Auburn, AL, Vol. 48, No. 3, pp. 189-221, 1995.

Fleming, Walter, *Civil War and Reconstruction in Alabama,* Reprint Company Publishers, Spartanburg, SC, 1978.

Frederick, Jeff, *Stand Up for Alabama: Governor George Wallace*, The University of Alabama Press, Tuscaloosa, AL, 2007.

Freyer, Tony and Timothy Dixon, *Democracy & Judicial Independence: A History of the Federal Courts of Alabama 1820-1994,* Carlson Publishing Inc., Brooklyn, NY, 1995.

Grady, Alan, *When Good Men Do Nothing: The Assassination of Albert Patterson*, The University of Alabama Press, Tuscaloosa, AL, 2003.

Gray, Fred, *Bus Ride to Justice: Changing the System by the System,* Black Belt Press, Montgomery, AL, 1995.

Greenhaw, Wayne, *Elephants in the Cornfields: Ronald Reagan and the New Republican South*, MacMillian Publishing Co., New York, NY, 1982.

Hackney, Sheldon., *Populism to Progressivism in Alabama*, Princeton University Press, Princeton, NJ, 1969.

Hamilton, Virginia., *Lister Hill, Statesman from the South,* University of North Carolina Press, Chapel Hill, NC, 1987.

Hayman, John with Clara Ruth Hayman, *A Judge in the Senate: Howell Heflin's Career of Politics and Principles,* New South Books, Montgomery, AL, 2001.

Hayman, John, *Bitter Harvest: Richmond Flowers and the Civil Rights Revolution,* Black Belt Press, Montgomery, AL, 1996.

Hettle, Wallace T., "Curing the 'Sir Walter Disease': The Politics and Fiction of Jeremiah Clemens," *The Alabama Review,* Auburn, AL, Vol. 52, No. 3, pp. 163-173, 1999.

Howard, Gene L., *Patterson for Alabama: The Life and Career of John Patterson,* The University of Alabama Press, Tuscaloosa, AL, 2008.

McGee, Val L., "Escape from Slavery: The Milly Walker Trials," *The Alabama Review*, Auburn, AL, Vol. 49, No. 4, pp. 243-252, 1996.

McMillan, Malcolm C., *Constitutional Development in Alabama, 1798-1901: A Study in Politics, the Negro, and Sectionalism,* The Reprint Company, Spartanburg, SC, 1978.

McMillan, Malcolm C., *The Disintegration of a Confederate State: Three Governors and Alabama's Wartime Home Front, 1861-1865,* Mercer University Press, Macon, GA, 1986.

McMillan, Malcolm C., "William L. Yancey and the Historians: One Hundred Years," *The Alabama Review,* Auburn, AL, Vol. 20, No. 3, pp. 163-186, 1967.

Mayer, Henry, "'A Leaven of Disunion': The Growth of the Secessionist Faction in Alabama, 1847-1851," *The Alabama Review,* Auburn, AL, Vol. 22, No. 2, pp. 83-116, 1969.

Moore, Albert B., *A History of Alabama and Her People,* The American Historical Society, Inc., Chicago, IL, and New York, NY, 1927.

Owen, Marie Bankhead, *The Story of Alabama,* Lewis Historical Publishing Co., Inc., New York, NY, 1949.

Owen, Thomas McAdory, *History of Alabama and Dictionary of Alabama Biography.* 4 vols., S. J. Clarke, Chicago, IL, 1921.

Pruitt, Paul M., Tony A. Freyer, Timothy W. Dixon, and Howard P. Walthall, *Alabama's Supreme Court and Legal Institutions: A History.* Unpublished MS.

Rogers, William Warren, Robert David Ward, Leah Rawls Atkins, and Wayne Flynt, *Alabama: The History of a Deep South State,* The University of Alabama Press, Tuscaloosa, AL, 1994.

Rumore, Pat Boyd, *Lawyers in a New South City: A History of the Legal Profession in Birmingham,* second edition, Association Publishing Company, Birmingham, AL, 2006.

Sikora, Frank, *The Judge: The Life and Opinions of Alabama's Frank M. Johnson, Jr.,* Black Belt Press, Montgomery, AL, 1992.

Swint, Kerwin C., *Mudslingers: The Top 25 Negative Political Campaigns of All Time,* Praeger, Westport, CT, 2006.

Taper, Bernard, *Gomillion versus Lightfoot: The Right to Vote in Apartheid Alabama,* 1962, The University of Alabama Press, Tuscaloosa, AL, 2003 edition

Thomason, Michael V. R., ed., *Mobile: The New History of Alabama's First City,* The University of Alabama Press, Tuscaloosa, AL, 2001.

Thornton, J. Mills, III, "Alabama Politics, J. Thomas Heflin, and the Expulsion Movement of 1929," *The Alabama Review,* Auburn, AL, Vol. 21, No. 2, pp. 83-112, 1968.

Thornton, J. Mills, III, *Dividing Lines: Municipal Politics and the Struggle for Civil Rights in Montgomery, Birmingham, and Selma,* The University of Alabama Press, Tuscaloosa, AL, 2002.

Thornton, J. Mills, III, *Politics and Power in a Slave Society: Alabama, 1800-1860,* Louisiana State University Press, Baton Rouge, LA, 1978.

Trest, Warren, *Nobody But the People: The Life and Times of Alabama's Youngest Governor,* New South Books, Montgomery, AL, 2008.

Venable, Austin L., "The Public Career of William Lowndes Yancey," *The Alabama Review,* Auburn, AL, Vol. 16, No. 3, pp. 200-212, 1963.

Watson, Elbert L., *Alabama United States Senators,* Strode Publishers, Huntsville, AL, 1982.

Webb, Samuel L. and Margaret E. Armbrester, eds., *Alabama Governors, A Political History of the State,* The University of Alabama Press, Tuscaloosa, AL, 2001.

White, Kenneth B., "Wager Swayne: Racist or Realist?" *The Alabama Review,* Auburn, AL, Vol. 21, No. 2, pp. 92-109, 1978.

Wiggins, Sarah Woolfolk, ed., *From Civil War to Civil Rights: Alabama, 1860-1960: An Anthology from The Alabama Review,* The University of Alabama Press, Tuscaloosa, AL, 1987.

Yarbrough, Tinsley E., *Judge Frank Johnson and Human Rights in Alabama,* The University of Alabama Press, Tuscaloosa, AL, 1981.

INDEX

K

L

M

N

T

PICTURE CREDITS

THE PUBLISHER WOULD LIKE TO THANK THE following individuals for their assistance in procuring photographs: Tim Lewis, Director and State Law Librarian, Alabama Supreme Court and State Law Library; Meredith McLemore, Alabama Department of Archives and History; Don Veasey, Birmingham Public Library Department of Archives and Manuscripts; Paul Pruitt and David Durham, Bounds Law Library of the University of Alabama School of Law; Christy Carl, Alabama State Capitol; Carol Ellis, University of South Alabama Archives; and Margaret Murphy, Alabama State Bar.

The following abbreviations are used for sources from which multiple images were obtained:

ADAH	Alabama Department of Archives and History
BPL	Birmingham Public Library Department of Archives and Manuscripts
LOC	Library of Congress Prints and Photographs Division

FRONT MATTER: i Robin McDonald. ii-iii Robin McDonald. iv-v Robin McDonald. vi-vii Robin McDonald. ix Robin McDonald. x-xi Robin McDonald. 1 (both Robin McDonald. **CHAPTER ONE:** 2 University of South Alabama Archives. 3 W. S. Hoole Special Collections Library, University of Alabama. 4 University of South Alabama Archives. 5 (above) ADAH, (below) LOC. 6 ADAH. 7 (above) LOC; (below) ADAH. 8 Robin McDonald. 9 Alabama Supreme Court. **CHAPTER TWO:** 11 ADAH. 12 Alabama Supreme Court. 13 (both) ADAH. 14 ADAH. 15 LOC. 16 ADAH. 16 ADAH. 17 Alabama Supreme Court. 18 ADAH. 19 Alabama Supreme Court. 20 LOC. 21 ADAH. 22 Alabama Supreme Court. 23 ADAH. 24 ADAH. 25 LOC. 26 ADAH. 27 (both) ADAH. **CHAPTER THREE:** 29 Alabama Supreme Court. 30 BPL. 31 Alabama Supreme Court. 32 Alabama Supreme Court. 33 Alabama Supreme Court. 34 BPL. 35 LOC. 36 Alabama Supreme Court. 37 W. S. Hoole Special Collections Library, University of Alabama. **CHAPTER FOUR:** 39 ADAH. 41 ADAH. 42 LOC. 43 ADAH. 44 Alabama Supreme Court. 45 ADAH. 46 ADAH. 47 (above) Alabama Supreme Court; (below) ADAH. 49 LOC. 50 (above) LOC; (below) Alabama Supreme Court. 51 (above) LOC; (below) ADAH. **CHAPTER FIVE:** 52 ADAH. 53 Erik Overbey Collection, University of South Alabama Archives. 54 LOC. 55 ADAH. 56 ADAH. 57 (left) LOC; (right) ADAH. 58 LOC. 59 LOC. 60 ADAH. 61 ADAH. 62 LOC. 63 ADAH. 64 LOC. 65 ADAH. 66 ADAH. 67 ADAH. **CHAPTER SIX:** 68 ADAH. 70 ADAH. 71 (both) ADAH. 72 ADAH. 73 ADAH. 74 (both) ADAH 75 (both) ADAH. 76 courtesy Thomas B. Albritton, Albrittons, Clifton & Moody, P.C. 77 ADAH. 78 (both) ADAH. 79 ADAH. 80 ADAH. 81 Erik Overbey Collection, University of South Alabama Archives. 82 LOC. 83 ADAH. **CHAPTER SEVEN:** 84 Alabama Supreme Court. 85 ADAH. 86 LOC. 87 (above) ADAH; (below) Erik Overbey Collection, University of South Alabama Archives. 88 (above) ADAH; (below) BPL. 89 (above) ADAH; (below) BPL. 90 (both) ADAH. 91 Erik Overbey Collection, University of South Alabama Archives. 92 (both) BPL. 93 (both) BPL. 94 (above) courtesy Cabaniss, Johnston, Gardner, Dumas & O'Neal, LLP; (below) BPL. 95 ADAH. 97 ADAH. 98 Eufaula Athenaeum. 99 LOC. 100 (both) University of Alabama School of Law. 101 (left) University of Alabama School of Law; (right) Erik Overbey Collection, University of South Alabama Archives. 102 ADAH. 103 LOC. **CHAPTER EIGHT:** 104 BPL. 105 Robin McDonald. 106 BPL. 108 BPL. 109 ADAH. 110 Erik Overbey Collection, University of South Alabama Archives. 111 BPL. 112 ADAH. 113 BPL. 114 BPL. 115 BPL. 116 ADAH. 117 BPL. 118 ADAH. 119 BPL. 120 BPL. 121 *Bench and Bar in Mobile, 1900.* 122 BPL. 123 BPL. 125 LOC. **CHAPTER NINE:** 124 LOC. 126 BPL. 125 LOC. 127 LOC. 128 (above) LOC; (below) Erik Overbey Collection, University of South Alabama Archives. 129 (above) Alabama Supreme Court; (below) BPL. 130 LOC. 131 (above) LOC; (below) BPL. 132 ADAH. 133 LOC. 134 LOC. 135 (both) BPL. 136 ADAH. 137 (above) ADAH; (below) BPL. 138 LOC. 139 Alabama Supreme Court. **CHAPTER TEN:**

140-141 ADAH. 142 (both) BPL. 143 ADAH. 144 LOC. 145 LOC. 147 ADAH. 148 (above) ADAH; (below) courtesy Mrs. Horace Weissinger. 149 (above) University of Alabama School of Law; (below) LOC. 150 LOC. 151 (both) BPL. **CHAPTER ELEVEN:** 152 BPL. 153 LOC. 154 copyright *The Birmingham News*. 155 Alabama Supreme Court 156 Alabama Supreme Court. 157 LOC.158 Alabama Supreme Court. 159 LOC. 160 LOC. 161 ADAH. 162 ADAH. 163 University of Alabama School of Law. 164 ADAH. 165 BPL. 166 BPL. 167 ADAH. 168 ADAH. 169 Alabama Power Company. **CHAPTER TWELVE:** 170 ADAH 171 Robin McDonald. 172 (both) BPL. 173 BPL. 174 BPL. 175 Erik Overbey Collection, University of South Alabama Archives. 176 University of Alabama School of Law. 177 (both) University of Alabama School of Law. 178 ADAH. 179 University of Alabama School of Law. 180 University of Alabama School of Law. 181 (all) University of Alabama School of Law. 182 Mobile Bar Association. 183 (both) Alabama Supreme Court. 184 Alabama Supreme Court. 185 BPL. 186 ADAH. 189 BPL. **CHAPTER THIRTEEN:** 190-191 ADAH. 192 BPL. 193 (above) courtesy Thomas B. Albritton, Albrittons, Clifton & Moody, P.C.; (below) courtesy Judge W. Harold Albritton. 194 Alabama Supreme Court. 195 ADAH 196 LOC. 197 ADAH. 198 Mobile Bar Association. 199 (both) BPL. **CHAPTER FOURTEEN:** 201 ADAH. 202 BPL. 203 copyright *The Birmingham News*. 204 ADAH. 205 ADAH. 206 ADAH. 207 ADAH. 208 BPL. 209 ADAH. 210 BPL. 211 BPL. **CHAPTER FIFTEEN:** 212 Alabama State Bar. 213 Montgomery County Archives. 214 copyright *The Birmingham News*. 215 Montgomery County Archives. 218 Erik Overbey Collection, University of South Alabama Archives. 219 ADAH. 220 ADAH. 221 ADAH. 222 BPL. 223 (both) BPL. 224 (above) BPL; (below) Burton Studio Collection, University of South Alabama Archives. 225 (above) Vernon Z. Crawford Records, University of South Alabama Archives, (below) Palmer Studio Collection, University of South Alabama Archives. 226 (above) John Leflore Papers, University of South Alabama Archives; (below) Mobile Bar Association. 227 Robin McDonald. **CHAPTER SIXTEEN:** 229 Alabama Supreme Court. 230 BPL. 231 ADAH. 232 LOC. 233 ADAH. 234 (both) BPL. 235 LOC. 237 BPL. 238 ADAH 239 copyright *The Birmingham News*. **CHAPTER SEVENTEEN:** 241 ADAH. 242 ADAH. 243 ADAH. 244 ADAH. 245 Robin McDonald. 246 (both) BPL. 247 (above) *Mobile Press Register* Collection, University of South Alabama Archives; (below) United States Senate. 248 Mobile Bar Association. 249 (both) BPL. 250 ADAH. 251 (both) BPL. **CHAPTER EIGHTEEN:** 253 University of Alabama School of Law. 254 University of Alabama School of Law. 255 University of Alabama School of Law. 256 Robin McDonald. 257 University of Alabama School of Law. 258 (above) University of Alabama School of Law; (below) Alabama Supreme Court. 259 (both) Alabama Supreme Court. 260 (above) Alabama Supreme Court; (below) University of Alabama School of Law. 261 (above) BPL; (below) University of Alabama School of Law. 262 (above) Robin McDonald; (below) Alabama Supreme Court. 262-263 (above) Robin McDonald. 263 (below) University of Alabama School of Law. 264 (above) Alabama Supreme Court; (below) University of Alabama School of Law. 265 (above) University of Alabama School of Law; (below) Louise Sheridan Collection, University of South Alabama Archives. 266 (above) BPL; (below) *Mobile Press Register* Collection, University of South Alabama Archives. 267 (both) University of Alabama School of Law. 268 Alabama Supreme Court. 269 University of Alabama School of Law. 270 Alabama Supreme Court. 271 courtesy Roy Moore. **CHAPTER NINETEEN:** 273 University of Alabama School of Law. 274 University of Alabama School of Law. 275 Alabama State Bar. 276 Alabama Supreme Court. 277 (both) Alabama Supreme Court. 279 Alabama State Bar. 280 (above) University of Alabama School of Law; (below) BPL. 281 Alabama Supreme Court. 282 (above) Alabama State Bar; (below) University of Alabama School of Law. 283 Alabama State Bar. 284 Robin McDonald. 285 Alabama Supreme Court. 286 (above) courtesy Drayton Nabers, Jr.; (below) University of Alabama School of Law. 287 photo by RCL Portrait Design, courtesy Pat and Sam Rumore. 288 Robin McDonald. 289 Alabama State Bar. 290 courtesy Maynard Cooper & Gale, P.C.